Indian Buddhist Philosophy

Ancient Philosophies

This series provides fresh and engaging new introductions to the major schools of philosophy of antiquity. Designed for students of philosophy and classics, the books offer clear and rigorous presentation of core ideas and lay the foundation for a thorough understanding of their subjects. Primary texts are handled in translation and the readers are provided with useful glossaries, chronologies and guides to the primary source material.

Published

The Ancient Commentators on Plato and Aristotle
Miira Tuominen

Ancient Scepticism
Harald Thorsrud

Confucianism
Paul R. Goldin

Cynics
William Desmond

Epicureanism
Tim O'Keefe

Indian Buddhist Philosophy
Amber D. Carpenter

Neoplatonism
Pauliina Remes

The Philosophy of Early Christianity
George Karamanolis

Plato
Andrew S. Mason

Presocratics
James Warren

Stoicism
John Sellars

Indian Buddhist Philosophy

Amber D. Carpenter

ACUMEN

First published in 2014 by Acumen
Reprinted 2014

Acumen Publishing Limited
4 Saddler Street
Durham
DH1 3NP

www.acumenpublishing.com

ISBN: 978-1-84465-297-6 (hardcover)
ISBN: 978-1-84465-298-3 (paperback)

British Library Cataloguing-in-Publication Data
A catalogue record for this book is available from the British Library.

Printed and bound in the UK by 4edge Ltd., Essex.

Contents

Preface vii
Acknowledgements xi
Abbreviations xiii
Chronology xvi
Development of Buddhist thought in India xviii

1. The Buddha's suffering 1
2. Practice and theory of no-self 20
3. *Kleśas* and compassion 48
4. The second Buddha's greater vehicle 72
5. Karmic questions 93
6. Irresponsible selves, responsible non-selves 117
7. The third turning: Yogācāra 137
8. The long sixth to seventh century: epistemology as ethics 169
   I. Perception and conception: the changing face of ultimate reality 171
   II. Evaluating reasons: Naiyāyikas and Diṅnāga 180
   III. Madhyamaka response to Yogācāra 189
   IV. Percepts and concepts: *Apoha* 1 (Diṅnāga) 214
   V. Efficacy: *Apoha* 2 (Dharmakīrti) 219
   VI. The path of the Bodhisattva 224

Epilogue 232

Background information
Appendix 1: The languages of Buddhism 242
Appendix 2: Intellectual context 244
Appendix 3: The Abhidharma 246
Appendix 4: Snapshot of Indian philosophy 248

Notes 251
Bibliography 289
Index 305

Preface

If ancient philosophy remains alive, this is because it is about life. However abstract the debate may get (and it does get abstract), however abstruse the discussion, a thread leads back, anchoring it in the inescapable concern with how to live and how to be. This is true of the ancient Greek philosophers, which is why their work remains alive for us still; and it is equally true of the philosophers of ancient India, including the Indian Buddhist philosophers whose work is the focus of this book.

I cannot hope to have given a comprehensive account of Indian Buddhist philosophy, which spanned several centuries, and involved an enormous variety of interlocutors. In what follows, I have aimed instead to present only sufficient breadth that the reader may become oriented within the terrain, develop a sense for which sorts of concerns weighed with the Indian Buddhists, and how they articulated these concerns. And I have otherwise tried to focus on following through particular arguments, so that one might come to see what it is to do philosophy *with* these Buddhist philosophers and their texts, and come to appreciate how rewarding – and how challenging – this is. For although Buddhist philosophers remained alive to the basic questions and concerns that may resonate with anyone, they developed sophisticated conceptual tools and arguments for pursuing these. They challenged each other to make more precise articulations of their understanding of the Buddha's teachings, and to give more sophisticated defences of these views. When Buddhist thinkers were not imagining new and better ways of understanding the Buddhist position, and justifying them to each other, they were responding to pressures from non-Buddhist philosophers deeply sceptical of Buddhism's main metaphysical and epistemological commitments – and therefore sceptical of Buddhism's basic ability to give a decent account of how we ought to live, think and understand ourselves.

The first chapter sketches the basic framework around which Buddhist thought was structured, and it offers an account of suffering that connects the metaphysical fact of suffering to the felt undesirability of it. Chapter 2 examines the claim for which Buddhism was, and remains, best known (or, indeed, most notorious): the absence of self. I explore whether this should be taken as a claim about reality or as advice for a kind of praxis of dis-identification, before examining the arguments of the early Buddhist philosophers, who took it to be a claim about 'what there is', in need of explanation and defence. Their arguments lead them to adopt a sort of trope-theory, which rejects not only selves as underlying subjects and unifying agents but also any such complex wholes that might be thought to underlie or unite diverse properties.

Whether meant as a claim about what there is or as advice about how to think, the aim of the no-self claim is the same: to eliminate suffering by eliminating the causes of suffering, above all craving. We might ask how exactly this is supposed to work (How does seeing there are no selves eliminate craving?); we might also wonder, however it works, whether the game is worth the candle (Should I seek to eliminate suffering at the expense of eliminating all desires?). Chapter 3 considers what exactly the Buddhist ideal is, looking at both the Bodhisattva ideal and the Arhat ideal it challenges, and asking whether either is an *attractive* goal, or should be expected to be. It also considers what there might be to say to someone who claimed that there was a higher aim than eliminating suffering. We continue the examination of Mahāyāna ethics in Chapter 4 with Nāgārjuna, the first named philosopher in the Buddhist tradition. His Madhyamaka interpretation of the Buddha's teachings claimed to go back to basics, to the more authentic meaning of the Buddha's words, and at the same time offered a systematic basis for the Mahāyāna view. His mode of argumentation is distinctive and difficult, relying on destructive tetralemmas that appear to countenance contradiction. I suggest that if we understand his form of anti-essentialism and anti-foundationalism, we may understand why he chose this elusive style of argumentation; yet foundationless metaphysics may also leave us without ground for moral improvement.

Central to moral thinking is not just the possibility for improvement, but the attribution of responsibility. Chapter 5 looks at *karma* (action) as the term through which Indian philosophers generally engaged with questions of moral responsibility. We ask what *karma* is for the Buddhists, how it works within the Buddhist view as a whole, and whether it can (and ought) to be revised, or even dispensed with altogether. The worry that a no-self view eliminates responsibility was one pressed by non-Buddhists, and we turn in Chapter 6 to look at the sophisticated Nyāya arguments for the existence of self. Experience itself, they say, demonstrates the unity-of-multiplicity distinctive of the self which the Buddhist would deny. Memory unites experiences at different times; desire unites different psychological modes (perception, memory) into a single moment. Buddhist minimalism, which seeks to eliminate all complex unities from the catalogue of really existing entities, may find it difficult to give an adequate account of memory, of individual responsibility, and even of desire – the supposed root of suffering.

Vasubandhu takes Buddhist minimalism to the extreme. Recognizing that nothing can be located in space and still be absolutely simple, he argues that Buddhists must therefore be committed to there being nothing spatially located at all. Chapter 7 considers his arguments, and whether the position he advocates should be called 'idealist'. Answering this requires understanding Vasubandhu's analysis of modes of existence, and of the preconditions for the possibility of any experience. The ultimate precondition, I shall suggest, is that of which Vasubandhu says nothing can be said, or thought – and recognizing this fact is just what thoroughly transforming ourselves consists in.

Any view that proposes, as Buddhism does, that 'seeing things as they are' is our central aim must take epistemology seriously. This is implicit in Buddhism's phenomenological bent, but made explicit above all in the work of Diṅnāga, whose revolution in theories of reasoning, logic and language were part of a larger explosion of intellectual activity that took place within Buddhist circles, and in India more generally, from about the middle of the sixth century. Chapter 8 takes a look at this 'epistemological turn' in Buddhist philosophy. Diṅnāga formalizes the Buddhist view that conceptualizing distorts reality, which itself is non-conceptual and, on Diṅnāga's account, directly perceived. This preserves our moral task as one of 'letting go' of clinging to conceptual contrivances – especially that of the self, and the distinction between self and other; but it does so at the risk of making all language-use equally false, and thus allowing no space to reasoning on the path towards moral improvement and eventual enlightenment. Diṅnāga and Dharmakīrti try to resolve these worries through an analysis of inference and its grounds, while their Madhyamaka contemporaries favour eliminating altogether the supposed distinction between 'mere conceptual contrivance' and 'the *really* real'. Thus, Bhāviveka argues vigorously against the Buddhist idealist claim that there is some ultimate, utterly unconceptualizable reality, while Candrakīrti supposes even such arguments concede too much to Vasubandhu and his epistemologist successors. The ultimate reality we are to see consists in seeing that there is no ultimate reality. If this seems to lead to an intolerable quietism – a philosophy that leaves everything too much in its place – Śāntideva offers one way in which a Mādhyamika might reject all metaphysical and epistemological asymmetry, and yet retain a notion of progress along a path of moral development.

This book ends when most of the crucial philosophical pieces have been put into play – the lay of the land has been surveyed, and claims staked. Non-Buddhist philosophers in India offer ever more serious and sophisticated challenges to this range of Buddhist views, eliciting ever more sophisticated replies. We do not investigate these here; but what we cover should enable an interested philosopher to carry on the discussion into the ninth to eleventh centuries, particularly as source materials from this period become increasingly available in English.

Acknowledgements

My own engagement with Indian Buddhist philosophy was enabled at a crucial moment by a grant from the Einstein Forum, where I was an Einstein Fellow in 2008. I am grateful to them for the rare opportunity to begin something genuinely new and open-ended; the benefits of their willingness to make that kind of investment, and take that kind of risk, will continue to reach far beyond this book. Thanks are also due to the University of York, which followed up with support in the form of an Anniversary Lectureship, allowing a sustained period of study over several months. The careful and encouraging comments of the anonymous reader for Acumen were appreciated, and have certainly improved the book.

Some of what appears here was presented first as talks: for their engaged and incisive comments I must thank colleagues at the University of Western Australia; participants in the "Making Sense of Suffering" conference in Prague, 2010; and residents at Thösamling, who in addition offered a marvellous spaciousness during my stay there in 2009. I must also thank my students at the University of York, on whom most of the ideas in this book had their dry run. Teaching a course with Graham Priest on Indian Buddhist and Greek philosophy was great fun as well as fruitful; Chapter 3 is particularly influenced by our conversations during my time as a visitor at the University of Melbourne, and I thank Graham for his tenacious disagreement, as well as for creating the opportunity for it. Rachael Wiseman has been a steadfast philosophical interlocutor, thrashing out together (among many other things) whether metaphysics does matter, if so then how – and is it still metaphysics? It is a joy to thank her, and Kadie Armstrong,

Fabian Geier, Joseph Hardwick, Seishi Shimizu and Ben Young, who kept up the spirit of inquiry, as well as the body sustaining it, through their lively discussion and wholesome food in the final stages of writing this.

All of my teachers have my heartfelt gratitude. M. M. McCabe and Verity Harte showed me how to do philosophy *with* Plato, and not just about him – a precious gift of how to work with philosophical texts whose influence extends to my engagement with the Indian philosophers treated in this book; Rai Gaita taught me that thinking clearly and speaking truly remain the hardest tasks in philosophy, and the most important. All three modelled a way of doing philosophy that is as uncompromisingly convivial as it is critical. I am particularly grateful to those early teachers – Jonathan Lear, Susan Neiman, Jonathan Glover – who did not ask me to make my field of interests more narrow than it is, or insist that philosophy be found only in a narrow range of texts. Without their ecumenical attitude, much less would be possible in philosophy – certainly not this book – and philosophy today would be much less alive.

The deepest gratitude is reserved for the earliest teachers: my sister, who taught me letting go of afflictive emotions; and my mother, who taught me dependent origination.

Abbreviations

Throughout this book, I have tried to take quotes from translations that are widely available, when that was possible. Abbreviations refer to the texts and translations detailed below, unless otherwise noted.

AK	Vasubandhu, *Abhidharmakośa* (*Treasury of Abhidharma*); see *AKBh*
AKBh	Vasubandhu, *Abhidharmakośabhāṣya* (*Commentary on the Treasury of Abhidharma*). Edited and translated into French from the Sanskrit by Louis de la Vallée Poussin, and from the French into English by Leo M. Pruden. 4 vols (Berkeley, CA: Asian Humanities Press, 1988)
AN	*Aṅguttara Nikāya*. Translated as *The Numerical Discourses of the Buddha* by Bhikkhu Bodhi (Boston, MA: Wisdom Publications, 2012)
BCA	Śāntideva. *Bohicāryāvatāra*. Translated as *A Guide to the Bodhisattva Way of Life* by B. A. Wallace & V. A. Wallace (Ithaca, NY: Snow Lion Publications, 1997)
CŚ	Āryadeva, *Catuḥśataka*. Translated as *Āryadeva's Catuḥśataka: on the Bodhisattva's Cultivation of Merit and Knowledge* by Karen Lang (Copenhagen: Akademisk Forlag, 1986)
Dhp.	*Dhammapadā*. Translated with annotations by Gil Fronsdal (Boston, MA: Shambhala, 2005)
KV	*Kathāvatthu*. Translated as *Points of Controversy, Or Subjects of Discourse* by S. Z. Aung & Mrs R. Davids (Oxford: Pali Text Society, [1915] 1974)
MA	Candrakīrti, *Madhyamakāvatāra*. Translated as *Introduction to the Middle Way: Chandrakirti's Madhyamakavatara* by the Padmakara Translation Group (Boston, MA: Shambhala, 2002)
MAl	Śāntarakṣita, *Madhyamakālamkāra*. Translated as *The Adornment of the Middle Way*, by the Padmakara Translation Group (Boston, MA: Shambhala, 2005)

MH Bhāviveka. *Madhyamakahṛdaya.* Books IV and V translated by M. D. Eckel in *Bhāviveka and His Buddhist Opponents* (Cambridge, MA: Harvard University Press, 2008)

MMK Nāgārjuna, *Mūlamadhyamakakārikā.* Translated as *The Fundamental Wisdom of the Middle Way: Nāgārjuna's Mūlamadhyamakakārikā,* by J. Garfield (Oxford: Oxford University Press, 1995)

MN *Majjhima Nikāya.* Translated as *The Middle-Length Discourses of the Buddha* by Bhikkhu Bodhi and Bhikkhu Ñāṇamoli (Boston, MA: Wisdom Publications, 1995)

MP *Milindapañhā.* Translated as *Milinda's Questions* by I. B. Horner (Oxford: Pali Text Society, 1963–64)

NS Gautama, *Nyāya-Sūtra.* Translated as *Nyāya-Sūtra With Nyāya-Vārṭika* by Ganganatha Jhā (Allahabad: E. J. Lazarus, 1910)

NV *Nyāya-Vārttika,* see *NS.* Section on *NS* I.1 translated by Matthew Kapstein in *Reason's Traces* (Boston, MA: Wisdom Publications, 2001)

PP Candrakīrti, *Prasannapadā.* Selections translated as *Lucid Exposition of the Middle Way* by M. Sprung (London: Routledge & Kegan Paul, 1979)

PS Diṅnāga, *Pramāṇasamuccaya* (*Compendium of Means of Knowing*): Chapter 1 translated by Masaaki Hattori in *Dignāga, On Perception* (Cambridge, MA: Harvard University Press, 1968); Chapters 2 and 5 translated by Richard Hayes in *Dignaga on the Interpretation of Signs* (Dordrecht: Kluwer, 1988)

PSV Diṅnāga, *Pramāṇasamuccayavṛtti* (*Commentary on the Pramāṇasamuccaya*); see *PS*

PTS Pali Text Society

PV Dharmakīrti, *Pramāṇavārttika* (*Commentary on the Pramāṇas*). Selections translated by John Dunne in *Foundations of Dharmakīrti's Philosophy* (Boston, MA: Wisdom Publications, 2004)

PVSV Dharmakīrti, *Pramāṇavārttikasvavṛtti* (*Auto-Commentary on the Pramāṇavārttika*); see *PV*

RĀ Nāgārjuna, *Ratnāvalī.* Verses remaining in Sanskrit translated by Guiseppi Tucci, *Journal of the Royal Asiatic Society of Great Britain and Ireland* 66 (1934): 307–25; 68 (1936): 237–52, 423–35. Translated from Tibetan translation as *Buddhist Advice for Living and Liberation: Nagarjuna's Precious Garland* by J. Hopkins (Ithaca, NY: Snow Lion Publications, 1988)

SN *Saṃyutta Nikāya.* Translated as *The Connected Discourses of the Buddha* by Bhikkhu Bodhi (Boston, MA: Wisdom Publications, 2000)

TK Vasubandhu, *Triṃśikā-Kārikā* (*Thirty Verses*). Translated by Stefan Anacker in *Seven Works of Vasubandhu, the Buddhist Psychological Doctor* (New Delhi: Motilal Banarsidass, 1984)

TS Śāntarakṣīta, *Tattvasaṃgraha*. Translated with the Commentary of Kamalaśīla by Ganganatha Jhā (Delhi: Motilal Banarsidass, 1939)

TSN Vasubandhu, *Trisvabhāva-Nirdeśa* (*Treatise on the Three Natures*). Translated by Stefan Anacker in *Seven Works of Vasubandhu, the Buddhist Psychological Doctor* (New Delhi: Motilal Banarsidass, 1984)

VK Vasubandhu, *Viṁśatikā-Kārikā* (*Twenty Verses*). Translated by Stefan Anacker in *Seven Works of Vasubandhu, the Buddhist Psychological Doctor.* (New Delhi: Motilal Banarsidass, 1984)

Vsm. Buddhaghoṣa, *Visuddhimagga*. Translated as *The Path of Purification* by Ñaṇamoli Bhikkhu (Onalaksa, WA: Pariyatti Publishing, [1975] 1991)

Chronology

Buddhist		Nyāya	Other
Buddha, *c.* 4th c. BCE; Nikayas and Vinaya shortly thereafter			Pāṇini, ?6th c. BCE; Grammarian
Abhidharma texts. Also the *Dhammapadā*; the *Milindapañhā*, 3rd–1st c. BCE			
		Gautama, 1st c. CE?	
Nāgārjuna, fl. 170? [2nd c. CE]			Iśvarakṛṣṇa, 2nd c. CE; Saṁkhya
Āryadeva (student of Nāgāruna), fl. *c.* 200?		Vatsyāyana, 2nd–4th c. CE	
	Asaṇga, 4th c. CE ['half-brother' of Vasubandhu]		Śabara, 4th c. CE; Mīmāṃsā
	Vasubandhu; Saṅghabhadra, 4th c. CE		
	Buddhaghoṣa, 5th c. CE [Theravāda]		
Buddhapālita, 470–540	Diṅnāga, *c.* 480–540		Bhartṛhari, 5th c. CE; Grammarian
Bhāvaviveka, fl. 570 [*contemp.* Dharmapāla]	Sthiramati, 6th c. CE [comment on Vasubandhu]; Dharmapāla, fl. *c.* 550–570 [comment on *MMK*?]		

Candrakīrti, early 7th c. CE	Dharmakīrti [either *c.* 540–600; or *c.* 600–660]	Uddyotakara, *c.* 550–650 [*contemp.* Dharmakīrti]	Prabhākara, 7th c. CE; Mīmāṃsā
			Kumārila, Mīmāṃsā, fl. 680; Śaṅkara, 8th c. CE Vedānta [*contemp.* Candrakīrti]
Śāntideva, 685–763			
[*syncretist*] Śāntarakṣita, 725–788			Bhaṭṭa Uṃveka, fl. 710; Mīmāṃsā
[*syncretist*] Kamalaśīla, 740–795 Dharmottara, *c.* 740–800; Jñānagarbha, 8th c. CE			
		Vācaspati Miśra, fl. 841 (or 976) Jayanta Bhaṭṭa, 840–900	
[*syncretist epistemologist*] Jñānaśrīmitra, fl. 980–1030		Udayana, fl. 984 CE	Śridhara, fl. 950–1000; Vaiśeṣika
[*syncretist epistemologist*] Ratnakīrti, *c.* 1000–1050		Trilocana, 10th c. CE Vācaspatimiśra, 10th c. CE	
Mokṣakāragupta, 11th–12th c. CE [*Tarkabhāṣā*, intro. to Dharmakīrti]			Pārthasārathimiśra, fl. *c.* 1075; Mīmāṃsā Śriharṣa (1075–1125); Advaita
		Gaṅgeśa Upadhyaya, 12th–13th c. CE	
		Śankaramisra, fl. 1450 CE	
		Raghunatha Siromani, 1477–1547	

Development of Buddhist thought in India

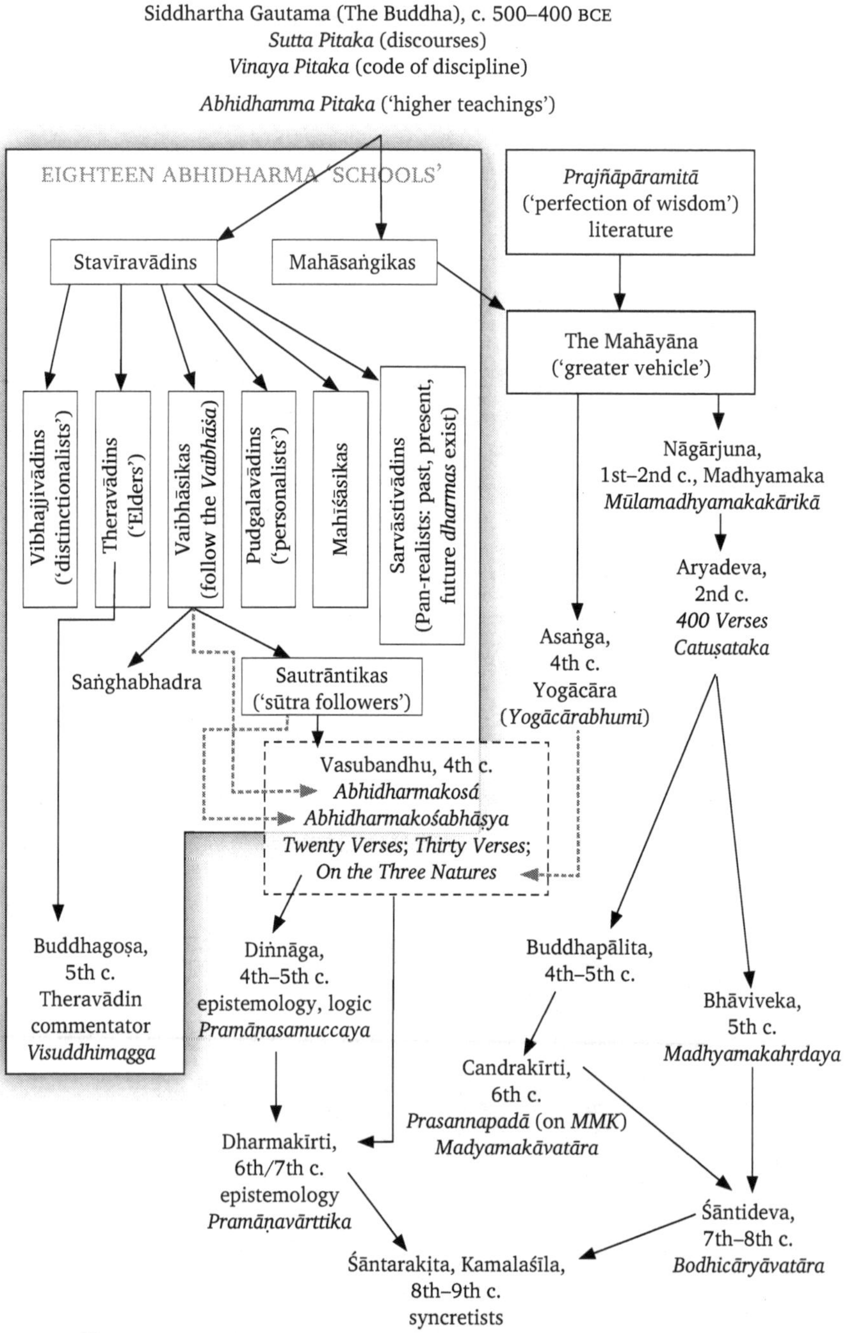

Siddhartha Gautama (The Buddha), c. 500–400 BCE
Sutta Pitaka (discourses)
Vinaya Pitaka (code of discipline)
Abhidhamma Pitaka ('higher teachings')
EIGHTEEN ABHIDHARMA 'SCHOOLS'
Stavīravādins
Mahāsaṅgikas
Vibhajjivādins ('distinctionalists')
Theravādins ('Elders')
Vaibhāsikas (follow the *Vaibhāsa*)
Pudgalavādins ('personalists')
Mahīśāsikas
Sarvāstivādins (Pan-realists: past, present, future *dharmas* exist)
Saṅghabhadra
Sautrāntikas ('sūtra followers')
Vasubandhu, 4th c.
Abhidharmakosá
Abhidharmakośabhāṣya
Twenty Verses; Thirty Verses; On the Three Natures
Buddhagoṣa, 5th c. Theravādin commentator *Visuddhimagga*
Prajñāpāramitā ('perfection of wisdom') literature
The Mahāyāna ('greater vehicle')
Nāgārjuna, 1st–2nd c., Madhyamaka *Mūlamadhyamakakārikā*
Aryadeva, 2nd c. *400 Verses Catuṣataka*
Asaṅga, 4th c. Yogācāra (*Yogācārabhumi*)
Diṅnāga, 4th–5th c. epistemology, logic *Pramāṇasamuccaya*
Buddhapālita, 4th–5th c.
Bhāviveka, 5th c. *Madhyamakahṛdaya*
Candrakīrti, 6th c. *Prasannapadā* (on *MMK*) *Madyamakāvatāra*
Dharmakīrti, 6th/7th c. epistemology *Pramāṇavārttika*
Śāntideva, 7th–8th c. *Bodhicāryāvatāra*
Śāntarakịta, Kamalaśīla, 8th–9th c. syncretists

ONE

The Buddha's suffering

The legend is familiar, and simply told. At the birth of the only heir to the family fortune, wise men confer and determine that the child will either be a great ascetic or else a great ruler. Greatly preferring the latter outcome for his son, the father does his best to bring up the boy in luxury, in a comfort designed to offer no occasion for untoward thoughts of renunciation or joining up with the wandering ascetics, society's dropouts, known even in far-off Greece for their naked insight.

Suddhodana, even in the fifth century BCE, would not have been the first father whose careful, well-meaning plans were thwarted by a headstrong son. For adolescent Siddhartha Gautama, the heir apparent, takes to stealing away from the comforts of home, riding about town to discover what his father has been keeping from him. What he discovers, to his shock and dismay, is sickness: disease, aged decrepitude and death – all the ugly, mundane miseries that befall a person. Just as Suddhodana thinks he has his son safely married off, Siddhartha determines to leave it all behind and go out in search of some answers. Shortly after the birth of his own son, and in spite of all temptations to enjoy the goods that wealth, family and status can confer, Siddhartha slips away.

At that time there is no shortage of seekers and wanderers, so Siddhartha Gautama joins them, enduring all manner of extreme deprivation and learning what he can from whomever has something to teach. He quickly surpasses all his teachers in meditational states and ascetic practices but none of this gives him what he was looking for. On the verge of starvation, Siddhartha accepts an offering of food, sits beneath meditate and wrestles with his demons – on some orty-nine nights – and in the morning he *understands*. at first convinced such understanding can be shared:

> onsidered: 'This Dhamma that I have attained is profound, ard to see and hard to understand ... this generation delights in attachment .... It is hard for such a generation to see this truth .... If I were to teach the Dhamma, others would not understand me, and that would be wearying and troublesome for me.' ... Considering thus, my mind inclined to inaction rather than to teaching the Dhamma."
>
> (*MN* 26, "Ariyapariyesana Sutta" [The Noble Search], §19)

He overcomes his reluctance, however, and without much confidence that he will be understood, Gautama – now awakened, *buddha* – begins to teach others what he has understood, and how. All his teachings are oral.[1] He never returns to the householder's life. After decades of teaching, the Awakened One passes away, without home, without possessions, without family, and without having written a word.

What he taught was collected after his death through the mutually verified recollection of those who were there. These *sūtras*, the discourses of the Buddha, form the basis of Buddhist thought and practice. The attempts by those who followed to make the descriptions of reality and of ourselves contained in these teachings clear, precise, consistent and compelling became the *abhidharma* – the higher teachings – and eventually became Buddhist philosophy.[2]

But what was it that *bothered* Siddhartha Gautama? What compelled him to abandon the palace? What was he looking for? The first thing the Buddha taught upon his enlightenment, and continued to teach for the rest of his life, was the truth of suffering; so this might provide some clue. But the banal, everyday misery we are all, to some extent, familiar with does not really explain anything, for it is precisely such misery that makes most of us long and strive for the cosseted life Siddhartha decides to abandon. Why did he not rather shrink back in horror when he saw the diseased man, decide his father was right, appreciate that he was himself a very lucky young man indeed and go on to become a powerful ruler over men? How was he seeing things instead?

The Buddha, Buddhism and Buddhist philosophy

Siddhartha Gautama, Sage of the Śakyas, belongs with Socrates and Diogenes of Sinope (called 'dog-like', *cynicos*) in being motivated to reflection by pressing practical concerns. The compulsion to philosophy comes from the question 'How should I live?', and this is a question in which everything is at stake.

Like the Greek tradition inaugurated by Socrates, followed through in various ways by Plato, Aristotle, the Stoics, the Sceptics and even the ancient Epicureans, the immediate and inescapable question 'How should I live?' leads Gautama, who will become awakened, just as immediately and inescapably to the question 'What am I?' and from there to 'How am I situated?' or 'What is the nature of that reality I am part of?' That is to say, ethics leads inexorably to metaphysics, to moral psychology, and to epistemology, as I ask about my relation to reality and capacities with respect to it.

The Buddhist tradition resembles the Greek in a more specific way, for both traditions favour strongly cognitivist, even rationalist, answers to these questions, although internal disputes remain about how that should best be understood. At the very least, *knowing* or *investigating* the true nature of reality and our own nature is part of the answer to the question 'How should I live?' The result is that, for the Buddhists, as for the Greeks, *metaphysics matters*.

From a contemporary perspective, this similarity between classical Greek and classical Indian philosophy is immediately striking because it is so strikingly at odds with contemporary academic philosophy. For the metaphysics that mattered to Plato and Vasubandhu alike was not some lofty examination of God, but metaphysics in that most mundane sense: the study of parts and wholes, of substance and attributes, and relations; questions about unity and multiplicity, identity over time and across distance, about causation – all those questions that arise in the examination of what things are real, and what is it for something to be real, and then by extension the study of our ways of relating to this reality.

Such everyday metaphysics and epistemology concern everyday life. Even if some kind of cognitive union with ultimate reality is itself a supreme good, the practice of seeing reality (and ourselves) as it is has practical consequences long before any such goal is reached. The way metaphysics matters *morally* is in the messy everyday of trying to live a better life and be a better person. In this, the similarity between ancient Greeks and Indians, and their distance from us, is manifested in a similarly comprehensive conception of the domain of the moral. We are concerned in both cases with living a life well, in all its aspects, and with improving our characters; for philosophers from both traditions such improvement and living well offered the only prospect for real happiness.

There are two ways in which metaphysics might matter morally, in this sense: (i) what is true makes a difference for ethical life; and (ii) seeking and understanding this truth matters. To say that metaphysics matters for the first reason is to see that one's metaphysical view can underwrite or undermine various moral positions, moral behaviour or even morality itself (the ability to conceive of the ethical). It can lead to, force or preclude particular moral views, kinds of moral thoughts or even the possibility of thinking morally. In the second sense, it is *doing metaphysics* that matters: the practice of reflecting on, questioning and thinking over the basic nature of reality is good for your soul and good for your life; it is morally edifying to think about whether, for example, wholes are anything distinct from their parts. In what follows, we shall find that psychology, epistemology and metaphysics matter morally in both these ways for the Indian Buddhist philosophers.

Some methodological remarks are in order here. Buddhism is a religion and not every Buddhist has been interested in critical inquiry any more than every Christian has been interested in critical inquiry. Most people practising a religion want to know how the practice goes, what the framework is for thinking about things, and that basic questions as to the coherence of the view can be answered (by someone) satisfactorily. Others have cared very much to examine and discuss with each other what exactly the view of reality and of human nature and the good *is*, and what the implications of this are. And they have cared very much whether this view can be defended against the objections of less sympathetic inquirers. These latter engaged in philosophical debate with each other and with non-Buddhists, and they expected to be giving and receiving reasons and evidence that did not presuppose agreement.

Some of what we want to know is how this discussion unfolded and what the salient questions and debates were as they arose 'from inside', so to speak; but we might also bring our own questions to this discussion and look to draw out implications that – as it happened – never arose in classical India. In the former case, we must come to participate in a discussion that our familiarity with the European tradition has not equipped us to understand; in the latter case, we must in addition actually generate a discussion that has not yet taken place.

In this we must follow our instincts about which kinds of questions matter and we must not do our Buddhist authors the disrespect of keeping at such a careful, sanitized distance from their answers that any old absurdity might pass unchallenged, with an insipid 'They thought differently then'. Refusing to engage critically is a refusal to take these thinkers seriously. At the same time, we must also engage respectfully, listening carefully to the texts we are reading, and making sure we do not simply force rigid preconceptions onto the material we are investigating. If we pose a question to which the texts seem only to offer stupid answers, or lame ones, we ought to consider whether our question is really as clever or deep as we suppose, or whether there might be a fundamental difference in orientation or aims, so that we are talking at cross-purposes. In the end, the whole exercise – like all good philosophical conversation – should reflect us back to ourselves, throwing into sharper relief our own categories, presuppositions and structures of thought, as well as illuminating new options for which we had not yet seen space.

What the Buddha understood: the four Noble Truths

There are four related claims at the centre of the Buddha's teaching. Refinements in our understanding of these and their implications form the foundations out of which Buddhist philosophical thought developed. The four so-called 'Noble Truths' are:

1. This is suffering.
2. This is the cause of suffering.
3. This is the cessation of suffering.
4. This is the way to the cessation of suffering.

There is much left underspecified in these but we can see already that there are explicit claims being made about the nature of reality and its dynamics. The first Noble Truth asserts something about how things are. The second responds by inviting us to look at the cause or explanation: what makes reality be like that? And again, the third Noble Truth makes a reality claim: there is a cessation of suffering. And the fourth invites us to consider the cause of that previous claim: what are the causes of the state of affairs described in the third Noble Truth?

This dynamic move between observing what is, or how things are, and then investigating how they came to be so, is central to the character of Buddhist practical and ethical thought. 'Seeing things as they are' is one way of describing both Buddhist practice and the end to be attained; that everything has causes, and consequences cannot be changed without changing the causes, is one of the central lessons that one learns, and must learn over and over again. *Pratītyasamutpāda* – mutually dependent origination, or the insistence that everything comes to be depending on other things as their cause – is one of the core concepts deployed in articulating the Buddhist view of reality, and its precise meaning and implications will figure in one of the most important intra-Buddhist debates.

These debates move swiftly from suffering to mereology and trope theory; from dependent origination to anti-foundationalism; from psychology to non-conceptual content and a linguistic theory appropriate to it; from giving reasons to theories of reasoning. But as our exploration of the view framed by the four Noble Truths becomes increasingly sophisticated, we must not forget that these are the central claims of Siddhartha Gautama, known as Śakyamuni, the Sage of the Śakyas, who abandoned a life of luxury, fame, power and family – all the things that move us – because he could not go on living without seeking and finding this truth and, having found it, could never live in the same way again. That is, this might be metaphysics, epistemology, ethics, semantic theory and moral psychology – all the abstract areas of classical philosophical inquiry – but it is philosophy with consequences. Answers to these questions move us dynamically between the four Noble Truths, a deeper understanding of which moves us along the path out of suffering. There is a fundamentally practical, and ultimately optimistic, structure to the four principles taken together: although suffering does exist, it does not arise arbitrarily or inevitably. It has causes that we can not only grasp, but also remove. Experience does not *have* to be one of suffering, and we ourselves can make it otherwise.

Exploring the four Noble Truths

The centrality of suffering to Buddhism is both difficult to overlook and difficult to accept. It is fundamentally unlike the role suffering plays in Christianity, where it is presented as ennobling and purifying.

For the Buddhist, suffering is simply how things are. In fact, it is how *everything* is: *sarvaṁ duḥkhaṃ*,[3] 'all is suffering', or 'everything suffers'.

This claim about the nature of reality – or of our experience of it – can strike one as either trivial or false, and not just at first blush. For it is not the case that every moment of life is miserable. But if the claim is merely that everyone suffers at some point or another, this is hardly news – and hardly worth leaving the comforts of a luxurious home to starve yourself for five years for, wandering homeless ever after. Granted that at some point or another everyone is faced with some suffering, it is hard to see what the *problem* is supposed to be here. On the other hand, if the claim is that *everything is suffering* – all our experiences are suffering ones – then this is just plainly false. There are moments of joy and rejoicing and pleasure and contentment, and even periods of life full of such things.

The claim might be the slightly more modest claim that *on balance* the miseries of life always outweigh the joys; or else that on reflection all those apparent joys are actually sufferings, whatever we might think or feel about them at the time. But again, both of these formulations remain highly contentious.

We can put the problem in terms of an equivocation on the notion of 'suffering': on a common understanding of suffering, it is *painful*. Suffering is something that happens too much to a few unfortunate people, or something that unfortunately befalls all of us from time to time – when we fall off our bicycles, or stub our toes, or get ill. But *this sort* of suffering, sheer pain – pain not chosen, and not adequately compensated for by greater pleasures – is not something constantly consuming us (at least not most of us lucky enough to have the leisure and security to consider matters like this); and such pain *is* something we can take measures to avoid. The threat of pain does give me good reason to take those measures, but for this I do not need the Buddha's 'Path'; I just need to look both ways before crossing the street. On the other hand, if the 'suffering' meant here is supposed to be something all-pervading, something inescapable and constant, but not necessarily painful, then I might be baffled about why I should bother taking measures – the Buddha's or any others – to avoid it. What is so bad about it? By calling it 'suffering' at all we are unjustly tarring everything with the same brush. After all, even the badness of evident pain might be questioned. If we could quantify it, even if there were always more suffering than happiness or joy, we might think the little bit of joy is of infinitely greater value: as we say, 'it makes it all worthwhile'.

Or, where the suffering and joy at issue are uncontroversial pains and pleasures, it may be after all the *meaningfulness* of my life I care about, not its overall pleasure–pain balance.

Some try to address this worry through translation. Thus, Thanissaro Bhikkhu chooses 'stress' and 'stressful' to translate *duḥkha* in *MN* 9, and 'distress' in his translation of *MN* 137. Other translators prefer 'dissatisfaction'. 'Stress', however, is a distinctively modern phenomenon; and while an assertion that stress is ubiquitous may strike a chord, and be appropriate to current conditions, it makes the claim about the overall nature of reality *less* plausible, rather than more so. 'Dissatisfaction' has the advantage that it does not imply physical *pain*; indeed, it suggests a mental phenomenon that can plausibly be low grade enough to be easily overlooked. Perhaps many more experiences *are* dissatisfying than are usually noticed. Furthermore, dissatisfaction has a direct connection to desires unfulfilled, which, as we shall see, is one of the primary sources of *duḥkha*. But it is still not obvious that whatever *dissatisfaction* could be said to be all-pervading is also of a kind to be regretted. Moreover, 'dissatisfaction' seems quite inadequate to capture the disease, old age and death that moved the Buddha to leave the palace: 'dissatisfaction' is hardly the relevant description for someone suffering a fatal or debilitating disease. *Duḥkha* is, like 'suffering', an inclusive notion, encompassing equally unhappiness, pain, misery, dissatisfaction and sorrow.

So the Buddhist has to convince us that suffering is indeed pervasive, and that this pervasive phenomenon is indeed *bad*: that the very suffering that is pervasive is something we have reason to do something about, if we can. If we cannot eliminate it (after all, the claim is that *all suffer*, suffering is a mark of existence), then recognition of it should so alter my perspective and behaviour that the comfortable life of indulgence and power is no longer attractive.

The second Noble Truth, the cause of suffering, might make it look as if the Buddhist opts for the 'redefinitional' interpretation of the first Noble Truth. For the cause of suffering is listed under three heads – greed (*lobha*), aversion or hatred (Pā: *doṣa*; Skt: *dveśa*) and delusion (*moha*) – often called the three roots of suffering.[4] The first two taken together are described as 'craving' (Pā: *tanha*; Skt: *tṛṣṇa*), and sometimes said to be rooted in delusion, confusion or ignorance of reality.[5] Although often translated as 'ignorance', *moha* should not be taken to be a mere blank, an absence of cognition or information. It is, rather, a cognitive state where thinking in a certain way actively interferes with correct understanding. If it is our basic ways of seeing things, our likes and dislikes, attractions and aversions that are the cause of suffering, this does sound rather like an ambitious programme designed to persuade us that either all our emotions and activities lead ultimately to suffering, or else they are themselves (unbeknown to us) forms of suffering. It is wanting that makes us (and others) suffer, whether we get what we want or not.

Indeed, one encounters much such talk among those describing the Buddhist view, and there is some merit in it. On reflection, we are suffering – in an obviously negative sense – much more than we might at first suppose, even in our laughter and loves, or perhaps especially there. We laugh out of pain, anger or bitterness or to cover over some unhappiness. Our loving is filled constantly with fear: fear for the beloved, fear of losing the beloved, fear of not loving well enough, fear of falling out of love. Even getting what we want fills us with terror at the inconstancy of ourselves and of others, and of the world. We then have to protect the material comforts we acquire for ourselves against the envy of others, as well as against the ravages of time and circumstance. The pleasure we get from objects, and even from other persons, carries with it the dim and poisonous awareness that the pleasure is fleeting and so elusive. When that pleasure fades, I will want more of the same or of another kind entirely, and I will have to exert myself to get it, with no guarantee of success. Whether or not the pleasure fades, I am constantly concerned about the potential sources of pleasure and pain, whether they will be mine in the future, whether they have been mine in the past. Thus, there is a great deal of sorrow, anger, frustration, disappointment and fear being enacted, fed and denied in everyday circumstances, even in the everyday circumstances we are likely to think of as pleasant. Each joy announces its own imperfection: this too shall pass; or if it does not, it sets us up for a cruel disillusionment when it does, in fact, pass away. Whether joy engenders the delusion that I am exempt from misfortune, or whether it carries within it the bite of fear, anxiety and desire, it is often not unequivocally pleasant, unsuffering and good. And this is because of our basic tendency to want to have things our way. Our attraction to some things, our aversion to others and the delusion that we can and should go out and get what we want – make over our reality and environment in the image of our wishes – only bind us more to the ongoing drama of desire, fear and disappointment.

But in the end, accepting the first Noble Truth will not turn on persuading us that all our experiences are, after all, unsatisfactory and feel so. Suffering, as we shall see, is a fact before it is a feeling.

And yet, although everything suffers, it is possible for suffering to cease. This is the third claim at the core of the Buddhist view. How is this possible, given the first claim? *Because of the second.* Precisely because there is a cause of suffering, it can be brought to an end by eliminating the conditions that give rise to suffering. And yet it remains the case that if *everything* suffers – if suffering does indeed characterize existence – this cessation will necessarily be unlike any experience we know or have the resources to articulate.

This ambition to articulate some aim quite unlike and outside ordinary experience picks up on a recognized ambition within Brahmanical culture of the time.[6] Already in the *Upaniṣads*, the futility of endless rebirth prompted a desire for liberation from all that, for *mokṣa*. Our ordinary state is one of bondage; our aim is to escape from this. But where the ascetics following the Vedas sought liberation, the Buddhist aim was *nirvāṇa*, 'cessation' or 'extinguishment'. This metaphor is telling. For if the aim is liberation, *mokṣa*, this invites the supposition that someone who was bound is now free. The metaphor of cessation or extinguishment, by contrast, does not.

'Extinguishment' in particular invites a different set of connotations, for it is above all something that happens to fire. The metaphor of fire is often appealed to within the Buddhist *sūtras* in order to illustrate a variety of points: the nature of dependency, the phenomenology of desire, the metaphysics of persons. Thus, the grass fire is so called according to its fuel. It arises owing to complex conditions; they are, so it is, constantly changing, and yet in some sense the same thing, and even the same fire. So similarly should we understand persons. Fire feeds on itself, creating the conditions for its continuation. Its intense, relentless pressure is, like desire, magnetically attractive, compulsive and dangerous. But most importantly, when a fire goes out there is nowhere that *it* goes *to*.[7] The metaphor of extinguishment thus deftly precludes the meaningfulness of the question 'Where has the one who has attained nirvāṇa *gone*?'

Although everything is suffering, then, there is a cessation of this suffering. Things do not just grind to a halt of their own accord; the conditions for cessation need to be generated. A fire's tendency is to replicate itself, appropriating whatever it can as its fuel, so long as fitting materials are available. Desire, aversion and ignorance are the fuel in this case: the causes of the ongoing suffering of everyday existence. If we do not want suffering – and that may still be an open question – then we should eliminate the causes of suffering.

The fourth Noble Truth offers an eight-point plan for doing just that. The way to bring about the cessation of suffering, called rather prosaically the Eightfold Path, comprises:

1. right view	3. right speech	6. right effort
2. right intention	4. right conduct	7. right mindfulness
	5. right livelihood	8. right concentration

The first two are collectively concerned with wisdom; the next three with action; and the last three with mental habit, cultivation or development.

This description of the way to the cessation of suffering is not a list of commandments, duties or prescriptions for action. In fact, of the eight, only three have to do directly with action; the rest are concerned with our 'inward' mental states. Thus we do not have, at least not at this level of description, anything like *rules* for living. What we have is rather a schema within which to reflect comprehensively on our lives, ourselves and our condition in all of its aspects.

And yet, however much we may not yet know how the 'right' is filled in here, the classification itself is by no means neutral. We might have imagined a rather different eightfold path, for instance: right external possessions; right adornments; right endowments; right accomplishments; right social status; right friends and family; right conduct, towards family, friends, foreigners, enemies; right livelihood.

We have here very apt headings for measuring the man and his life in ancient Athens, for instance; they reflect the tacit presumptions within and against which Greeks dwelt and thought, their conception of virtues and so on. In declaring, in the fourth Noble Truth, that these are the areas for consideration, choices have already been made, the shape of life outlined and a definite perspective recommended.

Right view and the path

Within this eightfold schema, 'right view' enjoys a kind of priority. To be sure, all elements are mutually reinforcing: none come without the others, and each needs to be addressed separately. If your livelihood depends upon things that harm others, then it will be difficult for you to develop mindfulness of the interconnectedness of things throughout everyday experience; if you engage in malicious or factional talk, it will be difficult to maintain right concentration, because your thoughts and emotions will be entangled and aggravated. Nevertheless, right view is the beginning and the end of the path, that in which all other aspects find their perfection.

> For one of right view, right intention originates. For one of right intention, right speech originates. For one of right speech, right action originates. For one of right action, right livelihood originates. For one of right livelihood, right effort originates. For one of right effort, right mindfulness originates. For one of right mindfulness, right concentration originates. For one of right concentration, right knowledge originates. For one of right knowledge, right liberation originates.
> (*AN* 10:121, PTS v.236)

Right view is what one begins with – and starting there, it is that by which one comes to recognize what right conduct, speech, intention, effort and so on consist in, in each case; it is that with regard to which one makes effort to practise mindfulness and concentration, establishing and impressing on oneself the right view; and it is that which – through right conduct, speech, livelihood, concentration and mindfulness – one comes fully to grasp, such complete grasp being what enlightenment and the cessation of suffering consists in.

The Eightfold Path is thus another substantive claim: how we understand the basic nature of reality makes a difference to how our life goes and to who we are as persons. Without a correct view of reality, life will not really go well. This is not just a philosophical claim; it is a claim that elicits philosophy. It is because of the centrality of this aspect of the path that Buddhist philosophy, metaphysics and epistemology especially, flourished with such vivacity in India for over a thousand years. That this understanding of reality must be *practised*, and fully incorporated into our way of feeling ourselves and our experiences, makes the Buddhist view unlike academic philosophy today – but makes it thereby *more* like, for instance, what the Hellenistic philosophers were getting up to.[8]

What is the content of the liberating right view? It is, primarily, correct understanding of the four Noble Truths themselves (see e.g. *MN* 141.24), especially (i) *that* everything suffers, or everything is suffering, and what this actually means; and (ii) the causes of suffering, in particular that it is our attachment that causes suffering, and that this attachment is itself rooted in ignorance or delusion. Which ignorance or delusion? "Ignorance of suffering", says the "Snake Sūtra" (*MN* 22). So we are back where we started.

At least this much is clear: the ignorance of suffering at issue is not the inexplicable failure to know that people get painfully sick and painfully die. Ignorance of suffering, rather, constitutes a fundamental misapprehension of the nature of reality, which misapprehension informs our cravings and aversions: "And what is ignorance? ... Not knowing about suffering, not knowing about the origin of suffering, not knowing about the cessation of suffering, not knowing about the way leading to the cessation of suffering – this is called ignorance" (*MN* 9, "Right View Sūtra", §66).

We want something because we think of it in a certain way, imagine it will be pleasant; we want to avoid something, judging it unworthy or hostile, in specific ways. Our aversions and desires themselves are part of seeing the world in a certain way. And if that is so, then these desires and aversions can be altered and eliminated by changing our beliefs about the world. The simplest example of this is the tempting glass of water sitting before a thirsty person. As soon as she knows it is poisonous, she loses all appetite for drinking that water.[9] This banal principle holds at each level. If my basic way of looking at the world – the concepts that frame my perceptions of what happens, what is valuable, what its causes are – if these basic, framing conceptions are mistaken, then so will be my desires, choices and actions. Since the four Noble Truths describe the nature of reality, our place and possibilities with respect to that reality, and the causes and connections between things, it is primarily non-delusion about these that constitutes right view and leads us out of suffering.

In order to get at this more specific and subtler form of delusion at the root of suffering, consider again the first two Noble Truths taken together, and their implicit claim that everything has a cause: that is to say, everything arises owing to conditions outside itself and cannot come into being without them. This might sound like good common sense or what European philosophers came to call the *principle of sufficient reason*. But it is an observation with serious implications. One of these is that there are no independently existing entities: no 'original existences', as Hume called desires.

You might think you already agree to this. But there is one area where almost none of us do, at least in practice, and that is with regard to ourselves. Of course, we all recognize that we are influenced by our environment; specific quirks or complexes were reactions to our upbringing, say; we respond to our environment. But we suppose that we ourselves are something: that there is something to us that is responsive to the environment. To our ordinary ways of living, thinking and experiencing ourselves, there is something about us that is independent of conditions, capable of being something more than just the resultant consequence of intersecting forces. This is, for instance, what it is to think of ourselves as agents, rather than merely subjects. But if everything arises depending on other things, then even the notion that we are something distinct from our experiences is a delusion. And indeed, this is the central delusion that leads to attachment, craving and aversion, and so to suffering.

An anatomy of suffering

All roads lead back to suffering. Ending it is impossible without understanding it. Let us, then, return to the unresolved question raised about the first Noble Truth: what is this 'suffering' that is supposed to be both pervasive and objectionable? How is the claim '*sārvam duḥkham*' not either trivial or false?

We need to find some sense of suffering that is broad enough to encompass the various sorts of phenomena we are familiar with – pain, dissatisfaction, frustration, disappointment, fear – and yet focused enough to ground the diagnosis that what is actually at issue is some one thing, plausibly called 'suffering'.[10] To that end, we might understand several different aspects or modes of suffering, each one more refined and more inclusive than the previous:

(i) One kind of suffering we might think of as brute, felt suffering: physical pain, of the sort that every ordinary natural creature feels under certain, specifiable circumstances. This is suffering as pain. Such brute suffering exists, certainly, but it hardly encompasses the whole of one's existence.

(ii) What have a broader reach, however, are the complex, felt sufferings that arise largely because sufferings of the 'brute' type are possible. These are feelings of misery, anguish, anxiety, fear, desire. For I want to avoid such brute suffering, am anxious to prevent it, and fear I may be unable to. This *phenomenological* suffering extends beyond episodic fears of imminent danger, for it is not just the fear of brute pain and the desire to avoid it, but extends to the general inclination to get *whatever it is* we want, and the wish to avoid *whatever* we do not want or like. This is because quite generally we experience 'getting what we do not want' as painful, while we generally experience 'getting what we want' as pleasant.[11] Thus, the description of suffering as 'not to get what one wants' and 'to get what one does not want' (*MN* 9.15).

(iii) This generic description, however, introduces a still wider and more subtle notion of suffering: suffering as lack of control, as impotence, as 'being at the mercy of another'. Presumably, we want to attain the object of our desires, and avoid the undesirable.[12] But the very reason these are *desires* is because the world does not always work out that way. In fact, it often does not. And the fact that, in spite of our desires and our strivings, the world does not grant us our wishes is itself a type of suffering. The fact of impermanence ensures that there will always be the possibility of the first two sorts of suffering, and thus brings us into permanent and inescapable contact with our impotence, our inability to control. This is reflexive, a generic dissatisfaction or discomfort felt at the second kind of pain, and the very possibility of it, even when it is not presently occurring.

(iv) It is in connection with impermanence that the universal scope of the first Noble Truth comes in. For it is not just desires and attempts to satisfy them that are liable to conditions beyond my control; *everything* is affected by other things. The obverse side of transience, together with the plausible claim that nothing arises without cause, is 'mutually dependent origination' (*pratītyasamutpāda*). Everything is subject to the effects upon it of other things, so that nothing is fully self-determining or free from external determination. We might call this 'metaphysical suffering'; *everything* that is a 'doer' with respect to other things is so only because it 'has things done to it'. Indeed, whatever is an agent is at the same time a patient, so that there is no 'agency' of the independent sort we take ourselves to have or, indeed, sometimes even to be.

This interplay and the way one form of suffering typically gives rise to another, according to complex patterns, all of it in a dynamic and unstable motion, is called *saṃsāra*. The claim that all is suffering is *not* the absurd claim that there are no moments of joy, no pleasant feelings and no periods during which objects stay as they are in the way we expect them to. Rather, it is the claim that even all these agreeable features are inescapably parts of this interconnected system, over which we have no ultimate or complete control: over which, in fact, there is not, anywhere, any overall control or guide. Thus, even the pleasant and desired experiences within our shifting, arising experiences invariably confront us with the fact of this impotence and dependence.

If the only kind of suffering were this rarefied metaphysical suffering, then we might suppose we could simply shrug it off. 'So everything is affected by other things? No sense getting excited about it.' And there is even less sense, we might think, in inquiring into the cause of any such 'suffering', for it is simply a descriptive claim about the nature of reality: that everything is liable to affect others and to be affected by others. This is, if you like, a definition of what it is to exist. But in fact, the felt suffering – the motivation to look to the causes and try to change things – comes from what that metaphysical fact *does to us*, and what we do with it, and especially from the way we misunderstand ourselves in relation to reality.

Consider for a moment the insight contained in a bit of grammar.[13] In ancient Greek, the ordinary verb for 'suffer' (*paschein*) functions as the ordinary form of the passive of the verb 'to do' (*poiein*). That is to say, the language itself allows no distinction between 'suffering' and 'having something done to one'. Defining suffering through its contrast with *doing*, being active, expresses an important insight into the human condition and our conception of ourselves. To act, or to do, is to have control and authority over your movements. Lack of such control is suffering, both grammatically and phenomenologically. This appeals to an implicit conception of ourselves as agents, and not just patients, in the causal structure.

Suffering is primarily rooted not in pain, but in impotence: in 'being done to' instead of 'acting upon'. Since pain is usually not something most of us choose, most of the time, pain is most often *suffered*, and a form that our suffering takes. But even not-painful states can be unwanted and so distressing; and if they arise anyway, we suffer them. Regardless of any 'raw feel', we suffer under such unwanted circumstances *because* they are unwanted; but also because, through their arising in spite of our wishes, we experience our impotence. More or less explicitly, we experience a new, mental pain at that very fact.[14] Thus the fact of suffering – being in a situation of 'being done to' rather than 'doing' – and the phenomenology of suffering are deeply entwined, even if they can be distinguished conceptually.

If this describes our condition, then living is the experience of an intractable problem, for *we are not in control.* Whatever marginal and transient success we may have in controlling our circumstances, we *always* fail to control them *completely* and *ultimately*,[15] and lack of complete control is no control at all. For without absolute control, there is no telling when and how something may come in to upset all one's plans, undoing whatever one had built up so far. And since there is no complete control, any partial success at making the world accord with one's desires must bring with it anxiety and fear for what unknown threats lie over the horizon, and protective energy exhausted in attempting to avert them. Striving to assert oneself as agent thus brings with it the fear and aversion towards whatever may limit or undermine that agency.

One might suppose that one does not, after all, seek *tyrannical* power; one may be content with some modest and limited areas of self-determination without wanting to control the world. Because of the vulnerability of one's accomplishments, this supposition may, in fact, be vain and disingenuous. But even supposing one could take oneself to be an agent, to act upon the world, without the anxious concern for preserving the results from unknown threats, the suffering internal to agency cuts deeper. The agent determines the world, or herself, through her action, without that action itself being determined by anything else. The agent, *qua* agent, should be self-determining, independent. This is how we distinguish action from other personal processes such as digestion. But if there is no such item in reality – nothing that is purely self-determining – then these supposed moments of intentional action are themselves something caused and created by other, non-agential factors. The shape and occurrence of our intentions and their related actions are determined by countless factors external to themselves, over which there is no control or oversight. Agency as self-determination is an illusion.[16] In so far as we are wedded to this idea of ourselves as agents, we badly mistake our situation, with inevitable practical costs. To the extent that we are aware of determiners of our actions, but experience them as alien intrusions, compromising the purity of our will, this awareness itself becomes felt as suffering: an unsatisfactory situation undermining our integrity and to be eliminated, which elimination is, of course, inevitably frustrated.

Such inadequacy can perhaps be tolerated if there is at least some meaningful purpose to this endless arising of transient things. Just as pain can be converted into non-suffering by our choosing it, and just as we might actively choose pain when we conceive of it as an inevitable part of a meaningful and worthwhile project, so too our metaphysical suffering could be embraced and made tolerable by conceiving of it as a necessary part of a meaningful order. Perhaps we are not in control, but *someone* is. Thus the prospect of a benevolent and rational creator-god, and the providential ordering of reality this brings with it, can offer solace for our own impotence. Our own plans and desires may be thwarted; our very having of plans that are our own may be an illusion. Never mind, for all this is necessary for the greater purpose of the universe. But, says the first Noble Truth, there is no such guide, controller, rational principle or purpose to redeem the unsatisfactory transience of things and our own inadequate authority over them.[17]

Here, then, is the *problem* of suffering: being vulnerable to forces outside our control, to no purpose, is suffering; the world being fundamentally outside our control, and not the unfolding expression of any hidden meaning, our attempts to assert and maintain control, to establish hidden meanings, and thus to avoid such suffering, only lead to more suffering.

The first Noble Truth is a profound appreciation of the inbuilt structure of reality, and therefore of our experience. It should prompt an exploration of its internal logic and manifestations: the second Noble Truth. And by putting 'right view', and systematic reappreciation of the world at the centre of the way to the cessation of suffering, the overall effect is an insistence that the only way out of the problem is *through* it, through facing it and understanding what we are facing.[18] We should address suffering by accepting it, and eliminate suffering by eliminating our misguided and self-defeating desire to avoid it by fleeing into transient sense-pleasures and delusions about our control.

The recommendation is to improve the *pathē* – the emotions, pleasures, desires that come over us – through metaphysics, rather than by attempting to exert control. We should practise seeing things as they really are in this specific respect: myself, others and the world as without essence, without ultimate bearers, or ground, or goals that justify whatever pain or suffering arises. This fundamental shift in perspective and presumptions will eliminate a great deal of self-created suffering: namely, all that which comes from lamenting our vulnerable state and trying to escape it, and that which comes from trying to hold on to what is transient. It breaks the feedback loop that makes more phenomenal suffering out of metaphysical suffering. If the first step in alleviating suffering is to accept it, this step is achieved by understanding correctly the nature of reality. That is, the path to happiness is the practice of metaphysics.

If suffering is a description of the nature of reality, then as long as we are a part of that reality, that suffering will not be eliminated entirely. All forms of suffering that depend upon our craving, our attachment, our wanting things to be other than they are, and the many conflicted emotions that this gives rise to, may be eliminated; but sheer physical pain remains one of those vicissitudes to which anything embodied is liable. Asked whether the Buddha, enlightened and without any remaining unwholesome or afflicted qualities, ever experienced pain, the Buddhist monk Nāgasena replies:

> Yes, when at Rājagaha, the Lord's foot was grazed by a splinter, when he was ill with dysentery, when his body was disturbed by humours and a purging was given him by Jīvaka, when he was troubled by wind and the Elder who was his attendant looked for hot water.
>
> (*Milindapañhā, MP* I.iv.8, PTS 134)[19]

What we can do is cease generating further suffering out of that, and cease creating the causes for further suffering. That is, we take aim at the ignorance, and at the craving and aversion that keep things suffering. Those few enlightened in this lifetime will still feel hunger when they do not eat, and they feel it as – in some sense – painful. Even enlightened ones feel pleasure at eating wholesome, rightly acquired food when hungry. But their relations to these desires, pleasures and pains are altered through their recognition that none of it amounts to a permanent satisfaction, or a reassurance that they are solid, powerful, in control. Everything is, and remains, as much agent as patient. Moreover, their relations to others are altered and consist partly of a heightened consciousness of the fact that others, too, are inevitably suffering: not only as a metaphysical fact, but in occurrent desires, pains and pleasures that invariably arise and over which they have no control. This is the basis of the compassion they inspire.

TWO

Practice and theory of no-self

> Formerly, one believed in 'the soul' as one believed in grammar and the grammatical subject: one said, 'I' is the condition, 'think' is the predicate and conditioned – thinking is an activity to which thought *must* supply a subject as cause. Then one tried with admirable perseverance and cunning to get out of this net – and asked whether the opposite might not be the case: 'think' the condition, 'I' the conditioned; 'I' in that case only a synthesis which is *made* by thinking.
>
> (Nietzsche, *Beyond Good and Evil*, §54)

No-self as practice

In ancient Greece, an inscription at the entrance to the Temple of Apollo at Delphi famously enjoined those who entered, 'Know thyself'. Socrates made this injunction central to his conception of philosophy and so of the good life, taking the pursuit of it to consist in an examination of one's own beliefs, especially beliefs about values, good and bad, right and wrong.[1] Plato refers twice to this intriguing injunction: in the *Phaedrus* (230a) and *Charmides* (164d), where the nature of the soul (simple or complex?) and of our access to it (transparent or occluded?) are under discussion. But in the *Alcibiades*,[2] 'knowing thyself' involves understanding your talents, family background, social status and material possessions, and how this places one to act in the world. For Aristotle, knowing oneself involves a special sort of reflexive consciousness, together with the understanding that such consciousness is the finest thing in us and, in some sense, divine.[3] The Stoics held that what we *really* are, and would exclusively identify with if we knew it, is our rational faculty, and they advocated practices for coming to appreciate this truth in everyday life. It is into this sort of discussion and debate that we should fit the Buddhist *anātmavāda*, which we might formulate, in a revision of Delphi, as 'Know thy lack of self!'

We have already stumbled upon one version of this injunction in our exploration of suffering. If suffering means 'to be affected', to be dependent rather than self-determining, and such suffering is pervasive, then it is true of us, as of everything: we are not in control; no one is. We are not independent. There is no supremely inviolable self, untouched by the vicissitudes of changing reality. This *anātmavāda* is the single most notorious and distinctive feature of all Buddhist views. Some call this the no-self claim and others prefer non-self, while still others call it non-Self or no-Self. This irresolution over fine differences is apt, for while it is clear from the etymology that there is something being rejected or denied (the '*an*' is like the English 'un'), and that this is something to do with self or soul (*ātman*) in some sense, little else is clear and beyond dispute. It is not even clear the Buddha held any definite view about the non-existence of self.[4]

The *sūtras* do, however, have much to say – most of it negative – on the topic of self, and especially clinging to self and to any idea or concept of self. We might start with the HAPPINESS ARGUMENT. In the "Snake Sūtra", the Buddha says:

> "You may well cling to that doctrine of self that would not arouse sorrow, lamentation, pain, grief, and despair in one who clings to it. But do you see any such doctrine of self, bhikkhus?" – "No, venerable sir." – "Good, bhikkhus. I too do not see any doctrine of self that would not arouse sorrow, lamentation, pain, grief, and despair in one who clings to it."
>
> (*MN* 22.22)

There is a definite claim here: clinging to a view of the self – any view – brings suffering. Why should this be so?

One thought is that as soon as I identify something as 'me', then I am immediately concerned with 'mine' as opposed to others'.[5] "There being a self," the *sūtra* goes on, "would there be for me what belongs to a self?" The mistaken claims addressed in the "Snake Sūtra" are that, for various selected candidates, "This is mine, this I am, this is my self".[6] It is appropriating something as *mine* that makes me act selfishly, in the interests of that self and to the detriment of others, for as soon as I say 'mine', I want only the good things for myself. Thus desire and aversion are generated, and from these lamentation, and so on, for myself and others. This is how the so-called 'three roots' of suffering – delusion, craving and aversion – are related. I think of some things as 'to be had', to be made mine, others as 'to be avoided'. I think of this precious thing, myself, as something to be protected and indulged at all costs. Valuing what is 'I' and, by extension, what belongs to it, I long to make as much as possible belong to it, to let it grow and have dominion over its environment.[7] This may be the sort of desire that is doomed to frustration – whether or not there actually is some such self – for it is an inherently unsatisfiable desire, and we do not even have control over *how much* success we shall have in satisfying it. It is the sort of desire that sets us up for constant battle, without much in the way of rewards for our effort.

Moreover, to distinguish a 'me' is to set off 'others' separate from me, who can therefore threaten me and take things from me. I think they are real: as real as I am, and every bit as concerned with themselves as I am with myself. If my desires are thwarted, my fears realized, then I am diminished, and so have more to fear and more need to assert my will so as to reaffirm myself. The more I act on such desires and fears, the more I believe that reality is the way my desires and fears tell me it is and that this is the only way reality can be. Asserting I, and then appropriating some things as 'mine' and disavowing others makes me rigid, inflexible, selfish. Self-oriented desires thus bring us into conflict with the world, as well as with others, to our own unhappiness, then, as well as theirs.[8] And this will be so no matter what my metaphysical conception of that self.

This diagnosis turns on positing an immediate psychological pressure, from 'I' to 'mine', from identification to appropriation, from distinction to preference for the side of the distinction identified as 'I' and 'mine'. If such observations about the psychological and behavioural effects of belief in self are correct, this might give us reason to abandon any view of the self, to do as the Buddha recommends and say for each thing 'This is not mine, this I am not, this is not my self'. The first-century CE Buddhist Nāgārjuna, about whom we shall have much more to say in what follows, puts it this way:

> 'The I exists, the mine exists.' These are wrong ultimates, for the two are not [established] by a thorough consciousness

> of reality just as it is ... Having seen thus the aggregates as untrue, the conception of I is abandoned, and due to abandoning the conception of I, the aggregates arise no more.
>
> (*Ratnāvalī*, I.27–28, 30)[9]

Christopher Gowans formalizes this diagnosis by saying that the false belief in a 'substance-self' – that there is a stable entity, distinct from phenomena with which to identify – leads to the sort of mental activity of grasping and aversion that *creates*, generates and constitutes the continuum that is what we in fact are, 'process-selves'.[10] This process-self has a kind of reality, but a temporary and dependent kind: it is *created* by the belief in a substance-self. Falsely taking myself to be substantial generates 'mine'-thoughts, and associated beliefs, perceptions and feelings; these cause myriad intentions, desires, aversions and so on, connected into a distinct stream of tight causal interactions. This interconnected casual stream, set in motion by I-thinking, is what we call a 'person'. Such process-selves are dissolved when we remedy our delusive belief in the substance-self, for without this, there is no activity of grasping that sets in motion the processes and continua constitutive of the phenomenal process-self.

This has the advantage of making it obvious why it is that the belief in the self is the most important mistaken belief to dislodge. But we may yet have two doubts. First, is it psychologically plausible? How, psychologically, does a fairly specific metaphysical belief about substances (in the philosophical sense), at best tacit in most of us, actually ground the attachment and craving that keep us actively disrupting others and causing suffering? (We shall return to this at the end of the chapter.) Second, does the argument in fact identify a mistaken belief in the self-*as*-substance as the root of the problem? Is *denying* substantial selves, then, the remedy?

The pragmatic argument stops short of actually asserting that there is no self in any sense. The claim is, rather, that *whatever* way we try to think about the self – whether as eternal or as perishing, and whether as quite separate from any of the physical and psychological properties belonging to us, or as identified with some one, or subset of these constituents, or with or all of them taken together, whether as one thing or as many – whatever way we try to assert 'This is myself', and believe it, leads to suffering.[11] Refraining from endorsing such claims alleviates suffering. The damage is done not by thinking of something as 'self', but, rather, in taking something as *my* self, or even as 'who I *really* am'. It is the process of identification rather than the positing of a metaphysical entity that causes the trouble; so, on this view, even the impersonal formulation of the Brahamanical philosophers 'I am that' would still fall foul of the Buddha's injunction to abandon self.

This argument may not yet move us. Certainly, *too much* focus on oneself is a recipe for misery; valuing it too highly is a vice (alas, an all-too-common one). But this does not entitle us to conclude that we ought to – or even can – dispense altogether with a concept of self, and with thinking in terms of it. For there remains the fact that I am, after all, something enduring: persisting through time and change, whether my hair is short or long, my eyesight good or failing, my memory quick or muddled. Persisting through change, I am the haver of my thoughts, the bearer of my changing desires, the enjoyer of my pleasures, the sufferer of my pains. Compare this description offered by King Milinda in the *Milindapañhā*:

> The life-principle [*jīva*] within that sees material shape with the eye, hears sound with the ear, smells smell with the nose, tastes flavour with the tongue, feels touch with the body, and discriminates mental states with the mind. Just as we who are sitting here in the palace can look out of whichever window we want to look out of – the east, west, north or the south window – even so, revered sir, this life-principle within can look out of whichever door it wants to look out of.
>
> (*MP* II.iii.6, PTS 54)

When I am conflicted, feeling both desire and aversion towards the same end – towards, say, taking a walk – then I am the chooser, the agent distinct from the desire to walk and the desire not to walk who adjudicates between the two, and *does* the one or the other. I am the one who remembers working hard to get where I am today; I am the one who anticipates a life that is easier than it is now. I am the one who has various talents and various weaknesses, and who therefore rightly benefits from the exercise of these talents, and sadly suffers the results of the inadequacies. This is a formal notion of 'I'; it plays a role in the structure of our thought and grammar, and may even have metaphysical implications about unity at a time and over time. But this apparently indispensable notion is *merely* metaphysical; it is not a concept that need necessarily provoke thoughts of 'mine', of appropriation, self-assertion and preference.

Those who suppose we can separate this innocent notion of self from the psychologically problematic notion at work in the happiness argument might be moved by a second sort of consideration, the MORAL IMPROVEMENT ARGUMENT. For example:

> If there is the view, 'The soul and the body are the same,' there is no living of the holy life; and if there is the view, 'The soul is one thing, the body is another,' there is no living of the holy life. Without veering towards either of these extremes, the Tathāgata teaches the Dhamma by the middle: "With birth as a condition, aging-and-death [arise]."
>
> (*SN* 12.35, PTS ii.61)[12]

The formulation here is still in terms of holding a particular view about the nature of the self. But these views are to be rejected because thinking them true is a hindrance to living well; in the absence of an elaborate error theory, for which there is no evidence, we must suppose that *thinking it* true is a hindrance because *if it were in fact true*, then living a better life would be impossible. So the source of the difficulty is now the self actually being *either* identical to *or* separate from the various bits that either constitute or belong to it, respectively. Thus, a *sūtra* appearing soon afterwards in the *Saṃyutta Nikāya* (*The Connected Discourses of the Buddha*) advises that "It would be better, bhikkhus, for the uninstructed worldling to take as self this body composed of the four great elements, rather than the mind. For what reason?" Because the body is experienced as relatively stable over time, while the mind "arises as one thing and ceases as another by day and by night" (*SN* 12.61, PTS ii.94–5). While identifying oneself with the body, or as distinct from it, makes the holy life impossible, even such identification would be preferable to misidentifying oneself as identical to the mental life.

The Buddha does not elaborate here about *why* identifying the self as the same or different from the body or mind should make 'the holy life' impossible. But perhaps the thought is that living the holy life requires some sort of transformation – hence the Moral Improvement Argument. On the one hand, if I am identical to all the various modes, moments and characteristics ordinarily thought to constitute or belong to the self, then I am the bad qualities as well as the good ones, the worse as much as the better. I cannot claim allegiance to only the subset of attractive properties and say that only these are 'me', for 'I' am the totality. On the other hand, neither can we instead suppose the self is an entity distinct from these various characteristics, unqualified by them. For then when I become more generous, say, there might be *something* better now than it was before (there is generosity now where there was meanness before), but this cannot be 'me', because the I which is eternal and independent of conditions cannot change at all. So, again, moral improvement is impossible. But there is no other possibility than for an existing entity either to be a distinct thing, or to be identical to some other existing thing. Therefore, if we are committed to moral improvement being even possible, we must reject the existence of self. Both passages conclude with substituting thoughts of continuity and causal connection in the place of questions about identity and individuals:

> The instructed noble disciple attends closely and carefully to dependent origination itself thus: 'When this exists, this comes to be; with the arising of this, that arises. When this does not exist, that does not come to be; with the cessation of this, that ceases'. (SN 12.61, PTS 95)

There are two lines of escape from this conclusion, for the one who would maintain the existence of a 'self'. First, one might challenge the ontological claim: any existing thing must be either identical to or distinct from other existing things. There *is* a third option, one might insist. We shall look at this later.[13] The second option is to bite the bullet: moral improvement is not possible. This would be the view, for instance, of a certain kind of monist, for change of all sorts is difficult to accommodate on a monist scheme. It is not an especially attractive option, either morally or metaphysically. But it should be acknowledged that the moral improvement argument, even at best, does not categorically disprove the existence of a self; the conclusion is conditional upon us being even more committed to the possibility of moral improvement than to the existence of self.

With a third, fairly common argument, we begin to get clearer on what exactly is supposed to be asserted or denied in asserting or denying the existence of self. It is a complex argument, working on two levels, bringing together practical and metaphysical thinking. This argument is also taken from the "Snake Sūtra"; but one finds essentially the same line of thought in the "Greater Discourse on the Full Moon Night" (*MN* 109), and elsewhere.[14]

> "Is material form permanent or impermanent?"
> "Impermanent, venerable sir."
> "Is what is impermanent suffering or happiness?"
> "Suffering, venerable sir."
> "Is what is impermanent, suffering and subject to change, fit to be regarded thus: 'This is mine, this I am, this is my self'?"
> "No, venerable sir."
> "... Therefore, bhikkhus, any kind of material form whatever, whether past, future, or present, internal or external, gross or subtle, inferior or superior, far or near, all material form should be seen as it actually is with proper wisdom thus: 'This is not mine, this I am not, this is not my self.'" (*MN* 22.26–7)

What is true for materiality will be true for feelings, volitions, perceptions, cognitions and even consciousness. Each of the identifiable constituents of ourselves is rejected in turn on the same grounds: it is impermanent, changing, suffering and so not *fitting* to be considered 'me'. Call this the WORTHLESSNESS ARGUMENT.

The Worthlessness Argument makes a surprising claim. Why should suffering make something *unworthy* of being the 'self', indeed so unfit that we can conclude it *is not* the self? Why should suffering make it undignified? After all, Christians seem to think that suffering *ennobles* a soul, can redeem and purify it. And why should we think that the self, if it is to exist at all, must be something especially dignified anyway? These surprising grounds for rejecting candidates for 'myself' invite some serious reflection on what it is we really want from *asserting* a self claim.

Recall our discussion of suffering. To suffer, in the broad metaphysical sense of it, is to be affected by another: that is, not to be self-determining but, rather, to have one's qualities, state, status, determined by another. Whatever is changing – at least if this change is not spontaneous generation (a sort of change Buddhists deny, along with most of us) – is affected by another just to the extent that it is changing. It is therewith dependent upon another, and again not self-sufficient. It is not the sole cause of its being how it is.[15]

One thing that we are often seeking, then, in supposing that we *are something* – whether for theoretical explanation or for reasons of self-esteem – is some claim to independence. There may be ever so many causes affecting us, but we are not *just* the effects of external causes; and we are not just passively affected. We can distinguish ourselves in thought and feeling from all of that – and, so distinguishing ourselves, we can choose to act on the world.[16] Liability to change touches a finer metaphysical point than mere indignity: anything liable to external determination cannot be in that respect self-determining, and so cannot be that executive deliberator and undetermined (free) chooser that we so immediately identify ourselves as being.

As a matter of fact, so distinguishing oneself from the causal flow of changing conditions was one of the predominating spiritual exercises and goals of the Brahamanical ascetics at the time of the Buddha and during the centuries that followed. Seeking the *true* self, and not being satisfied with false substitutes, is a leitmotif from the *Upaniṣads*, philosophical reflections on the Vedas composed before and contemporaneous with the beginnings of Buddhism. "Come! Let us search out that Self, the Self by searching out whom one obtains all worlds and all desires!", enjoins the *Chāndogya Upaniṣad*.[17] Correct understanding of the real nature of self promised the dedicated ascetic liberation from the cycle of rebirth and redeath.[18]

Especially against such a background, we can appreciate how vulnerability to alien influences disqualifies a potential candidate from being that thing, the 'self', that we thought we were looking for. Such a changing, externally determined thing may in some technical sense be a self, but in which sense, exactly? Well, it is at least what we are really like, and what our experiences are like. It is an accurate account of the phenomena and the phenomenology. But such a 'self', so described, does not invite identification. Seen for what it is, it would not prompt 'mine'-thoughts, or hold out occasion for something to protect from misfortune, or to aggrandize by accumulation of honour, fame, wealth or love. For none of that could alter its liability to be affected, and its lack of control over how it is affected. So this technical sense of 'self', while in one sense true to the phenomenology, cannot be how we are taking ourselves to be when we crave, appropriate, assert and generally attempt to exert control over our experiences. These unwholesome emotions arise precisely when we take ourselves to be something more or other than the changing, suffering, impermanent sort of thing familiar from all of our experiences.

Unlike the HAPPINESS ARGUMENT, the WORTHLESSNESS ARGUMENT makes a claim about what actually exists (or does not exist), rather than just about what is a useful belief to hold or to abandon, and it does so less equivocally than the MORAL IMPROVEMENT ARGUMENT. Its conclusion might be put: *There is no self worthy of the name.*

The mode of presentation, however, is not at all as we have extracted it. Instead the point is expressed as a practical exercise in metaphysics. The exercise begins with a list of all the identifiable existing things. These are classed into five broad kinds, and together instances of these five kinds of things exhaust the constituents of reality. Since we are most interested in investigating ourselves and our experiences, there is a heavy bias towards psychological categories, which are given a more finely specified analysis. 'Form' (*rūpa*), is the physical; 'feeling' (*vedanā*) is that portion of experience that can be pleasant and painful; perception or cognition (*saṁjñā*) is that part of experience that can be true or false; the *saṁskāras* are a capacious category, including most importantly volitions and various emotions; finally, consciousness (*vijñāna*) is awareness of object, the union of content with the mental activity that has content.[19]

There are, in fact, several different ways of categorizing things in the Buddhist Abhidharma, depending on the purpose of the analysis.[20] Analysis is for some purpose, to understand something or other. And for our purposes it will mostly be adequate and appropriate to use the schema sketched above, according to which existing things are divided into five *skandhas*, or 'heaps'.[21] Each *skandha* is a succession of moments or events of a particular kind, and the name itself declares one of their most significant features: like heaps, the *skandhas* have no necessary internal structure definitive of what they are. Each instance of feeling, or whatever, arises owing to suitable causes and conditions, of course, and not out of nowhere; but nothing about it belonging to the feeling-*skandha* dictates which sorts of feelings should arise when. Thus *skandha* is often aptly translated 'aggregate', for this brings out the notion of *mere* aggregation, as opposed to development or structure, which are teleological notions. Just what is aggregated and why will be made more precise as the discussion unfolds. For now, it is enough to know that it is feelings, cognitions and so on that are aggregated.

The WORTHLESSNESS ARGUMENT draws on this analysis of reality into five *skandhas*. In a detailed catechism, each one is held up for consideration, and each rejected on the same grounds. In order to reach the explicit conclusion that there is no 'self', these candidates for self must exhaust all possible candidates. This stronger claim is not actually made; however, one might regard it as implicit in what follows:

> Seeing thus, bhikkhus, a well-taught noble disciple becomes disenchanted with material form, disenchanted with feeling,

> disenchanted with perception, disenchanted with formations, disenchanted with consciousness.
>
> Being disenchanted, he becomes dispassionate; through dispassion, liberated. When it is liberated, there comes the knowledge: "It is liberated". He understands: "Birth is destroyed, the holy life has been lived, what had to be done has been done, there is no more coming into any state of being".
>
> (*MN* 22.28–9)

It seems reasonable to presume that dispassion follows disenchantment from the five *skandhas* because, after these, there are no further candidates for enchantment, nothing else to potentially become attached to. One might also note the impersonal formulation of the oft-repeated description of the liberated insight. Even here, thoughts of *who* has done this are resisted; there is no place for 'I'.

But the strength of this argument can also be measured in practical terms: we are not just informed that (according to the Buddha) changing things are not worthy to be considered 'me'; we are enjoined to engage in an ongoing practice of recognition about every thought-feeling-experience that arises, that this too cannot be 'me'. For it passes away, and the 'me' that I want to protect and defend had better actually *be there* once I've protected it, and the 'I' that acts should not be just a nervous tic, an involuntary reaction to external forces. But nothing in our experience is like that. So what we shall discover over time is that it turns out there is nothing there to be defended, and no independence to pride ourselves on. Each candidate for holding on to and centring a life around has been 'let go', for it was not the sort of thing that one *could* base one's life on.

Remember that the Buddha says that we practise seeing no-self primarily for moral reasons: if there were a view of self, clinging to which did not cause suffering, then he would be happy for someone to embrace that view. But no such view of self has been found.

> Therefore, bhikkhus, whatever is not yours, abandon it; when you have abandoned it, that will lead to your welfare and happiness for a long time. What is it that is not yours? Material form is not yours. Abandon it. When you have abandoned it, that will lead to your welfare and happiness for a long time. Feeling is not yours. Abandon it ... Perception is not yours. Abandon it ... Formations are not yours ... Consciousness is

> not yours. Abandon it. When you have abandoned it, that will lead to your welfare and happiness for a long time.
>
> (*MN* 22.40)

This gives us what we might call a *practice* of no-self, as opposed to a claim.[22] We are not just enjoined to abandon any view of self, as in the first argument. We are engaged in an ongoing practice of recognition and dissociation: first identifying clearly a distinct individual, recognizing what it is in order to actively dis-identify with it. This should be not just an informative process, learning each of the particular things in the world that are not self; it should become, more importantly, a sound mental habit and perspective, responding to what presents itself (howsoever urgently and immediately it presents itself) with a preparedness to recognize that seeing it for what it is, clearly identifying it, is at the same time to see that it is 'not-I'.

We might compare this with Stoic practice, especially as it is articulated so eloquently by the first-century CE Stoic, Epictetus. When anything vexing arises, he encourages us to bear in mind that the supposed cause of the vexation is nothing to do with 'me', properly considered. "Know that a thief or an adulterer has no place among the things that are your own, but only among the things that are another's and that are not under your control" (*Discourses* I.18.12).[23] Being not under my control, it is not really mine, so no part of my virtue, and therefore no part of what is good or bad, helpful or harmful, desirable or undesirable.

The practice has one significant difference, however. Epictetus supposes that there is, in the end, *something* – just one thing – that is under my control and worthy of identifying with: "your power of rational choice [*prohairesis*]. This is why the ancients gave us the injunction, 'Know thyself'" (I.18.18).

> What then should a man have in readiness in such circumstances? What else than "What is mine, and what is not mine; and permitted to me, and what is not permitted to me." I must die. Must I then die lamenting? I must be put in chains. Must I then also lament? I must go into exile. Does any man then hinder me from going with smiles and cheerfulness and contentment? "Tell me the secret which you possess." I will not, for this is in my power. "But I will put you in chains." Man, what are you talking about? *Me* in chains? You may fetter my

> leg, but my will [*prohairesis*] not even Zeus himself can overpower. (*Discourses* I.1.21–23)

The Buddha, by contrast, never suggests that, after all the other candidates have been rejected, there may be some final one that 'makes the cut' and should be properly identified as 'me'. In fact, the first argument claims that taking ourselves to have chanced upon such a candidate would be misguided and unbeneficial.

But recommending the cultivation of a certain habit of mind still stops short of the outright denial of any metaphysical self, on *any* conception of it whatsoever. Perhaps there is some self 'not worthy of the name' that nevertheless must be posited to make good sense of our experience. And indeed, although the Buddha says that questions such as "For whom is there this ageing-and-death?" (the question that prompts the advice at *SN* 12.35, quoted above) and "Who gets liberated?" are ill formed,[24] there are other places where he seems perfectly happy to talk in terms of individuals, distinct from one another and persisting through time and change. For instance, the Buddha characterizes his own 'omniscience' as consisting, in part, in the ability to recall each of his prior births at will. And in the much-contested passage on the Burden (*SN* 22.22–32, PTS iii.25–6), in answer to the question "what, bhikkhus, is the carrier of the burden?", the Buddha advises, "It should be said: the person, this venerable one of such a name and clan. This is called the carrier of the burden" (*SN* 22.22).

Some Buddhists knew each and every such passage well, and took them for evidence that the Buddha did not deny the self, in every sense of it, after all. It is simply not among the items of experience, nor can it be thought coherently in relation to these items, not even through the relations of 'different' or 'separate from'. It is not, therefore, something to seek or to find; there is no practical or soteriological value in experiencing it directly, as the Brahamanical ascetics supposed. It is, perhaps, a bit of metaphysical glue, making it possible for us to re-identify the same person over time and through change; it is perhaps a bit of psychological glue, preventing us from falling off the steep precipice into nihilism. If the continuity between different psychological events is real – as it must be if the no-self position is not itself to fall on the horns of the dilemma set by the MORAL IMPROVEMENT ARGUMENT – then the self must be equally real, for it just is this continuity. The person is, according to these Buddhists, *really* real; ultimately, there *are* persons, although as continua they are neither identical to nor existing separately from their constituents.[25] Although vociferously rejected by other Buddhists, the *pudgalavāda* – the person-claim – flourished for at least the first millennium of Buddhism in India; Xuanzang (Hsüan-tsang), a seventh-century scholar visiting India from China, records that more than a quarter of Buddhists of his time adhered to the *pudgalavāda*.

Nearly three-quarters, however, did not. And perhaps for good reason.

There are moral and practical reasons for dismissing any *doctrine* of 'self'. Such beliefs lead us to action that is inappropriate, and lead us to develop character traits that make ourselves and others unhappy; a fixed notion of the self as permanent or impermanent would make the very possibility of moral improvement conceptually impossible; and holding any particular variety of self-belief invests the thing believed in with a kind of importance it could not possibly live up to. It is not evident that supposing there to be a person, as the real continuity between certain things (and not others), avoids these problems. Moreover, a policy of 'de-selfing' – of rejecting any positive view of self and dis-identifying with any candidate self – cannot, on reflection, be metaphysically neutral. The plausibility of some of the happiness argument, for instance, rests on believing a certain metaphysical picture of the world: namely, a picture of reality as in constant flux, with nothing stable and enduring, and so on. Otherwise, it is not clear why holding some idea of self and trying to appropriate things as 'mine' should be guaranteed to lead to frustration. Even the self as the mere witness accompanying my experiences, but different from them and so unaffected by them and changeless throughout, gives me something to identify with, and identify as my own, and so to prefer to the exclusion of others.[26] If that is who or what I *really* am, then this is what I will value, promote and prefer, with corresponding aversions for all that has been identified as 'not really me'.

The Worthlessness Argument in particular appears to be trying to show that there is at least no self worthy of the name, and so nothing warranting inviting the pernicious consequences that follow from identifying something as 'myself'. If every candidate for self is changing, suffering, impermanent, then there is no distinct and unifying agent and subject enduring over time. And this is a metaphysical claim.

This impulse towards the outright assertion of no-self is given explicit expression in the voice of the nun Vajirā. The fifth part of

'Book of Verses' in the *Saṃyutta Nikāya* concludes with a description of how Māra, a disruptive force, attempts to distract and disorient the accomplished Vajirā:

> He approached and addressed her in verse:
> "By whom has this being been created?
> Where is the maker of the being?
> Where has the being arisen?
> Where does the being cease?" (*SN* 5.10, PTS i.135)

To these, Vajirā, identifying the mistaken presumption in the questions, replies:

> "Why now do you assume 'a being'?
> Māra, is that your view [*diṭṭi*/Skt: *dṛṣṭi*]?
> This is a heap of sheer formations [*saṅkhāra/saṁskāra*]:
> Here no being [*satta/sattva*] is found.
> "Just as, with an assemblage of parts,
> The word 'chariot' is used,
> So, when the aggregates exist,
> There is the convention 'a being'.
> It is only suffering that comes to be,
> Suffering that stands and falls away.
> Nothing but suffering comes to be,
> Nothing but suffering ceases." (*SN* 5.10, PTS i.135)

The *sūtras* leave us with an equivocal picture, then, about what the *anatta* claim is.[27] At the same time, it is very clear that understanding the claim is a central part of following the Buddha's path, and eliminating suffering. And, as the "Snake Sūtra" emphasizes, it is very important not to grasp the teachings in the wrong way:

> Suppose a man needing a snake ... saw a large snake and grasped its coils or tail. It would turn back on him and bite his hand or his arm or one of his limbs, and because of that he would come to death or deadly suffering. Why is that? Because of his wrong grasp of the snake. So too, here some misguided men learn the Dhamma ... (*MN* 22.10)

No-self as a metaphysical claim

The chariot as an analogue for the person turns up again in the *Milindapañhā* (*The Questions of King Milinda*), an Abhidharma text from about the beginning of the Common Era, purporting to be the record of a conversation between Nāgasena, a Buddhist monk, and the Greek king, Menander (Pā: *Milinda*), who reigned in Bactria in the second century BCE.[28] Nāgasena is evasive when the king asks who he is. My family call me Nāgasena, he says, "yet it is but a denotation, appellation, designation, a current usage, for Nāgasena is only a name since no person [*puggala*] is got at here" (*Milindapañhā* II.1, PTS 25]). The king retorts by calling him a liar. If Nāgasena himself is not found among existing things, then the person speaking to the king cannot be Nāgasena at all. Nāgasena replies by turning the tables:

> N: You, sire, are a noble delicately nurtured, exceedingly delicately nurtured. If you, sire, go on foot at noon-time on the scorching ground and hot sand, trampling on sharp grit and pebbles and sand, your feet hurt you, your body wearies, your thought is impaired, and tactile consciousness arises accompanied by anguish. Now, did you come on foot or in a conveyance?
> K: I, reverend sir, did not come on foot, I came in a chariot.
> N: If you, sire, came by chariot, show me the chariot. Is the pole the chariot, sire?
> K: O no, reverend sir.
> N: Is the axle the chariot?
> K: O no, reverend sir.
> N: are the wheels the chariot? [... *and so on for each part*...]
> K: O no, reverend sir.
> N: But then, sire, is the chariot the pole, the axle, the wheels, the body of the chariot, the flag-staff of the chariot, the yoke, the reins, the goad?
> K: O no, reverend sir.
> N: But then, sire, is the chariot apart from the pole, the axle, the wheels, the body of the chariot, the flag-staff of the chariot, the yoke, the reins, the goad?
> K: O no, reverend sir.
> N: Though I, sire, am asking you repeatedly, I do not see the chariot. Chariot is only a sound, sire. For what here is the

> chariot? You, sire, are speaking an untruth, a lying word. There is no chariot.

This conclusion is only the interim conclusion and it is probably good for Nāgasena that it is so, because you do not usually want to start your audience with the king by calling him a liar. Milinda is allowed his rejoinder:

> K: I, revered Nāgasena, am not telling a lie, for it is because of the pole, because of the axle, the wheels, the body of the chariot, the flag-staff of the chariot, the yoke, the reins, and because of the goad that 'chariot' exists as a denotation, appellation, designation, as a current usage, as a name.
>
> N: It is well; you, sire, understand a chariot. Even so it is for me, sire, because of the hair of the head and because of the hair of the body … and because of the brain in the head and because of material shape and feeling and perception and the habitual tendencies and consciousness that 'Nāgasena' exists as a denotation, appellation, designation, as a current usage, merely as a name. But ultimately [*paramattha*] the person is not got at here.
>
> (*Milindapañhā* II.1, PTS 26–8, trans. mod.)

The structure of the argument is straightforward, and resembles the dis-identification practices of the WORTHLESSNESS ARGUMENT, but with wider scope. For the argument is now a general metaphysical one regarding the (ultimate) reality of complex wholes. The chariot (or take any complex whole you like, the table, the tree, the astronaut) is either identical to one or the other of its parts; or it is identical to all of its parts together; or it is something distinct from its constituents. Milinda agrees, however, that although these are the only available options, the chariot is none of these things. By process of elimination, then, the chariot itself is eliminated. Nāgasena draws this false conclusion: that the chariot does not exist in any sense at all – the king was *lying* when he claimed to have journeyed by chariot. This prompts Milinda to draw the correct conclusion, which Nāgasena confirms by transferring the point back to its original context: the reality of Nāgasena.

The correct conclusion is that neither Nāgasena nor Milinda was lying in referring to the complex wholes, 'I, Nāgasena' and 'a chariot', respectively. There is no *really existing* thing, ultimately or in the last analysis, that 'chariot' or 'Nāgasena' refers to, or picks out; and yet, it is neither a *lie* nor a *mistake* to use such words. Notice, it is actually Milinda's *eliminativist* conclusion that prompts Nāgasena's rejoinder, not any theory the king has presented about 'the self'. Nāgasena argues not only against the supposition that there is a specific entity 'Nāgasena' among the existing things, but also against Milinda's presumption that if something does not exist *like that*, then it does not exist *at all*.

The fifth-century scholar Buddhaghoṣa, perhaps the most prominent and influential Theravādin commentator, also has no hesitation in seeing explicit metaphysical connotations in the *anatta* claim. Also picking up on Vajirā's chariot, Buddhaghoṣa quotes the verses, and refers to "many hundred suttas", in support of his claim that "above mere mentality-materiality [*nāma-rūpa*] there is nothing else that is a being or a person or a deity or a Brahmā" (*Vsm.* XVIII.24–28). Seeing reality correctly confirms this, and is why seeing reality correctly matters:

> After defining mentality-materiality thus according to its true nature, then in order to abandon this worldly designation of 'a being' and 'a person' more thoroughly, to surmount confusion about beings and to establish his mind on the plane of non-confusion, he makes sure that the meaning defined, namely 'This is mere mentality-materiality, there is no being, no person' is confirmed by a number of sutta.
>
> (*Vsm.* XVIII.25)

Buddhaghoṣa concludes with clear reference to the *Milindapañhā*:

> Therefore, just as when the component parts such as axles, wheels, frame poles, etc., are arranged in a certain way, there comes to be the mere term of common usage 'chariot', yet in the ultimate sense when each part is examined there is no chariot ... so too, when there are the five aggregates of clinging, there comes to be a mere term of common usage 'a being', 'a person', yet in the ultimate sense, when each component is examined, there is no being as a basis for the assumption 'I am' or 'I'; in the ultimate sense there is only mentality-materiality. (*Vsm.* XVIII.28)

Space is opened up for this complex conclusion by one of the oldest epistemological–metaphysical distinctions in Buddhist philosophy.

Eschewing any categorial metaphysics,[29] the Abhidharmikas instead make a distinction between *paramārthasat*, 'ultimate reality', and *saṃvṛtisat*, 'conventional reality'. The distinction commonly goes by the name of the 'two truths', but *-sat* can equally be 'truth' or 'reality', and it is probably best understood as the 'two realities', as it distinguishes two different ways of being real. Nāgasena, Milinda and chariots are conventionally real. But ultimately there is nothing more there than the constituent parts.

The distinction between the 'two truths' makes extremely minimal claims about the respective natures of ultimate and conventional reality, or about the correct criteria for determining into which class a candidate truth might fall. Different Buddhist philosophers will have different ways of cashing out this fundamental distinction, and philosophers have different interpretations of what those ways are.[30] In fact, one thing the chariot argument does is to take a minimal stand in asserting what the distinction amounts to, and so specifying what any ultimately existing entities must be like.

The trick is to see how it is that the 'conventionally real' can be real in any sense at all, and how nevertheless the 'ultimately real' can be, at the same time, prior – and, moreover, how the activity of discerning what is in fact ultimately real from that which only looks so at first but is in fact a conventional reality can be a meaningful and even necessary intellectual process.

Take Nāgasena and chariots as our paradigm 'conventional realities', and conventionally (but not ultimately) real for the reasons given in the chariot argument. The hallmark of such conventional realities seems to be their *dependence*. Notice how it is *because of* the wheels, axle and so on that we correctly say, "There is a chariot". In virtue of its constituents, the whole exists. In fact, conventional reality is dependent upon three things:

(i) the nature of ultimate reality: the chariot-constituents actually have to be there, together;
(ii) our conventions: the shared practice of picking out such groups with the word 'chariot' must be in effect (notice how Nāgasena's first response to the king invokes a community of people among whom 'Nāgasena' is the recognized appellation); and,
(iii) our purposes: only with reference to these can it be *useful* to think of, or group together, ultimately existing things in one way rather than another (the king would like to address his interlocutor, and

he would like to travel comfortably, without hurting his delicate feet).

Being conventionally real, it is dependent entirely and only on these for its identity as the complex unity we name with words such as 'chariot' and 'Nāgasena'. It is in virtue of its dependency on conventions and convenience that it gets its name, 'conventional reality' (*saṁvṛtisat*), and is also called 'conceptual reality' (*prajñāptisat*); it is in virtue of its dependency on ultimate reality, and in virtue of its efficacy in serving our practical purposes that it gets to count as 'real' at all.

Thus, while ultimate reality contains nothing answering to the name 'chariot', it does contain items that, together with our own aims and conventions, make it effective to conceive of certain bits of reality *as a chariot*. If I called the chariot a 'waterfall' and tried to act and elicit behaviour accordingly this would be *just plain* false, false in all ways. But to call certain collections of distinct individuals – wheels, axle, staff, goad – a chariot is correct: where there are these items co-located, together with intentions and conventions such as we share, then there is a chariot. To deny this, as Milinda does when he calls Nāgasena a liar, would be a mistake. However, it would be equally mistaken to suppose ourselves to have picked out or referred to any 'chariot-essence' when we successfully deploy conventional language. So, too, I neither refer to nor imply any personal essence, any 'you' apart from the multitude of phenomena, when I call your name.

How did we get to this anti-holist conclusion? Milinda is offered three options about the chariot's relations to its constituents: it is identical (i) to one part; (ii) to all parts; or (iii) to none, and so is a quite distinct thing. A fourth option, that chariot's absolute nonexistence, is presented as the provisional conclusion. But that, too, like the other options, is rejected.

Now it is clear why the first option is rejected: there is no one part with which a whole is identical (otherwise, it would just *be* the part, and not the whole). More strictly, the only case in which that could be correct would be in the case of absolute simples. But we are concerned here with the status of complex wholes. And the third option, although less obviously false, is still *prima facie* implausible. One might be a realist about wholes, and think that there is the chariot, and then the various parts belonging to this substantial individual. Similarly, one might think that there is a tree, for instance, and that leaves, bark, branch and roots *belong to* the substantial particular, the tree. This adds extra items to one's ontology – all the tree-parts *and* the tree are distinct existing things; but ontological generosity is not itself a reason against a view. Yet consider: what is this 'tree' *apart from* root, bark and branch? What is this 'chariot' quite distinct from all the chariot-parts, and why can it never occur in the absence of its constituent parts? How is this strange sort of object supposed to be related to the parts, and why do I need it, if I have the parts? If the chariot is supposed to be some abstract object, realized in the material parts, then we might wonder again in what sense it was *the chariot* that brought the king to his meeting with Nāgasena. Surely it was the parts.

The second option, however, looks more promising, and it is surprising how readily Milinda dismisses it out of hand. Why shouldn't the whole be all of its parts together? Perhaps because a heap of chariot-parts is not a chariot. But this difficulty is easily remedied by specifying that it is the chariot-constituting elements *in their chariot-constituting relations* that are 'the chariot'. We might say 'chariot relations' are among the chariot-constituting parts, or we might suppose this is just what it means to take all the parts *together*. And this seems like a fairly good stab at articulating what the chariot itself is. Three considerations, however, should give us pause.

First, if we mean literally *every single* particle constituting the chariot to be included in 'all the parts', then it quickly becomes clear that this cannot be identical with the chariot. For the paint may flake off, the wood splinter, the canopy be removed, without it ceasing to be a chariot. So 'chariot' cannot be strictly identical with the set of all chariot-constituting elements. But if it is identical with only some subset of these, we would need some principled way of specifying which.

Second, it is true of the constituents, taken collectively, that they are many; but the chariot is one thing, not many. And what is many cannot be one. This may sound like mere sophistry. But to reject the claim that there is a real contradiction here is merely to put the initial question again: how *can* many things be one thing?[31] What *is* a complex whole? Is it anything at all?

Third, the constituents change without the whole changing. It may not be *the same* axle (perhaps the old one broke), but it is still the same chariot. How far this can go on – how many parts can be changed while the whole remains 'the same thing' – is a puzzle associated by venerable tradition with the Ship of Theseus, which has exercised philosophers. But for our purposes, the grey area and what we want to say about it is not relevant. In the clear and agreed case of a single small substitution of a part – instead of these leather reins, we have those – the whole remains 'the same individual'; the same chariot has different reins. And if this is correct, then the whole cannot be identical with all its parts taken together.

This third consideration poses a challenge even to the more sophisticated version of 'all the parts', which took all the parts *together*. In fact, adding relations into the list of parts exacerbates this problem. For anything with moving parts – and in this respect, 'chariot' is a good analogue for the individual person – the relations between parts *will* change, while it remains collectively the same chariot. In fact, that some relations between some parts *must* change in certain ways belongs to what a chariot is. As in our incomplete response to the first consideration, we need some principled way of specifying which *alterations* in relations and parts are constitutive of the chariot, which are permissible and which entail that we no longer have a chariot, or no longer have the same chariot.

For those familiar with Aristotelian philosophy, a suitable principle is to hand: those parts and relations, and changes in these, are constitutive of the chariot which are necessary for the whole to perform its chariot function – to get the king to his meeting with Nāgasena. This function itself, then – carrying persons comfortably and quickly over land – has claim to be what the chariot *really is*: the essence or being of the chariot, or what Aristotle calls the 'form' of the chariot. The parts are a real unity – and there is really a single unity there – because together they serve to make certain functions, purposes or capacities possible.

This may sound diametrically opposed to Nāgasena's position, and in so far as Aristotelian functionalism has not been engaged with, Nāgasena's argument may look sadly incomplete. For he has not entertained all the available options. But these two positions are in fact closer than at first appears, differing primarily in the reality they accord 'the chariot', so described. For Nāgasena agreed that 'chariot is as chariot does': that is, it is genuinely *useful* to think of all these distinct individuals *as* a chariot, because only such arrangements of such-like elements perform a function that we are highly interested in. Only they 'convey a person swiftly and comfortably over land', and it is *this capacity* of theirs, when taken together, that makes it useful and convenient for us to designate 'many' with a single term, 'chariot', and to think of them as a single thing.

This, then, is indeed the criterion for specifying which subsets *within* the chariot-constituting elements are variable and in which ways, and which are not. But this criterion for sorting subsets is not just rationally given, independent and unchanging. It has no mind-independent reality, no reality independent of our practices and purposes. It requires the cooperation of mind-independent reality for its *existence* – no chariot without wood; but the *unity* of the several constituents is due entirely to our practices and purposes. Unlike the Aristotelian forms, which are given and to be discovered, the Buddhist alternative recognizes a vital flexibility and fluidity in our appreciation of identity criteria in varying circumstances and contexts. Sometimes, the same chariot gets a new coat of paint; sometimes, new paint makes it a different chariot, or perhaps not a chariot at all, but a fairground piece, say, a work of art, or a poisoned chalice.

The identity criteria in our practices of individuating persons are similarly fluid and this is a familiar fact from ordinary practice and language. Buddhaghoṣa demonstrates this with the following example and analogy, from the *Visuddhimagga*, the *The Path of Purification*:

> Now it is asked, "Whose is the fruit, since there is no experiencer?" Herein: "Experiencer is a convention, for mere arising of the fruit; They say 'It fruits' as a convention, When on a tree appears its fruit." Just as it is simply owing to the arising of tree fruits, which are one part of the phenomena called a tree, that it is said "The tree fruits" or "The tree has fruited", so it is simply owing to the arising of the fruit consisting of the pleasure and pain called experience, which is one part of the aggregates called 'deities' and 'human beings', that it is said "A deity or a human being experiences or feels pleasure or pain". (*Vsm.* XVII.172)

A tree has fruited; the tree has lost a branch in a storm; the tree sheds its leaves; the tree puts down new roots – in each case, this is the same tree. And yet in each case, we are distinguishing *within* the potentially tree-constituting elements, designating some of them as 'the tree' and others as 'the fruit', or 'branch' or 'leaves', or 'roots'. Moreover, in each case, what is picked out as 'the tree' differs: in the first case it does not include the fruit; in the last case it may well. 'The tree' that has lost a branch in a storm includes leaves; but the name cannot pick out a group including the leaves when we say 'the tree has shed its leaves'.[32] All the time, within a constant shifting but overlapping set of elements, we pick out some subset or another as 'the tree' (or chariot or person), different in each case according to the pragmatics of the situation.

The chariot principle: all the way down

If Nāgsena has reasons for his conclusion, and they are something of this sort, then it is clear that what is good for the chariot counts equally for the chariot's wheel, axle, yoke, body, goad; and what counts for the wheel counts equally for the spoke, rim, axis – and so on. If the argument is good at all, it must apply all the way down. And if 'chariot' is meant to model 'Nāgasena', then what is true for the chariot is true also for the tree and the elephant. So from Milinda's chariot, we can distil the CHARIOT PRINCIPLE:

> Whatever has constituents depends upon those constituents for its existence, and depends upon our conceiving this 'many' *as* a 'one' for its unity, and so does not exist ultimately, but only (at best) conventionally.

The principle has far-reaching consequences. Wherever there are multiple distinguishable and distinct properties or parts jointly referred to by a single word, we must identify one or the other constituent as the thing named, *or* discover some separate entity as the thing named, *or* accept that the name picks out several distinct individuals together, without there being some one thing thus picked out. In every case, the last option will turn out to be the only viable one.

The upshot is that nothing complex can be ultimately real; the only fundamental constituents of reality, out of which each part, and each part of a part, and so on, is constituted, are absolute simples. So, for instance, if water is both fluid and cold, then it is complex, so *qua* water it exists conceptually but not ultimately. Ultimately there is an instance of coldness and an instance of fluidity, co-located. Vasubandhu's way of defining the distinction between ultimate and conventional reality is seen in the *Abhidharmakośa*:

> The idea of a jug ends when the jug is broken; the idea of water ends when, in the mind, one analyzes the water. The jug and the water, and all that resembles them, exist conventionally [*saṁvṛtisatya*]. The rest exist ultimately. (*AKBh* VI.4)

If either coldness or fluidity itself were constituted of distinct aspects or parts, then it too would be a conceptually real thing, in virtue of the ultimate reality of its constituents.

According to the Chariot Principle, whatever is ultimately real could neither have properties nor be a property of something else. Any such supposed case would be a case of two (or several) distinct individuals, with no common ground uniting them. The only source of complex unity is the conceptualizing activity proper to the construction of conceptual reality. This is what it means for the Abhidharma ontology to be resolutely non-categorial. There are no qualities *of* substances, no relations or quantities *inhering in* or *belonging to* substances or qualities. Ultimately, there are only absolutely simple individuals of various kinds.

These absolute simples are called *dharmas*. Much of the canonical Abhidharma texts are devoted to enumerating the various kinds of *dharmas,* their natures and their relations to each other.[33] The *dharmas* are 'atoms' in the strictest sense: there is no conceivable divisibility in them. They are, then, *atomos* (indivisible) far more literally than in any ancient Greek atomism, for there are no single bits of reality that have *both* shape *and* size, for instance. *Dharmas* are unqualified and unqualifying. Nor does *dharma*-atomism have the least association with materialism, as is particularly the case with early modern atomism. For nothing in the foregoing gives any reason to suppose there will not be indivisible bits of *mental* reality. Indeed, the Buddhists need such *dharmas*. For these are the objects of meditative observation, as we attend to our arising and passing experiences, full of feeling, volition and thoughts.[34]

Dharmas are elements in that anything else that is real is ultimately composed of them. They are substances in the sense that they are genuine individuals, with a distinct identity. They are also that which 'underlies' reality in that anything real is constituted by *dharmas*; but they cannot be substances in the sense of bearers of properties. They *are* their (respective) properties. This view has been likened to trope theory; and we could think of *dharmas* as property-particulars.[35] If we bear in mind the emphasis the Buddhist puts on the causes and conditions of things, on the impermanence of everything, then it is clear that such property-particulars could not endure (since it is the mark of existence to be impermanent, and liable to the changing conditions around it). Indeed if we consider, as the Abhidharma philosophers themselves did, that temporal parts will be just as susceptible to the same treatment as physical and conceptual parts, then it seems unavoidable that any such entity could have only momentary existence. Its very arising must be the cause of its passing away.[36] For this reason, it may be most apt to think of *dharmas* as property-particular *events*. A *dharma* is an episode of a simple, specific existence.

These events are continually occurring, constituting together with others the conditions for subsequent such events. The *skandhas* are thus not just heaps, but streams of *dharmas*, over time. This undermines our notions not only of complex unity at a time, but also of identity *over* time, or persistence through change. As Buddhaghoṣa describes it:

> With a stream of continuity there is neither identity nor otherness. For if there were absolute identity in a stream of continuity, there would be no forming of curd from milk. And yet if there were absolute otherness, the curd would not be derived from the milk. And so too with all causally arisen things. And if that were so there would be an end to all worldly usage, which is hardly desirable. So neither absolute identity nor absolute otherness should be assumed here. (*Vsm.* XVII.167)

These streaming simples come in many different kinds, and the fact that they have some very specific nature that is theirs, and that constitutes the whole of what there is, is expressed by saying that they have *svabhāva*: a distinct nature of their own. So denying that the chariot is anything distinct from its parts is the same as denying it has *svabhāva*, a nature of its own, in virtue of which it is what it is. The wheel has no *svabhāva*, and so on. Milk and curd likewise lack *svabhāva*, for if they had real, individual identities, they would have to be either the same as or different from each other, and either way the process of curd *coming from* milk would be impossible. Only the fundamental elements have some definite nature, constituting what they are, and not merely a label for further, smaller and simpler elements. While the Abhidharma texts offer several elaborate taxonomies of *dharmas*, these kinds can be usefully categorized as each belonging to one or another of the five *skandhas*. So if we ask, "What is a heap (a *skandha*) a heap *of*?", it is a heap of *dharmas*. And where we were unreflectively inclined to presume the endurance of individual entities over time, we see now that there is transient but causally dependent arising of successive moments or streams of discrete *dharmas*. Continuity replaces identity over time, just as (to use the favoured metaphor) a fire burning through the night or across a field is not numerically identical at various times, and yet the various moments are suitably causally connected that we might speak correctly of 'a single fire'.

The consequence is a concertedly anti-holist picture. There are no essences of complex things – no properties that constitute the essence of things; no substance in which properties inhere at a time or over time; no one thing there to which many things might belong. The only 'substances' are simple substances, which inhere in nothing and to which nothing belongs as a property.[37] There is, then, no asymmetry between an object and its properties; no *ways of being* at all, in the way that Aristotelian metaphysics outlines, or the way the non-Buddhist Vaiśeṣika school came to describe. On such a view, any purported ultimate reality of relations, continuity or unity will become inarticulable. In fact, this is precisely what the Buddhist personalists, the Pudgalavādins, claimed about their 'ultimately real person': it could not be expressed.[38]

We might compare it to nominalism – recall, 'Nāgasena is a name ...', 'chariot is a name ...' – but it is not exclusively, or even primarily, a theory concerned with universals. The chariot principle is primarily about the complex wholes of everyday experience, and the obverse of denying real unity to the many constituents is to emphasize that *individuation is something we do.* We are constantly active in the production of the world as we experience it. This does not make such experiences *illusory*; after all, the complex items of everyday experience are properly grounded in really existing simples. In the absence of these, it would be just plain false to talk of chariots, and so on. But a full account of these experiences requires appeal not only to ultimate simples, but also to conventions, and those conventions must actually be in place, and so regarding 'many' as 'one' must *in fact* help us to satisfy our aims and fulfil our purposes. Desires, then, are an important factor in the construction of everyday reality.[39] Without them, there is no way of grouping the innumerably interacting *dharmas* that is 'more convenient' than any other. This is one way of spelling out how it is that ignorance of (non-)self and desire – craving for and attachment to things conceived of as complex and unified – are the roots of suffering. Returning to the question postponed at the beginning of the chapter, we can see now why taking the non-personal view of reality should indeed involve the dissipation of desires.

Thinking of things and myself as substantially existing, I conceive desires with respect to them; conceiving desires, I conceive things as substantially existing. The "Right View Sūtra" (*MN* 9) does not declare either of these is exclusively prior to the other.[40] But once set in motion, the desires cause me to *feel and act* in such a way that I *create* unities – connected continuities – between things where they otherwise would not exist. Acting from a desire to meet Nāgasena, Milinda has a chariot built. Identifying himself as the one with such a desire, he further identifies himself with that desire's satisfaction or frustration, acts delighted or cross accordingly, and takes this gratification for reason to think well of himself (or the opposite), to have confidence regarding future projects, think himself more powerful or happier than his fellows, and so on; thus he generates a whole host of *psychological* and *psycho-physical* interconnections and continuities that would not otherwise arise.

And all because a Greek king asked a Buddhist monk how he was known.

THREE

Kleśas and compassion

> About liberation (the idea), that it is indeed gruesome, consisting of a cessation of all activity. With such a liberation which divorces us from everything, so many good things of life would be finished. How, therefore, can any intelligent person find that sort of liberation characterized by absence of all the pleasures and even of consciousness at all palatable?[1]

The extirpation of desires is not an immediately and universally attractive state to strive for. Even if there are ultimately no selves, even if all suffers, withdrawal of care may seem an uninspiring ideal to adopt in the light of that – and what else could 'detachment' be than this? What else does the Buddha mean, when he exhorts us to give up all forms of clinging? If suffering is rooted in desire, attachment and aversion, so that we must 'cut off' these roots if we are to end suffering, then it may seem that the game isn't worth the candle – or that the life one is left with (dispassionate, detached, desireless) is just the best of a bad job.

Nor, even if recognizing non-self goes together with the diminution of desires, is it particularly plausible psychologically that we could simply review a reductive mereological argument and thereby leave off desiring, even if we believe the argument sound, and review it clear-headedly many times, so that we are utterly convinced of it. Detailed study of the structure of reality as 'suffering, impermanent, no-self' may be necessary for such a transformation of outlook. But it is appreciation of the particular way and reasons that there is 'no self' that will make the difference. This is metaphysical reflection as a spiritual practice, and is in character rather different from the setting out and challenging of a metaphysical argument, for it takes whatever phenomena arise for us as the occasion and material for reflection. Such reflection does not take the metaphysics as the object of study but engages in a practice of seeing the wide and sometimes baffling diversity of experience as belonging to this metaphysical picture.

The Nietzschean Objection

The opening objection – which, if valid, would render the question of practicability otiose – was perhaps most incisively and most eloquently put by Nietzsche, who absorbed an amalgam of Buddhism and Vedānta from Schopenhauer. I shall call this the Nietzschean Objection, although there are various non-Nietzschean forms the general objection might take. Nietzsche's critique extends well beyond Buddhism, but might be thought particularly fatal to the overall Buddhist ethical orientation. For instance, "the real opposition", Nietzsche writes, is between:

> the degenerating instinct that turns against life with subterranean vengefulness (Christianity, the philosophy of Schopenhauer, in a certain sense already the philosophy of Plato, and all idealism as typical forms) versus a formula for the highest affirmation, born of fullness, of overfullness, a Yes-saying without reservation, even to suffering, even to guilt, even to everything that is questionable and strange in existence.
>
> This ultimate, most joyous, most wantonly extravagant Yes to life represents not only the highest insight but also the *deepest*, that which is most strictly confirmed and borne out by truth and science. Nothing in existence may be subtracted, nothing is dispensable – those aspects of existence which Christians and other nihilists repudiate are actually on an infinitely higher level in the order of rank among values than that which the instinct of decadence could approve and call good.
>
> (*Ecce Homo*, "The Birth of Tragedy", §2)

Our highest calling and proper orientation, according to Nietzsche, is "saying Yes to life even in its strangest and hardest problems; the will to life rejoicing over its own inexhaustibility"[2] – rather than rejecting some or all of it on account of its unpleasantness, painfulness, unsatisfactoriness or suffering. One must "think pessimism through to its depths ... beyond good and evil and no longer, like the Buddha and Schopenhauer, under the spell and delusion of morality" in order to:

> have opened his eyes to the opposite ideal: the ideal of the most high-spirited, alive, and world-affirming human being who has not only come to terms and learned to get along with whatever was and is, but who wants to have *what was and is* repeated into all eternity. (*Beyond Good and Evil*, §56)

Being life-affirming means, among other things, subscribing to a different order of values than pleasure and pain, or the socially accepted-and-rejected, or the comfortable or uncomfortable – and one that is incompatible with these. Instead of asking "Is it suffering or not?", Nietzsche encourages us to guide our evaluations according to how something expresses and affirms vitality: life itself fully recognized as both suffering and sweet. Measured by this standard, the Buddhist ideal of *nirvāṇa*, extinguishment, makes a pretty miserable showing.

The worry that the Buddhist outlook is fundamentally life-denying is, perhaps surprisingly, not at all foreign to Buddhist thinkers. The very early *Kathāvatthu*, a record of points of controversy between Buddhists that was incorporated into the Abhidharma canon, describes such a debate over the disputed claim that, according to the Buddha, "all conditioned things are, without distinction, cinderheaps" (*Kathāvatthu*, II.8).

Buddhaghoṣa, in his commentary on the *Kathāvatthu* (II.6), concisely summarizes the point at issue. Some Buddhists "by thoughtlessly grasping the teaching of such Suttas as 'All is on fire, bhikkhus!', 'All conditioned things [involve] *dukkha*', ... hold that all conditioned things are without qualification no better than a welter of embers whence the flames have died out, like an inferno of ashes. To correct this by indicating various forms of happiness, the Theravādin puts the question", namely:

> *Th.*: You affirm this; but is there no such a thing as pleasurable feeling [*sukhā vedanā*], bodily pleasure, mental pleasure, celestial happiness [*sukhaṃ*], human happiness, the *sukhaṃ* of gain, of being honoured, of driving, of resting, the *sukha* of ruling, of administrating, of domestic-and-secular life, of the religious life; *sukha* related to taints [esp. sense-desires] and those

> of untaintedness; the happiness [of *nirvāṇa*] with remainder and without remainder; worldly happiness, unworldly happiness, with zest and without, *jhāna-sukhaṃ*, liberation-pleasure, pleasures of sense-desire, renunciation-*sukhaṃ*, the *sukha* of solitude, of peace, of awakening [*saṃbodhi-sukhaṃ*]?
>
> (*Kathāvatthu*, II.8, 1, trans. mod.)[3]

From the first Noble Truth, that all is suffering (*duḥkha*), we should not conclude that there is nothing that is its opposite, *sukha*. There are, as the Theravādin elder points out, very many different forms of pleasure and happiness that are perfectly recognizable to us.

This, however, may not seem to meet the objection, precisely because it includes such a motley jumble of attractive feelings, several of which are specifically said to lead to suffering if one pursues or is attached to them. They might feel good for a moment, but we have every reason to treat them – as the Gokulika Buddhist recommends – as worthless cinders. Was not this, in fact, precisely the conclusion to which our metaphysical meditations on the lack of selves should lead us by another route? The objects of pleasure are transient and mentally constructed, this activity of mental construction and the pleasure itself a shifting kaleidoscope of mental events, without bearer or basis: without anything *worth* being considered 'myself'. The Gokulika interpretation does not seem to be an overly assiduous application of the Truth of suffering, but a fair way of capturing the attitude we ought to adopt – or which ought to be induced in us – by reflection on the impermanence and dependency of all things. All these fleeting events, attractive though they may be, are as dust, burnt out remnants of an imperfect reality temporarily constructed by our own craving desires. To this, observations that we do feel pleasure when we eat, or rule a kingdom, or go for a drive, are beside the point.

Of course there are pleasurable sensations in one obvious sense. If there were not, what would it be that we craved, became attached to and constructed our actions around? But if by virtue of being pleasant they counted as 'not-suffering', we should have no reason left *not* to pursue them, value them, accumulate them and seek to spend our lives so. Yet this is certainly not the attitude we are to adopt towards sense-pleasures. In fact, while matters of belief were largely considered irrelevant to one's standing within the Buddhist monastic community, the one *view* for which one could be expelled from the *saṅgha* was the persistent assertion that there was no danger in sense-pleasures.[4]

Although Arittha is not expelled, in the "Snake Sūtra" (*MN* 22), he is severely and publicly admonished for his assertion that sense-pleasures may not be obstructions to enlightenment, if one goes about them in the right way. "Sense-desires", he is reminded, "bring little enjoyment, and much suffering and disappointment" (*MN* 22.6). As part of good practice, we should therefore "guard the doors of our sense-faculties", not allowing ourselves to be distracted by physical sensations, pleasant or painful – "if we were to dwell without restraint over the faculty of the eye [ear, nose ...] evil, unskilful qualities such as greed or distress might assail us" (*MN* 39).

And it is not just sense-pleasures that are to be abjured. The vexed emotions of pride and resentment at praise and blame respectively should dissipate in the person who recognizes they are without foundation (*MN* 22); mixed mental states such as envy, anger, idleness and dissipation are considered 'afflictions' (*kleśas*),[5] and as such will not be felt at all by someone of healthy mind and correct understanding. The disputed point, then, is not whether anything at all might appear pleasant and happy for a time, but whether anything appearing so has a right to be *treated so*, rather than to be diagnosed as suffering-in-disguise: whether "all things without qualification are no better than embers".

The Theravādin's inclusion of the pleasures of untaintedness, the happiness of the renunciant, the joys of awakening, are more to the point here. These seem to be pleasures whose pursuit and enjoyment initiate a virtuous circle; they do not lead to more suffering but rather to less. Pressed on this point, the Theravādin invites us to consider the virtue of generosity:

> Take giving: does that bring forth fruit that is undesired, unpleasant, disagreeable, adulterated? Does it bear, and result in, sorrow? Or take virtue, the keeping of feastdays, religious training, and religious life: do they bring forth such fruit, etc.? Do they not rather have the opposite result? (*KV* II.8.7)

This friendliness towards selected forms of pleasure and happiness has good basis in the *Nikāyas*, which paint a complex attitude towards the attractive feelings and states available to us. On the one hand, the sense-pleasures (and aversion to their corresponding pains) are primarily misleading and dangerous. But we should not, for all that, cultivate contempt towards them. "On being touched with pleasant feeling", a well-cultivated person "does not become impassioned with pleasure"; when it ceases and is replaced by a painful feeling, she "does not sorrow, grieve, lament, beat her breast, or become distraught" (*MN* 36). But one should not therefore deliberately abjure all possibility of natural pleasure, as the extreme ascetic does (*MN* 57). One *feels* pleasure and pain – as long as there are psycho-physical aggregates arising, so too will pleasure and pain arise – but without becoming attached to either. Not being attached, one does not pursue pleasure, or relate to the world as so many opportunities to obtain pleasure and foresee and stave off pains.

Some pleasures, however, are good states or lead to good states, or both. There is the distinctive joy of awakening, *saṃbodhisukha*, referred to in the *Kathāvatthu* passage; the "Māgandiya Sutta" (*MN* 75) has the Buddha call *nirvāṇa* the greatest happiness (*paramaṃ sukhaṃ*). Other discourses in the Pāli canon have the Buddha discussing the increasing pleasures of successive states of meditational insight (e.g. *MN* 36, *MN* 59). Vasubandhu offers, among others, faith, respect and energy as instances of good mental states. Buddhaghoṣa reminds us that the 'divine abidings' are loving-kindness (*maitri*, Pā: *metta*), compassion (*karuṇa*), gladness (*muditā*[6]) and equanimity (*upekṣa*). Although 'divine abidings' are privileged objects of meditation, the first three at least are also indisputably what we call 'emotions', and the point of each meditation is not only to *analyse* the respective feeling, but also to *cultivate* it.[7] It is presumably here that the pleasures of generosity, used in the Theravādin rejoinder to the Cinderheap Objection, would fall.

We shall have to ask what the principle of distinction is between afflictive feelings and emotions and non-afflictive ones, for it is clear that it cannot lie in whether they are painful and pleasant, respectively, in any obvious sense. And in order to address adequately the Nietzschean Objection, we shall have to consider just what these non-afflictive feelings are like, and what a life that endorses these but not the others is apt to look like. This will force us to address the still more difficult question of just how it is that this is compatible with the view that all is suffering. But at least this much is clear: whatever we are to make of the cessation of desire recommended by the Buddhist, it should not be thought to induce or consist in an affective blank or emotional deadness. It is not the 'life of a stone' that is recommended, so it is not this that the Buddhist must make attractive to us if we are to be persuaded to devote ourselves to seeking *nirvāṇa*.

Teleological ethics

The Nietzschean Objection accepts that there is unavoidably much suffering mixed up in life. We must therefore either reject suffering, and so life, as the Buddhists recommend; or we must affirm life and its suffering too. Nietzsche recommends the latter. True, his characterization of the Buddhist position as life-rejecting may be unfair. As we just saw, although some Buddhists endorsed it, most Buddhists rejected the notion that the elimination of suffering, and of the desire and attachment to self that cause suffering, entails the equal rejection of *all* lived experience as unqualifiedly worthless. But this may not yet meet the objection, either in its particular form or in its general form. The generalized form of the objection asserts that there is something (plausible candidates are life, love, justice, meaning, God) that is more important than the elimination of suffering, and it is this other good that should be the measure of which suffering is bad and to be eliminated, and which suffering is instead inconsequential or even wholesome. But the Theravādins, as we noted above, have not given us a principle for distinguishing afflictive from non-afflictive emotions, so it is not clear that they are entitled to their claim, against the Gokulikas, that some happy states are to be welcomed or even pursued, while still maintaining that whatever exists is impermanent, dependently arising, and suffering, and the fully awakened state is the complete cessation of any possibility of suffering.

The objection, and considering how the Buddhist might meet it, focuses our attention on the teleological structure of Buddhist ethics. This basic structure is, of course, already evident in the four Noble Truths. 'There is an end of suffering' is the third Noble Truth, and it is towards this that the other three truths lead. That is to say, we do not just observe that suffering exists, and has causes. We are supposed to be bringing about the elimination of suffering – *following* the Eightfold Path set out in the fourth Noble Truth, in the first instance by understanding better what it is (the first Noble Truth, discussed in Ch. 1); and then by examining its causes (the second Noble Truth), fundamentally greed, aversion and confusion, and primarily confusion about one's own insubstantiality (discussed in Ch. 2). There is a *telos* implicit in the four Noble Truths, an ultimate goal with respect to which activities, thoughts and feelings are evaluated as good or bad – the good ones being those that move us along the path towards that goal.

We might think that we could helpfully divide the field of teleological ethics into two: those that offer some transcendent and unexpected end that you never knew you had (say, 'knowing God'); and those more modest accounts that seek simply to describe the ends we all, in fact, have (say, 'desire-satisfaction').[8] But such a dichotomy would miss out the greater part of all Greek *eudaimonist* ethics, which seeks to be descriptive *and* reformist: by getting us to think more clearly about our actual ends and their relations, they seek to move us to modify our behaviour and even reform our conceptions of our ends. We all want to be happy and live well – to be *eudaimon*; but while many unreflectively assume this has to do with being able to enjoy satisfying our desires, Greek moralists and philosophers try to persuade us that it has rather to do with living virtuously, exercising our rational faculties, fulfilling our human nature, or something of that sort. Only this, they tell us, enables us to truly have the power to enjoy satisfying our *real* desires.

Teleological ethics can be still more complex than this. Plato, for instance, wants to be both reformist *and* revisionary. That is, on the one hand, we should reflect on and reform our conception of happiness; but, on the other hand, in the process of doing this, we shall discover that there is something else entirely – the Good itself – that is in fact the ultimate and worthiest *telos*, and that by reference to which anything else good counts as good. Something like this, I shall suggest, is the most helpful way of getting at the shape of Buddhist ethical thought.[9] There is a path, and there is somewhere the path leads: ultimately, to the cessation of suffering, or 'crossing over' as it is often called. But our conception of that end, and so also of how to get there, alters as we progress along our journey; and at some point our understanding of what is possible and desirable may radically alter into something we could not have conceived of before we began the journey.

So, for instance, if it is obvious that *duḥkha* is bad, it should by the same token be equally obvious that *sukha* is good. And it is recognized that *sukha* is indeed what everyone goes for. But in going for *sukha*, we creatures sadly get it quite wrong about how to find it; we think that following our desires and appeasing our aversions, hatreds, fears, angers and jealousies will bring happiness, whereas in fact if we are to become happy we must be generous, fair, without pride or malice, and willing to restrain our appetites in order not to harm others. This is a reformation of our conception of happiness, according to reflection on what actually increases and decreases suffering in our everyday lived experiences. However, in the course of coming to understand this, and becoming so, we may *also* discover that even this reconceived happiness is not, after all, the absence of all suffering. Indeed, it may rather be that the whole enterprise of going for *sukha* is the problem, creating suffering inevitably. At this point, we have the option of switching our ultimate goals, for a new one has become intelligible to us through the process of coming to clarify and better attain the original goal. The elimination of suffering is not, after all, the replacement of it with happiness, but something that dissolves the causes and conditions of any possibility of suffering arising.

This radical revision of what the ultimate goal is, from happiness or *sukha* as lack of suffering to *nirvāṇa* as the comprehensive elimination of suffering, consists significantly in increasingly understanding reality as selfless. This specification of the reality to be understood makes the complexion of Buddhist ethics rather different from the more familiar neo-Aristotelian virtue ethics, which is decidedly person-centred. Classic virtue ethics is person-centred in two ways: normatively and extensionally. First, Aristotelian-style virtue ethics takes its conception of well-being from its conception of the human being; but if, as the Buddhists claim, there are no complex wholes, and so no essence of a human being – no 'true' self – then this cannot set the standard to live up to and measure our success by. This means that, on the Buddhist teleological picture, instead of trying to become the best thing of our kind, we are trying to become quite unlike the kind of thing we are. Second, in virtue ethics, persons are the primary beneficiaries of excellent activity; in the Aristotelian version, it is primarily one's own well-being that is a guide to the good. This may require having healthy loving relationships, and it may be that we should also take a general interest in the well-being of others. But it is the well-being of particular, distinct individuals that is the object of concern. Since Buddhist metaphysics recognizes no distinct individuals, it can in the end take only a radically impersonal concern for the elimination of suffering. It is the cessation of suffering (which benefits what we conventionally call persons) that is the aim, not the benefiting of individuals. Such an aim is virtually unintelligible without the radical revision introduced by the *anatta* principle.

If correct, this could go some way towards addressing two misgivings one might be inclined to have about the ultimate Buddhist goal, and about the shape of Buddhist ethics. About the latter, one might worry that Buddhist ethics changes horses in mid-stream – that the 'suffering' we originally agree is bad and worth eliminating is not the same 'suffering' that we discover pervades everything; and it is not nearly as obvious that this latter, subtle and pervasive, 'suffering' *is* bad, and to be eliminated. Related to this, one might worry that the goal of complete cessation of all suffering, *nirvāṇa*, is not obviously attractive and desirable. Extinguishment is a difficult thing to find a compelling goal, the more so as we learn that it is the extinguishment of all desire, attachment (even to other persons), pleasure and so on.

But if the foregoing reflections on complex and dynamic teleological ethics are apt, perhaps these difficulties need not trouble us. To the worry about the shape of Buddhist ethics, we see that the apparent 'changing horses in mid-stream' is in fact an acknowledgement of the dynamics of embarking on a journey of comprehensive moral transformation, and it may be part of the view that these two ends are not after all as disconnected as they may seem before the nature of the psychological development envisaged is taken into account. To misgivings about the ultimate Buddhist goal, it should not surprise us that *nirvāṇa* may not be immediately attractive: our ordinary way of looking at the world does not have space for articulating the value of *nirvāṇa*, which is good in a quite different way, a way for which we could hardly have the language, since language takes its bearings from the everyday, the conventional. If Buddhist ethics has this complex teleological structure, it might well be that the ultimate goal appears as such only once one is some way along the path towards the (retrospectively) proximate goal of happiness.

Measures of value: *kuśala* and *akuśala*, *puñña* and *pāpa*

Buddhist moral thought begins from the perfectly evident observation that we do not want to be miserable. By this, we ordinarily take it that we want to be happy instead; and happiness is, broadly, getting what you want and not getting what you do not want. But of course the devil is in the detail, and the moralist invites us to consider what we really do want. The basic virtues of Buddhism – generosity, patience, and good conduct – and the basic precepts defining good conduct – refraining from harmful speech, from taking life, from taking what is not given, from intoxicants and from sexual misconduct – reform one's conception of what one actually wants, and correspondingly one's conception of what will bring this about. My desire for happiness leads me to see that being generous, kind and helpful, and refraining from intemperance, pettiness and deceit, actually best contribute towards that end. The best way to attain happiness is to aim at virtue. There is a certain sense in which one aims at the cessation of suffering. But one may not yet be fully convinced of the first Noble Truth, that everything suffers. Comfort, pleasures, contentment and peaceful relations with others are still thought to be non-miserable, and desirable. Decent conduct and a generous attitude is the best way of attaining these, and perhaps even the truest form these take.

Here Buddhism measures the qualities of one's actions, words and states of mind according to whether they are harmful or beneficial. Generosity brings about pleasant results, and not the opposite, as do refraining from anger, not indulging in malicious talk and so on. Within a schema of rebirth, such actions serve to bring about a good rebirth, while their opposites bring about the opposite. The former actions are called 'meritorious', generating merit (*puñña*); the latter are unmeritorious, generating demerit (*pāpa*). These are the measure of whether an action is good, which intentions are to be cultivated or eschewed, whether temporary pains and pleasures might be sought or avoided.

But living such a life is also beneficial in a rather different way. For it puts one in a position to recognize the real and pervasive nature of suffering, and the futility of just that pleasant rebirth and the sort of pleasant results that make action meritorious. If we attend to and focus on the nature of things and their causes, we will see that what exists suffers, and does so as part of a scheme no more grand or meaningful than the sheer fact of accumulated cause and effect. Even the consolations we build around us to make life meaningful become themselves the source of further suffering. "If one clings to the idea that the Lord, etc. is the cause of the world," Vasubandhu writes, "this is by reason of false conceptions of permanence and personality. Thus this clinging is to be abandoned through seeing (the truth) of suffering" (*AKBh* V.8). According to the first Noble Truth, the universe is not arranged providentially; it does not progress according to any plan or purpose. It just goes on and on. This is one of the deep truths conveyed through the cosmology of rebirth, even if that cosmology is not literally true. And it is this that makes the Buddhist ethical outlook so striking compared to its Greek and Roman counterparts: for while the latter conceive of human beings as (potentially) orderly parts of a well-ordered cosmos, and so can take realizing this as our aim, the Buddhist ethical outlook is teleological within a resolutely non-teleological reality.[10]

If you are not already fed up with the empty futility and repetitiveness, you may not have reason to adopt the radically transformed goal, and there is no further argument that could persuade you to do so. There is only the confidence that greater attention to the subtle forms of suffering embedded even in desired, non-harmful events will reveal them as ultimately less satisfactory than the complete elimination of suffering. It is this that would effect a radical transformation in one's understanding of the ultimate aim. Now it is no longer happiness in any conceivable sense, in this life or in any future one, that one is aiming at, for the complete cessation of suffering includes the cessation *even of the results of meritorious action.*[11] These, which include all the goods recognizable in our reformed conception of happiness, are no longer worth aiming at, and are good only incidentally: that is, in so far as freedom from acute pain and distress, and some material security, are extremely useful in allowing one to focus one's attention on practising the virtues that will give rise to the complete cessation of suffering.

Such virtues and practices are *kuśala* – wholesome or skilful; their opposites are *akuśala.*[12] We thus have two partially overlapping scales of value: whatever is meritorious, *puñña*, is also *kuśala*, inasmuch as the ordinary life of non-harming makes for optimal conditions for one to reorient one's attention towards *nirvāṇa.*[13] But some things may be *kuśala* without being meritorious. For actions of mind and body, whether meritorious or not, give rise to further nodes in the endless causal nexus of dependent origination, and so are eschewed entirely by the person who has reconceived the end of suffering as consisting not in happiness but in *nirvāṇa*. As Nāgārjuna puts it in his *Ratnāvalī*:

> In brief, the no-existence view consists in denying there are fruits of actions. It is non-meritorious, and leads to low rebirth; it is called a wrong view. The existence-view is that there are fruits of actions. It is meritorious (*puṇya*) and causes rebirth in happy conditions of existence. It is called right view. But through knowledge, one subdues both existence and non-existence; one is beyond merit and demerit (*pāpapuṇyavytikramaḥ*). Therefore the saints say this is salvation from good as well as bad conditions of existence.
>
> (*RĀ* I.43–5)[14]

For one with true knowledge, the wholesome or skilful alone remains as the criterion of evaluation, indicating whether something is or conduces towards the complete elimination of suffering and its causes in all its forms. The person who has accomplished the ultimate end, the Arhat whose mental states are entirely *kuśala*, engages in no deliberate action whatsoever, and so sets nothing further in motion, generates no further results of any kind whatsoever. As the stock phrase has it: "Birth is finished; the noble life has been lived; that is done which was to be done; there is no more coming to any state of being".[15] This is what complete cessation, *nirvāṇa*, involves.

Alleviating afflictions, replacing passions with compassion

We bring an end to suffering by understanding it, and by understanding its causes. The fundamental cause of suffering is ignorance of reality *as* suffering, transient, and without 'self' – that is, the ordinary objects of experience, including ourselves, are dependent upon their constituents and their causes, which are themselves dependent upon others for their existence. But it hardly seems credible that the arguments alone should suffice to extinguish suffering. The habit of mind – itself one of these dependently arising phenomena – of taking there to be complex wholes, ourselves among them, is firmly entrenched, so that simply seeing a metaphysical argument to the effect that there are no wholes (as in Chapter 2, for instance), does not suffice to alter that momentum of the mental habit of grasping the world in terms of complex wholes and, in particular, in terms of what things are useful to us or otherwise, desirable and beneficial or harmful and threatening. As long as we perceive things as desirable and undesirable, we will inevitably have reactive emotions with respect to them, and finally act accordingly.

The Stoics, who also recommended a radical revision of our sense of what is worthwhile and what is not, understood this, and so developed handy mental exercises that one might use in the course of a day in order to retrain the mind to look at things in a new way. The Buddhists, whose revision was so much more radical, developed this into a science. The Eightfold Path includes right mindfulness and right concentration, and these were worked out into a range of specific mental disciplines in which one practises seeing reality aright, and in particular seeing one's own experiences as transient, dependent, non-personal phenomena. Such recognition should directly affect the phenomena that then arise, making for experiences that are less painful, less filled with disappointed striving and fearful clinging to what cannot in any case be held on to.[16] Attending to mental phenomena in a relatively unpressured environment should not only make distressing, distracting and unwholesome mental phenomena arise less but also better enable one to take the right stance – of dis-identification and dis-investment – towards them when they do arise in the heat of the moment.[17] For this emphasis on attending to our experiences as they arise, Mrs Rhys Davids called her translation of one Abhidharma text of such analytic exercises *A Buddhist Manual of Psychological Ethics*.[18] And similarly, because of the practice of close attention purely to the psychological, while bracketing all questions regarding the metaphysical status of the experiences or that which is presented as their content, some contemporary scholars are inclined to regard Buddhist ethics as 'phenomenological', rather that *eudaimonist*, consequentialist, a form of virtue ethics or deontology.[19]

The mental phenomena we observe arising in meditation might be cognitive and sensory impressions generally; the *skandha* theory that we developed in the search for some candidate to play the self role offers apt categories for the classification of the interrelated constituents of our experiences. While *rūpa* (form, body) is not itself a mental event, it plays a role in describing and explaining the varied contours of the feelings, cognitions, volitions and consciousness events that do arise. Close attention to the patterns of the arising mental events reveal that our feelings and emotions drive the whole business forward. Attitudes of attraction and aversion, approval and disapproval, 'right' and 'wrong', 'ought' and 'ought not', arise from grasping things as definitely *this* or *that*, and perpetuate this mode of engagement, as well as themselves, and thus lead to an endless proliferation of other such thoughts. Even if they are not themselves immediately unpleasant, they arise based on misguided apprehensions of things that do lead to suffering; and they cause grasping, controlling behaviour that leads to suffering in ourselves and others. Desires and aversions are thus both the *source* of suffering and are themselves afflictions (*kleśas*), or instances of suffering.[20] They arise dependent upon fundamental misapprehensions of the nature of reality, and their emotional momentum reinforces and proliferates these misapprehensions.

Meditative practice involves observing how afflictive mental states give rise to further aggravating thoughts and emotions, where they come from and how they grow. We should observe, for instance, how awareness becomes awareness *of* something or another, thus giving rise to feelings or perceptions regarding it. These are pleasant and painful, and give rise to craving – wanting one and not the other; and this in turn gives rise to clinging to the object of desire, no longer contented to let it pass.[21] Uninterrupted, it is from such mental states that we then choose and act. But revealing the stages of this chain gives us the opportunity to break the connections at various stages, to interrupt the development of a feeling into a desire.

Notice that, again as with their ancient Greek counterparts, we should conceive of ethics here as primarily concerned with the qualities and states of a person. The field of ethical concern is not delineated by the moment of choice, or the principles of action; acts and choices are treated rather as the practical effects of the 'inner structure' or the mental events constituting the person. Precepts may guide, when necessary. But progress requires attention to the causes and conditions that give rise to the choices and actions for which precepts are a crude second best. Concentrate on these causes, and the choices and actions will take care of themselves.

Arhats and Bodhisattvas

Philosophical ethics thus takes shape in part as the articulation and exploration of ideal persons – consider for comparison the role in ethics of the figure of Socrates, the Stoic sage, or Aristotle's *phronimos* (the person perfect in practical wisdom). In being good and doing well, one aspires to be a certain kind of person. The peculiarity of the Buddhist version of this is that it is the aspiration to be no person at all. The Arhat, the accomplished person, is the one who no longer sets in motion anything that will cause further personal factors to arise in the future. So long as one remains alive after having been released from the grip of delusion and desire, this is merely the residual momentum of previous forces playing themselves out: '*nirvāṇa* with remainder' it is called, as opposed to '*nirvāṇa* without remainder' when there are also no longer any results from previous events to arise.

In case I should fail to fully appreciate the implications of selfless metaphysics, meditational practice should reveal to me the greater part of my mental life as in fact entangled in suffering and delusions of self that cause further suffering. Practice in discerning the patterns of dependent origination offers opportunity for breaking the links that keep the cycle of *saṃsāra* in motion. And there is no gainsaying the fact that these meditational practices should persuade me where the metaphysical arguments may fail.

We may yet wonder, however, whether we *want* to break these links. Even considering the great joy and loving kindness the Arhat's life involves – primarily through meditational states – the life can still appear forbiddingly austere, for it does not include many of the emotional ties that give meaning to an ordinary life. Indeed, the Buddha is explicit about this: "Household life is crowded and dusty; life gone forth is wide open. It is not easy while living in a home to lead the holy life utterly perfect and pure as a polished shell" (*MN* 100.9).

Again, this potential failure of the Arhat ideal to get a grip on a person's motivation should not surprise us. Our ways of perceiving things as attractive now are the accumulated result of countless misguided judgements and feelings, which we should only expect to be able to alter incrementally. This is why we have two different ends – happiness and *nirvāṇa* – and why we acknowledge some genuine merit in good actions, even if these are ultimately incompatible with *nirvāṇa*. While movement from one goal to another may describe a single person's trajectory along the path, we can also distinguish distinct lives aimed at these two different ends, and related symbiotically. The monastic community, made up of those for whom worldly happiness holds no charms, concerns itself exclusively with attaining *nirvāṇa*. Living a life uncompromised by worldly affairs, monastics present an opportunity for others to practise giving (since monastics are in need of material sustenance), and are the suitable cause and recipients for worthy acts of generosity. The laity, meanwhile, aiming at happiness (or good rebirth) rather than liberation, are able to share in true virtue-based happiness by sharing some part of their worldly goods with renunciants. Such a symbiotic relation between '*kammic* Buddhism' and '*nibbanic* Buddhism' may have been a social and practical fact in some Buddhist societies.[22]

However, the strict separation of these two forms of Buddhist life has been challenged in point of fact, and as an adequate ideal in principle. While it is obviously difficult to attain liberating insight while engaged in the mundane task of making a living, still it should not be in principle impossible. So we should expect even those who do not devote their lives to meditation to be aiming at understanding selflessness and incorporating this into their outlooks and lives. For insight into selflessness benefits whoever can realize it, in so far as they can realize it, and is part of what enables anyone to live better by being less in the grip of neurotic craving. Yet lay Buddhists were often presumed not to be capable of enlightenment in this lifetime. Also, there is no obvious reason why great portions of humanity – all women, for instance – should be considered, as the conservative Buddhists did consider them, incapable of fully attaining such liberating insight in this lifetime. Such restrictions seem to betray an excessive attachment to conventional distinctions that selfless metaphysics shows up as ultimately without ground.

Moreover, for all that the Arhat has renounced the greater portion of ordinarily recognized pleasures, his scope of concern seems peculiarly restricted. While concerned above all with the cessation of suffering, the aspiring Arhat's life is organized around eliminating that suffering which would be a direct causal consequence of the volitional action of *this* particular group of *skandhas* here. The greater mass of suffering – although lamentable and worthy of compassion – is not his affair, and is not incorporated into his conception of the ultimate end he seeks, and what it would be to realize it.

In these respects, the way of the Arhat came to seem unacceptably narrow to some Buddhists: narrow in who could conceivably walk that path, and narrow in the scope of concern of the one so walking. Such Buddhists envisaged a 'greater community', a *mahā-saṅgha*: whoever aspired to liberating insight, and to perfecting the virtues necessary to attaining it, might be a member of the community; and the aspiration is to eliminate *all* suffering, not just to bring to a conclusion the momentum of *saṃsāra* occurring 'here'.[23]

The Buddha referred to himself in his previous lives as a "bodhisattva" – an awakened being – and these Mahāsaṅghikas aimed to emulate the devotion to enlightenment for the sake of all beings characteristic of the Buddha through his many incarnations as an accomplished being, and in particular in his decision to teach the Dharma for everyone's welfare, even though it was troublesome and unnecessary for him (*MN* 26.19–21[24]). Instead of aiming merely for the liberation of the Arhat, these Buddhists vowed to continue working for the cessation of suffering until *all* beings were liberated.[25] This is the Bodhisattva vow, and the project of fulfilling it, consisted not only in following the Eightfold Path – as this might be understood with its emphasis on attaining and sustaining liberating insight – but also in understanding right speech, conduct and thought as consisting in the six 'perfections' (*pāramitās*) of generosity, self-restraint, patience, energy, concentration and insight. While these and other virtues were naturally acknowledged by all Buddhists, they increasingly became for some a way of organizing a conception of advancing along the trajectory of the Bodhisattva path.

These two different ideals coexisted within single Buddhist communities, more or less happily, for a period. Neither the Arhat ideal nor the Bodhisattva ideal is positively harmful, and insisting on one rather than the other would be an excellent case of attachment to views raising unnecessary friction and faction. Gradually, those adopting the Bodhisattva ideal, infused with the influence of the *prajñāpāramitā* literature,[26] would come to coalesce and distinguish themselves from the others as belonging to 'the Greater Vehicle' – the Mahāyāna – in contrast to the lesser one (the *hinayāna*). Of the great plurality of non-*mahāyāna* views and communities from antiquity, the only one to exist unbroken to the present day is the Theravāda.

The Nietzschean Objection revisited, revised

The general form of the Nietzschean Objection was that there was some other good than the elimination of suffering that could act as the criterion for distinguishing bad suffering from that which should be accepted or even embraced. There are few things that could be realistically thought to play this role. Now that we have looked more closely at what the Buddhist ideals are, what a life organized around the aim of awakening looks like, and why its attractiveness should come into view only once one has progressed along the path, we are in a position to see why characterizing the difficulty as the Nietzschean Objection is, after all, apt.

Virtue

> You are wrong, sir, if you think that a man who is worth anything should weigh up the risk of life and death; he should look to this only in his actions, whether what he does is right or wrong, whether he is acting like a good or a bad man.
>
> (Plato, *Apology* 28b[27])

So says Socrates, in provocative defence of his perverse habit of antagonizing people by interrogating them publicly about their understanding of their own actions, values and lives. He does not say here that virtue is the only good (that extreme stance is reserved for the Stoics); but he does say that the only question to consider is virtue, for without that nothing else is good either – "it is virtue that makes wealth and everything else, both public and private, good for a person" (*Apology* 30b3–4). Virtue and justice – moral goodness – is, one might say, more important than suffering; suffering in itself is irrelevant, although it can be made good or bad according to how it relates to justice.[28]

But in fact the Buddhist need not dispute the claim about virtue, for it only introduces the question: in what does virtue consist? Excellent conduct and character may be that which conduces to the elimination of suffering. Socrates does not here offer an alternative suggestion, and articulating alternatives without appeal to divine command is no simple matter. Plato himself endorses the general principle that whoever is good cannot, *qua* good, be the source or cause of damage or harm. So to be good, and virtuous, involves not being the source of any harm. Is 'harm' significantly distinct from 'suffering'?

Perhaps so, but determining this involves extensive specific and refined metaphysical commitments, of which Plato and Kant give us two possible examples. It is no simple matter to articulate what value it is that the Buddhist version of the supremacy of virtue – conceived of as aiming at the elimination of suffering according to the Buddhist understanding of the human condition – necessarily leaves out or overlooks, compared to its rivals.

Love

There seems to be a kind of miraculous originative goodness in love. Philosophers have not known well what to do with this and, of course, much is written of love in a hyperbolic vein. Nevertheless, some version of the thought that our highest calling and highest good is to 'love one another' has remained compelling. Actual experiences of love in human intercourse are admittedly highly equivocal. Not all that goes by that name is suited to play the role of the highest good in human life and certainly not the messy, demanding, often painful and selfish stuff of erotic love. We should love our neighbour as we love ourselves (Leviticus 19:18), or as God loves us (John 13:34–35); such love might reasonably lay claim to being an irreducible, unequivocal good in human life.

But this unselfish direct concern for the well-being of another – often presented in paradigmatic form as maternal love, neighbourly love or Christ's love – is hardly distinguishable from the Buddhist virtues, or 'divine abidings', of loving-kindness, compassion and joy in another's well-being, which are loving care purified of all egoism. So again, if one wants to present 'love' as an alternative to the Buddhist ideal, it is quite difficult to see what there is worth saving that the Buddhist view, taken in all its complexity, actually leaves out. Selfless care and concern for the well-being of others is not another name for the highest goal of eliminating suffering; but it is a quality of consciousness enjoyed by those who have attained that goal, and enjoined upon those aspiring to attain it.

God (knowing God, loving God)

If one believes there is a highest principle – an ultimate ground of being and source of all reality, whether this is conceived of as a creator-god or not, or as a person or not – with which one may come into some kind of unity, then this aim would make suffering in its ordinary sense irrelevant. Not only certain Christians and Jews, but also some Brahmanical thinkers held some such view. The Buddha excoriates extreme asceticism, which presumably aimed at some such goal, as an unnecessarily painful existence leading *only* to more pain (*MN* 57). The weight of his rejection, that is, rests on there being no such good to be obtained. This battle is one to be fought on metaphysical grounds, and cannot simply be stipulated as an available good. The same holds for the conception of "the first, the last purpose of the human soul" as loving God.[29] It may typically enjoin a less austere life, but its potential value depends upon postulating the existence of some such supremely deserving object of love.

Truth

Truth and wisdom may be thought ultimately more valuable than all else, and the proper measure of the worth of other things. Feelings of pleasure and pain might be thought only valuable when they aptly capture the truth of things. Of course, like love, knowledge and the search for it is evidently not unambiguously worthwhile. Knowledge of all possible facts, in a Faustian sense, could not play the role of the ultimate good. But there is another way of valuing truth. Someone might place an absolute value on truth and truthfulness, "such that they would hazard all their prospects for it",[30] not as an accumulation of facts but as an orientation of soul. Only knowledge of truth in some such robust sense and an adherence to a principle of valuing reality over fantasy could lay claim to be the search for understanding in which wisdom consists.

Here again, however, once such a rival claimant to the title 'highest good' is spelled out, it is difficult to make out whether there is any real rivalry. For after all, the Buddhist path centrally involves right view, and the insight won by meditative concentration on this correct view of the fundamental nature of reality. A common expression of the aim is 'to see things as they are', and rooting out confused, delusive misapprehensions is the fundamental, ongoing and transformative task. The Buddhist path consists in valuing reality over consoling fantasy, and is a path towards that insight into the fundamental natural of reality that liberates from suffering and the causes of suffering.

Life

For all that, we might – confronted with the Buddhist ideal of the Arhat, or even of the Bodhisattva – find ourselves lamenting the rich, vexing emotional life of particular loves with their ups and downs, proximate goals and achievements that only sometimes work out and always admittedly leave something to be desired. There is something beautiful and true and infinitely precious in all the messy variety that life, in all its imperfection, has to offer.

To feel sympathetic to this view, and to feel that something of irreplaceable value – however imperfect and unsatisfactory it might be – has been lost, one need not be a full-blown Nietzschean. Bernard Williams's selective Humean Nietzscheanism gives powerful voice to the incommensurable importance of personal projects, and particular personal relations.[31] And one need not go to Nietzsche's heirs at all to find sympathizers: there is a whiff of the same spirit in Ecclesiastes:

> He hath made everything beautiful in his time: also he hath set the world in their heart, so that no man can find out the work that God maketh from the beginning to the end. I know that there is no good in them, but for a man to rejoice, and to do good in his life. And also that every man should eat and drink, and enjoy the good of all his labor, it is the gift of God. (3:11–13)

And Susan Neiman, a much more recent defender of the European Enlightenment, eloquently articulates the virtue of being life-embracing in her exposition of a 'grown-up idealism'.[32]

The Buddhist might reply by insisting that their diagnosis of our common unhappy condition, and programme for its amelioration, actually offers to allow us all these goods but in a better form. If we cure ourselves of our neurotic fears and cravings, and the bad habit of interposing ourselves between our experiences and the things experienced, then we in fact experience all of life much more directly, fully and truly. It is being imprisoned in the partial conceptual frameworks built up by our greed and fundamental attachment to self that prevents us from fully experiencing all the riches life has to offer; and it is our perverse attachment to getting what we want and repudiating what we do not want that prevents us from doing just as Nietzsche recommends: affirming life and the experiences that come to us, exactly as they are, without judging them constantly according to fixed notions of good and bad, desirable and undesirable.

This reply is apt but it can only go so far. It can only reflect what following the Buddhist path may do for someone still seeking some version of happiness as the solution to suffering. Once one has reconceived non-suffering as *nirvāṇa*, and pursues the state of the Arhat or of the Bodhisattva as the ideal, one can no longer consistently affirm the intrinsic value of having any worldly experience at all.

Delusion, attachment and aversion are eliminated together. Uprooting attachment and aversion eliminates the strong desires and passions that underpin outstanding accomplishments and life-projects, adventurous embracing of life's diversity and the abandon of great love affairs. Siddhartha could not become both a great ruler and the Awakened One.

Feeling our way forward

Feelings, emotions and volitions might be thought bad because they (i) are painful, or (ii) are false: more carefully, because they (i) require, involve or lead to more pain than pleasure, or (ii) arise from, are expressive of or lead to confusion (ignorance).[33] On the Buddhist picture, is it ultimately on conative (hedonistic) grounds, or on cognitive (rationalist) grounds that the greater part of emotions are to be rejected?

There is no doubt that the Buddhists think many emotions are bad on straightforwardly hedonistic grounds, and they expect us, on reflection, to agree. Irritation, for instance, or envy, is not fun, and I am happier when I am not feeling these or something worse. One of the standard Buddhist strategies is to argue that even pleasant emotions are only had along with pain, whether as necessary causes, as internal to the pleasure or as invariably arising because of the pleasure; more subtly, one might argue that the overall mindset that enables pleasant emotions to arise is one structured so as to involve more pain overall than pleasure.

But this ground alone is inadequate. For I might agree so far as it goes, and yet claim about at least some of my negative emotions that they are warranted ("He *really is* being irritating!"), positively motivating ("Well, I'll get a house twice as big as his!"), or worth more than the negative feeling is bad. If it is better to have loved and lost than never to have loved, this is not because the pain of losing is vastly outweighed by the pleasure of loving, but because being in love is either valuable in its own right or makes other things so. Acknowledging the unpleasantness of obviously uncomfortable emotions might be enough to persuade me to take a modest dose of Buddhist medicine – sage advice about the transience of things – but it cannot give me a reason to let go of those emotions that seem true, or in some other way sufficiently meaningful to render the pain irrelevant. However valid such hedonistic arguments against emotions, however many more of the emotions they encompass that we might at first have been inclined to count pleasant, such hedonistic arguments cannot make headway with the second sort of reason for finding emotions valuable: their relations to truth and meaning.

This is where we need metaphysics, and where we appreciate just how much a presumed metaphysical picture supports our ethical outlooks. For it is here that we shall be invited to reflect again on the four Noble Truths, and particularly on the first of these: everything is suffering, transient, without substantiality or independence. That is the very nature of being, and it resists any possibility of 'higher meaning', 'greater purpose', or 'final good'. The meaningfulness we think we find in our various emotional attachments is created by us, and while we might do a better or worse job of that, and while creating some or another of these might be provisionally necessary given the delusions we are starting from and dwelling within, the greatest – most dangerous – delusion of all is supposing that there is or could ever be any kind of ultimate validity in the meaning we give things. When I appreciate this fully, my romantic attachment to grand narratives that cast myself as the heroic protagonist will be replaced by an unbounded compassion for whatever suffers. This is a compassion that neither seeks nor depends upon finding meaning, for this and related emotions are the only affective states that are true to the world as it is.

FOUR

The second Buddha's greater vehicle

> The Bodhisattva Avalokiteśvara, while moving in the deep course of Perfect Understanding [*prajña paramitā*], shed light on the five *skandhas* and found them all equally empty. After this penetration, he overcame all pain. ("The Heart Sutra"[1])

With Nāgārjuna, we encounter the first *named* Buddhist philosopher. His impact on the character of Buddhist thought was so massive that he is sometimes hailed as the 'second Buddha'. But he is an elusive figure. Very little is known of him personally, except that he is probably from an educated Brahmin family in the south of India, and was working in the first to second centuries CE. Trained in the Vedic tradition, Nāgārjuna established the practice of discussing Buddhism in Sanskrit, the shared language of the educated classes, rather than in Pāli or some other vernacular, thus bringing Buddhist and non-Buddhist thought into a common linguistic and intellectual space.

Nāgārjuna is elusive in another way. Such was his eventual popularity and esteem that, like Pythagoras in the Graeco-Roman world, Nāgārjuna had many views and texts retrospectively fathered on him, so that it is particularly difficult to discern the man from the myth. If we take 'Nāgārjuna' to refer to 'the founder of Madhyamaka', then we can use one prominent text, the *Mūla-madhyamaka-kārikā* as criterial. The author of this text may reasonably, although not indisputably, be considered the author of about half a dozen other works, among them: the *Vigrahavyāvartanī* (*The Dispeller of Disputes*), which, like the *Mūlamadhyamakakārikā*, is more focused on metaphysics and epistemology; the *Suhṛllekha* (*The Good-Hearted Letter*) which focuses more on ethics; and the *Ratnāvalī* (*The Precious Garland*), which treats of ethics and metaphysics together. These together set out a distinctive interpretation of the Buddha's teachings.

And it is here that Nāgārjuna is most elusive of all. The primary text setting out the distinctive interpretation that became known as 'Madhyamaka', or 'Middle Way', is the *Mūlamadhyamakakārikā* (*Verses on the Core of the Middle Way*) – and the title is telling: it is, like many texts of the period, written in verse. These are extremely compact, for ease of memorization, with no expectation that explanations were to be found here. Explanations of the verses – the meaning of the claims and the reasoning behind them – were to be carried by those memorizing the verses, and passed on orally to their students, who in their turn used the root text as an *aide-memoire* for the elaborate, finely articulated view under discussion. Although Nāgārjuna may have written a commentary on his own work, articulating the position he sets out and the reasoning behind it, if it ever existed it has been lost to us. His most immediate successor, Āryadeva, wrote treatises defending the Madhyamaka view against its critics; but these too were not initially very influential in India, and almost none of his work survives in Sanskrit. Beyond that we are largely left with much later interpreters who, writing in rather different intellectual climates, had their own distinctive philosophical aims and projects. Such commentaries are unreliable, but inescapable.

It is clear enough that Nāgārjuna is picking up central aspects of the Mahāyāna movement; he allies himself explicitly with the Greater Vehicle in the *Ratnāvalī*, for instance. He also picks up on a related and growing body of 'perfection of wisdom', *prajña-pāramitā*, literature,[2] among which the "Heart Sūtra" might be taken as emblematic:

> Śariputra, form does not differ from emptiness; emptiness does not differ from form. Form itself is emptiness; emptiness itself is form. So too are feeling, cognition, formation, and consciousness.
>
> Śariputra, all *dharmas* are empty. They are not born, not destroyed, not defiled, not pure; and they neither increase nor diminish. Therefore, in emptiness there is no form, feeling, cognition, formation, or consciousness; no eyes, ears, nose, tongue, body, or mind; no sights, sounds, smells, tastes, objects of touch, or *dharmas*; no field of the eyes up to and including no field of mind consciousness; and no ignorance or ending of

> ignorance, up to and including no old age and death or ending of old age and death. There is no suffering, no accumulating, no extinction, and no Path, and no understanding and no attaining.
>
> Because no attainment, the Bodhisattva relying on *prajña-pāramitā* is free of any impediment, rid of the fear bred by it, has overcome confusion and in the end reaches utmost Nirvana.[3]

Śūnyatā (emptiness) figures prominently in Nāgārjuna – all *dharmas*, he says, are *sūnya*, or empty – but precisely to what end is not at all clear. On a very modest reading, Nāgārjuna is not actually saying anything substantially different from the Abhidharmikas; he is just giving a new (and more obscure) terminology for it. Such a deflationary reading is, admittedly, at odds with the description of Madhyamaka, with its emphasis on emptiness, as 'the second turning of the Wheel of Dharma', after the Buddha's own teachings.[4] But the more revolutionary we take Madhyamaka to be, the more ambitiously we understand the insistence on *emptiness*, the more the position smacks of nihilism.[5] And, in fact, although Nāgārjuna's decidedly Mahāyāna interpretation of the Buddha's teachings turned out to be incredibly influential, it took some time before it was taken seriously. About two centuries after Nāgārjuna was writing, Vasubandhu, in his "Treatise on the Person" (*AKBh.* IX), relatively swiftly dismisses the Madhyamaka view as nihilism, without much labour.

We shall try to find a middle way between these two extremes. Taking seriously his Abhidharma contemporaries, Nāgārjuna engages with them in order to offer what he takes to be a truer interpretation of the Buddha's teachings than that embodied in the increasingly intricate Abhidharma schemas of classification. His critique of core Abhidharma metaphysics gives systematic and substantial ground to the difference between Mahāyāna and Abhidharma, so that the differences between them could never again be papered over as merely methodological. At the same time, this critique of Abhidharma Buddhism should not leave Madhyamaka a form of extreme nihilism.[6]

The Precious Garland (Ratnāvalī)

In the *Ratnāvalī*, the twofold structure of a revisionist *eudaimonism* sketched in Chapter 3 becomes explicit. Presented as a letter of advice to a prince, the *Ratnāvalī* begins by declaring two goals, and relating them hierarchically to one another:

> The elevated state is considered to be happiness [*sukha*], and the final good is liberation [*mokṣa*]. In brief, the method of realizing them is summed up in faith, and wisdom. (*RĀ* I.4)

> Due to faith, one partakes of Dharma; due to wisdom one apprehends things as they are. Of these two, wisdom is foremost; but faith comes first. (*RĀ* I.5)[7]

The faith that Nāgārjuna puts forward as the means to happiness is not the blind belief in metaphysical claims, as it has mostly been in the Christian tradition.[8] It is rather an attitude embodied and enacted in keeping the precepts, and generally living a decent life: "He who does not transgress the Dharma on account of worldly cravings, hatred, fear, and mental bewilderment is one who has faith" (*RĀ* I.6a–c).

Verses I.8–20 enumerate the familiar virtues and vices: refrain from killing, from theft and sexual misconduct; be generous, self-restrained and patient. These are conventional virtues and vices, from which – following the one and avoiding the other – one wins an end conventionally considered unquestionably worth having, namely *sukha* or happiness. Āryadeva sums it up as follows:

> Heaven is attained by means of moral conduct [*śīla*]; one attains the highest level by means of the [right] view. (*CŚ* XII.11cd)

> In brief, the Tathāgatas explain non-violence [*ahiṃsā*] as virtuous behaviour [*dharma*], and *nirvāṇa* as, in fact, emptiness [*śūnyatā*]. Here [in our system], there are only these two. (*CŚ* XII.23)

We must, of course, educate and revise our conception of happiness. The genuinely elevated state may not turn out to consist in the sorts of things people unreflectively assume will make them happy. It is rather "the happiness of the gods" (*RĀ* I.24a), which, according to Nāgārjuna, consists in meditative states of undisturbed bliss. But even this revised happiness is not the highest good attainable. The highest good is liberation, attained through insight into the nature of reality.

But these two are related so that happiness is good not only because it feels good, or is attractive to us, or is itself a state of being well-off. It is *also* good because living the life that yields true happiness paves the way for the attainment of a quite distinct and higher good.[9] The person of faith, described above, is "the supreme vessel for the final good" (*RĀ* I.6d).

These two ends are thus correlated to the two truths, and similarly related – and they display a similar tension. The real happiness of 'elevated status' is, on the one hand, genuinely good; but on the other hand, it is so in virtue of its relation to a more ultimate good. And while we might be satisfied with conventional goods, just as we might be satisfied with conventional wisdom, it would be better to understand ultimate reality if we can. Nāgārjuna's *Ratnāvalī* thus gives practical advice about which things are good, and to be done, in everyday life (particularly by a prince); and he warns of the dangers of mistakenly grasping ultimate reality, or attempting to understand it when one is not psychologically prepared for it.

> If this doctrine is not well understood, it causes the ruin of the unintelligent man, since he sinks into the impurity of nihilism ... By food badly digested a man gets his ruin ... even so, those who do not properly understand the doctrine will get their ruin ... If one does not thoroughly understand this doctrine, egotism is originated; from this, *karma*, both moral and immoral ... Therefore as long as this doctrine, which annihilates egotism, is not thoroughly understood, so long apply yourself with great care to *dharma*, which consists in generosity, self-restraint, and patience. (*RĀ* II.22–25)[10]

In spite of these dangers, Nāgārjuna continually returns to the ultimate good (e.g. *RĀ* IV.67–70), and the wisdom by which it is attained, as if mere happiness – even the highest bliss of the gods – will not actually be satisfactory after all. The greater part of Book I consists in articulating the no-self view of reality in which proper wisdom consists (I.25–100); and Book II opens with a continuation of the same (II.1–25).

Nāgārjuna is explicit that different goods, the means to them, and ways of articulating them, are appropriate to different persons. For some people, it would be quite wrong to attempt to attain the highest good, even if every other good is in some way deficient by comparison.

> The Buddha taught the Dharma to some to free them from negativities [*pāpa*]; to others so that they could do meritorious deeds [*puṇya*]; to others he taught a law based on duality. To still others he taught a *dharma* beyond duality ... to others again the dharma consisting of the two tenets of compassion and emptiness, the means leading to awakening.
>
> (*RĀ* IV.95–96)

This is an exercise of the Buddha's skilfulness in teaching: that he presents his interlocutor with a truth that allows them to progress from wherever they are. These various truths are largely only provisional: approximations to truth whose value and veracity ultimately consist in enabling one to get closer to being able to attain the insight of full awakening.

This 'skilful means', as it is often referred to as, has its basis in the earliest discourses of the Buddha, and was a hermeneutic device employed to render consistent diverse teachings that seemed to contradict each other. One discourse may say that there is no concept of self that does not cause suffering, but another (as we saw in Chapter 2) speaks of the self as the bearer of the burden of craving and aversion, and another speaks of the Buddha's previous lives – which seems to presume an individuation impossible without a subsisting self. So the distinction between 'interpretable' (*neyārtha*) and 'definitive' (*nītārtha*) statements, even within those agreed to be words of the Buddha, was indispensable for any Buddhist intellectual. Most, for instance, would take 'no concept of self which does not cause suffering' as definitive; talk of 'bearers' and 'burdens' should be interpreted as an imprecise but useful way of speaking. This latter point was of great importance in argument against the Pudgalavādins, who took the bearer/burden claims as definitive.

The notion of the Buddha's skilful means, of provisional and definitive expositions, and of withholding the latter where appropriate, was crucial especially to the Mahāyāna. For Mahāyāna Buddhists had to explain how it could be that some of the most dedicated Buddhist renunciants could have overlooked the teachings of the Greater Vehicle, and how they nevertheless were good Buddhists, after a fashion. This polemical purpose of stressing 'skilful means' is apparent in Nāgārjuna's exposition of it, for just before the passage quoted, he is distinguishing the Greater Vehicle from the rest according to views and practices: "In the vehicle of the Auditors [*śravakas*],[11] there is no mention of the vow of the Bodhisattva, nor of his virtue of devolving upon others the fruits of his career" (*RĀ* IV.90).

While there are limited truths, suitable for advancing persons of limited abilities, only the Mahāyāna promises the complete picture, and so the complete complement of available goods: "By having faith in the Mahāyāna and by following the precepts enjoined in it, one attains the supreme illumination, and along the way all happiness [*sarvasaukyāni*]" (*RĀ* IV.98).

Nāgārjuna's project: form and content

If there is genuine innovation in Nāgārjuna's interpretation of the Buddha-Dharma, it is not to be found in which things are considered good, nor even – at least nominally – in why they are good. No Buddhist would dispute that keeping the precepts is good, *kuśala* (wholesome, skilful), nor that the precepts consist in not killing, not stealing, speaking truly and compassionately; nor that keeping them leads to genuine well-being, which well-being enables one to attain the ultimate insight in which final goodness – liberation from *saṃsāra* – consists.[12]

The emphasis, of course, is different. The perfections, generosity above all, are emphasized as suitable for all persons. Articulating ethics in terms of 'perfections', rather than the Eightfold Path, orients one more towards attitudes we take towards our actions, thoughts, perceptions and feelings. And since they are perfections, it is clear that 'the path' consists in continual improvement in all these areas, rather than sequentially fulfilling one step after another. But such differences are more of emphasis than of principle.

It is by this favouring of 'perfection', and the aspiration to end all suffering, that we recognize the *Ratnāvalī* as a Mahāyāna text; and it is in specifying what 'final goodness' actually is, and what attaining it therefore consists in, that Nāgārjuna's view shows up as distinctly Mādhyamika. Where all Buddhists will relate liberation to correct grasp of ultimate reality, Nāgārjuna specifies that we must correctly grasp 'emptiness'.

Yet the difference between Nāgārjuna and his Abhidharmika predecessors is still difficult to make out. For the Abhidharmika would be the first to acknowledge that what we know, in knowing ultimate reality, is that ultimate reality is without self; and Nāgārjuna's emptiness claim is precisely that all reality is empty *of* self. No Buddhist, not even the infamous Pudgalavādin, rejects *anatta*.

Yet Nāgārjuna clearly means to be more revolutionary than that. He directly criticizes Abhidharma views of momentariness (*RĀ* I.66–70), and atomism (*RĀ* I.71[13]), and frequently insists that the key to correct understanding is avoiding commitment to both existence and non-existence (*RĀ* I.62, for instance). At the same time, Nāgārjuna infamously claims to hold not views at all: "[For us] there is no thesis to be demonstrated, no rules of conduct, and on account of our taking shelter in the supreme illumination, not even mind, our doctrine is really the doctrine of nothingness. How then can we be called nihilists?" (*RĀ* I.60).[14] His distinctive style of destructive critique of classic metaphysical categories in the *Mūlamadhyamakakārikā* should persuade us to reject these in favour of his own position, which position, Nāgārjuna nevertheless concedes, is, like everything, empty.

Foregrounding this absence of a positive alternative, the *Mūlamadhyamakakārikā's* examination of classic Abhidharma categories takes shape as a series of destructive tetralemmas: the *catuṣkoti* (tetralemma) should show that for any category, each of the logically possible positions regarding it, or implied by it, turns out to be untenable. For instance:

> Neither from itself nor from another, nor from both, nor without cause, does anything whatever, anywhere arise.
> (*MMK* I.1)

> Everything is thus, and not thus, neither thus nor not thus. That is the Buddha's instruction. (*MMK* XVIII.8)

> One may not say that there is emptiness, nor that there is non-emptiness, nor that both, nor that neither exists.
> (*MMK* XXII.11)

For any *A*, we should reject *A*, not-*A*, both *A* and not-*A*, and neither *A* nor not-*A*.

While it is easy to see why one might be inclined to designate such a rhetorical performance 'emptiness', it is otherwise difficult to see what lesson we are meant to draw from it. Since the third limb looks like a straightforward contradiction, and the fourth simply redundant, much scholarly effort of the past century has gone into a debate over the logical form of the *catuṣkoti*: can the arguments be recast in terms of classical logic? Or does Nāgārjuna offer an alternative to classical logic? If so, what form does it take? Or should the destructive tetralemma be taken as a rejection of logic altogether? Perhaps Nāgārjuna is a mystic and irrationalist, a paradox-monger with spiritual intent: the paradoxes should so befuddle and baffle the mind that it jars one into 'seeing beyond' conceptual reality to some other ineffable reality.[15] There is in fact no lesson to be drawn; Nāgārjuna is simply trying to induce a state of non-conceptual awareness by whatever means possible. "The true doctrine", Nāgārjuna tells us in the last verse of the *Mūlamadhyamakakārikā*, "leads to the relinquishing of all views".

This last, most evasive, alternative may seem to find further support in Candrakīrti's fifth-century CE introduction to Madhyamaka, the *Madhyamakāvatāra*, where he places the aim within the ethical context of freedom from attachment: "Attachment to one's own belief, aversion for another's view: all this is thought. Once clinging and aversion are dispelled through reason and analysis, we will be swiftly freed" (*MA* VI.119).

But if the 'freedom' referred to here is some experience of non-conceptual consciousness, one might well wonder what the benefit of such a state was supposed to be, and whether metaphysics can be so easily escaped. For the very notion of non-conceptual awareness implies a metaphysics of mind, and the presumption that such a thing is possible commits us further. Moreover, we cannot simply take it as obvious that there is any point in striving for such a state, even if it were possible. If the value of such a state is in any way related to its veracity, then this implies a view about what reality is actually like: for instance, that it is not structured in a way that any concepts could accurately reflect. If its value is not connected to its veracity, then some other account of its value must be offered, for it is not self-evident. Finally, if the *Mūlamadhyamakakārikā* is a device for getting us into that – or any other – mindset, it can only be effective in its aim if we actually find the claims, and the arguments for them, persuasive. Notice that Candrakīrti acknowledges that it is *through reason and analysis* that we are freed. If the arguments against all possible positions are no good, I have no reason to abandon the attempt to make coherent claims using such concepts.

If Nāgārjuna's aim were to get us to withhold belief (or assent to propositions), like the ancient Greek Sceptics, then he could have done as they did, and presented convincing arguments on *all sides* of any questions, rather than merely negative arguments. Although there is some dispute in the later Madhyamaka tradition over what sorts of arguments can legitimately be used to articulate the 'Middle Way' proposed, Nāgārjuna clearly favours the *via negativa*, called '*prasaṅga*': showing for whatever one may want to assert that it is untenable on its own terms. This preference is unlikely to be due merely to aesthetic considerations.[16] Rather, the process of rejection of all possible alternatives is closely related to the content of the Madhyamaka position.

Although the 'mystical' or irrationalist interpretation of Madhyamaka does justice to this, it obscures the fact that Nāgārjuna's purpose is more ambitious, and more specific: he hopes, as Candrakīrti says, to make us become unattached to the holding of views as such; this is his ethical aim, and the virtue in non-attachment to views is well attested in the earliest Buddhist literature. To that end, Nāgārjuna intends to show that all views, each on its own, in its own right, is incoherent. Therefore, he takes each potentially metaphysical category in turn – cause, motion, agent, element, connection, essence, time, entity, to name a few – and demonstrates that these are, one and all, incoherent, at least *when taken to be asserting something about the fundamental nature of reality*. They all have a perfectly serviceable everyday meaning, and there is no reason to jettison them in that role; precisely because everyday usage does not purport to grasp the deep nature of things, such uses escape the charge of incoherence. But as soon as they claim any deeper meaning, they become incoherent.

If successful, this strategy has unmistakable metaphysical implications. For if all possible versions of our basic categories of thought cannot be pressed into the service of describing how things *really* are, this is either because reality itself is ultimately incoherent, or because there is something incoherent in the very attempt to distinguish ultimate reality from the everyday.

From anti-holism to anti-foundationalism

"Whatever is dependently co-arisen," Nāgārjuna tells us, "that is explained to be emptiness" (*MMK* XXIV.18).[17] This may seem a disappointingly unrevolutionary interpretation of *sūnyatā* (emptiness). For what Buddhist ever denied that everything was dependently co-arising? This is a basic part of the second Noble Truth, the causes of suffering. Wholes depend upon their parts and everyday worldly experience depends upon our conceptualizing activity and volitions; the ultimate parts, the *dharmas*, do not depend upon their parts (they have none) so neither do they depend upon conceptualizing activity (there is no mental act artificially unifying distinct things). But they do assuredly depend upon each other for their arising. Meditational exercises should get us to attend to precisely this fact. So where is the Madhyamaka revolution?

It is distinctive of the Brahmanical thinking in which Nāgārjuna was brought up that at least one thing (namely, the Self) is sublimely free from the messy vulnerability of whatever is dependent upon others for its existence. Nāgārjuna's objection to his Abhidharma colleagues is that they have inadvertently done the same, re-establishing the independence distinctive of selves in their simple elements, the *dharmas*. *Dharmas* may not create a separate, personal Self; but so long as they have a distinctive nature all their own, *svabhāva*, then they can lay claim to a stability and independence that one could be tempted to cling to.[18] In particular, one might cling to it as the 'real truth' about their 'real nature': for instance, whatever chariot-parts depend upon for their arising here and now, they are *really* co-located brown-events, solidity-events and so on, and that is what they *really are*, quite regardless of whatever else may be. The Abhidharmika, Nāgārjuna claims, thus evades the Buddha's challenging exhortation to give up all attachment. This failure to grasp the fundamental truth of dependent origination properly becomes a moral and spiritual failing, preventing one from reaching happiness and enlightenment.

The difference between the two positions is real, then, and the charge a serious one. Nāgārjuna likens the *svabhāva* (individual nature) proper to each *dharma* to the 'self' in important respects. The Buddha's teaching, he claims, is not just that there are no personal selves, but that there is no 'self' of any sort, anywhere; all things, concepts, *dharmas*, are empty of intrinsic nature. This, he suggests, is the unavoidable implication of the core Buddhist claim that all arises dependently. If true, this would explain why concepts invariably become incoherent when taken as capturing the nature of distinct entities. But can he substantiate the claim?

The irreality of the chariot was based on the fact that these different *dharmas*' being a chariot depended upon our taking them so. The principle illustrated was:

> Whatever has constituents depends upon those constituents for its existence, and depends upon our conceiving this 'many'

> *as* a 'one' for its unity, and so does not exist ultimately, but only (at best) conventionally.

Whatever depends on its parts for its identity exists only conceptually, because it is our conceptualizing that makes a 'one' out of 'many'. Nāgārjuna needs to adopt the stronger principle:

> Anything dependent upon another for its existence does not have any independent identity or nature of its own.

This granted, he need only point out that, as is agreed, everything arises through dependence upon something else; it would follow that everything is dependent for its nature, for 'what it is', on another. One cannot, then, take the 'inherent nature' out of complexes and rest it in simples without encountering the very same philosophical difficulties that reification of the complexes posed in the first place.

But why should this be so? Why grant the stronger principle? No doubt, *dharmas* depend upon something other than themselves for their arising. But why, from this, should they also depend upon another for their respective *natures* or identities – for 'what they are like', which is for *dharmas* the same as 'what they *are*'? The Abhidharmika opponent agrees that nothing exists independently of anything else. Is he thereby forced to conclude that nothing can have a distinct identity: that there are no individuals whatsoever? He may well reject the implication. For it looks as if Nāgārjuna's principle requires an equivocation on *svabhāva*, sometimes needing it to mean 'nature' or 'essence', sometimes merely 'existence', in order to make his argument work.[19] Nāgārjuna seems to argue from the admission that changing things are dependent upon conditions for their arising (they *are* dependent), to the conclusion that such dependent things cannot have, nor be, distinct and individuating *natures* of their own (their *being* is dependent).

But perhaps the move is a legitimate one, after all, and no mere equivocation. Consider how we might understand the first verse of the *Mūlamadhyamakakārikā*: "Neither from itself nor from another, nor from both, nor without a cause, does anything whatever, anywhere arise". Once we have identified all the conditions for something's arising – whether something simple or something complex – are we supposed to think there is something left over, something still unaccounted for? Is there 'some thing', over and above the various ways the consequences of several conditions manifest? What would this thing be?

Where would it come from? Is it supposed to just be there, always, waiting to be 'actualized' – whatever that means – by the arising of the associated conditions? (In what sense, then, would it not be dependent upon those conditions, and therefore analysable into them?) Is it supposed to be caused by something else entirely? (But then, it would in this respect too just be a manifestation of some other previous condition, and not something quite independent of all else.) But surely it is not supposed to be utterly without cause: independent characteristics just popping into and out of existence, randomly, for no reason whatsoever. And, *if all of that is correct*, then there can be no aspect of any existing thing, no matter how simple it may be, that is not due to some condition or set of conditions. But the chariot principle (Nāgārjuna argues) tells us that whatever depends upon other things for being what it is, is not truly and ultimately existent at all. So from the fact that everything, in every respect, arises from conditions we can conclude that nothing is independent, and that is as much as to say that no characteristic is distinct, independent and really existent as such, just on its own.

Now generalize this picture. Ask "Are they something, or are they nothing?" about all the various conditions responsible for any one thing arising and the Middle Way answer will be – they are not something, nor are they altogether nothing. The conditions themselves are effects of other conditions, lacking any determinate and abiding nature of their own. The upshot is there are no foundations; we cannot scratch beneath the surface of apparent complex wholes and find really existing simples. All identity is derivative; all supposed existence is dependent. The phenomena depend upon each other, upon our conceptualizing, but not upon anything else more fundamental or independent.

We might illustrate the point by entertaining a common objection to Aristotelian common-sense metaphysics. Aristotle claims that substance is primary. For our purposes, let 'this cat' be a substance. To be 'this cat' is to be in the most primary sense of 'being'. Other ways of being depend for their being upon substance: the greyness of the cat, for instance, exists by inhering in or belonging to the cat, and not in any other way. And in general, qualities are dependent upon substances. Confronted with this position, so argued for, a natural objection is to concede the point in one way – yes, the greyness of the cat depends upon the cat – but to reject the asymmetry. For does the cat not depend just as much upon its various qualities as the qualities depend upon the substance? Without the greyness, furriness, whiskeriness, and so on, there is no cat. Whether or not Aristotelian metaphysics has a response to this, Nāgārjuna's Madhyamaka can be understood as making some such observation as this: qualities and so-called substances, relations and relata, all things exist dependently. Inherent 'stopping-points' such as Aristotelian substances are a fantasy. In so far as *dharmas* as tropes (or property-particulars) were taken to be such stopping-points – the endpoints of analysis and bedrock of reality, or *ultimately* real instead of merely conventionally real; existing *really* as opposed to existing only dependently upon mental construction – this too was a fantasy, the last fantasy of the self-illusion.

If you suspect that this line of thinking does away with objects altogether, you may very well be right, and you can see why for centuries Madhyamaka might have been synonymous with 'nihilism'.[20] Candrakīrti does not exactly help this impression: "The elements do not exist, as we have generally shown, when proving, as we have done, that not from self, nor from other, nor from both, nor yet without cause does birth occur. Refuted thus, the elements are lacking all existence" (*MA* VI.103). Worse, the argument so construed seems to rely on just that equivocation – or unargued assimilation – between existence and essence that was identified above.

Now Candrakīrti goes on to explain the denial of 'all existence' as: "since phenomena are not produced Uncaused, nor are the handiwork of God, Do not arise from self, from other, nor from both these things, They do indeed emerge dependently" (VI.114), reminding us that the point about emptiness is a point about dependent origination. It is to this examination of causation and dependent origination, then, that we should look more closely, in order to discover whether Nāgārjuna may be acquitted of the charge of equivocation.

Dependent origination as lack of self

The Abhidharmika naturally concedes that 'seeing-blue-consciousness' depends upon a blue-event and on all the *dharmas* constitutive of the organ of sight (the eye), and on perception *dharmas*, and on all of these coming into contact.[21] But the blue-*dharma* does not require anything else *for its being blue* (rather than red, or hot). Naturally its arising here and now depends on appropriate conditions – a preceding blue-*dharma*, say; but why exactly should that impugn the non-dependence of the *blueness* of the *dharma*? Nāgārjuna needs to show that any kind of causal dependency impugns the self-sufficient identity of a *dharma* in just the way that conceptual dependency impugns the ultimate reality of complex wholes. Rather than equivocating, however, he does this by showing that causal dependency is *itself* a conceptual construction, and yet it is impossible to think *dharmas* without thinking them *as causally dependent.*[22]

The first chapter of the *Mūlamadhyamakakārikā* thus attempts to show that thinking causation requires drawing together distinct things, the 'cause' and the 'effect', and thinking them *as one*, while at the same time keeping them distinct; it aims to show, in fact, that it requires just that 'thinking the many as one' that is involved in thinking 'chariot' or 'Nāgasena'. This has far-reaching metaphysical implications, for on close examination the idea of 'existence' falls apart into two incompatible parts: to exist implies identity;[23] and it implies a location within a causal order.[24] But the former requires a distinctness from all else, which the latter cannot grant.[25] This is why in the *Ratnāvalī* Nāgārjuna relates conceptions of causation to existence claims: "when one has recognized the arising of cause and effect in this way, he cannot maintain either that this world *is*, nor that it *is not*, in reality" (*RĀ* I.38).

To think something as 'caused' requires simultaneously taking cause and effect *as one*, and *as distinct* from each other. A notion of cause is useful of course, just as appeal to chariots and persons is useful; but it is not simple. Not being simple, it is by the Abhidharmika's own criterion conceptually constructed.

Now Abhidharmikas agree that to think any thing at all is to think it *as caused*; or, put metaphysically instead of epistemologically, they grant that everything arises due to conditions, and is a contributory condition to what subsequently arises. That is, to exist is to be within the causal order. But to think something as causal is, Nāgārjuna points out, already to construct unities and relations that are incompatible with the absolute simplicity and independent identity that were supposed to warrant our treating *dharmas* as privileged, and ultimately real.

Causal dependence implies conceptual dependence. 'Blue-*dharma*' depends on our conceptualizing it *in so far as* we think it *as* a causally arising thing. To the extent that causal language succeeds in relating phenomena, it thereby succeeds in showing supposedly discrete entities to be somehow unified. And this 'thinking the many *as one*' is just the mark of the conceptually constructed that warranted considering the chariot and the self merely conventionally, and not ultimately existent. Thus to concede that something is 'dependently arising' cuts against the meaning of 'exist' usually reserved for 'ultimate existence' – namely, to have reality independent of our conceptualizing, and able to be individuated from all other such ultimately existing things.[26] If *this* is what we mean by 'exists', then it is indeed true that – in so far as any (existing) thing is within the causal order – nothing *exists*, and we should avoid all existence claims. But this is not a nihilistic position.[27] It is the rejection of the supposition that there are discrete individuals, each with their own identity, discernible from the conditions making it possible for them to arise. Nothing exists *like that*.

One advantage of this way of taking the argument is that it need not be piecemeal, the way Madhyamaka arguments often are presented. One might offer a series of pairs of concepts – short–long (cf. *Ratnāvalī* I.49), mountain–valley, fire–fuel – showing in each case that both members of a pair are equally dependent upon their partner for their meaning, and so presumably for their existence. Such a strategy leaves scope for exceptions, or even for the suspicion that the argument depends upon the Mādhyamika having cleverly chosen her examples. Moreover, relying on simple reflections on the meanings of words takes for granted that conceptual dependence implies actual, metaphysical dependence, and this is a strange thing simply to presume, as consideration of terms such as 'barbarian' quickly reveal.[28]

Indeed, even for the Buddhist, there *are* exceptions. There is some debate over whether things like 'space' should be considered to be outside any causal order, and therefore not dependently arising as do all the spatial phenomena. But there is general agreement that *nirvāṇa* is not dependently arising. *Nirvāṇa* does not 'exist' in the same way that we speak of existing things in the four Noble Truths – it is not among the 'everything' that suffers, or is transient. None of those categories apply. Nāgārjuna follows the argument in the opposite direction, and concludes that *nirvāṇa* is not exceptionally uncaused, but is in fact within and even identical to the causal order called *saṃsāra*. "There is not the slightest difference between *saṃsāra* and *nirvāṇa*. There is not the slightest difference between *nirvāṇa* and *saṃsāra*" (*MMK* XXV.19).

The emptiness of emptiness and the identity of *nirvāṇa* and *saṃsāra*

Rather like Wittgenstein, Nāgārjuna wants philosophy to leave everything in its place. Our ordinary use of ordinary language is unexceptionable. It is not *dysfunctional*; it should not be junked, and replaced with a better sort of language. Our words, our concepts and our thinking perform their services well. But Nāgārjuna differs radically from Wittgenstein in this respect: Nāgārjuna, unlike Wittgenstein, thinks that we will be fundamentally altered and improved by examining ordinary concepts, bringing out, and ultimately rejecting their pretensions to be informative about how things *really* are.

Ordinary language in its everyday use does a job; but in order to do that job, it necessarily presents itself as making claims about how discrete individuals relate to one another. Not only is our everyday language riddled with talk of causal relations, but every basic category through which we communicate – 'this', 'is', 'moving', 'changed', 'different', 'in the same place' – presents itself as being metaphysically committed in this way. It cannot do otherwise – to say '*X* is *Y*' requires thinking two separate things, thinking of them both as existing, distinctly, and as being related. It requires a movement of mind that simultaneously grasps as *one* and *many*. As this is incoherent, it cannot be how things really are. How they 'really are' is mutually determining, and therefore without any principle of individuation, so that distinguishing any portion of this mutually determining reality involves just that sort of act of mind that is the mark of conventional reality. Articulating this – asserting, that is, the emptiness of all things – itself requires just these same conceptual interdependences, so is likewise empty of any intrinsic, independent nature.

That language is necessarily inadequate to the task of capturing ultimate truths, or conceptualizing reality as it really is, cannot help but be informative about ultimate reality, even if only negatively. It might be thought to imply that there is some ineffable real reality behind the everyday illusions we live in. Or, it might alternatively imply that there is no ultimate, deeper truth or fundamental reality, beyond the mundane sort of things that we use it to say in practical everyday life. The claimed identity of *nirvāṇa* with *saṃsāra* speaks rather for the latter.

If there is nothing deeper that stands behind the phenomena, if our thinking itself does not require grounding in some more fundamental reality of some sort, then the surface is all there is. This is particularly so if our thinking itself partially determines any possible object of thought. Metaphysical examination of the categories of thought indicate that there is nothing there to be found: all these concepts are empty, including all attempts to conceive of emptiness itself as some surrogate fundamental metaphysical ground. For 'empty' is just the character of anything thinkable, in virtue of the fact that it is thinkable; it is descriptive, not explanatory. This, in turn, means that there is no *other*, ultimate reality that is somehow lying in wait, beyond the phenomena. The phenomena are all that there is.

Nirvāṇa, therefore, cannot be some reality standing beyond, and sublimely immune from, the selfless suffering of *saṃsāra*. And indeed, the *Ratnāvalī* confirms: "*Nirvāṇa* is not even non-existence; how can it be existence? *Nirvāṇa* is called the suppression of any notion of existence and non-existence" (*RĀ* I.42). And further: "From the standpoint of absolute truth, both this world as well as *nirvāṇa* are equally non-existent, either in the future or in the past or in the present; how can then any difference between them be real?" (*RĀ* I.64).

This may seem, alarmingly, to do away with *nirvāṇa* altogether, and thereby with the whole point of Buddhist practice and theory. The accusation of *nihilism* strikes again, this time tinged with a moral aspect.[29] The escape from the accusation will be the same, however. This 'neither-existence-nor-non-existence' is true of everything, for it is notions of existence that are inappropriate, implying, as they do, an unattainable independence. But this means that the very feature which prevents there being some ultimate, mind-independent reality – namely, the dependent origination that is at the same time the essencelessness of all things – is the same feature that makes *nirvāṇa* possible for us. As Nāgārjuna puts it, negatively, "If (the world) were not empty, then action would be without profit. The act of ending suffering and abandoning misery and defilement would not exist" (*MMK* XXIV.39). For if all reality is conditioned by our cognition, then a change in our cognition can substantially alter the character of reality as we experience it. *Nirvāṇa is saṃsāra*, properly understood. And it is proper understanding that transforms one into the other. Thus, while Nāgārjuna is sometimes read as an irrationalist, a mystic, he could also be seen as the staunchest defender of the power, and ethical relevance, of reason.

Conclusion

Nāgārjuna has a position, and makes claims, in our perfectly commonplace sense of those terms. His central claim that 'everything is empty' is neither a sceptical nor a nihilistic claim – for one thing, the former would be an epistemological claim and the latter an ontological claim;

and Nāgārjuna wants to say something equally epistemological and metaphysical. 'Empty' means for Nāgārjuna 'lacking self-sufficiency'; it indicates dependency. Epistemologically, the claim is that any claim – including this very claim – is *provisional* and *contingent*. All claims depend for their full meaning and truth on claims outside themselves; they are not true of necessity, either their own or a borrowed one. The full meaning of any one claim can only be ascertained and established by looking outside that claim to others, and its truth can only be established by relying on other claims. It is in no way contradictory or self-defeating to say that the emptiness claim is itself dependent (or empty) in this way. Metaphysically, 'emptiness' is a description of ontological relations; specifically, everything is dependent for its existence *and* its identity on the existence-identity of others, outside itself. There is no 'given', no metaphysical lynchpin, no core of reality exempt from this. And this sounds like a plausible version of the canonical Buddhist view that everything suffers, is transient, without self, and arises dependently.

In a way, Nāgārjuna's Abhidharma opponents were certainly anti-essentialist already. Any complex whole was without an essence of its own (in ultimate reality). And it is generally where there is complex unity that we seek for some real essence to ground that unity, to explain and justify the 'oneness' of the 'many'. For with absolute simples, whose nature is just the one thing that they are, there is no place for an essence–attribute distinction; there is no need to suppose some one thing to which many properties belong, or in which they inhere. Perhaps Abhidharma *dharmas are* essences, but they could hardly *have* essences. So on one criterion, the Abhidharmikas have done away with essences already in adopting an anti-holist position.

On the other hand, there were two senses in which it was correct to think of *dharmas* as substances: (i) they are that which 'underlies' all else, which grounds the reality of complex objects; and (ii) they are discrete individuals, wholly distinct from one another. Although they may require conditions for their arising here and now (i.e. for their existing), *what* they are when they arise is dependent upon nothing but themselves. That *this* is a blue-event; that *this* is a seeing-blue-event; that *this* is a consciousness-of-blue-perception – these are not dependent upon anything else for their respective natures, or specific identities. This is the sense in which one might well want to say that the *dharmas are* essences (of themselves), although neither they nor anything else *has* an essence. And it is at this part of the Abhidharma view, the vestige of essentialism in the atomist picture, that Nāgārjuna takes aim in his critique of causation.

To grasp a presumed property–particular event requires simultaneously distinguishing it from all else, and grasping it *as arising* – that is, as related to others. Seeing it as a caused event means seeing it as somehow unified with what is, at the same time, somehow distinct from it. This inescapable grasping of many as one just is the mark of the conceptually constructed. To suppose there is something of a *dharma* – not its arising here and now, to be sure, but its *blueness* or its *solidity*, its specific character – that escapes this is to suppose that these specific characteristics are *uncaused* – anathema both to reason (for 'uncaused' means 'without explanation') and to any Buddhist of any stripe, where understanding the causes of suffering is the key to its elimination.

In so taking aim, Nāgārjuna has in his sights primarily the presumed foundationalism of *dharma*-theory, the explanatory priority and adequacy granted to *dharmas* over the admittedly conventional wholes that they constitute. Taking aim at this is, on the Buddhist picture, tantamount to undermining the presumed priority of 'ultimate' over 'conventional' reality, and perhaps the very distinction between them.

One may worry, however, that such undermining can go too far. Although Nāgārjuna claims that the 'emptiness' of *nirvāṇa* – non-difference from *saṃsāra*, and so the conventionality of the ultimate – is necessary for the possibility of attaining it, we must not forget that the framework of 'two truths' was a useful way of distinguishing our everyday ways of thinking from another, more accurate way that we might aspire to. Although they are related, the priority of ultimate over conventional reality grounds the recommendation that we learn to understand the latter as merely conventional, and to regulate our perceptions and emotions by ultimate reality: by what is really so, rather than by what is merely thought to be so. If we collapse the distinction between these two truths altogether, then it is not just eliminativism, metaphysical nihilism, that lurks in Nāgārjuna's Madhyamaka, but moral nihilism.

For if there is no difference between these, there is no transition to make. If the ultimate reality is simply that there is only conventional reality, then there is, it seems, no improvement to be made in our grasp of reality, and no grounds for radically transforming our desires and emotions. If the identity of *nirvāṇa* and *saṃsāra* means that the only truth is the one we already believe in and live every day, then it cannot ground a *change* in that perspective. If *nirvāṇa* is *saṃsāra*, then we are all already liberated right now, and there is nothing for us to do differently.

Some later Buddhists inspired by Nāgārjuna speak as if this is indeed literally the case, although taking it seriously is incompatible with the notion of suffering as something to be eliminated by following a path, that is, with the four Noble Truths. On the other hand, the four Noble Truths are themselves treated to destructive examination by Nāgārjuna in the twenty-fourth chapter of the *Mūlamadhyamikakārikā*. The challenge is to find some sense in this that is compatible with Nāgārjuna's own claim, in the *Ratnāvalī*, that gaining insight into selflessness provides a good distinct from, and better than, mere happiness.

FIVE
Karmic questions

> [*Karma*] stands out by virtue of its consistency as well as by its extraordinary metaphysical achievement: It unites virtuoso-like self-redemption by man's own efforts with universal accessibility of salvation, the strictest rejection of the world with organic social ethics, and contemplation as the paramount path to salvation with an inner-worldly vocational ethic. (Max Weber, *Essays in Sociology*, 359)

Action and result

Karma means 'action'. Actions are typically distinguished from the class of all bodily movements by being what someone *does*. Eating is an action; digesting is not. It is also typical to characterize the difference as that between what we deliberately do, or choose to do, and those bodily movements over which we have no control. This does not imply all actions are *well* thought through, or *carefully* deliberated; the threshold for 'intentional' here is quite low. I might act in a rush, in haste or without attending to what I am doing. Nevertheless, the behaviour can still be sufficiently intentional to call it an 'action'. And, finally, it is commonly thought that it is *for that reason* – because of the element of intentionality involved – that actions can be evaluated along a new dimension while other bodily changes cannot. My digestion can be good or bad according to whether it performs its job efficiently. And while many actions are liable to this same sort of evaluation, actions can also be good or bad in a quite different way:

'morally', we might call it, or 'ethically' good and bad. The 'good shot' in archery can be a bad or wrong thing to do. And this latter judgement, many think, is a measure of the quality of the intention, or of its object as one that is intended.

So far, so familiar, and thus far Buddhist discussions of *karma* do not diverge much from more familiar discussions of action. Actions are the focus of moral evaluation, in virtue of being the sort of thing that is related to a certain kind of mental state. On some views, the moral quality of the intention directly affects the moral quality of the act; so if, for instance, I save your life in order to extort money from you, one might be disinclined to consider my act of life-saving a morally good one. And the Buddhist view of *karma* (but not all other Indian views) would probably concur.

One step, however, transforms a familiar discussion of action into the 'doctrine of *karma*'. According to the Buddhists, and indeed to nearly all of their Indian contemporaries, the moral quality of an action has effects of corresponding valance (good or bad) on the *happiness* of *the agent*. On most accounts of *karma*, this is happiness as naively understood; pleasure and pain, wealth and poverty, reputation and ignominy are, respectively, the consequences of morally good and bad intentional acts. And these effects are on the agent herself. That happiness and well-being *ought* to correspond to virtue seems to be a deeply held intuition. Kant calls it the 'highest good' (*Critique of Practical Reason* 5:110–11; see also 5:124–5), and our common practices of punishment reflect a sense that the proper consequences of morally bad action *should be* physical pain and deprivation of the goods in which happiness is ordinarily thought to consist. But the Indian views of *karma* appear to be writing this conviction about what ought to be into the very fabric of reality, incorporating it into the natural functioning of the universe.[1]

And indeed, according to the Buddhist view of which the doctrine of *karma* is a part, there is no agent or judge presiding over human affairs, punishing wickedness with misery. There is no being transcending the natural world, whose Word or will makes some acts right, and others wrong. Instead, this is just the way the natural world works: one of the dimensions along which causes and conditions give rise to effects.

Except, of course, this is conspicuously *not* the way the world works. The wicked sometimes flourish like the green bay tree; the virtuous sometimes suffer the trials of Job. Since it is quite obvious that happiness is not proportioned to virtue *in this life*, the Indians – Buddhist and non-Buddhist alike – stretch out the cause and effect process over several lifetimes.[2] The "Shorter Exposition of Action" (*MN* 135.3-5) offers a typical statement of the view:

> Here, student, some man or woman kills living beings and is murderous, bloody-handed, given to blows and violence, merciless to living beings. Because of performing and undertaking such action, on the dissolution of the body, after death, he reappears in a state of deprivation, in an unhappy destination, in perdition, even in hell. But if on the dissolution of the body, after death, he does not reappear in a state of deprivation ... but instead comes back to the human state, then wherever he is reborn he is short-lived.

Someone who is not murderous, if they return as a human, they are long-lived; someone who injures living beings, if they return as a human, they are sickly; if they did not injure living beings, they are healthy – and so on.

Notice the degree of uncertainty here: someone who behaves badly may or may not be reborn as a human being. This is because there is never just one act, and intentions are rarely simply black or white. There are countless actions, varieties of nuance in the exact intention, innumerable other complicating causal factors, so that discerning any direct line will be impossible, and unnecessary. Eventually, in this lifetime or the next, or the next, the actions sown will bear fruit according to their kind.[3] Thus, the doctrine of *karma*, so understood, is bound inextricably to a belief in rebirth.

It is difficult to know how best to approach and assess these claims.[4] If *karma* and rebirth are meant to be scientific claims – claims about the natural organization of empirical reality – then we can delegate the matter to physics: either the natural scientists find evidence of these cause-and-effect relations or they do not. And the matter is closed.

But it may be that natural science as it is presently constituted is not well placed to investigate and deliver clear verdicts on *moral qualities* of intentions and actions, nor on the presence or absence of factors of *happiness*, and still less to investigate any purported connection between the two. Moreover, there are other questions to consider in order to get a clearer idea of just what the *karma* claim is, for the Buddhists, and how it fits (or does not fit) into Buddhist ethical thought. We can do that in part through addressing the following challenges:

1. First, an ancient objection asks whether or how any doctrine of *karma* could be consistent with a metaphysics of non-self.
2. A second, similar question of consistency might be raised. If we take seriously the edifying consequences of abandoning any concept of the self, or thinking in terms of self, then we might wonder whether a belief in *karma* does not cut against this. A doctrine of *karma and rebirth* seems to invite me to think in terms of *myself*, and consequences on *my own* happiness; and just this sort of thinking was supposed to lead to suffering.
3. Addressing this second question will take us to a third area of inquiry looking at how the doctrine of *karma* functions in Buddhist metaphysics and ethics. Here there are two sides to the inquiry. On the one hand, there is a question of what role the doctrine plays in a theory; on the other hand, there is a question of how it is, in fact, appealed to in context – what sort of psychological work is meant to be done by invoking *karma*. (Concerns that appeals to *karma* invite us to blame the victim of misfortune would belong here.)
4. Finally, having identified what work a doctrine of *karma* is meant to be doing within the Buddhist framework, we can consider whether that work itself is negligible or even dispensable, and so whether and how we might drastically revise or reinvent the doctrine of *karma*. Can we de-couple it from dubious claims about rebirth, without making still more dubious claims about the inevitable poverty of every thief? Or might we just as well drop the doctrine of *karma* altogether? After all, on the Buddhist view it is ultimately cessation, not worldly happiness, that we should be aiming at.

Karma in Buddhism

According to the Buddhists, *karma* is just one sort of cause. Not everything is the result of moral qualities of previous actions:

> Certain experiences, Sīvaka, arise here originating from bile, ... from phlegm, ... from wind, ... resulting from the humours of the body, ... born of the changes of the seasons, ... of being attacked by adversities, ... of spasmodic attacks, ... of the effect of kamma. And this ought to be known by yourself,

> Sīvaka, that certain experiences arise here as originating from bile, ... as born of the effect of bile. Now, Sīvaka, those recluses and Brahmins who speak thus, who hold this view: "Whatever a human being experiences, whether pleasure, or pain, or neither pleasure nor pain – all this is by reason of what was done in the past," – they go beyond what is personally known, and what is considered as truth in the world. Therefore, I say of these recluses and Brahmins that they are wrong.
> (*SN*. 36.21, PTS iv.230–31)[5]

Moreover, as we saw above, we cannot necessarily draw a direct line between action and consequence, so we cannot make precise claims about such connections in any general way:

> Therein, Ānanda, when a recluse or Brahmin says: "Indeed, there are evil actions, there is result of misconduct," I grant him this. When he says: "I saw a person here who killed living beings ... and held wrong view, and I see that on the dissolution of the body, after death, he has reappeared in a state of deprivation ... even in hell," I also grant him this.
>
> But when he says, "On the dissolution of the body, after death, everyone who kills living beings ... and holds wrong view reappears in a state of deprivation ... even in hell," I do not grant him this. And when he says: "Those who know thus know rightly; those who think otherwise are mistaken." I also do not grant him this. And when he obstinately adheres to what he himself has known, seen, and discovered, insisting: "Only this is true, anything else is wrong", I also do not grant him this. (*MN* 136, "Greater Exposition of Action", §13)

Although no reason is explicitly given here for resisting the generalization, we might recall from the "Shorter Exposition of Action" that results of actions could vary, presumably according to other causal factors involved.[6] Actions are far too many, their precise moral complexion far too complex, their interaction with and conditioning of each other far too complicated to draw universal one-to-one lines between type-A acts and type-B effects. "The succession of kamma and its result in the twelve classes," writes Buddhaghoṣa, "is clear in its true nature only to the Buddhas' 'knowledge of kamma and its result'" (*Vsm.* XIX.17). We can know tendencies – positive, negative and neutral

– and that this tendency will be a contributing factor in what eventually results. But precise outcomes defy systematic treatment. It follows from this that it cannot be necessary that we have such knowledge in order for belief in *karma* to be edifying (or efficacious in whatever way it is supposed to be); and it suggests that it is probably *unedifying* to search for such knowledge.[7] The Buddha adopts the prevailing view that those who are now humans can be reborn as non-humans, and that the options for non-human lives are much broader than those available in the everyday world. In addition to the animals' modes of being, familiar from the everyday world, there are pleasanter realms and more miserable ones, with happier and more miserable beings, respectively; we saw a reference to this in the quote from the "Shorter Exposition of Action", above. Buddhists today differ about how literally we should understand the existence of such worlds. But Buddhists always agreed that rebirth in any one of these realms, even a 'higher' one, did not constitute success. The only ultimate success is *nirvāṇa*; everything else is just another station-stop within *saṃsāra*. This will make the appeal to *karma* as motivational of equivocal benefit.

Although *karma* means 'action', Buddhism is clear and consistent in maintaining that physical bodily motions are not, as such, the source of morally inflected consequences, and they are not the primary locus of evaluation as 'wholesome' or 'unwholesome' (*kuśala* or *akuśala*). Rather, "Intention, I tell you, is *karma*. Intending, one performs deeds of body, speech and mind", as the Buddha famously (or infamously) puts it in the "Nibbedhika Sutta" (*AN* 6.63, PTS iii.415; my translation).[8] It is by thinking things in a certain way that we formulate plans that we then act on. As the early *Dhammapadā* puts it, "All conditions have mind as forerunner, mind as master, are accomplished by mind. If one speaks or acts with an impure mind, suffering follows him like the wheel that follows the ox" (*Dhp*. I.1).

Intention is a specific sort of mental event, of course; it is different from, say, pleasure and pain, which are also (at least) mental events. But we ought not to think of the intention that is identified as 'action' as something so specific as an explicit choice or plan that one self-consciously puts to oneself. Our intentional activities have much wider scope, including those thoughts and feelings formed due to our values, preferences and so on.[9] For our perceptions and thoughts are not ordinarily neutral; they are motivated. We perceive things *as* this or that, we think of them in this way or that. But, as we saw in Chapter 2, perceiving or conceiving things *in a certain way* already involves our active mental participation, turning our attention this way rather than that, holding this rather than that feature to be salient, approaching things with this or that attitude, ordering the manifold of sensation for the sake of some end or another. If I aim to leave the room, I see the room accordingly, attentive and inattentive to various features according to their relevance to this end. If my attitude towards my leaving the room is one of timidity, or of hostility, or grudging or respectful or impatient, this colours the intention, the relevance of various perceptions, the acts possible for me and manner of these.[10] As we seldom have only one aim, end, desire, care or interest, few accounts of the intentionality of perceptions will be as simple as 'leaving the room'. But however complex, competing and variable, how we see the world, what we perceive as experience arising for us, is pervasively intentional.[11]

This is why we see 'right view' and 'wrong view' sometimes credited with exactly the same role as intention in the creation or mitigation of suffering, as in the *Numerical Discourses*:

> Bhikkhus, I do not see even a single thing on account of which unarisen unwholesome qualities arise and arisen unwholesome qualities increase and expand so much as wrong view ... Bhikkhus, I do not see even a single thing on account of which unarisen wrong view arises and arisen wrong view increases so much as careless attention ... (*AN* 1.306–10, PTS i.31)[12]

> Bhikkhus, I do not see even one other thing that, when undeveloped and uncultured, brings such suffering as the mind.
> (*AN* 1.29, PTS i.6)

This may put one in mind of the weak philosophical sense of 'intentional', where it means simply 'having an intentional object'. And this may very nearly capture the same range of items. What Buddhist psychology observes is that such objects are never neutrally constructed, or just given. That we come to have the 'intentional objects' we do is itself a product of broadly intentional mental activity. It is intention in this sense that is *karma* or 'action'; intention in this sense is the source of corresponding positive and negative consequences, and it is the locus of moral evaluation, the ground of responsibility.

This is how the Buddhist will meet the rhetorically brilliant objection put by the Jains, who favoured the results as the locus of evaluation and source of merit. In the *Sūtrakṛtāṅga* II.6, the Jaina author mockingly adopts the Buddhist perspective:

> If one thrusts a spit through the side of a granary, mistaking it for a man; or through a gourd, mistaking it for a baby, and roasts it, he will be guilty of murder according to our views (26). If a savage puts a man on a spit and roasts him, mistaking him for a fragment of the granary; or a baby, mistaking him for a gourd, he will not be guilty of murder according to our views (27). If anybody thrusts a spit through a man or a baby, mistaking him for a fragment of the granary, puts him on the fire, and roasts him, that will be a meal fit for Buddhas to breakfast upon (28).

And the text concludes, now in earnest:

> Well-controlled men cannot accept (your denial of) guilt incurred by (unintentionally) doing harm to living beings. It will cause error and no good to both [those] who teach such doctrines and who believe them (30).[13]

The debate over whether good intentions or actual results should more attract our admiration and opprobrium is not special to Buddhists and Jains. It has been a favoured way of putting the debate between Kantians and consequentialists in moral philosophy. In the terms set by that debate, the Buddhist position is complicated. For if we ask what the source of normativity is – what makes things good or bad – the Buddhist answer may well look consequentialist: it is *because* suffering results that certain actions are considered bad.

> If you know, "This action that I wish to do with the body would lead to my own affliction, or to the affliction of others, or to the affliction of both; it is an unwholesome bodily action with painful consequences, with painful results", then you definitely should not do such an action. (*MN* 61.9)

However, if we want to determine just what the action was that was performed, we look not to the results but to the intention, for it is this that has the right to be considered 'what one does'. It is my intention that determines this adding of white powder to the mix as baking a cake, rather than a failed attempt to poison my aunt.

What makes an intention right is that it is the appropriate attitude towards the correct objects under the right circumstances. The normative terms here might be cashed out by reference to the creation or amelioration of suffering; but what makes an *action* right is that it arises from a right intention, not its immediate results.[14] Thus, for instance, in the "Right View Sūtra" (*MN* 9), after baldly stating a list of unwholesome activities – a practice looking more deontological than consequentialist – the Buddha goes on to specify that the *roots* of unwholesome acts are greed, aversion and delusion. The state of mind with which one acts determines whether an action is a greedy, and therefore unwholesome, one, regardless of the immediate results.

Locating responsibility in intention rejects responsibility for what is done unwittingly but thereby raises the usual complications about when and where we are responsible for our ignorance. In its generous conception of the 'intention', the Buddhist view may have resources to meet the Jaina objection that are unavailable to the Kantian. For the Buddhist, there need be no maxim, however tacit or suppressed, upon which one is acting. Acting wittingly is not a matter of what propositions one explicitly entertains. One need only be deliberately or consciously doing whatever it is one is doing. If, for instance, we failed to notice something relevant because we were caught up in all kinds of other useless thoughts and emotions, then we could be held responsible inasmuch as the irrelevant thoughts express and constitute the intentions we did have, which thus excluded consideration of what should have occupied our attention.

In the grotesque example put by the Jaina *Sūtrakṛtāṅga*, there is *something* going on in my mind when I thrust a spit through a man or a baby, and it is *not* having the presence of mind to ensure that it is a gourd I am about to roast. Let us suppose that I am in haste, because I wish to complete my journey. I am indeed focusing my attention *somewhere* – on dining quickly; but I am *thereby* not focusing it correctly – on checking just what it is I am preparing for my meal. Generally, when one is not attending to what one ought, there is something else that one is attending to, other volitional states that preclude the proper intentional states. And this preclusion is why they are *akuśala*, unwholesome or unskilful.[15] So the Buddhist need not roll over in the face of the hyperbolic objection, and may continue to enjoy her breakfast – thoughtfully.

What both the conception of *karma* and the objection should have made clear already is that discussions of *karma* are not only about sorting out the metaphysical niceties of a certain purported form of causation. It is in terms of *karma* that debates about and explorations of moral responsibility, its ground, and the sources of moral value take place. Thus when we come to our first, most obvious and perhaps most ancient challenge to the Buddhist view in relation to *karma*, we find a metaphysical difficulty with practical bite. If there is no self, the objection goes, this makes a nonsense of any doctrine of *karma*. If this were merely a metaphysical matter, one might be inclined to say 'so much the worse for *karma*' and wonder that the Buddhists were not inclined to say the same. At stake, however, is not just an arcane claim about a certain kind of causal relation but, rather, the very coherence of attributing moral responsibility. And *this* is something one might well be more circumspect about junking altogether.

Action and result without selves: a question of moral responsibility

The *Milindapañhā*, or the *Dialogues with King Milinda*, from which we drew the chariot argument discussed in Chapter 2, engages with a host of delicate and difficult perplexities. Milinda, depicted asking the Buddhist Nāgasena who he was, also has worries about *karma*, as well he might. Having grasped that there is on the Buddhist account no 'self' enduring over time, nothing remaining the same through change as the 'bearer' of those changed properties, he is concerned that this undermines any doctrine of *karma* (see *MP* II.ii.6–7, PTS 46–9). The same person who commits a wicked deed or a fine one *cannot* enjoy the fruits of his actions, if there are no persons who are the same over time at all.[16] If the Buddhist no-self view is correct, then it is *always* a different person who receives the later benefits of previous actions. This was a problem that the Nyāya pressed.[17] One might wonder, then, what sense it makes for a Buddhist to believe in rebirth, and there is a ready Buddhist reply to this. But this ready reply must meet the more difficult demand of preserving *moral* sense; if persons do not endure over time, then wrongdoers cannot suffer the evil effects of their own wrongdoing. This presents a problem, even if the question of rebirth is set to one side. Although the problem is discussed in terms of *karma* and the naturally occurring consequences to the agent of her own deeds, the problem is the same even if we consider such appropriate consequences do not occur naturally but, rather, require human intervention, in the form of systems of reward and punishment. At stake is the justice and coherence of holding each other responsible for our respective deeds.

How can a Buddhist believe in rebirth? Frequently challenged on this point, Buddhists consistently offer the same reply: the same continuity that warrants regarding a series of interconnected, constantly changing phenomena as 'this person' suffices to account for the perceived unity of persons across lifetimes.[18] There is no more, and no less, unity in Nāgasena over different lifetimes than there is in Nāgasena within this lifetime, as infant, child, adolescent, adult, old man. In each case there is sufficient integrity of causal continuity that it is meaningful to think of these numerically different events as 'the same person'. In the case of rebirth, the Buddhist will have to insist that this causal integratedness pertains entirely to the non-physical person-constituting *dharmas*, since it is agreed that there is no physical continuity between the Nāgasena's corpse and the body of the infant Nāgasena becomes. And the greater part of the *integrity* of this causal continuity among mental phenomena is meant to be provided by the necessary connections between volitions and their consequences: that is, by *karma*. Nāgasena's characteristically carefully worded claim is: "This *nāma-rūpa* [psycho-physical bundle] does not itself reconnect, sire; but, sire, by means of this *nāma-rūpa* one does a fine or a wicked deed, and because of this deed another *nāma-rūpa* reconnects" (*MP* II.ii.6, PTS 46, trans. mod.). So in one way *karma* provides the answer to the purely metaphysical question of rebirth in the absence of strict, or numerical, identity over time and through change.

Does such causal continuity suffice to ground claims of moral responsibility? Nāgasena thinks so, making analogies with mangos fruiting, fires burning through the night, and girls growing into women. And Milinda is content: "You are dexterous, revered Nāgasena", he finally replies, his appetite for analogies answering to that particular worry being satisfied. Evidently the Nyāya-Vaiśeṣika opponents of the Buddhists did not think this sufficed, for we see the fourth-century CE Buddhist Vasubandhu still entertaining objections that without a self, the results of actions cannot accrue to the agent, and indeed there is no one to be happy or miserable as a result of their actions.[19] Steadily offering 'continuity' in place of endurance, as Vasubandhu does, may seem not to be meeting the objection.

But in fact the Buddhist reply, and position on the self, is more sophisticated than the objection suggests. If the response to the rebirth objection outlined above is correct, the Buddhist account reverses the expected order of explanation; it is *because* there are these relations of causal continuity, not just physical but also and especially mental – it is *because*, above all, there is continuity between intention and results, between action and its fruits – that we are warranted in thinking of a disunified set of phenomena *as* a person at all.

> In all kinds of becoming, generation, destiny, station and abode there appears only mentality-materiality, which occurs by means of linking of cause with fruit. One sees no doer over and above the doing, no experiencer of the result over and above the occurrence of the result. But one sees clearly with right understanding that the wise say "doer" when there is doing and "experiencer" when there is experiencing simply as a mode of common usage. (*Vsm.* XIX.10)

To suppose there could be a tension between no-self and *karma* is to mistake the no-self claim, and to get the explanation of unity exactly the wrong way round. *That there are these relations of cause and effect* is what grounds the correctness of the designation of several (phenomena) as one (person) in the first place. This is why one of the rejoinders to the Nyāya is that their own view, maintaining the existence of a distinct and unchanging Self, precludes moral improvement, and so is itself the end of all morality.

So to the charge that no-self metaphysics entails holding one person responsible for another's deeds, or (what is the same) giving up on moral responsibility altogether, the Abhidharma Buddhist reply is: responsibility is prior. The fact that these conditions here give rise to those consequences there is one of the primary reasons it was convenient, and so conventionally true, to distinguish some phenomena from others, and to designate them collectively as 'Nāgasena' or 'Milinda', respectively. There is no 'person at time *t*2' held responsible for the deeds of some 'person at time *t*1'; the only legitimate sense in talk of persons is that which names the *continuity between* a circumscribed set of phenomena at *t*1 and a numerically distinct set of phenomena at *t*2.

One might suspect that this way of putting the position commits the Buddhist to the ultimate reality of the self, after all. For if the person-constituting elements really are, ultimately, connected to each other in some way in which they are not connected to all the other things they interact with and cause, then is this very fact not the elusive principle of unity that the Self is supposed to be: the principle, distinct from the constituent parts of a whole, enduring over time and through change? The Buddhist personalists, the Pudgalavādins, seemed to think this. The 'person', they maintain, is the necessary continuity or connectedness of personal-elements referred to, for instance, when the Buddha says in response to Subha, the student, in the "Shorter Exposition of Action": "beings are owners of their actions, heirs of their actions; they originate from their actions, are bound to their actions, have their actions as their refuge" (*MN* 135.4).[20] In their concerns about transition, development and *karma* the Pudgalavādins seem convinced that rejecting the ultimate reality of *the integrity* of the person – of the relatedness of person-constituting *dharmas* – really would leave the *anatta* view without the necessary resources to ground attributions of moral responsibility.[21] They were reluctant to call this principle a 'self', preferring the term 'person' (*pudgala*) to designate this real unity holding between person-constituting phenomena.[22] And since complex facts have no clear ontological standing in Abhidharma metaphysics, they called the person 'ultimately real but unsayable', *avaktavya*: a way of being neither conditioned nor unconditioned, nor in any other familiar way.

Such an ultimately real person was thought by other Buddhists to fly in the face of the Buddha's injunction to abandon attachment to anything as 'self' and to any conception of self. And perhaps the Pudgalavādins need not have been concerned. Other Buddhists thought it was enough to point to the *de facto* causal connections to dissolve any concerns about the relations between actions and their appropriate consequences (whether naturally occurring or otherwise) for the agent. The principle that appropriate fruits accrue to the agent, and not to someone else, is preserved by insisting that it was the continuity, and not a static heap of elements at 'time *t1*', that grounded whatever talk of persons that was legitimate in the first place.[23]

Psychological effects of *believing* a doctrine of *karma*

But this will not address a more subtle version of a similar worry about the compatibility between *karma* and no-self. For notice that, whether or not the Pudgalavādins are correct about what we must be committed to as *ultimately* real, to think in terms of *karma* inevitably draws us to thinking in terms of self. The no-self claim was not merely a position in metaphysics; in fact, it is only secondarily that. It is primarily a project for psychological transformation: giving up 'I' thoughts should cure me of the compulsion to say 'mine', to appropriate. It is not only important that we reject the view that there is a self; we must thereby systematically cease thinking in terms of 'self' – or at least, cease endorsing any I-thoughts that encourage 'mine'-desires. But *in so far as* I think in terms of *karma*, in so far as I am focused on and care about the causal connections between intentions and their affective consequences, I am just to that extent still directing my thought in a fundamentally selfish way. I am distinguishing between those intentions that are 'mine', and those that are not, between those future experiences *of mine* that will be painful or pleasant; and I am motivated by the thought that they are *mine*. To think in terms of *karma*, that is, turns our thought in exactly the wrong direction. So it is perplexing to see the emphasis many Buddhist texts put on acknowledging *karma*. In fact, denying this sort of connection between actions and fruits is one of the forms of that terrible vice 'nihilism'. And yet, if I should stop thinking in terms of self, in terms of 'me' and 'mine', then how can I *not* thereby leave off concern with which events are *my* fruits of *my* actions and *my* intentions?

There may be no way out of this muddle. The sociologist's response has been to distinguish between '*kammic* Buddhism' and '*nibbanic* Buddhism'.[24] There were, on the one hand, renunciants aiming at *nirvāṇa*, and, on the other hand, ordinary folk, aiming at a better rebirth through practising good deeds. Renunciants pursue their aim by devoting their whole time to meditation, to transforming the mind and bringing the causes of mental suffering to an end in themselves; the laity pursue their end by practising virtuous activity, including making gifts of food and clothing to the renunciants. There is an aptness here similar to that we saw in Nāgārjuna's recognition that it was better, for some people, that they not try to learn the no-self view; similarly, if one cannot devote one's life to the absolute cessation of suffering, then a second-best aim is to create and aim for happiness by cultivating good intentions and good actions rather than their opposites.

While bad action leads to bad results, then, and good action to good results, the higher aim is for no action at all; this is associated with following the Path, and is a precondition for bringing suffering to an end.

> And what is *kamma* that is neither dark nor bright with neither dark nor bright result, leading to the ending of *kamma*? Right view, right resolve, right speech, right action, right

> livelihood, right effort, right mindfulness, right concentration. This is called *kamma* that is neither dark nor bright with neither dark nor bright result, leading to the ending of *kamma*.
> (*AN* ii.235)[25]

So one might address the worry by distinguishing between interlocutors. If the discussion is one of metaphysical technicalities, with someone not particularly committed to the Buddhist project of the ultimate elimination of all suffering, then the simple reconciliation of no-self and *karma* in terms of continuity is unobjectionable. If the concern is raised by someone sympathetic to the Buddhist view, but not dedicated to realizing the highest end now, then it is useful for them to continue thinking in terms of *karma*. Since they are not seriously going to transform the whole of their thinking in terms of no-self anyway, recognizing *karma* as a part of the language and logic of a world of persons is a useful and correct way of conceiving things. Although it does not lead anyone towards recognizing the impersonal nature of reality, it does lead one towards creating the causes of happiness rather than of further misery, and that is a good second-best.

We also need not give up altogether on maintaining some connection between the two ends, happiness and cessation. For we can bear in mind the dynamic processes involved in adopting the Buddhist view as a *path*. While one is still thinking in terms of persons, supposing unhappiness to come to oneself following one's own misdeeds may be useful in learning and embedding wholesome practices of body, speech and mind. On the way to enlightenment, interest shifts away from *whose* intention gave rise to *which* events, and turns instead towards which factors could be usefully altered in order to eliminate suffering, and how. Once one has internalized good practice, *karmic* fruits should be a less necessary or less central incentive. The right actions appear to one as desirable in their own right. Once this transformation in perspective is in place, one is in a position to appreciate the badness of suffering *tout court*, and the suffering implicit even in ordinary happiness.[26] For the one committed to the impersonal view of reality, thinking in terms of *karma* will indeed be abandoned in favour of a practical and impersonal regard for causes and consequences, or dependent origination. Karmic thinking has no place in the enlightened perspective.[27]

One might naturally want to object that if the higher aim is to eliminate action altogether, so as to bring to an end all consequences of action, this must also eliminate *compassionate* action. How is it that someone enlightened is meant to *act*, at all? In particular, how are they supposed to manifest the compassion for suffering in which their wisdom at least partially consists? The pessimistic answer would be that enlightened beings no longer act at all; having attained enlightenment, there is nothing more for them to do. Even acting from compassion would presume that suffering individuals can be assisted out of their suffering, rather than having to walk that path for themselves. And there is an element of truth in this.

But we must also remember that after his enlightenment the Buddha decided, however reluctantly, to teach. So an enlightened being *can* be responsive to the claims of compassion. If we bear in mind that *karma* is *intention*, we might understand this enlightened behaviour is radically non-intentional; that is, one's aim is simply to respond to the situation that is there, rather than to engage in conceptualizing it, thinking of it with respect to various cares and concerns that usually order our perception, conceptions and action. Such notions of enlightened behaviour as non-conceptualized immediate responsiveness became more prominent in later Buddhist thought. Or, less drastically, one might consider that since enlightenment partially consists in recognizing the mere conventionality of our conceptual reality, the enlightened person could in one sense entertain such thoughts – sufficiently to do what we unenlightened people would call 'alleviating suffering' – without endorsing what those thoughts represent or mistaking the conceptual for ultimately real or substantial: that is, without clinging or attachment to those conceptions.

The place of *karma* in moral thought

Being mindful of this pragmatic, impersonal concern which should result from truly engaging in the view of no-self and its practices will be useful in addressing one of the most persistent of the external objections to any doctrine of *karma*. Whether compatible with Buddhist views of no-self or not, *karma* has been thought to be a corrosive and positively immoral view. If we suppose that current suffering is the result of the past ill-deeds of the one suffering, the objection goes, this will undermine whatever fragile motivation we might have had to help people who are in need, or to alter structures of society that create suffering and distribute it unfairly, for we must regard disadvantaged and needy persons as deserving their fates. Thus, even worse, a doctrine of *karma* encourages us to positively blame those on the receiving end of injustice for their suffering. If we are the ones on the receiving end of injustice or misfortune, a doctrine of *karma* would have us blame ourselves.

Implicit in the foregoing discussion is the presumption that a doctrine of *karma* functions as a motivator: belief in *karma* should provide incentives and disincentives for right and wrong action, respectively. But in ethical discourse, appeals to *karma* arise in contexts of explanation as well as exhortation: that is, when our concern is backward-looking, as well as when it is forward-looking. Thus the "Shorter Exposition of Action" starts from a concern with explanation:

> Master Gotama, what is the cause and condition why human beings are seen to be inferior and superior? For people are seen to be short-lived and long-lived, sickly and healthy, ugly and beautiful, uninfluential and influential, poor and wealthy, low-born and high-born, stupid and wise. What is the cause and condition, Mater Gotama, why human beings are seen to be inferior and superior?
>
> Student, beings are owners of their actions, heirs of their actions; they originate from their actions, are bound to their actions, have their actions as their refuge. It is action that distinguishes beings as inferior and superior.

The objection that *karma* reinforces self-regarding patterns of concern pertains to its forward-looking, hortative role; the objection that it entails passivity and victim-blaming pertains to its role in explanation or justification.

In addressing this objection, it will be important to consider whether, when, and in which ways the doctrine of *karma* is in fact appealed to as explanatory or justificatory, and also what weight is placed on such justifications or explanations, and what is supposed to follow from them.

First, we should recall the indeterminacy of our knowledge of *karmic* causation. Because no unenlightened person is in a position to determine which actions give rise to which results, definite inferences from an instance of suffering to some specific previous ill-deed cannot be drawn. Any supposition would have to be vague. Charles Hallisey and Anne Hanson, recognizing its moral significance, call this the "opacity of *karma*".[28] Moreover, since not everything experienced is a result of one's own previous actions, any supposition regarding specific experiences would have to remain uncertain. We find the *sūtras* acknowledging the moral relevance of this uncertainty in the "Tittha Sūtra" (Sectarians, *AN* 3.61), where preserving moral motivation is offered as a reason for rejecting the view that everything is the result of previous actions: "Those who fall back on past deeds as the essential truth have no desire [to do] what should be done and [to avoid doing] what should not be done, nor do they make an effort in this respect" (*AN* 3.61, PTS i.174).

Such an insistence on the opacity and indeterminacy of *karma* resists inclinations to regard current sufferings as *punishments*, especially since for the Buddhist there is no one we have disobeyed, no law that has been violated. Instead, the doctrine of *karma* offers the believer in it only the diffuse notion that 'there are things I've done that are somehow related to some of what I am experiencing now, in some ways'. And as Candrakīrti reminds us, we are in fact "warned against investigation of the karmic process" (*MA* VI.42d). *Karma* is, in the first person, more a reminder of our own embeddedness in our lives and our experiences; a reminder that no experience ever comes entirely from outside us, but also is a function of what we are bringing to a situation, in virtue of the sorts of thoughts, desires and values with which we perceive and act in the world. That one of the causes may well have been rooted in the previous intentions of the one suffering may be a salutary reminder. It may help to mitigate resentment and festering bitterness, for I do not perceive or experience myself as wholly passive, as *only* a victim or object being acted upon. If every agent is patient, so too is every patient agent: that is, correctly seen, we are neither, for both notions are too artificially distinct to capture the mutual conditioning that is *saṃsāra*. If we can work on improving our attitude towards our lack of independent self-determination, we can likewise work on our attitude towards the opposite, equally illusory extreme.

In the third-personal case, epistemic modesty about causes of another's suffering likewise demands that questions of blame and guilt do not arise with the same force. In fact, mere recognition that someone suffering may have played some role in bringing this suffering about does nothing to answer the question of what is to be done about it now, whether regarding one's own suffering or another's. This is a wholly pragmatic question, and is guided by the simple recognition that suffering is bad, and to be eliminated. All of us have committed innumerable, incalculable deeds, good and bad and neutral, and there is no point in trying to draw up some ultimate accounts sheet. Rather, bearing in mind the forward-looking aspect of *karma*, the salient question is how to act now in the face of the suffering with which one is confronted.[29]

These observations do not ensure that a doctrine of *karma* will not lead the one who believes in it into poisonous victim-blaming and apathy, any more than they ensure that the one who pursues the end of happiness will eventually come to recognize that the higher aim is beyond this, and requires ceasing all intentional action. They can at best show why such morally dire consequences are not psychologically inevitable, and indicate what can in fact be fruitfully done with belief in a doctrine of *karma*. Coupled with other Buddhist principles, such as compassion and the basic undesirability of suffering, *karma* can play a useful role in reminding us of our embeddedness in situations, and of our potential and responsibility for affecting future situations.[30]

The potential pernicious effects of *believing* a doctrine of *karma* are perhaps less likely to arise if one, first, does not hold on to the metaphysics of well-individuated agents, determining phenomena and not determined by them; and second, if one does not come to the view by transferring thoughts about justice and punishment from such a substantial-individual-centred view. In fact, it may be that *karma* does not serve primarily to motivate or to justify at all, at least as the Buddhists actually appeal to it. It may serve rather, as suggested above, to recall us to the unknown interconnectedness of things, and so if anything to soften – or make less absolute – judgements about blame and desert. Similarly, *karma* may be appealed to precisely when the contradictions in life bring out the tensions in our judgement that must simultaneously attribute responsibility and yet recognize the vulnerability and ultimate impotence of that very 'agent'.[31]

Can *karma* be 'naturalized'? Can it be eliminated?

The traditional conception of *karma* and rebirth need not be inconsistent with Buddhist no-self metaphysics. Where others say 'identity', the Buddhist appeals to continuity, with its elastic identity conditions: the very same continuity that makes sense of ordinary attributions of praise and blame in everyday life. However, attending to *karmic* fruits, and unity across lifetimes may be in tension with the pragmatic aims of the no-self claim; making *karma* morally relevant may introduce tensions within Buddhist ethics. These tensions may be resolvable, and the contours of Buddhist ethics better appreciated by looking to how they are resolved, and at how appeals to *karma* in fact encourage us to act in and think about the world. However, any doctrine of *karma* appears firmly wedded to a doctrine of reincarnation, and literal rebirth has the status of a natural scientific claim that is not substantiated by modern science.[32] If anyone wishes to be bold enough to try to show literal *karma*-and-rebirth is consistent with what natural science tells us about the structures and forces of the natural world, that is a matter to be taken up with the physicists. Philosophers are best off taking the natural world to be as the natural scientists describe it, and so far this leaves no room for literal rebirth.

Given this, it is worth asking whether any account of *karma* that is functionally equivalent to that which arises in Buddhist ethics could be disentangled from a commitment to rebirth. If it cannot, without flying in the face of experience, then in light of its moral dangers (apathy, victim-blaming), in light of its potential to reinforce rather than undermine I-thinking, and in light of its merely provisional utility at best, we might prefer to abandon the doctrine of *karma* altogether. In either case, the question will be: is what remains a coherent view? Is it still a Buddhist view? Have we disfigured Buddhist ethical thought beyond all recognition, or only brought out more clearly its real contours, by shaking it free of culturally specific conceptual constructs?

Stephen Batchelor adopts the more extreme position. *Karma* and rebirth, he argues, was *never* part of the Buddhist view, except incidentally.[33] It was a cultural accretion, a widely shared belief among his contemporaries, which the Buddha used without endorsing in order to make his view intelligible to that particular audience. He would say it differently now, to us. In demonstration of the claim, Batchelor translates *sūtras* omitting all reference to *karma* and rebirth; nothing of ethical import has been lost (or so goes the claim implicit in the exercise). The claim is worth taking seriously and carefully, not as a historical claim about the belief state of Gautama (which is surely unrecoverable to us anyway), but as a practically forceful thought experiment. If we systematically refrain from appeals to *karma*, what *are* we left with?

If we allow the distinction made above, between the aims of monastics and those of the laity – between *kammic* and *nibbanic* Buddhism – then nothing of relevance has been lost to those seeking the highest and ultimate goal, *nirvāṇa*. And surely it is seeking this goal that is distinctive of Buddhism.[34]

And yet, this leaves non-renunciants in the lurch. Buddhism, it seems, should not have *nothing* to offer them in terms of guidance or a framework for thinking about what to do and be and how to live. The omission is a serious obstacle if we think that a connection is retained between *kammic* and *nibbanic* Buddhsim, between seeking happiness and seeking enlightenment, between virtue and renunciation. *Karma* and its results enter into discussion wherever action and intention are at issue, and these are surely at issue wherever we are interested in developing from an ordinary state of confusion to one of clarity. What is more, they enter the discussion in ways that are not immediately and inevitably connected to untenable rebirth claims, for much of what is under discussion are questions of responsibility, and cultivating an appreciation of dependent origination.

So a less extreme alternative might be to 'naturalize' *karma*: to turn it from a claim about physics to a claim about psychology.[35] Accounts of *karma* typically distinguish two sorts of effect, 'internal' and 'external'. This is not the difference between consequences for the agent and consequences for others, for the distinctive feature of the *doctrine of karma* is that it is a claim about the effects of the action *on the agent*. The difference is rather between effects on an agent's internal, 'spiritual' condition, and effects on their material condition. (Pleasure and pain, we might note, may fall indiscriminately into both.) The *karma*-claim that becomes grossly implausible in the absence of rebirth is the claim that good intentions lead to worldly happiness and prosperity; this is so patently not the case that only an appeal to actions and their effects stretching across several lifetimes could support it. But perhaps we could retreat to the more modest claim: actions invariably have an effect of a corresponding quality on the *character* of the agent.[36] Just how much of a *revision* this amounts to is unclear, since it was contested among Buddhists as early as the *Kathāvatthu* whether the 'fruit' of *karma* should, strictly speaking, include only subjective states.[37]

This is, in effect, Dale Wright's recommendation, for which he brings both moral and metaphysical arguments.[38] The idea is that talk of *karmic* fruit is not vacuous or vain; it picks out the psychological effects that episodes of willing, forming intentions and acting according to them have on the character of the person forming and acting upon such an intention. We can put this 'impersonally' by saying that *karma* picks out the effects of an intention-event on the cognition-, perception-, consciousness- and volitional-causal streams that lie within intimate causal proximity to that event.

Such a conception of *karma* would relieve us of complicated physical and metaphysical questions about the relation of *karmic* to other sorts of causes. Since the connection between, say, my greedy and adversarial way of looking at the world and my emotional isolation and fear is an internal one, it is not at all mysterious; and there is no gap opened up between intention and result, and so no question of their fittingness to each other, or the justice of results from actions. It also maintains the characteristic emphasis in Buddhist ethics on the mental and psychological as the primary areas of concern.

This revised doctrine of *karma* may even perhaps be a moral improvement, since it would not recommend good action in virtue of pleasure, but in virtue of its internal consequences – to be got only from such a will, and intelligible as good from that perspective. This is a more compelling account of action and result, more insightful, it seems, and of obvious relevance to someone undertaking to reform and habituate their patterns of willing and seeing in new ways. It seems entirely likely – obvious, even if too often overlooked – that there is some kind of effect on my further mental state made by the sorts of intentions I form and ideas I entertain. Indeed, how else is our character formed and reformed? Attending to this fact would be an integral part of the project of reforming the attitudes and actions that currently give rise to suffering. To believe this *karma* claim would have the edifying effect of reminding one not to take short cuts with morality, and that every thought counts. It would point out the way in which we really do have a role in determining our experiences.

This conception of *karma* cannot be reconciled with those Pāli *suttas* that explicitly cite physical pleasure and pain, or ordinary happiness and success, as the results of action.[39] But it thereby takes a position in a long-running debate among Buddhists, reaching back at least to the early Abhidharma period, over exactly which items could be considered the 'fruits' of intentional actions: the material constituents of worldly happiness, or (as the Theravādins claim) only the psychological effects of suffering or happiness.[40] If Buddhist philosophy is to be taken as a living tradition, then it must be open to critique and responsive to it, and its current practitioners must be part of this practice.

One might yet object, however, that this particular revision is too radical. For 'naturalized' *karma* as outlined above does not, as the

Theravādins of the *Kathāvatthu* might have argued, merely confine the fruits of *karma* to felt states. For felt states include all the misery of disease, discomfort and deformity, the gustatory delights of fine food. But the naturalized *karma* outlined above does not want to include these in the effects of *karma*. It aims rather to confine the fruits of *karma* specifically to the effects on the moral quality of one's character. It thus cannot do the motivational work the doctrine of *karma* was meant to do, the objection goes, precisely because it drops any claim about the connection between moral and non-moral goods, between virtue and (ordinary) happiness.

Such resistance to the proposed reform must come, it seems to me, from a deep cynicism about human nature, and an artificially dichotomous view of moral and non-moral goods. For the presumption seems to be that at least most if not all persons could see no reason to act unless they were themselves materially benefited by the action, nor see any reason to refrain from an action unless they themselves were materially harmed by it, or at least that there must be non-morally inflected sensual pleasures and pains in the offing. But human beings are not like that. Even ordinary moral mediocrities like most of us are can be directly motivated by both the material and psychological effects of our actions on (at least *some*) others; and most of us can be motivated by concern for the effects of intention and actions on our future mental states. We are motivated not only by crude categories of 'happy' or 'sad', but also by whether these future mental states are calm, open, loving, confident ones, instead of anxious, isolated, defensive. Concern for this latter is all that one needs in order for the revised, 'naturalized' conception of *karma* to be motivating, and to play essentially the same functional role within Buddhist ethics.

A lingering doubt may remain over whether what we are left with is in any way a distinctively *Buddhist* account. For by internalizing the whole business to individual psychological 'streams', we seem to end up with an account of moral improvement and moral psychology not essentially different from a Platonic or a Stoic one. There, too, virtue is its own reward because the goods at issue are the direct, internal consequences of the moral quality of our intentions. Perhaps naturalizing *karma* has turned Buddhism into just another form of Greek *eudaimonism*.

Such a worry would be precipitous. Buddhist ethics remains distinctively non-personalist, its non-self metaphysics recommending distinctive views, values and ambitions. Happiness still has its real but provisional place in the hierarchy of final goods. And all these features will determine the details of psychological cause and effect called '*karma*'. The Buddhist doctrine of *karma* remains distinctively Buddhist; but it does so *because it is informed by a distinctively Buddhist moral psychology, account of the final end, and description of how that is attained.* So while Buddhism's unique contributions to ethics, to metaphysics, to moral psychology and epistemology – and to the connections between them – are manifold, they are perhaps best found elsewhere, and not directly in any version of its doctrine of *karma*.

SIX

Irresponsible selves, responsible non-selves

The fourth century or so of the Common Era saw an explosion of intellectual activity in India, accelerating into the ninth century, at which point Buddhism as a whole, and so Buddhist intellectual activity, began to decline in India. Non-Buddhist philosophy continued to flourish in India for several centuries, especially intensively from about 1000 CE, while Buddhist thought moved into separate geographical and intellectual contexts, particularly in Tibet and in China, which took up different parts of the Indian inheritance in substantially different ways.

Vasubandhu is perhaps the finest flower of this fourth-century activity. He was trained in the prominent Sarvāstivādin tradition of the Abhidharma, mastering in particular the version of the higher teachings set out in the *Mahā-Vibhāṣa*, the Great Commentary, whose adherents in Kashmir bore therefore the name Vaibhāṣikas. Vasubandhu was particularly reputed as a fierce debater, so it was not a welcome move when he subtly brought his fellow Vaibhāṣika Buddhists to account. His compendious *Abhidharmakośa* (*The Treasury of Abhidharma*) sets out the mature Buddhist position on all points of the 'higher teachings' – metaphysics, psychology, phenomenology, ethics – as these were understood by the Vaibhāṣikas. His own extensive commentary (*bhāṣya*) on this text, however, goes on not only to elucidate and explore but also to *criticize* several of the Vaibhāṣika positions, particularly those that tend towards metaphysical elaboration, rather than metaphysical minimalism.

In fact, it is not just the Vaibhāṣikas who come in for criticism. Vasubandhu's *Abhidharmakośabhāṣya* is one of our best sources of information on a variety of contending Abhidharma positions, of which there were by this time many, each offering a different interpretation of what it meant for reality to be impermanent, no-self and suffering, and of how understanding this properly should free us from attachment, to self and to other things, so that ultimately suffering may be brought to an end. Vasubandhu engages with and adjudicates between these alternative claims, defending in the *Bhāṣya* what seems to be a Sautrāntika (*sūtra*-follower) position, which presents itself as returning to the simplicity of the *sūtras* over the perceived 'innovations' of later interpreters.[1]

But it was not just the interpreters of the Buddha-*dharma* who were getting more systematic and precise in their interpretations, and clearer about their points of disagreement. Non-Buddhist philosophers had meanwhile begun formulating more precisely exactly what they found objectionable in the Buddhist view.[2] Differences between Buddhist and Brahamanical views were thoroughgoing and systematic. The Vaiśeṣika philosophers, in particular, had a comprehensively different metaphysical picture from the *dharma*-ontology of the Abhidharmikas. The Nyāya (analytical, 'reasoning') school, focusing primarily on epistemology and logic, helped themselves to Vaiśeṣika metaphysics in making their arguments against Buddhist philosophy of mind in particular.[3]

Categorial and non-categorial metaphysics

At least as early as the *Milindapañhā*, Buddhists recognized that they were making claims about the nature of reality. Impermanence is a metaphysical claim; so is dependent origination. These are not isolated dogma to be recited, but integrated parts of a comprehensive view. The principle elicited from the conversation between Nāgasena and Milinda seemed to warrant a radical anti-holist account of the nature of reality. If chariots and Nāgasena are, in some important sense, 'mere names', this claim seemed to rest on showing that chariots and individual persons cannot be identical with one of their parts, nor with all of them, nor do they have some existence quite separate from the parts. Thus, support for no-self came via a mereological argument about the relations between, and respective natures of, wholes and parts. But that reason, if it is any good at all, is equally good for all complex unities, as Vasubandhu recognizes in his canonical formulation of the distinction between ultimate and conventional reality, cited in Chapter 2:

> The idea of a jug ends when the jug is broken; the idea of water ends when, in the mind, one analyzes the water. The jug and the water, and all that resembles them, exist conventionally [*saṁvṛtisatya*]. The rest exist ultimately. (*AK* VI.4)

The resulting *dharma* ontology sheds not only wholes from its accounting of (ultimately) existing things, but also universals, and the essences of any complex wholes, such as 'self' was supposed to be. Such entities were instead conventional realities, which meant their reality was dependent upon facts about the useful, and judgements about the desirable, as well as on the ultimately existing simples. Ultimate reality consists only of absolute simples – momentary events of property-particulars, or tropes – causally conditioned by their predecessor tropes. Nāgārjuna's critique of Abhidharma, which we explored in Chapter 4, challenged the possibility of even such entities carrying their identity in themselves, rather than dependently on other events; and he insisted on the merely dependent reality of causal dependence itself. Nāgārjuna's position was not just anti-holist; from impermanence and dependent origination together Nāgārjuna extracts anti-essentialism and anti-foundationalism – even 'ultimate reality' was not the sort of thing that could function as a foundation for the reality of everything else, in particular the familiar complex unities of experience.

But how minimal can you get, and still account for the phenomena? This point was pressed against Buddhist philosophy for the duration of its time in India. And none pressed harder than the Nyāya and Vaiśeṣika philosophers, working together in defence of a categorial metaphysics that recognized *ways* of being, and substances as that in virtue of which qualities, relations and so on existed.

The radically minimal metaphysics of the Abhidharma Buddhists cannot acknowledge varieties of ways of being, with structured relations between them. There are no categories of 'substance', 'quality', 'relation' and so on, whose ways of being differ, and depend upon their structured relations to each other. Everything existing is the same *sort* of thing, ontologically: a simple property-particular event.[4] Such events may occur in succession, or they may co-occur; but there is no relation of 'belonging to', 'inhering in' or 'being predicated of'. On a non-categorial metaphysics, nothing qualifies or is qualified.

Contrast this with the Vaiśeṣika picture, which has a claim to be much closer to capturing our common-sense ways of thinking.

Everyday experience suffices to tell us that you do not get colours floating around, unattached to anything; you do not have motions, without any *thing* that is moving. Moreover, you can tell the motion is distinct from the thing moving because the moving thing can come to rest, and yet still exist. Similarly, the table's colour is distinct from the table; the colour can be utterly eliminated without harm to the table, but utterly eliminate that table and that instance of colour goes with it. So we do not want to add colours and motions as separate items in our ontology *if* that means we are counting up the entities in the universe, and we count the table, and the colour of the table, and the motion of the table each as distinct but equally existing things, as if they were somehow all on a par. Yet surely the colour exists, *in some way* – namely, *in the table*; and the motion also *exists* rather than being non-existent, for *the table moves*. Only, without the table, no motion; and without the table, no colour. So we say that the motion and the colour *belong to* the table.

This excursion into common sense suggests that there is some special priority in table-like things. The Vaiśeṣika categories, like Aristotle's, thus put 'substance' at the centre of an account of ways of being, or categories of being. A substance is a bearer of properties: of motion and colour, in the examples given above. These exist by virtue of their relation to an existing substance. But not all properties are themselves of the same kind. Colours and motions qualify substances in fundamentally different ways. At the same time, two individuals can be the same colour, or can move in the same way. How are we to understand the sameness in type across numerical diversity? Given the vast number and variety of properties, as well as their repeated occurrences, what is the most efficient way of classifying them? What are the bare minimum of *types* of characteristics required to explain what individuates one thing from another, and how it is possible for there to be *things* – individuals such as we experience, similar to and different from each other, and both changing and persisting through time?

What Nāgārjuna saw as deeply paradoxical, the Vaiśeṣikas take as a challenge to fundamentally rethink the way we go about thinking about the nature and structure of reality.

According to the Vaiśeṣika, after (i) *substance*, we need (ii) *quality*, (iii) *motion*, and – or so later Nyāya-Vaiśeṣika philosophers thought – (iv) *absence* in order to capture all the different sorts of predicates there are, or ways in which a thing is modified. In addition, we require (v) a way of relating the properties to their bearers, namely, *inherence*; (vi) a way of explaining similarities across distinct cases, *universals*; and (vii) something that explains distinctness of otherwise identical individuals: individuators.[5] Without at least these ways of being, one cannot account for the diversity and unity of the world as we experience it.[6] With them, one has a powerful way of expressing how complex, unified entities endure and change over time, resemble and differ from each other – all of which is necessary if our modes of reasoning about such entities are to be well grounded.

The Vaiśeṣika system of categories bears comparison with the Aristotelian one, both in the nature of the project attempted and in the details of execution. Both are attempting to lay out what the structure of perceptible reality must be if it is to remain the same through change – as it seems evident it does – and to be intelligible, the proper object of thought and inference. On the Vaiśeṣika view, as on the Aristotelian, the most fundamental way of existing is to be a fully determinate individual. To be is to be a well-defined, distinct thing; and such beings are the ground for the possibility of other, dependent ways of being, such as colours existing qualitatively. Where Aristotle is somewhat vague about exactly which categories are necessary and mutually exclusive, the Vaiśeṣika consider that exactly their six (or, later, seven) categories are necessary and sufficient to account for the full complexity of the world and experience.[7] Aristotelian categories include 'relation', of which there are several kinds, but what Aristotle can only explain by appeal to several different relations, the Vaiśeṣika promise to explain by appeal to just the one type of relation: inherence.

While there are many categories, the Vaiśeṣika can still lay claim to economy in explanation. For, they claim, theirs is the simplest account of the structure of reality that is also *powerful enough* to ground basic predication (asserting *of* something *that* something is the case) and so ground reasoning; and also complex enough to enable us to conceptualize change (that is, unity and diversity over time), and unity *in* diversity generally. The Vaiśeṣika categorial metaphysics resists the pressure to put all existents on a par, as if they must all be the same sort of thing. Such a move is necessary to avoid the sorts of confusions that a Mādhyamika, for instance, might fall into by trying to treat all entities as ontologically distinct and exclusive individuals, as their Abhidharma brethren do. A relation is a different sort of thing from an entity, so we do not have to ask how relations and their relata get stuck together; in fact, it is more apt to say that a relation is not a *thing* at all – 'inherence' is a way of describing how different sorts of things relate to, or stand with respect to, one another.

A categorial metaphysics is thus superior, one might think, to talk of 'bundles'. Bundles are at best vague and unspecific, and likely to be misleading. A very minimal theory might be, in a qualified sense, *true*; but it may not be sufficiently fine-grained, or sophisticated, to capture and adequately describe, or do justice to, the details. That is, such a way of conceiving reality is not as informative. It is not *false*, but it under-represents and so fails to capture the real structure that is there. The Vaiśeṣika theory of categories, on the other hand, illuminates the *structure* of reality. It shows how various bits fit together, and are suited to one another. If the Buddhist wishes to persist in her radically minimal *dharma* ontology in the face of such an option, she cannot avoid commitment to the stronger claim that such a minimalist view does not fail to capture the finer structure of reality because *reality is not in fact so structured.*

What the Vaiśeṣika approach gives us, above all, is a way of thinking of what a self is and what it is for a 'self' to be a substance. It is tempting to caricature the self-view (a temptation not every *anātmavādin* avoids), depicting it as the belief in some strange, inner appendage, gratuitously added alongside all the other, more respectable, items in one's ontology. Such a view is easily dismissed as ridiculous. But this is not the self-as-substance view. To claim there are selves, and that they are substances, is to place personal identity within the categorial schema.

Vasubandhu recognizes this. The Self that is to be abandoned is not some theoretically otiose postulate that only some odd religious commitment could induce one to seek in the first place. The general principle from the Buddha's discourses is: 'That conception of self is to be abandoned which leads to "mine" – leads one to clinging',[8] and Vasubandhu formulates the relevant senses of self with precision: "The three kinds of grasping after self are grasping for one central entity, grasping for an 'enjoyer', and grasping for a 'doer'."[9] That is, agent, subject and unifier are the grounds of grasping, or attachment to self, that are to be abandoned. But an originator and locus of change which is at once the subject or bearer of properties and the ground of unity in diversity is just what a 'substance' is.

So when the fourth-century Naiyāyika Vatsyāyana turns the tenth verse of Gautama's second-century *Nyāya-Sūtra* into an argument for self, all parties to the debate recognize this is no mere semantic difference. The Vaiśeṣika alternative endorsed by the Nyāya philosophers constitutes a challenge to two related pieces of the Buddhist metaphysical picture: (i) the adequacy of an ontology that does not include wholes, or substances, in general; and (ii) the dispensability of selves, or of persons as substances, in particular. At stake is the nature of self and implicitly the structure of reality.

How *not* to pass like ships in the night

Where the philosophical positions and the extra-philosophical commitments are so widely divergent, it is difficult to see how the contending parties can even enter into productive debate, rather than simply talking past each other. If I say there are selves – meaning persons are among the substantial individuals existing – and if you reject the claim on the grounds that there are no *substances* at all – that is, by challenging the whole framework within which I make sense of any existence claims – it is difficult to know where and how we are to begin resolving our disagreement. This was a widely recognized concern within the highly diverse Indian philosophical community, and its members took care to address it by giving attention to *epistemology*. Such pressure from metaphysical disagreement to epistemological clarity is one reason the Nyāya and Vaiśeṣika were such natural allies.[10] There was, therefore, active discussion of permissible and impermissible moves in debate and persuasive speech,[11] and the attempt to establish agreement about what counts as permissible and impermissible evidence, which sources are reliable and unreliable. Reliable sources of valid cognition, *pramāṇas*, were thus themselves the subject of investigation.[12] But where this, too, is disputed – as it was between the Nyāya, the Buddhist and the Brahamanical Mīmāṃsikas (which latter acknowledged the greatest range of sources of legitimate evidence in argument) – then debate between two contending parties may appeal only to those forms of evidence and argument that are acknowledged as legitimate by both.

Thus Vasubandhu begins his so-called "Treatise on the Person", *Abhidharmakośabhāṣya* IX,[13] with a clear articulation of the terms of the debate:

> How is it known that this designation 'self' applies to the bundle-continuum alone, and not to some other designatum? Because there is neither acquaintance with nor inference to [the posited self]: Thus, whatever things there are

> are apprehended by acquaintance whenever there is no obstruction ... On the other hand, [they may be apprehended] inferentially.[14]

If we are to suppose there is a self, we must have some reason for thinking so. Direct, immediate and incontrovertible experience – *perception* – of a self (or of selves) would be a very good reason to suppose there were selves. This everyone can agree to. Alternatively, one might establish there is a self by a sound inference. Provided we can agree about what makes an inference a sound one, this too is undisputedly a reliable source of valid cognition.[15]

Some non-Buddhists, indeed some Naiyāyikas, did indeed think that there was direct perception of the self. But Vasubandhu's imagined opponents in the *Abhidharmakośa-Bhāṣya* do not press the suggestion, and neither does the fully real Buddhist opponent Vatsyāyana. There is good reason for devoting energies elsewhere. For if it comes to direct perception, and someone – someone not otherwise obviously insane and incapable of navigating the world, and several such 'someones' at that – claims sincerely not to have any such perception, it is difficult to see how you would go about proving to her that she *did* in fact have such a perception.

So when Gautama's *Nyāya-Sūtra* declares that "Desire and hatred, wilful effort, pleasure and pain, and knowledge are the marks of the self" (I.i.10), Vatsyāyana sees in this just so many grounds on which the self-hypothesis is either inescapable, or at least an inescapable part of the best account of phenomena we all agree on. "The self is not grasped through direct acquaintance," Vatsyāyana says, but "it is to be established through inference", and then cites *Nyāya-Sūtra* I.i.10 to show how. Where the Buddhist puts the burden of proof on the self-theorist, with the challenge 'If I don't directly experience it, why should I believe there is such a thing?', Vatsyāyana replies by coming up with some very good reasons: because there is desire and aversion, intentional action, pleasure, pain and knowledge, there must be a self. Who would dispute there are these phenomena? The work for the Naiyāyika, and every *ātmavādin* who would follow him, is to show *how* these indisputable experiences are grounds for a reasonable inference that there is a self.

Kinds and cross-modality, kinds of cross-modality

Vatsyāyana explains:

> The self, having [previously] acquired pleasure through contact with an object of a certain type, desires to possess an object of that very type when it perceives it. It is the mark of the self that this desire-to-possess occurs, because a single seer unites [*pratisaṃdhā*] the [individual acts of] seeing.
>
> (Kapstein, tr., 378)

The idea seems to be straightforward: I look with desire upon something of which I have some previous pleasant experience. I smell the coffee and feel a desire to drink the coffee; this is because I have seen, smelled and tasted coffee in the past – I can now recall having done so – and I felt pleasure from drinking it (I remember this, too). That is, the subject of coffee-perceptions previously must be the same as the subject of pleasure-at-drinking-coffee on that occasion; *and* moreover, this previous perceiver-enjoyer must be the same as the current perceiver of coffee-aroma, in order for this current desire for coffee to arise in me: "When, for example, its object is an established cause of pleasure, then perceiving an object of that type, it strives to possess it, and this would not be the case if there were not one seer of many that unites [the individual acts of] seeing" (*ibid.*: 378).

The phenomena cited are grounds for postulating a self because they are all so many ways in which experience demands that there be genuine unity in multiplicity. Knowledge and memory require unity over time; intentional action implies unity of diverse mental modes at a time (cognition and agency, or willing). Call the first sort 'temporal unity' and the second 'cross-modal unity'. Vatsyāyana first observes that desire implies memory, and then that it must join that memory with current perception and with a rather different sort of capacity for conceiving oneself as an agent of change.[16] "In the same way, wilful effort with respect to the cause of suffering is explained. Recalling pleasure or pain, this one, undertaking the means to achieve that, realizes pleasure, or realizes pain" (*ibid.*: 378).

Straightforward but complex, desire thus combines both sorts of unifying: unity over time (previous coffee-perception and current coffee-perception), and unity of distinct phenomena at a time (previous coffee-perception and previous pleasure; current coffee-perception and current desire). It is thus a powerful argument for self as subject, agent and unity, at once. Since the Buddhists themselves give desire such a central role in their explanations of dependent origination and suffering, the evidence is especially to the point.

Vatsyāyana does not clearly distinguish these kinds of unity-in-difference, for desire brings them together.[17] But the self they seem to imply is different; or, rather, they imply two different features of the self. The demand for the same subject at different times requires a self that persists through time and change. This does not say anything about what this self must be like; perhaps it is *just* a substratum of experience, a subject, a passive recording device. The cross-modal argument, by contrast, requires a self that is distinct from any particular sort of phenomenon, and so is able to unify diverse phenomena. Only that which is neither *essentially* agent nor *essentially* subject could ground the possibility of an agency *based on* subjective states. This argument makes no claim on the longevity of the 'self'; but it does require that it be a certain kind of thing: namely, the kind of thing to which a diversity of subjective states, volitions and agency equally properly belong. What this argument precludes is that either volitional or perceptual capacities could be called in to do duty of being 'the self' required.

Attending to the complexities of desire tells against the *anātmavāda* because, as Vatsyāyana observes, the connection between the two moments of perception expressed in desire cannot be based on distinct mental events. For in distinct mental events, there is only difference, and difference itself cannot explain *connectedness*.

> It is a commonplace that [regarding] one being, memory is of what he himself has perceived, not of what another has perceived. Similarly, it is a commonplace that what one has perceived is not remembered by another. Neither of these two [points] can be established by the non-self advocate.
>
> (*Ibid.*: 379, trans. mod.)

The Buddhist, Vatsyāyana contends, cannot account for this connection *between* different moments of perception, and for the fact that such a connection fails to hold between different persons. For on the Buddhist view, there is no agent, and no subject existing at different times to unite these experiences from different times in an act of *re*cognition: 'This now is like that then was'. This means that the Buddhist must consider different moments of the 'same person' as being just as distinct as different persons – whether they want to or not. If, as the *anātmavādin* claims, there is no self, no metaphysical 'glue', making this person(-bundle) at this moment anything other than simply different from any person-bundle at any moment, then every person-moment is equally non-identical with every other.[18] But if the difference between different persons at the same time is the same as the difference between the same person at different times, then the same person will be no more able to have these unifying experiences than two separate persons are able to, or will be just as able to. That is, it should be as correct to say that Yajñadatta recalls Devadatta's previous experiences as it is to say that Yajñadatta recalls 'his own' previous experiences, for the connection, or lack thereof, is (on the no-self account) the same in both cases. Yet, as we know, it is not equally correct. "It is a commonplace ... that memory is of what he himself has perceived, not of what another has perceived" (*ibid.*).

Desire also requires that diverse modalities of experience – memory, perception, volition – belong to the same individual. In striving to satisfy a desire, the subject of the desire and the agent of the effort to satisfy the desire must be the same. If the experiencer of desire is not numerically the same as the agent, then the action cannot count as 'attempting to satisfy a desire'. There may be a felt desire here, and an action there nearby, but without them belonging to the same being, there is no more 'effort to satisfy a desire' than there would be when Karen wants and Kenneth acts. Vatyāyana's use of knowledge as grounds for inferring a 'self' works essentially by way of the desire argument: "Desiring to know (*buddhutsamāna*), moreover, one reflects, 'What is...?' And, having reflected, it knows, 'This is...'" (*ibid.*: 378). If there is no self, then the questioner (desiring to know) cannot be the same as one who later understands the answer. This would make seeking knowledge and coming to know impossibilities, a demoralizing conclusion that most philosophers have tried to avoid.[19]

So, Vatsyāyana concludes, "Therefore, it is proven: the self is." And we have a clear view of *what* sort of self it is that is demonstrated: only one that is as 'mystical' or 'substantial' as necessary to do the work that ordinary experience tells us must be done, if such experiences are to be at all possible.

Replying to the memory (temporal unity) objection

The Buddhist replies, simply, "those two [Devadatta's act of seeing and Yajñadatta's apparent memory] have no connection as do two [mental events] belonging to the same continuum, because they are not related as cause and effect" (Kapstein, tr., 367). At least, that is Vasubandhu's response in *Abhidharmakośa-Bhāṣya* IX, where he imagines a non-Buddhist interlocutor with objections very much like Vatsyāyana's here.[20]

Thus the response to these objections is the familiar replacement of identity with causal continuity. That is all, and it is considered sufficient. But if we consider how our bodies are in constant interaction with our physical environments, and indeed with other minds, we might be tempted to think that Vasubandhu has missed the point. For there are causal connections between *dharma*-streams constituting different persons; so causal connectedness alone cannot ground the principle that one only ever recalls *one's own* previous experiences. Even Buddhaghoṣa seems to think this is a problem, for he lists '*life faculty*' as one of the 'derived' material (*rūpa*) *dharmas*, apparently attributing to it the maintenance of and connection between living-creature-constituting *dharmas*, thus acting as "a condition for distinguishing what is living".[21] This naturally raises considerable difficulties about the life faculty's duration, power over and relation to other material *dharmas*, which Buddhaghoṣa attempts to answer. So it is no wonder that Vasubandhu does not wish to avail himself of any such devices in his answer. But we can see why the seventh-century Naiyāyika Uddyotakara is still insisting, in his own elaborations of Vatsyāyana's objections, that the Buddhists have only explained *difference*, not unity; thus the Buddhists are committed to supposing that Yajñadatta can recall what Devadatta perceived. Appealing to sameness of causal stream *presupposes* just the individuation that needs accounting for.[22]

Vasubandhu's observation that different individuals do not have each others' memories because there is a lack of causal connection seems simply to miss the point: unless the subject of the two experiences is *the same in number*, there is just as much 'connection' between Jane's perception and John's desire or John's recollection, and we must think of our own experiences as structurally identical to cases of John recalling what Jane saw; not only is this a situation that does not occur, but also it would be absurd to call it 'recollection' if it did occur.

But is Vasubandhu's reply really so feeble as that? It may be that, in pressing the objection, we have missed the point of the Buddhist position. Causal connection is sufficient to explain memory, Vasubandhu thinks, and the unity over time implicit in desire. John never recalls Jane's perceptions because there is no unbroken causal stream from Jane's perception to John's recollection. This is a good answer, and not a feeble one, because it recalls us to the nature of the Buddhist claim: individuation of persons is a conclusion that is drawn in light of the observed phenomena; it is not a precondition for drawing conclusions. All the facts are agreed and remain in place, but the order of explanation is – the Buddhists say – the other way round: It is *because* certain causal relations obtain, and others do not, that we find it useful and correct to designate certain groups of events as 'Devadatta' and a different group of events as 'Yajñadatta'. The same connectedness that makes Devadatta (conventionally) one person and Yajñadatta another person is what makes it the case that Devadatta has access only to Devadatta's previous experiences, and not to Yajñadatta's, or, more literally, to immediate consequences of previous events in Devadatta's causal stream. The fact that causal connections are thus and so is prior; it is this which makes sense of our talk of Devadatta recalling what he had seen before, and of Yajñadatta seeing now something he (Yajñadatta) previously experienced as pleasant.

However, as Uddyotakara makes clear, Vasubandhu's continuity alternative has not engaged with the cross-modal version of the unity argument for self, and this is the truly difficult objection to meet.

Uddyotakara's rejoinder: cross-modal unity

Uddyotakara draws together Vatsyāyana's arguments for self into a single, concise objection to the *anātmavāda*. "How is it that desire, etc., cause there to be knowledge of the unapprehended self?"[23]

> [T]he sharing of a single object with memory; for singularity of agency is established because desire, etc., have the very same objects as memory. For [otherwise] there is no unification of diverse agents, diverse objects and diverse stimuli ... According to those who propound the non-self view, there can be no determinate objects whose forms are here and there differentiated, and thus there is no reason for unification. (Kapstein, tr., 379)

For those familiar with it, this looks reminiscent of Kant's argument that some unity of apperception must be posited in order for there to be the experience of individuated, enduring objects that we undoubtedly have (however falsely or unjustifiably). A disintegrated subjectivity would entail disintegrated objects (or objectual representation).[24] But that is not how we experience the world. On the contrary, we are capable of such judgements as "what form I have seen, that is this texture, and what texture I have felt, that is the form I see" (*ibid.*). And such complex cognitions are possible only if there is a single subject of diverse modes of experience, at different times. Uddyotakara, too, conjoins these two sorts of unity in diversity. Vasubandhu may be able to build the experience *as of* the same object enduring over time into the peculiar nature of the original perception whose effect is experienced as a mental event of 'memory'. But if we focus on the cross-modal diversity in such judgements as 'I see what I touch', it becomes clear that the same response will not work. There must be the same person, simultaneously aware *in different modes* – simultaneously aware of texture and of colour – in order to unify them in a single judgement. But that subject cannot be any one of the particular modes of perception themselves, since they preclude each other (one does not *taste* a texture).

In simple cases like this, there is a single experience of that yellow thing tasting sour, or of that shiny thing sounding melodious, as when we eat a lemon, or hear the bell we are looking at ringing. Now, we do not hear colours, and we do not see sounds. Hearing is the distinct faculty it is by virtue of the fact that it processes only its special type of information, and not information of another type – and likewise with seeing, tasting and so on. So a cognition of this shiny thing *as* loud, or this yellow thing *as* sour, cannot be the work either of seeing or of hearing, or of taste. Something distinct from these must be involved if such complex cognitions are to be possible. But this distinct thing must also have the deliverances of the various sense-modalities available to it.

Appealing in the *Theaetetus* to such 'common terms' as 'one', 'being', and 'same', 'different', which are not the privileged content of any particular sense-modality and yet are constantly represented together with our sensory experiences, Plato says it is the activity and responsibility of the soul (*psychē*) to receive and coordinate disparate information (*Theaetetus* 184c–186c). Aristotle says it is the 'common sense' (*de Anima* III.1–2). The Brahmanical philosophers say it is 'the self'.[25]

Vasubandhu may have a response to simple cross-modality: namely, to reject the phenomena. At *Abhidharmakośabhāṣya* III.8–9, he denies that shape can be a really existing *dharma* on the grounds that any sensory object can be perceived *only* via its proper sense-modality. This may be a slightly stronger claim than the converse: that any sense-modality can only perceive its proper objects. But it seems warranted, and is generally an accepted part of distinguishing sense-modalities at all; strictly speaking, 'visibles' are *only* seen, audible objects as such are *only* heard. Such an implication is indeed required by a *dharma* ontology that rejects any really existing complex objects. If no one thing can be both seen and touched, then Vasubandhu will in any case explain any apparent instance of seeing what I touch as two successive moments, rather than a single one, and likewise for seeing what I hear, and so on. Whether this is an adequate reply must be tested.

But there is also a sophisticated variant of the cross-modal objection, one which forces the issue of complex unity, refusing to let it be dissolved into successive distinct moments. Any such item would constitute an argument against the extremely minimal metaphysical picture the Buddhists offer.

Sophisticated cross-modality

Using tensed sentences, as we saw he does, and relating this to the phenomenon of desire, Uddyotakara presents a considerably more sophisticated variety of cross-modal experience.

Suppose I eat a lemon. I see that it is yellow and I taste that it is sour. And – let us say I am otherwise unfamiliar with lemons – I judge, 'that yellow fruit is sour'. This is indeed a sequence of events, just as Vasubandhu's model of mind supposes. But they are not related *causally*; nothing about the yellow-perception makes my subsequent gustatory experience a 'sour' one. Nevertheless, these experiences *are* connected somehow: the judgement 'that yellow fruit I saw is sour' combines the two. And it can do this only if both the previous visual perception *and* the current gustatory experience are available to the same consciousness. But this requires not only the union of different sense-modalities, but also the union of different *mental*-modalities, namely, memory and perception, for on Vasubandhu's own account, I must remember the colour of the previous moment and perceive the flavour in the current moment in order to construct the complex judgement. "There is unification with memory owing to there being one object of both earlier and later cognition; but such memory cannot occur according to your [*anātmavādin*] side" (Kapstein, tr., 381).

Thinking of this as 'the memory objection' can obscure the diverse modalities, and their significance to the point. For if we think of memory as merely 'the preservation of perception', we might think there is no real diversity here: nothing, at any rate, that is not amenable to Vasubandhu's causal account. For surely previous perceptions can unproblematically be considered part of the cause of subsequent perceptual experiences, even if the subsequent ones are not of currently present objects. That is, one can simply reject the Naiyāyika's demand that the contents of memory be identical to the contents of perception.

But from the context in which Uddyotakara raises the objection, it becomes clear that memory cannot be so easily dealt with. Memory is relevant at all because it is a necessary part of desire. And desire even more clearly requires that distinct *modes of cognition* or experience be available to a single being. In desire, not only must the object experienced at different times be the same (in some sense), not only must the subject of the two perceptions be numerically the same, but also the *subject* must be identical to the *agent*. It is not clear whether Uddyotakara thinks the sort of unification of diverse perceptions is *itself* an activity, requiring agency and not mere subjectivity. Even if not, he is at least connecting the representational aspect of desire with its volitional aspect. A desire is 'agentive'; but it is also always a desire *for* something or another. And taking an object requires that volitions be also representational: that is, agency as expressed in desire involves unification of the active and passive, the 'doer' and the 'enjoyer'. Thus the very three forms of self Vasubandhu encouraged us to abandon are necessarily implied in any desire.

Consider how the Buddhist herself puts desire at the heart of suffering. Clinging and craving lead to unhappiness of all sorts. The simplest, and most pervasive, sort of craving – the sort almost impossible to detach ourselves from – is the desire for what is pleasant, and the aversion towards what is unpleasant or painful. I dislike the painfulness of being with other people, so I desire an alcoholic drink that will relieve the painful stress, and replace it with a spreading feeling of pleasant warmth and relaxation and joy. I want a drink.

But how do I come to want a drink? I must have had a drink before in order to know it now to be something that *would* be pleasant if

I *were* to have it. For desire is always for what is not present to me now – that is why it is painful; so I cannot know the pleasantness of the desired object through an immediately occurring perception. Yet I must in some way be in contact with the fact of its pleasantness; I must, indeed, *remember* that having a drink occasions such-and-such sensations, which are pleasant.[26] So in order for desire to be the sort of thing the Buddhist says it is, *if it is going to be the source of suffering*, then it must be a complex and unified mental state, involving the ability to recognize *as* 'the same' diverse experiences, and the ability to coordinate forms of experience (perception, recollection, imagination, thinking, volition) with each other. Similarly, in the *satisfaction of desire*, the subject desiring must be the same as the subject satisfied; otherwise, there is no 'satisfaction of a desire' occurring, only unrelated episodes of desiring and pleasure.

That is, *something* must be the receptacle and coordinator for all sorts of information: about what something felt like (whether pleasant or painful or neutral), about how one found it last time (so that we can judge in which circumstances our desired object is likely to be found next), about how much effort it took or did not take in order to acquire the pleasant thing (so one can consider whether the amount and quality of gain is worth the amount and quality of effort to be expended). There must be some one thing, distinct from any particular faculty of cognition, volition, perception and so on, in order to coordinate and preserve together the sort of complex mental state necessary for feeling a desire for something – at least, necessary for feeling the sorts of desires we feel, or for feeling desires in the way that we recognizably do feel them.

That this some one thing must be distinct from any of the particular *skandhas* can be seen by running a repeat of the cross-modality argument: no one of the bundles, in virtue of the distinct sort of bundle it is, could be the sort of thing capable of *having* or *being* the experiences of another bundle, in the way the other bundle has it. Cognition cannot have sensations or provide sensible qualities, just as hearing cannot see or provide visible qualities; consciousness cannot will, even if I become conscious *of* a volition, just as I might hear something visible without hearing providing that visible content. A moment of consciousness remains a moment of consciousness, no matter what it takes as its content; it cannot become a volition, and so cannot unite volition and, say, recollection or perception. It can only be aware of these various mental events as objects of awareness. So no one *skandha* could host the unified recollection of what before caused a pleasant sensation and is likely to cause that pleasant sensation in future. But if I do not have that unified complex experience, I cannot come to feel desire.

Such a universal receptacle and coordinator, say the Naiyāyika, just is what 'self as substance' means. 'Self' is that which is distinct from all the various sorts of properties and faculties that a person has; and that which, in virtue of this distinctness, can collect, retain and coordinate the various types of experiential event into single coherent experiences: that of wanting a drink.

The Buddhists themselves, say the Nyāya philosophers, must posit some such self, if they are to maintain that desires exist at all, and that they have the complex psychological structure and impact that the Buddhists themselves claim desires have.

This sort of argument against the Buddhist tries to foist on her a richer ontology than she had wished to endorse, and a more reflective metaphysical position about what it is for anything to 'be', and about what sorts of ways of being there are, and how they can and cannot relate to one another. The claim is an especially pointed one: for not just common experience, but the very common experience that Buddhism puts at the centre of its moral ambitions, seem inexplicable on the mere bundle-and-process view, and by contrast very clearly explicable on the self-as-substance view.

Dharmas, no-self and cross-modality

Does the Abhidharma position have any resources for responding to this sophisticated version of the cross-modal objection or, indeed, even to the simple one? If there is nothing distinct from the various experiences *to whom* these experiences belong, or are available, then how is the coordination of these experiences possible and, more crucially, how can there be single complex experiences integrating what must be distinct modes of experience? If there are no such things, then we need to explain what memory, desire and cross-modal sensory judgements are instead of this. If there is some such thing, the Buddhist would have to explain how this is not just the very 'Self' that the *ātmavādins* were talking about all along.

It seems the Buddhist has three options; on all of them, Vasubandhu's continuity response to the memory objection, and other unity-over-time objections, is accepted as sufficient:

- *Option 1*: Deny that there are, in fact, any complex phenomena; there is only the illusion of such. In fact, there is only the co-occurrence of distinct phenomena in close spatiotemporal mutually conditioning proximity. One might think that clarifying such connections, and thus giving proof that such an account is adequate, is the project of the extensive Abhidharma books and their commentaries, which identify each kind of mental phenomena and their mutual relations.
- *Option 2*: Accept that there can be complex phenomena: there is something that is neither perception nor grasping, which has these two phenomena available to it somehow and thus is able to *be* a desire *for* a recollected pleasure. But such a thing is still only an event; it has only momentary existence, and so is not a 'self' in the pernicious sense. This would be attractive if we find it hard to deny the internal multi-modal complexity of some of our experiences. It would have the disadvantage of allowing a substance-property metaphysics, although an entirely momentary one. This would be a fundamental change in metaphysical orientation, which may give an opponent grounds to insist that if there *can be* items which 'inhere' and 'are inhered in', and if that strange relationship can exist at all, why should it not be our account of beings in general?
- *Option 3*: The Buddhist might deny the essential complexity of phenomena that nevertheless do permit of analysis. This seems to be the line later philosophers working in the Yogācāra tradition did indeed take. The idea would be that there are phenomena, such as desire, that can be usually analysed into various components – perception, recollection, will; but the splitting up into components is a result of our mental activity. So the complexity has only conceptual reality; it does not belong to the phenomenon itself, which does not consist in some divided way of separate individuals or aspects whose coherence then requires an explanation. Such a line requires moving away from *dharma* ontology, and from the Abhidharma, significantly, although not in the direction of substance-property, Vaiśeṣika-like metaphysics.

Uddyotakara's argument is strongest when it focuses on multi-modal unity at a time, rather than on unity over time. When he allows the objection to be primarily about unity over time, he opens up space for the Buddhist 'causal continuity' picture. This picture may or may not be adequate, but it will seem much weaker when addressing multimodal complexity at a time. Now, to the extent that he does focus on such cross-modality, Uddyotakara pins his argument to the phenomenon of desire, and this may well provide a powerful, and perhaps even unique, necessary union of subjective and agentive. It may also, however, open space for a uniquely Buddhist rejoinder, one not included in the options outlined above.

Desire proves the self, says Uddyotakara. But the Buddhist might reply by granting the logical and psychological point: desire implies a subject–agent unity, called 'self'. And this is precisely why desire is to be abandoned, if suffering is to be eliminated. The phenomenon of desire is indeed a complex one. And such a complex conjunction *is* the self, and *creates* the self. This is just what it means to say that we are bearers and inheritors of our actions, and to say that this self is a constructed, conventional reality. All Uddyotakara has pointed out is the psychological fact about what conjunctions of complex *dharmas* give rise to a sense of self and to activities reinforcing further such complex conjunctions. In using desire to prove 'self', Uddyotakara has only given us a clearer reason why desire implies self, and how it is then that eliminating desire (so understood) is necessary in order to root out self-thinking fundamentally.

SEVEN

The third turning: Yogācāra

> Who can believe that Vasubandhu, to say nothing of his acquaintance with the Sāṁkhyā, was a Vaibhāṣika in his youth, a Sautrāntika in his mature years, a Vijñānavādin in his old age, and a Pure Land follower of Amitābha at his death?
>
> (Lamotte, *History of Indian Buddhism*, 39)

Vasubandhu is a slippery customer. Trained in the Vaibhāṣika tradition of Abhidharma – either a variant or dissenting offshoot of the Sarvāstivādins – he nevertheless criticizes his own exposition of Vaibhāṣika orthodoxy as being too opulent, offering too much elaboration on the simplicity of the Buddhist view as articulated in the *sutta-pitaka*. Buddhists thus inclined came to be called Sautrāntikas: *sūtra*-followers.[1] Of course, all Buddhists follow the *sūtras*; the Sautrāntikas, we might say, made a particular point of it, rejecting or challenging elaborations of the discourses of the Buddha, as these might be found in the Abhidharma canon, for instance. "What is the meaning of *sautrāntika*?", asks the early commentator, Yaśomitra. "Those who take *sūtra* as their authority, not *śāstra*, are Sautrāntikas."[2] The *śāstras*, in this context, are the recognized Abhidharma texts, which Vasubandhu reminds us are *not* the word of the Buddha, and so their truth is open to dispute.[3]

This boast was not necessarily recognized by other Abhidharma schools, who may have referred to this group of Abhidharmikas as Dārṣṭāntikas ('those who employ examples'), but distinctions (if any) and relations between various positions, schools of thought, and thinkers during this period and earlier is uncertain and much contested in the scholarly literature.[4] Perhaps even more important than doctrinal faithfulness in Vasubandhu's critique of Vaibhāṣika is the insistence on metaphysical minimalism. (No doubt, Vasubandhu would not have supposed the two came apart.) So, for instance, many *dharmas* that are an accepted part of the Abhidharma ontology – accepted in particular by the Vaibhāṣikas or Sarvāstivādins – are considered merely conceptual, *prajñapti*, by Vasubandhu, not ultimately real. 'Forces dissociated from mind' fall by the wayside, as do any 'unconditioned *dharmas*', such as space and *nirvāṇa* were thought by some Abhidharmikas to be. Difficulties about 'who perceives?' and 'what is perceived?' are dissolved by insisting that, ultimately, there is neither agent nor object: perceiving arises in dependence on organ and perceptible quality.

From rejecting unnecessary *dharmas*, through a denial of motion, to denial of spatiotemporally located atoms

We can see this preference for minimalism also in one of Vasubandhu's shorter works, *A Demonstration of Action*. Action, or *karma*, is central to Indian thought, and unavoidable; one must have something to say about it. And if one is taking a Buddhist line, one must say something about what it means to interpret *karma* as intention.

In the *Demonstration of Action*, Vasubandhu tries to show that all the concepts through which we might attempt to make sense of a physical, as opposed to a mental, act turn out to be incoherent, confused beyond remedy. So, for instance, to distinguish bodily from mental action, we might naturally appeal to the configuration of physical parts in the latter case; but 'configuration', Vasubandhu argues, cannot be anything ultimately existing. Shape must be conceived on the basis of the aggregated colour-*dharmas*, and is thereby a conventional reality. The distinction between mental and physical action on this basis would be grounded merely in our convenient conceptualizations. Likewise, appeal to motion as characterizing physical but not mental action will not do, because motion too is merely a handy way of thinking what is in fact the arising and passing away of successive similar *dharmas* in contiguous spaces at different times.

But if configuration and motion are problematic concepts, there is much more at stake than a distinction between mental and bodily action. For it is not only in considering bodily action that we avail ourselves of notions of shape, spatial relation and motion. Whenever we think or perceive visual or tactile objects of any sort, shape and spatial relation at least seem to be inescapable. So perhaps it should be no surprise to see Vasubandhu turning his hand in the *Twenty Verses* to a direct critique of spatially extended objects *tout court*.

Scholars have been surprised by this, however – so much so that one prominent twentieth-century scholar went so far as to argue that the *Twenty Verses* and similar pieces must have been written by a different Vasubandhu than the Vasubandhu who authored the *Abhidharmakośa* and its *Bhāṣya*.[5]

The reason for their surprise is that the difference between these texts has not been received by the tradition as a mere extension of a line of thought; it has been taken, rather, as a radical change of sides. The *Abhidharmakośa* (The treasury of Abhidharma) is, as the name suggests, a straightforward Abhidharma text, articulating a widely accepted position among a range of acceptable lines defended by Abhidharma Buddhists interpreting the view of the earliest Buddhist texts, and of the seven canonical Abhidharma texts in particular. The relation of the *Bhāṣya* itself to its root text is admittedly complex: it seems to defend points disputed among Abhidharmikas along a different, Sautrāntika line, a line perhaps not quite as widely accepted as the Vaibhāṣika view presented in the *Treasury* itself, but still clearly recognized as a viable interpretation of the 'higher teachings'. This, however, means that the *Abhidharmakośa* and its auto-commentary were *not* participating in what had, by Vasubandhu's time, become a widespread and cohesive Mahāyāna movement, involving different practices and distinct goals, and claiming a new set of *sūtras* (particularly, but not exclusively the *prajñāpāramitā*, perfection of wisdom, literature) as legitimate representatives of the Buddha's teaching.

Nāgārjuna had given philosophical articulation to the Mahāyāna movement in ethics and especially in metaphysics, by emphasizing 'emptiness'. But the Greater Vehicle was greater than Nāgārjuna, whose arguments – in so far as he offered any – did not make their massive impact on Indian Buddhist philosophy until centuries after he had written the *Mūlamadhyamakakārikā*. Instead, those moved by the distinctive goals of the Mahāyāna took on board Nāgārjuna's emphasis on 'emptiness' and incorporated it into what they styled the 'third turning of the Wheel [of Dharma]'.

After the Buddha's first discourses and their immediately related texts, there was Nāgārjuna's Madhyamaka, teaching 'emptiness' (*śūnyatā*), to counteract the tendency of the old guard (*Sthaviravādins*) to reify its analysands into substantial objects. This contributed to the Mahāyāna cause of widening the franchise, by taking a certain sort of expertise – expertise in a certain sort of analysis – off the table, and replacing it with a single insight open in principle to whoever dedicated themselves to it. One did not need special scholarly education in the lists of *dharmas* – their kinds and relations – in order to understand emptiness, and reciting such lists to oneself was not likely to be particularly beneficial to anyone. And the Madhyamaka resistance to reification could also be interpreted as serving the Mahāyāna cause of foregrounding compassion. For, to the extent that we attend to mutual origination, to the extent then that we do not focus on individual *dharmas*, to that extent our attention is on the flexible and permeable nature of the convenient boundaries defining individuals, rather than on the distinct causal streams constituting Abhidharma conventional persons. And this diffusing of agency, associated as it is with the appreciation of all beings as suffering, should undermine tendencies towards blame and thus replace vindictiveness with compassion. This is the 'second turning of the Wheel': emptiness, the resistance to reification, and the recognition of dependence that this implies.

But this second turning is liable to its own extremism. Exclusive emphasis on 'emptiness' tends towards nihilism, and there were Mahāyāna Buddhists sensitive to this danger, and so keen to put Madhyamaka in perspective. These Buddhists became known as Yogācāra Buddhists, or Yogācārins: an uninformative title that seems to mean 'the way (or, conduct) of exercises (or, practices)'. The Yogācāra strand of Mahāyāna was, like Nāgārjuna's Madhyamaka, influenced by the *prajñāpāramitā* literature, which foregrounded emptiness (*śūnyatā*). But many Yogacārins were also influenced by another set of *sūtras* that grew up from perhaps the third century CE, associated with the *tathāgatagarbha* (Buddha-Nature, or literally Buddha-womb).[6] And they had come, at some point or another, to recognize additional *sūtras* – including the *Daśabhūmika-sūtra*, the *Laṅkāvatāra-sūtra*, and the *Saṃdhinirmocana-(mahāyāna)-sūtra*, texts whose legitimacy conservative Abhidharmikas never recognized.

According to Yogācārins, the elimination of substantial selves was a first move towards the 'right view', which will eliminate craving, and so suffering. The recognition of the non-substantiality of reality as a whole was an important second move. But this must be completed by a third step: the return to the reality of experience. Ultimately, regardless of kind, quality, number or change, there is experience. This can be conceived of as neither an activity, if activity requires an agent, nor an object, for that implies a kind of individuation that is not provisional, dependent, liable to change. It is sometimes called consciousness (*vijñāna*) or mind (*citta*), and for that reason the Yogācāra position has also, retrospectively, been called the *Vijñānavāda* (the consciousness doctrine) or *Cittamātra* (mind-only) – for on their account *only* this is ultimately, unqualifiedly and unconditionally real.[7]

So when the commentary (*vṛtti*) on the *Twenty Verses* (*Viṃśatikā-Kārikā*) opens with a preamble, claiming allegiance to the Mahāyāna – "In the Great Vehicle, existence is determined as being cognition-only [*vijñapti-mātra*]" (*VK* 1[8]) – this can be difficult to reconcile with the Abhidharma master of the *Abhidharmakośa*.

The critique of mind-independent, extended objects that follows argues, first, that such supposed entities are unnecessary in explaining experience; second, that the non-mental entities supposed to serve as objects of cognition are not up to that task anyway. And so the commentary to the twenty-first verse of the *Twenty Verses* concludes with an allusion to the true self of the Buddhas, through which one knows directly, without distinction between subject and object: in an important sense, not like knowledge at all. "The enlightened have been liberated from ignorance and have transcended subject–object consciousness. They know their own minds as well as the minds of others. They have achieved true Selfhood."[9]

This is not the only willingness to use *ātman* in the *Twenty Verses*.[10] Presuming, as we must, that this is not heralding the triumphant return of the Brahmanical *ātman*, 'self' seems here rather to indicate a realization through recognition of a modest Buddhist self – consciousness that is neither subject nor object nor agent – as a sheer fact of experience; for this, as we shall see, is all that is left by this point in the *Twenty Verses*. This conclusion, after the *vijñaptimātra* opening, puts the text squarely in the Yogācāra camp. And *this* is startling, given Vasubandhu's known Abhidharma training, his able articulation of that view in the *Abhidharmakośa* and its *Bhāṣya*, and the radical gulf by now separating Mahāyāna-adherents and Abhidharmikas.

Tradition has it that Vasubandhu, the great Abhidharmika, was in fact converted to the Mahāyāna by his half-brother, Asaṅga, the first great exponent of the Yogācāra. Such traditions need not be taken literally, and evidence to establish this one beyond doubt is probably beyond us. But neither need tradition be absolutely disbelieved and replaced with complicated hypotheses of two different philosophers by the same name, each working in a distinct context, time and place within Indian Buddhist culture and history, and yet forever confused with one another. For on the one hand, the sorts of moves that take Vasubandhu in the *Twenty Verses* in a Yogācāra direction are entirely in keeping with the sort of Sautrāntika moves he makes against the Vaibhāṣika *Abhidharmakośa* in his own *bhāṣya*; they are moves towards metaphysical minimalism, arguments in favour of reducing rather than inflating the principles we appeal to in explaining experience as we find it.[11] On the other hand, it is not so clear just when Mahāyāna came to be seen as radically distinct from, and intellectually incompatible with, Abhidharma Buddhism. What retrospectively looks like a chasm too wide to bridge may have been a full and contested assortment of views in the process of being clarified and distinguished, and set alongside and against each other.

At any rate, for most of Vasubandhu's texts, it is reasonably clear which position he is articulating, whether Abhidharma (like the *Abhidharmakośa*, and its *bhāṣya*) or Yogācāra (*Twenty Verses, Thirty Verses, Treatise on the Three Natures)*. We can, therefore, for pragmatic purposes, distinguish between Vasubandhu as Abhidharmika and Vasubandhu as Yogācārin, while remaining agnostic about the conventional-historical identity of these two.[12]

In considering Yogācāra Buddhism, we shall look at how it is set out by Vasubandhu, for although Asaṅga sets out the view extensively, Vasubandhu offers the arguments. In the *Twenty Verses*, these arguments should move one from Abhidharma atomism to the mind-only interpretation of the Buddha's teachings, but they should also put any realist about mind-independent reality on the defensive. After weighing these arguments, we shall turn to Vasubandhu's two expositions of where this leaves us: one positive (*Treatise on the Three Natures*), the other negative (*Thirty Verses*).

Twenty Verses

Twenty Verses initially follows a standard way of structuring discussions in Indian philosophy,[13] beginning with a statement of a position, followed by the entertainment of objections and responses to them. So the first preamble to verse 1 states and clarifies a claim:

> In Mahāyāna ... [reality is] determined to be cognition-only [*vijñapti-mātra*] ... Mind [*citta*], intelligence [*manas*], consciousness [*chit*], and perception [*pratyakṣa*] are synonyms. By the word 'mind' [*citta*], mind along with its associations is intended here. 'Only' is said to rule out any (external) object.[14]

Verse 1 clarifies further: "All this is cognition-only, because of the appearance of non-existent objects, just as there may be the seeing of non-existent nets of hair by someone afflicted with an optical disorder."

Vasubandhu goes on immediately to canvas objections, and the *Twenty Verses* may be said to consist in a series of objections and replies to the carefully stated thesis. We can, however, discern order in this dialectic by recognizing that the philosophical strategy of the *Twenty Verses* consists in four key moves.

1. *Mind-independent reality is an unnecessary hypothesis I*
   All the phenomena can be explained without appeal to mind-independent causes. Verses 1 to 7 consider experiences as of spatially extended, mind-independent objects. "If perception occurs without an object," an imagined objector says (*VK* 2), "any restriction as to place and time becomes illogical, as does non-restriction as to moment-series and any activity which has been performed". All such experiences, Vasubandhu will argue, are perfectly explicable without recourse to the spatially extended, mind-independent reality hypothesis.
   But if these are not grounds for concluding such entities do exist or *must* exist, the onus is on the mind-independent realist to show that there is nevertheless good reason to believe the hypothesis.
2. *Consider the alternative*
   There are more virtues to a theory than its positing fewer kinds of entities. Minimal ontological commitment is admirable. But so are simplicity, explanatory power, elegance, internal coherence and intelligibility. Anyone advocating a theory so contrary to common notions as Vasubandhu is has an obligation to consider the claims of common sense. He does this in verses 8 to 10, which appear to be introducing an issue merely for the faithful: didn't the Buddha say there were such objects and refer to them? In the guise of this doctrinal question, Vasubandhu gives voice to the concern that the realist metaphysical picture is at least equally

viable, and has the advantage of being how most people, and the wise too, seem to view the world and their experiences of it. Why give up on a perfectly familiar metaphysical picture just because some circuitous appeal to untrackable mental causation might also be made to explain the same?

Here, the sort of burden-shifting arguments considered in (1) are not enough; even if experience as of mind-independent objects does not *entail* or *necessitate* the actual (mind-independent) existence of such objects, their actual existence might after all be the better explanation of our experiences. The Buddha – who actually knew about such things – does not hesitate to appeal to mind-independent *dharmas* in his teaching.

Vasubandhu's reply has resort to that tried and trusted Buddhist hermeneutical device, the distinction between '*sūtras* of definitive meaning [*nītārtha*]' and '*sūtras* of interpretable meaning [*neyārtha*]', based on the Buddha's avowed policy of using 'skilful means' in teaching. Talk of *rūpa-dharmas* – the Buddha's, and so presumably our own, in so far as we are wise – should be understood as merely provisional, to be interpreted according to more literal statements. But any appeal to this distinction immediately becomes a *philosophical* problem, for it is not agreed which *sūtras* are to be taken literally, and which are to be interpreted in their light.

3. *The mind-independent extended objects hypothesis is incoherent; it* could not *explain experience*

This prompts the third move, in verses 11 to 14, in which Vasubandhu tries to show that the realist alternative cannot offer an equally good explanation of experience, because in fact the realist picture is incoherent and so cannot offer any account of our perceptions. The best evidence we have, says Vasubandhu, that the Buddha did not mean his references to mind-independent objects literally is that such objects simply cannot exist or do the work asked of them in explaining experience. And the Buddha, being wise, would not therefore have invoked them in this way. The work is being done here not by claims about the Buddha's special insight into things otherwise unknowable, but by the claim that no intelligent, reflective person *could* seriously believe in mind-independent reality, for such a thing is riddled with incoherence. The arguments here are what I refer to as the 'positive arguments' for the thesis set out in the preamble to verse 1. They aim to show that the mind-independent objects hypothesis *cannot* be right.

4. *Mind-independent reality is an unnecessary hypothesis II*
Granting the incoherence of extension, even some mind-independent reality of some other, unspecified sort is, Vasubandhu argues, unnecessary to explain the phenomena. Here in verses 16 to 21, the phenomena at issue are not as of extended objects. Rather, it is the distinction between veridical and non-veridical perception, continuity between action and result, knowledge of, and interaction with, other minds that should require some extra-mental reality of some sort or another. Vasubandhu will try to show they do not.

This, in outline, is the strategy for a comprehensive argument for the claim that 'reality is thought-only [*vijñaptimatra*]': a kind of idealism, perhaps. Whether it is an adequate defence depends particularly on making good two claims: (i) all the phenomena really can be explained without appeal to mind-independent objects; and (ii) the mind-independent objects hypothesis is incoherent. In fact, as we shall see, Vasubandhu only aims to defend a weaker version of (ii), namely, that spatially extended and mutually related objects are incoherent. This may be relevant to how we understand his overall aims, for it allows the possibility that there may be *some sort* of mind-independent reality that is not flat-out incoherent (even if, according to (i), it need play no role in explaining experience). A great deal will depend upon what 'mind-independent' means by the end of the argument, which conclusion is only fully drawn out in the *Thirty Verses* and the *Treatise on the Three Natures*.

The negative arguments of the Twenty Verses

The direct evidence for mind-independent, spatially extended reality is simply that we experience the world that way. Further, we could not experience the world in this way, goes the objection (first raised at *VK* 2, above), unless it actually were like this. Vasubandhu imagines his opponent citing three respects in which experience of the sort we have is anchored in reality actually being that way: First, spatiotemporal locatedness is a feature of our experience, and impossible to explain without appeal to there being objects causing such experiences that are themselves spatiotemporally located; second, shared experience requires shared objects, and since these are not proper to any one person, they must exist independently of these persons; third, there is efficacy between experiences that holds in some cases and not in others, and this differential efficacy implies a difference in the mind-independence or otherwise of the objects so related.

In addressing these objections, Vasubandhu relies largely on appeals to cases where we do, in fact, have such experiences as of spatiotemporal, mind-independent objects, although there are no such objects present. In dreams (*VK* 3a) and hallucinations, for instance, we have experiences as of mind-independent objects, located spatially and temporally with respect to one another, without there in fact being any such thing there. In mass hallucinations, we all experience 'the same thing'; in fact, such perceptual experiences, grounded wholly in mental causes, can even prompt us to act, and to act in ways that have effects on future experiences counted as non-dreaming. Vasubandhu's own example is not what we would recognize as a likely mass hallucination, for it appeals to his contemporaries' popular tales of other realms of existence. In lower realms, where some have suffering inflicted upon them by others, we know the whole 'realm' must be jointly imagined by those suffering it, for those supposedly inflicting the harm cannot deserve to be there (*VK* 4b–5d). They must, therefore, not actually be there, but be collectively imagined by those who experience suffering 'inflicted' upon them. Similarly, such unfortunates may drink the very same water as you or I, but, owing to their distorted psychological state, they can only taste it as pus or excrement (*VK* 3b–c).

To show that perceptions as of physical objects can cause results even in the absence of such objects, Vasubandhu uses the monk-appropriate example of wet dreams (*VK* 3d–4a). We might as easily consider a sleepwalker, or someone acting under the influence of hallucinated experience. So neither shared nor solitary experience as of external objects located in specific places with respect to one another need be grounded in actual mind-independent objects in order to arise, and indeed to play its normal role in guiding action.

All Vasubandhu has done so far is show, by giving examples, that it *can* happen: there are cases where experiences of mind-independent, spatiotemporally located objects can arise, be shared and be efficacious in causing action, in the absence of any such objects as our experiences represent. Vasubandhu does not explain *how* it happens, what the causal mechanisms are.[15] But this is implicit in the original statement of the position being defended: if what exists is only consciousness, then the causes we must suppose in the absence of non-mental causes are mental ones. And this, indeed, is how one might naturally understand dreams: there are certain mental impressions and events, perceptions and desires, that set in motion the images and events that arise for us in dreams. The claim is carefully *not* that *karma* is exclusively responsible, for the mental causes may not be just intentions, and they may not be conveniently individuated according to distinct persons. Thus the claim that all experience is mental, and arises owing to exclusively mental causes, should not give rise to the perverse thought that, for each of my experiences, if only I introspected strenuously enough, I could identify *the one* desire, occurring earlier in *my own* mental stream, which is responsible for my experiencing just this now.

Indeed, there is never just one cause explaining events, and there is no reason to suppose that causation respects conventional boundaries drawn between persons. In fact, there is every reason to expect it will not. This is why Vasubandhu is able to meet worries that *vijñaptimatra* leads inevitably to solipsism, raised in verses 18–21, to which we shall return, below.

The positive arguments of the Twenty Verses

But Vasubandhu does not leave things there. Not only is there no good reason to posit extra-mental reality of the sort perceptual experience suggests, but there is good reason *not* to posit any such thing. The basic reason, explored in a variety of ways in the *Twenty Verses*, is that one cannot aggregate true atoms into perceptible objects with extension, shape and relation. Nor can one experience an atom. Nor can one have complex, mind-independent perceptible objects unless they are composed of mind-independent simples (here called *paramānu*). These true, partless 'atoms' are the *dharmas* of Abhidharma ontology, and it was already recognized that any logic that denied ontologically distinct reality to complex wholes at any level must deny it to them at every level, so that only absolute simples could ground the reality of anything complex.[16] But if extra-mental reality should be fundamentally constituted by simples, there is no way we could perceive it.

> An object of perception is neither one unit, nor several units, nor is it even an aggregate; so atoms cannot be demonstrated. (*VK* 11)

The first option is simple enough: whatever one perceives spatiotemporally, one can distinguish parts within it, even if only conceptually, even if it is as minimal a distinction as 'the left hand side vs. the right hand side'; and one cannot experience the whole without experiencing those parts. Something genuinely partless would have no shape or size or colour at all (even tonal colour, which itself is never simple), and so could not be perceived. If we cannot perceive one indivisible simple, however, then we cannot perceive several. It is equally impossible, says Vasubandhu, to perceive an aggregation of what cannot themselves be perceived.

Another reason we cannot perceive aggregations is that there cannot even *be* aggregations of simples. No genuine atoms could be related to one another spatially.

> If there is a simultaneous conjunction of six atoms in six directions, then the one atom comes to have six parts. For that which is the locus of one cannot be the locus of another.
> (*VK* 12a)

But an atom, by definition, is indivisible; it can have no parts. So atoms are not the sort of thing that *can* conjoin with one another.[17] Nor, by the same reasoning, could they even be spatially related to one another:

> [I]f there are such divisions as to directional dimensions [e.g. 'in front of', 'on the bottom'], how can the singleness of an atom, which partakes of such divisions, be logical? (*VK* 14a)

If atoms cannot be related spatially, neither can they collectively be opaque (or solid, one might add). Several simples incapable of taking up space, and so blocking what is behind it, cannot together take up space or block what is behind or beneath them:

> [H]ow could there be shade and blockage? (*VK* 14b)

> If there were no divisions as to directional dimensions in an atom, how could there be shade in one place, light in another, when the sun is rising? For there could be no other location for the atom where there would be no light. And how could there be an obstruction of one atom by another, if divisions as to directional dimensions are not accepted? For there would

> be no other part of an atom, where, through the arrival of another atom, there would be a collision with the other atom. And if there is no collision, then the whole aggregation of all the atoms would have the dimensions of only one atom.
> (*VK* 14b)

It is quite clear that these sorts of arguments against the very possibility and coherence of mind-independent reality are restricted in two ways: first, they target only *perceptible* mind-independent reality; but one might think that real mind-independent objects are not objects of sense-perception. A Platonist, for instance, will think that it is the categories and objects of intelligence that are given mind-independently. Second, Vasubandhu's arguments target only one account of mind-independent reality, namely, an atomist account. This latter might be one restriction too many, for it would follow that the arguments here offered – and the only arguments that extra-mental reality is positively incoherent – need only be taken seriously by realists offering an atomistic account of extra-mental reality.

Indeed, if we think of the *dharmas* central to Abhidharma ontology, it is quite likely that Vasubandhu has his old Vaibhāṣika and Sautrāntika *confrères* in his sights. For it is they who thought through the logic of atomism with such remarkable tenacity, discovering and exploring the implications of composition and partlessness. And it is, above all, other Buddhists who would have been unwilling to try to address these problems by admitting that "an aggregation of atoms is something different from the atoms themselves" (*VK* 14c). However, while the Abhidharmikas were the most consistent in their atomism, such a picture of extra-mental reality is by no means limited to them, and may indeed be hard to avoid. The Nyāya-Vaiśeṣika categorial metaphysics admitted both atomistic and non-atomistic simple substances, and familiar substances like elephants and coconuts were composites of these. Even a high rationalist like Leibniz recognizes the inexorable logic pushing towards atomism.[18]

So although Vasubandhu has shown the incoherence of just one account of the supposed nature of mind-independent reality, it is an account of the nature of perceptibles that is much more widely shared than Abhidharma Buddhism, and was even shared by their primary opponents. The burden is thus on the realist to offer some intelligible alternative account of extended objects – or else to show how atoms survive the criticisms brought.

There is one very prominent such attempt in Leibniz's successor, Kant. According to Kant's 'transcendental idealist/empirical realist' picture, extra-mental reality must be posited to explain the nature and possibility of the sorts of experiences we have; but while we can know there must be some such cause of our experiences, we cannot know anything about what it is *like*. For it is also a condition of our having sensible experience at all that, however things might exist in themselves, we experience them *as* spatiotemporal, or not at all. In so far as the causes of the content of our sensible experiences are not able to be represented *as* 'external', extended and unified individuals, they cannot be experienced by us. Yet our modes of experience, the conditions on which we have spatiotemporal experience, are not alone sufficient to account for the fact that there is any content to sensation at all, nor to account for its variability. By the fact that there is some way that objects appear to us, we know they must exist somehow or another, and in some way not conditioned by, or determined by, the fact that we experience them, or by our modes of possible experience. Thus, some such extra-mental cause is necessary; but what it is like apart from our modes of cognizing is epistemologically unavailable. What the necessary non-mental causes of our various sensible experience are like *in themselves*, as opposed to *as experienceable by us*, is beyond our ken. It is by retaining this robust principle of reality not conditioned by our experience that Kant remains a realist rather than becoming a metaphysical idealist, while fully recognizing that all our experiences are *also* conditioned by our available modes of experiencing and not only by the objects of experience.

Mind-independent reality is an unnecessary hypothesis, II

Vasubandhu cannot, of course, be faulted for failing to have an explicit reply to Kant's transcendental idealism. However, he comes very close to something like it in the verses that follow.[19]

There are at least three things that one might think require that we postulate some sort of mind-independent reality. It need not be extended, and let us even grant that it could not be; we cannot know the nature of this mind-independent reality, perhaps. Nevertheless, we must appeal to some such thing in order (i) to explain the knowledge of, and interaction with, other minds; (ii) to ground a distinction between veridical and non-veridical cognitions; and (iii), closely related, to distinguish that for which we are morally responsible from that for which we are not – indeed, even to preserve the coherence of the notion of responsibility.

Let us turn first to Vasubandhu's reply to the solipsism objection. In brief, the 'question of other minds', doubt about their existence or mutual interaction, cannot arise in a serious way on a metaphysical picture according to which distinctions among phenomena into 'this person' and 'that person' are only ever convenient measures of relative degree of causal relatedness in the first place. The question is not how various minds can interact, as if individuation of minds were prior. The question is rather how, in the manifold ceaseless dependent arising of events, divisions are made designating some as 'this person' and others as 'that person'. And the answer here is that there are no such divisions ultimately, but it is nonetheless convenient to draw such boundaries in certain ways, owing perhaps to density of connections and also to our aims being better served when we so distinguish things.

Thus I might consider: is there good evidence that the conscious events present to me, and recollectable by me now, do not exhaust the causal conditions required to explain my current experiences? Yes, the full causal explanation of current experiences does not seem available from within recollectable experiences, no matter how good my memory. Do I have good reason for dividing the hypothesized necessary complete causal conditions according to various qualitative experiences as of distinct human and other bodies? Yes, it is convenient and effective to regard things that way, even though these divisions and assignments shift, are partial and defeasible, and do not pick out any real division in nature. This is all there is to say about 'my' mind and 'other minds' and their interaction.

So if you hear me say something, what happens on a micro-level is that an intention to speak arises here (in 'me'); it causes further mental events that represent, or have content as of, my uttering intelligible sounds; the conditions are suitable for these mental events to give rise to further 'hearing'-type events – that is, they directly affect 'your' mental stream. The events that we represent to ourselves as 'acting on one another' are to be explained similarly: there are indeed causal links, we represent these links as bodies acting on one another, but that is just a way of representing the purely mental interacting events. Thus is a sheep 'killed', and someone rightly considered responsible for 'a certain modification' in the sheep-'aggregate-series' – for it is still in the malevolent intention of the sheep-killer that the wholesale disruption of the unfortunate sheep lies (*VK* 19).[20]

On this view, it may be not only permissible but actually *required* that we posit some mental events that it is in no wise convenient to attribute to any person at all. That is, not only do feeling-events, cognition-events and so on not inhere in or belong to a subject (Abhidharma *skandha* analysis of persons had already dispensed with that), but there may be some such events that do not belong, conventionally, within any person-constituting stream at all.[21] Such 'free-floating' mental events would explain, for instance, how it is that once the potter has filled his potting shed with freshly thrown pots and leaves them to dry, I might unwittingly stumble across the same shed, empty of sentient life, three hours later and have experiences as of freshly thrown pots.[22]

Obviously part of the explanation of my having pots-experiences now will appeal to the mental causes that brought me to stumble upon the shed, and enable me to have any spatiotemporal colour–shape experiences at all. But why suppose that the only conditions giving rise to an event within my mental stream now are to be found located somewhere among the mental events belonging in what is conveniently designated 'my' previous mental stream? Down that road lies solipsism. Instead we should draw on the way that your intention to speak may give rise to a hearing event in me, and model my seeing pots in the empty shed on that. The potter's intentions set in motion several chains of consequences, among them those events that are contributory causes to my seeing pots now in the shed. Such events would be 'free-floating' not in the sense that they do not inhere in a body – we have done away with extended bodies altogether, anyway; nor in the sense that they do not inhere in a mental substance – there never was any mental substance, and in that sense *all* mental events are 'untethered'. So the mental events set in motion by the potter that cause me, later and alone in the shed, to see pots are 'free-floating' in the sense that it is not convenient, customary or in any way useful to assign them either to the potter's mental stream, or to mine, or to anyone else's. This may have to do with their relative unconnectedness to other mental events. But the fact that is tracked here is a difference in degree, not in kind.[23]

This line of defence does not address the reasonable objection that the *vijñanavāda* leaves us without resources to distinguish between dream experience and veridical experience at all. The mind-independent reality hypothesis gives us that crucial touchstone or criterion by which to distinguish in principle between veridical and non-veridical experiences. Without it, the idealist must provide some other way of making good the distinction;[24] failure to provide a principle for distinguishing imagined from veridical experience is ordinarily taken as a decisive blow against an idealist theory. But the Buddhist idealist is no ordinary idealist. In the discussion of *Twenty Verses* 17c, Vasubandhu is happy to compare ordinary veridical experience to a dream; if we were truly awake to reality, we would realize that our everyday 'veridical' experiences were just as unreal as we now suppose dreams to be. Perhaps, indeed, this is precisely what he wants us to understand: there *is no substantial difference* between dreaming experience and waking experience.

But this bald willingness to dispense with what is normally thought to be a vital factor in the coherence of our epistemic practice does not let Vasubandhu off the hook entirely. Even if there is no such distinction, Vasubandhu must explain why this distinction is nevertheless so widely recognized, and so useful. When Vasubandhu goes even further (*VK* 18b), asserting that there is in fact no difference *in kind* between dreaming and waking experience, he offers instead a difference in intensity. This intensity has an effect on which events follow, so dreaming of killing a sheep does not in fact give rise to the sorts of mental events that a 'waking' intention to kill a sheep does (*VK* 18–19). This is not because the latter intention is 'real' and the former 'only dreamed'. Both are intentions in the very same way; but the dream-intention is significantly weaker, and so has radically less potency in setting other events into motion.

Consider it this way: the mental event constituting a dream-sheep is relatively isolated, and not causally connected to many other mental events, past, present and future. Thus the mental event that is my killing that sheep has very little effect on other events. Notice that it may well have some consequences on my own future mental states: dreaming of murder probably does affect me somehow, even in what I would call my 'waking' states. Vasubandhu does not say that it has *no* effects, but only that it has so many fewer, in virtue of it not being an action performed with clarity and general alertness, that it is not something conventional morality deems as being within its purview. Contrast that with the killing of a real sheep. The disruption of that sheep-constituting mental event has serious consequences, for it is tightly embedded within a vast and complex web of other mental events, all of which will be disrupted and eliminated. Such an event, particularly when caused by explicit and clear intentions, are significant enough to be within the domain of morality, and significant enough to have a marked consequence on my own future mental states.

As in our speculative discussion of personal and impersonal mental events, Vasubandhu here explicitly responds by replacing a difference in kind with a difference in degree. There is no difference in kind between waking and dreaming states; all mental states are caused exclusively by other mental states, and there are no experiences of what is non-mental. Nevertheless, we can retain the correctness of our usual presumption that one is not guilty of a dreamt murder (but is guilty of a 'waking' one) by pointing out the considerably diminished intentional force and consequences of those mental events we commonly designate as 'dreaming'.

In sum, our starting-point is not with distinct mental substances in which mental qualities or acts differentially inhere; our starting-point is not with individuals at all. And so we do not have to explain, after the fact as it were, how two such minds could interact or be confident of their evidence for the existence of each other. There are momentary mental events with distinguishable content, arising in a kind determined by the overall conditions in which they arise: that is, by the other mental events occurring. Which of these conditioning mental events or consequent mental events belongs to you or to me is a matter of drawing convenient lines, not discerning nature's lines. But we have as good evidence as we could wish that there are mental events other than those immediately present here now: namely, they are necessary for a complete explanation of the currently occurring mental impressions. The difference between veridical and non-veridical is again a conventional and useful distinction, grounded in difference in *degree* of causal integratedness, and not in any difference in kind.

It should be clear by now that Vasubandhu's aim here is not mere scepticism. If the arguments are good, they should show rather more than that we lack certainty about the nature of the causes of our experiences. They show that we (so far) lack good reason to posit non-mental causes; appeal to mental causes suffices. Direct evidence turns out not to speak decisively in favour of mind-independent objects; indirect evidence does not force us to draw the realist conclusion. Until there are new and better arguments, then, it would be intellectually disreputable to suppose there were such spatially extended objects, and gratuitous to postulate any other sort of mind-independent reality. Without some better reason than 'because my cognitions represent it that way', adopting the mind-independent objects hypothesis would be like appealing to fairies as causal agents when one can point to nothing that they cause, and one has available a coherent non-fairy-ontology, fully adequate to the task of explaining the phenomena. Although this may not yet constitute a proof that there are no such things as fairies – proving a non-existence takes a special kind of argument, something that would show the incoherence of any conception of mind-independence – it does mean that such belief would be, in an important sense, *irrational* as well as intellectually irresponsible.

Maintaining belief in non-mental reality would require an argument of one of two kinds. Either one must show that Vasubandhu's arguments here are no good: they do not show what he claims and, specifically, he has not in fact accounted for the phenomena without appeal to extra-mental reality. (For instance, one might ask – as Bhāviveka will in fact ask – whether our experiences *as if* of spatiotemporally organized phenomena would be possible if one had *never* had experience of actual spatiotemporally organized phenomena. One might, alternatively, ask whether moral responsibility and personal interaction has indeed been satisfactorily accounted for by Vasubandhu.) Or, one might instead offer an alternative metaphysical picture, a realist one, and show how the phenomena are *better* explained on this view, where the real work at issue will be to identify what makes an explanation a better one. There is space left open for this latter alternative because, although Vasubandhu has arguments against the coherence of extended extra-mental objects, he does not argue that the very notion of extra-mental reality, on any description, is incoherent. About the latter, he argues only that it is unnecessary.

Thus, those who would want to minimize Vasubandhu's conclusions, likening his position to the modest realism of Kant, emphasizing only that none of our actual experiences are devoid of 'conceptualization', miss the crucial radicalism of the *Twenty Verses.*[25] Such a view fails to take seriously the intent of the arguments against spatial extension and relation in the middle of the *Twenty Verses*. And, more importantly, such minimizing fails to acknowledge the radical transformation Vasubandhu thought his arguments should make us undergo. In the *Thirty Verses*, he speaks of a "revolution at the basis"[26] – a common Yogācāra notion[27] – a fundamental reorientation of our thinking. Exactly what this revolution consists in and amounts to is only hinted at in the *Twenty Verses*, in the occasional enigmatic aside about the 'real self' and the knowledge proper to Buddhas. But whatever the 'revolution at the basis' is, the modest Kantian account does not even *want* to achieve this. Kant's 'Copernican revolution' is for philosophers only.

This is related to another stark contrast between Kant and Vasubandhu, or indeed any Buddhist, over the possibility of experiencing non-conceptual reality. While both are at pains to indicate the ways and extent to which our conceptual activity insinuates itself into our experience, only Kant thinks this is both necessary and innocuous. For most Buddhists, this is not at all innocuous, and indeed our aim is to strip away the conceptualizing that distorts our perceptions, leaving us, on the Yogācāra view, with a direct experience of ultimate reality.

While the arguments Vasubandhu offers in the *Twenty Verses* seem, indeed, to lead to what should properly be called a kind of idealism, the view he arrives at is not liable to some of the standard problems of idealism with which we might be familiar. Distinguishing veridical and non-veridical experience – a besetting problem if there is no mind-independent reality to ground that distinction – is not a problem for Vasubandhu; on his view, there is no difference. At least, there is no difference in kind. There is what works and what does not work, and this criterion depends on our aims. Changing our ambitions is where the important work is done, not primarily in replacing false beliefs with true ones.

Nor is solipsism a worry for a Buddhist idealist, for according to the Buddhist, there never were distinct substances that then had to interact and give evidence for their existence. Similarly, Buddhist idealism introduces no special worry about enduring objects: you don't like that the tree in the quad needs God's oversight to persist over time? Yogācāra, like all Buddhism, does not suppose there was ever identity, in the first place, but only continuity. Neither does eliminating mind-independent entities threaten to eliminate morally significant actions: those who are no friend of transcendental idealism will appreciate that there is no need to posit, or identify oneself with positing, some reality that must necessarily remain unknown to us in order to conceive of ourselves as moral agents.

So if one is going to be an idealist, it matters very much how one gets to one's idealism: whether through a critique of material substance, as George Berkeley does, or through a critique of the very notion of substance, as the Buddhist does; whether by insisting on the consequences of substantialist metaphysics, like Berkeley, by turning metaphysics into epistemology, as Kant does, or by dropping substance-property metaphysics altogether, as the Buddhist does.

Is there, according to Vasubandhu, anything existing in the last analysis that is not mental – not a mental event, nor a substance or property of the same? If the answer is yes, it will only be in a very unexpected way – through a distinction between ultimate and conventional reality – and it will have very little to do with attempts to account for the phenomena.[28]

The positive picture: the *Thirty Verses* and the *Treatise on the Three Natures*

Identifying Yogācāra as a particular form of idealism is not the end of the story. Vasubandhu, remember, is in the business of ending suffering. The question will be whether reality so understood leaves us space for uprooting suffering, and whether so understanding reality is at least part – perhaps the whole – of that process of uprooting. To that end, merely recognizing reality as 'cognitions only' does not yet go far enough.

Working through the arguments of the *Twenty Verses* may radically challenge our ordinary conceptions of things. Yet this may still leave all ordinary practice in place. After all, discovering that all my experiences of physically extended reality are constituted of the experiences themselves, and not causally related to the mind-external objects they represent in their content, does not change the fact that experiences of bumping against tables cause pain, and so on. So recognizing reality as 'cognitions only', as we have done in the *Twenty Verses*, does not yet get us the 'revolution at the basis' of our experience that Vasubandhu promises from Yogācāra. For this one must turn to elaborations of what these critical arguments should leave us with.

From two realities to three 'natures' (svabhāva) *– and three 'non-natures'* (niṣvabhāva)

According to the *Treatise on the Three Natures* (*Tri-Svabhāva-Nirdeśa*) and the *Thirty Verses* (*Triṃśikā-Kārikā*), representations of a mind-independent, spatially extended reality are fabricated (constructed and illusory, *kalpita, TSN* 1a; *parikalpita, TK* 20c), with respect to their representational content. The basic form of this illusion can be described as a mistaken distinction between 'self' and 'other': between perception and object of perception, whether at a confused, complex level ('me', as opposed to 'that table') or at the precise, particular level ('this table-perception here', as opposed to 'the table there being perceived').

The complementary implication, and the constructive lesson of the *Twenty Verses*, is that understanding truly the nature of our cognitions means understanding them *as* cognitions: recognizing that they, and all the causes we can infer from them and their effects, are not mind-independent spatially extended entities, but are instead more events of the same kind.

Reality on Vasubandhu's version of idealism consists in ceaseless series of mental events differentiated, and differential in their efficacy, according to their kind and content. Their specific, varying content depends upon preceding conditions, that is, upon the varying content of other mental states, themselves likewise dependent. For this reason, Vasubandhu says that the nature of all these is 'dependence on other' (*parantra, TSN* 1a; other-dependent nature, *parantasvabhāva, TK* 21a). That is the sort of thing they are, their way of being, so to speak.

Contrasting and relating the two 'natures', Vasubandhu writes:

> Whatever range of events is discriminated by whatever discrimination is just the constructed nature [*svabhāva*], and it isn't really to be found. The dependent nature, on the other hand, is the discrimination which arises from conditions.
>
> (*TK* 20a–21b[29])

The more succinct formulation of the *Treatise on the Three Natures* brings out the inseparability of the two natures: "That which appears is the interdependent; 'how it appears' is the constructed" (*TSN* 2a–b).

Thus we have a contrast between the ostensible objects of such cognitions ('this table', 'the cat'), and the cognitions whose content they are ('table-thought', 'cat-seeing'). The former are misleadingly presented to consciousness as if mind-independent. *As* 'tables' and 'cats', in the ordinary senses, the objects of everyday experience are wholly unreal, without those experiences thereby being wholly untrue. They are not untrue because they are indeed the content of dependently arisen mental events, which arise owing to suitable causes and conditions: there really is an event of table-thinking or cat-seeing occurring, whose nature as a mental event depends upon other such events.

We might think of the description Plato gives of ordinary life in Book VII of the *Republic*: we are all engrossed in watching shadows of objects cast upon a wall, convinced, without even putting the question, that the shadows are all there is – not shadows *of* anything at all, but the very things themselves. But however mistaken and unreflective we might be about their ontological nature, we perceive nevertheless that there is an order among these phenomena; there are patterns in events, and we can learn these, and become better and worse at discerning and predicting these patterns. And there is some sense in which the person who anticipates that the sprout follows the seed, rather than the seed the sprout, is *correct*, even while being fundamentally mistaken about what sprout and seed actually are. Similarly with Vasubandhu's 'fabricated' nature: there is a real standard of correctness in such uninformed and misleading judgements (e.g. 'There is a brown table') because this fabricated reality is the mistaken construal of genuinely causally interdependent mental phenomena.

'Constructed' or 'fabricated nature' and 'other-dependent nature' are not, then, two different classes of beings. Rather, these two different 'natures' can be two different ways of grasping the same thing: the misleading realist way, or the more accurate idealist way. If all Vasubandhu wanted was to point out something that all phenomena have in common, he could as well have observed that they are all mental events. This is as far as the *Twenty Verses* takes us. Distinguishing two 'natures' (*svabhāva*) in the *Treatise on the Three Natures* and in the *Thirty Verses*[30] goes a step further by indicating something of their character. Being 'dependent upon other' should capture how they exist, or the kind of existence they have; cognitions exist dependently, and it is of their very nature to be thus dependent. Their representational content as of extra-mental reality exists *constructedly*. The constructed content, however, is not an item distinct from the other-dependent mental event distinguished from others by this particular fabricated content.

Each experience thus has two natures, 'fabricated' and 'other-dependent'. This may look like a Madhyamaka version of the distinction between conventional and ultimate reality, which realities are co-occurring and mutually implicating. This impression would be heightened by the care with which Vasubandhu insists, in the *Thirty Verses*, that each of these natures is also without nature, *niṣvabhāva*, in their respective ways.

> The three different kinds of absence of nature [*niṣvabhāva*] in the three different kinds of nature: The first is without nature through its character itself; but the second, because of its non-independence; and the third *is* absence of *svabhāva*.
>
> (*TK* 23c–24d)

It is the nature of the 'constructed' to lack the sort of reality it presents itself as having, which includes lacking any kind of mind-independence; this is its proper sort of 'emptiness', or lack-of-essence. What is 'other-dependent' is without essence, or nature, in a different way. Much like Nāgārjuna's *sunyāta*, the *niṣvabhāva* of dependent nature consists precisely in its other-dependency. Mental events themselves are dependent for their nature and existence, and thus do not have their nature 'in themselves', intrinsically, or independently.

Such a description of the nature of mental phenomena (now including all phenomena) acknowledges Nāgārjuna's critique of essentialism and his interpretation of dependent origination: there is a way in which the fact that things arise dependently infects the kind of reality they can be thought to have, and makes problematic the individuateability of phenomenal experience. Talk of *dharmas* as if they were discrete mental moments is a convenient approximation, but inevitably disregards their basic nature as implicated in the quality or characteristics of others. This is *their* proper 'lack of nature', the species of 'emptiness' proper to mutually dependent mental processes constituting our experience.

But here is where the Yogācāra lays claim to being the *third* turning of the wheel of Dharma. To suppose this mutual muddled-togetherness of dependent-origination-as-lack-of-essence exhausts what can be said about reality does not attend sufficiently to what has been uncovered by this analysis of reality. This is where Nāgārjuna goes wrong, and his Mādhyamika ends up a sort of nihilism in spite of itself. This 'other-dependent' nature that Nāgārjuna stresses so keenly is in fact an expression of yet another, more refined, self–other illusion, and so is firmly conceptual and *not* ultimate reality. There is, Vasubandhu claims, a third 'nature', which is also 'natureless' in its own distinctive way. This is 'perfected' or 'consummate' nature. It is natureless (*niṣvabhāva*) by way of being undifferentiated and without characteristics: "It is the ultimate truth of all events, and so it is 'suchness', too, since it is just so all the time" (*TK* 25a–c). And yet, in spite of its undifferentiatedness, it is not what a Madhyamaka would call 'empty', for it is not *dependent* for its nature – or naturelessness – on anything else.

Of course, if consummate nature is undifferentiated and different from other-dependent nature – that is to say, from all our experiences – it will necessarily be difficult to get a grip on just what this consummate nature is supposed to be. This elusiveness, together with the refusal to grant that consummate nature was *dependent*, even though it is without intrinsic nature, led Buddhist opponents of the Yogācāra to accuse Vasubandhu of thus surreptitiously reintroducing Self into the foundation of reality – and not without good reason.[31] As we saw, Vasubandhu's commentary on the *Twenty Verses* makes oblique reference to some unconditioned reality, calling it the ungraspable self (*anabhilapyenātman;* v. 10c and v. 21b).

What, then, is pushing Vasubandhu to make the claim that there is this 'perfected' nature, as well as this other-dependent and fabricated nature of experiences? What exactly *is* the claim? And can we acquit him of the charge – which will dog Yogācāra in the centuries to come, pressed especially by the Mādhyamika Candrakīrti – that he has reasserted the Self that the Buddha so insistently rejected?

Consummate nature: phenomenology as metaphysics

Just as the Yogācāra styles itself the 'third turning', after Abhidharma and Madhyamaka, so Vasubandhu is not happy with merely two natures, 'constructed' and 'other-dependent'. On a Madhyamaka account these two look very much like conventional reality and ultimate reality – the 'emptiness' that is the ultimate nature of all things just is their other-dependence; while, not separate from that, conventional reality is all these very same other-dependent beings, not considered as such but rather, taken as each is misleadingly conceived, as a distinct identifiable thing. According to Vasubandhu, these mutually defined 'constructed' and 'other-dependent' natures remain within conventional reality, yet point to the still unrecognized nature of ultimate reality.

If I attend properly to my experiences, I will realize that they neither are, nor imply, nor are of a mind-independent, spatiotemporal reality. There are just the manifold cognitions. Attend to *these*, as such, and we would notice that, amid the complex, shifting patterns of mutual dependency, there is, after all, a constant – besides their other-dependency. If we practise overcoming objections to eliminating *rūpa dharmas* from our ontology, the process of thinking through the revised Yogācāra picture of what is actually happening in ordinary, everyday experience reveals a recurring pattern. Whatever arises is always a complementary and mutually exclusive pair of 'mode of cognition' (the other-dependent mental events) and 'content of cognition' (out of which fabricated reality is fabricated). These might be determined in any countless number of ways, with respect to their content and with respect to mode. But it is always the case that wherever there is the one there is the other associated with it, and excluded by it. However various, experienced reality yet has a common structure: all moments have a mode of awareness – volition, say, cognition, perception, bare awareness; and they all have some content differentiated from and related to that mode – the colour perceived, the object desired, the proposition thought. All of reality is double-sided, the side of one kind (call it 'mode of cognition') implying the side of the other kind (call it the 'object' or 'content of cognition').

This might be seen as a sort of Cartesian point, although much more precise and modest than Descartes' 'I am'. Wherever any perception, cognition, feeling, emotion or volition arises, there must likewise be some mode of awareness. Consciousness is implied by anything that could be evidence – distorting or otherwise – for anything else. It is incontrovertible bedrock. For, where that fails, so does everything else, and indeed the very possibility of anything else. And wherever there is a mode of awareness, there is that of which it is aware: logically distinct from it, even if that object is a qualitative blank or placeholder. This mutual implication of mode and content of cognition is epistemologically as well as metaphysically incontrovertible. No one maintaining any theory of the nature of reality, or none at all, can deny that all their experiences are also, whatever else they may be, modes or instances of awareness.

This pervasive pattern went unnoticed by Nāgārjuna, who attended only to the pervasive similarity ('emptiness', other-dependence) and infinite diversity of constructed or conceptual reality. And so Mādhyamikas also miss something of the logical structure of reality. If mode of cognition logically implies contents, and vice versa, we cannot suppose that there are – at a fundamental level – bits of modes of cognition flying about, and bits of contents, which then somehow get married up together. Ontologically, if they are not different aspects of the very same thing, then we would need some further explanation of how mode of cognition gets connected to content: what the connector is and why it cannot go wrong. But if these complementary pairs are, in one sense, not *pairs* at all, but logically entailing aspects of a single thing, this means there must be something capable of differentiating into infinitely varied complementary pairings, without itself actually being – essentially, in its own nature – either. All reality is double-sided, yet that which has these sides cannot have either side as *its* nature.

And this is how Vasubandhu gets to the 'third nature' claim.[32] Attending carefully to what experiences are actually like, and refusing to rest with a mere rejection of mind-independent reality, Yogācāra has been regarded as primarily a sort of phenomenology. And this seems a correct description of its priorities, all the more so as such attending should have the practical effect of transforming the mental stream, and this is why we do it. Still, this does not exempt Yogācārins from having metaphysical interests and commitments. Even phenomenology can imply metaphysics – especially in order to support the Yogācāra contention that such phenomenological exercises will result in a recognition of ultimate reality that is at once the unblemished realization of such reality.[33] Vasubandhu calls this third *svabhāva* 'consummate' or 'perfected' inasmuch as it is undistorted or unaffected in its nature by any conceptualizing activity, and inasmuch as it is not dependent for its being on any of the differentiated other-dependent events that arise out of it.

The ultimate determinable

We are, I think, in the area of the mythical Aristotelian 'prime matter', and the 'receptacle' of Plato's *Timaeus*.[34] Vasubandhu's 'perfected nature', or third mode of being is the 'ultimate determinable': that which becomes all things by virtue of not being, in itself, anything. Its 'nature' is to lack any determinate nature, and thus it grounds the possibility of varied and incompatible differentiations, without determining any.

The dependently arising, specifically informed moments of consciousness (other-dependent nature) are just so many determinations of the ultimate determinable, which we could perhaps think of as consciousness, except that this term is already in service to indicate one of the differentiated content-bearing modes, or determinations of ultimate reality.[35] More precisely, 'subject' and 'object (of perception)' are themselves the primary determinations of the ultimate determinable, for which we have and can have (by the nature of the case) no words. For words differentiate; if they do not do that, they are meaningless. But if they *do* differentiate, then they necessarily distort any description of what is wholly undifferentiated. This is the very strict sense in which perfected nature is 'inconceivable' (*TK* 30a).

Because it lacks determinate characteristics of any kind, it therefore lacks individuation and substantiality.[36] It is not a *stuff* underlying. It is, rather, the potential or possibility of specific determinations arising. Yogācāra would agree it is not a substance, nor an individual, in Aristotle's sense, nor even in the Buddhist sense: this is why it too is empty of *svabhāva* (without essence) and non-dual ("consummate nature exists through non-duality, but is simply the non-being of 'two'"; *TSN* 13a–b), without internal distinction or differentiation. The difference is, for the Yogācāra Buddhist, this does not count against its being real, and indeed *ultimately* real.

Again, we cannot say that this ultimate determinable is consciousness, or that its two primary (most proximate) determinations are determinations *of consciousness,* if we take consciousness as an item-event that can take content differentiable from the having of content (*TK* 26–7). And changing words here will not help. It is not that we could perhaps exchange 'awareness' for 'consciousness' or some other cognitive vocabulary. All our words for any such states imply, or open up, logical space for an *object* of awareness, the *content* of cognition, the various qualitative variations that distinguish moments of awareness from each other, not by reference to their quality as awareness, for that is what they have in common.[37]

Although we can have no words to assert what consummate nature positively *is,* we need not be utterly tongue-tied, for it is informative to consider what the determinations of a determinable are. The most proximate determinations of the ultimate determinable are 'self' and 'other' manifested as 'awareness of' and 'content of awareness' – form and content of experience. There are countless determinations of these pairings, distinguished from one another by their determinate mode–content pair, and dependent upon each other for their arising as 'this now'. Moreover, when we consider the related three natures as exercises of transformation, first from naive experience, then to appreciation of mutually causing mental events, and finally to the constant ground (*TK* 30b) of such events – as, indeed, Vasubandhu presents them – the final transformation cannot bring about some *non*-mental reality.

> When consciousness does not apprehend any object-of-consciousness, it is situated in consciousness-only; for with the non-being of an object apprehended there is no apprehension of it. It is without *citta,* without apprehension, and it is super-mundane knowledge; it is revolution at the basis.
>
> (*TK* 28a–29c)

Thus, while we have – and can have – no word for the non-duality of subject–object, the fact that *just these* are the modes of determination of that non-duality, and that *just these* are the transformations at issue, nevertheless gestures towards its nature. It is that which bifurcates into mode of cognition/content of cognition, logically prior to the particular determinations these pairs might take.

But is it Self?

Is this megalomaniacal monism? Has Vasubandhu, as Candrakīrti will later contend, simply re-introduced 'self' at the foundation of reality?

On the one hand, no. The ultimate determinable meets the criterion of Nāgārjuna's emptiness of having no determinate characteristic of its own, in virtue of the thing it is. It is *niḥsvabhāva*: without essence. Yet, on the other hand, it is not dependent. It does not rely on anything apart from itself for its lack of determining characteristic or 'nature'. It cannot be 'empty' in Nāgārjuna's sense, because its utter undifferentiatedness is not dependent upon other.[38]

Does this independence make Vasubandhu's 'consummate nature' a 'self'? Since self has long since travelled far from its primary meaning as a 'personal self', the answer to the question can be determined only by the answer to the pragmatic question: does it lend itself to 'clinging', to attachment? Is it the sort of thing one might fasten upon, and construct a vexed, confused and distressing emotional life around? And to that, I think, the answer is no.

Regarding consummate nature so understood, it is, importantly, impossible to think 'I am that', as the Vedic philosophers would have us do. This is for two reasons. First, in practice, this is because the process of coming to understand the metaphysical picture has been simultaneously a process of letting go of the very question and of the impulse to identify anything as 'I'. The impulse to suppose there might be an 'I', identified with anything or qualified by anything at all, has been thwarted at every turn, and remorselessly, without holding out any pretence of a prospect that we might finally be able to identify with *something* so long as we give up on enough of the ordinary objects of identification. One would not say 'I am that', with respect to Vasubandhu's 'consummate nature', but not because one recognized instead that 'I am *not* that'. Neither is true; but this is because 'I am' gets no foothold here.

Second, the psychological practice has theoretical underpinnings: first, in the process of understanding Abhidharma trope-theory; and second, in thinking through how a Buddhist idealism can answer objections about solipsism, interacting persons, and so on; and finally, through considering carefully what this actually leaves us with. Eliminating substance-property ontology from the ground up takes away any sense one could give to the notion of identifying *oneself*; first this is dissolved into a fluctuating 'many' by the Abhidharma philosophers, and then, with Nāgārjuna's attention to the implications of dependent origination, the individuation necessary for identification is no longer secure at any level. Moreover, that with which we might have identified 'ourselves' is itself no individual, nothing that can be grasped. Like Aristotelian 'prime matter' and the receptacle of Plato's *Timaeus*, it has no determinate qualities. It therefore cannot be the object of self-directed desires, or 'I-thinking'; nor can it ground self-affirming striving or appropriation. It is of such a kind that nothing can belong properly to it *as such*: everything belongs equally, nothing belongs in particular. Seeing, through attention to 'cognitions-only' reality, that even distinguishing between the activity of cognition and the content is an artificial contrivance, and does not identify absolute articulations of reality, one loses one of the few remaining grounds for a self–other distinction, disrupting any sense that we might ever get a grip on some 'that' with which 'we' are identical.

In short the ultimate determinable cannot be a bearer of identity, and nor can coming to understand it in the progressive way that we do – through undermining successively rarefied forms of substantialist thinking – leave us within the conceptual space where deploying concepts such as 'I' and is-identity can gain traction.[39]

And in practice?

This may acquit Vasubandhu of the charge that he has reintroduced self-oriented thinking – a substantial Self – at the most fundamental level. Can he, however, do any better than Nāgārjuna at showing how understanding reality as he recommends is beneficial – will improve my soul, and ameliorate suffering?

The wholly undifferentiated ultimate determinable is not a hypothetical posit or a mystical claim; it is what one arrives at by considering the interrelated, dependently arising pairs of 'mode of cognition'–'cognitive content'. Arriving there in this way implies a distinctive perspective on our everyday experiences, radically different from the ordinary one. This perspective on our experiences, which acknowledges them as both dependently arising *and* misleadingly dual, transforms those very experiences. They are not just mutually dependent, but are themselves artificial and transient distinctions of what by its nature has no differentiations.

Contrast the Mādhyamika's claim that the sheer possibility for such interdependent processes is itself dependent, and there is no reality but the other-dependent. This claim is not just gratuitous, and perhaps barely meaningful, but also dangerously quietistic. Supposing we must make such a claim will cause us to miss the nature of ultimate reality; we will dwell instead in the recognition of dependent arising that leaves everything in its place (conventional reality, remember, is ultimate reality, so nothing needs to change nor can), and offers no transformational insight into the nature of that experience.

Recognizing ultimate reality does not just matter because truth matters. Recognizing reality connects us to reality; in fact, it is the only such connection that is not at the same time a separation from it. The view Vasubandhu sets out offers a distinctive aim: to know reality and *thereby* to make it real. What is thereby made real is a non-dual state; it cannot even be called non-conceptual awareness, for that implies an awareness that has no thing as its content. But it is not awareness-*of* at all, not even awareness of emptiness. It is an undifferentiated event prior to any distinction between subject and object/content. Realizing this state presents the transformational perspective on the infinite differentiability, which we might recognize as our emotions, perceptions and all the rest of what constitute *saṃsāra*. We see them as what they are and, so seeing them, we recognize that while they are suffering *we* are not – there is no 'we'; and while they are suffering, impermanent and vulnerable, they are not ultimately real and neither is their suffering.

Vasubandhu offers a different diagnosis of just *what* it is in self-thinking (thinking within a metaphysics or categories of self) that does the damage, and sets the cycle of suffering in motion. Nāgārjuna seems to think that problems come – attachment arises – owing to supposing things have stable and well-defined natures. Supposing there are such things leads to attachment because it offers the opportunity of *something* to get attached *to*.

Vasubandhu sees it differently. The damage done by thinking in terms of 'self' starts with the drawing of lines, with the distinguishing between two things. As soon as there is a distinction there is the opportunity to identify with one side of the distinction, and thereby to dis-identify with the other. If I distinguish between persons, one is me and the others are not; if I distinguish between mental and physical, the one is me and the other is not; if I distinguish between mode of cognition and object of cognition, that too allows me to identify with one and thus to distinguish myself from the other – if only in a very rarefied way. (I am, of course, the *subject* of my cognitions, not their content.)

If, however, I recognize that ultimately these two are themselves not distinct from one another, then there is nothing left whereby to distinguish myself by contrast with what I am not. The *activity* of identifying is dissolved, fundamentally. And this is how one roots out the very possibility for attachment from the basis.

EIGHT

The long sixth to seventh century: epistemology as ethics

Vasubandhu really put the cat among the pigeons. Orthodox Vaibhāṣikas, like his near contemporary Saṅghabhadra, devoted themselves to disproving Vasubandhu's Sautrāntika innovations in Abhidharma, possibly with some success.[1] The Yogācārins were bursting with new energy, insisting that we focus on the mental nature of all *dharmas* in order to realize the ungraspable ultimate reality that this implies. And the Mādhyamikas, meanwhile, previously largely quiescent intellectually, are roused into a defence of their version of emptiness over the Yogācāra alternative. Nāgārjuna's close successor, Āryadeva, does not seem to have troubled the intellectual waters much. But when Buddhapālita writes his commentary on the *Mūlamadhyamaka Kārikā* at the beginning of the sixth century CE, he unleashes a furore of Madhyamaka activity, igniting disputes that carried on into Tibet and up to today.

Within all this metaphysical controversy, there are at least two distinct pressures towards epistemology. First, the contested claims about ultimate reality, or the distinctions and related natures of conventional and ultimate reality, become easily converted into disputes about what grounds one has for one's position, and then over what count as good grounds at all. This pressure towards epistemology comes not just from inter-Buddhist dispute, but also from the broader intellectual context. Non-Buddhists had not been idle in the face of the proliferation and refinement of Buddhist views. The intellectual world of India was a dynamic and contested space. Arguments were meant to give reasons to those not already persuaded. Debates were public, and had consequences. Clever debaters discovered all manner of sophistical argumentative tricks, giving birth inevitably to a systematic study of the distinction between real and merely apparent reasons and arguments, or inferences.[2] This is in the interests of all parties to debate, for no argumentative trickery can be kept to oneself and used only for one's own cause. As soon as one uses a sophistical trick, it becomes common property and may well be taken up by the opponent. In a philosophical context in which the most basic metaphysical claims are contested, articulating and agreeing valid modes of reasoning was critical.

There is a second pressure towards epistemology from within Buddhism itself. Buddhist thought emphasizes constantly attending to *how we experience things*: a sort of phenomenological inquiry, perhaps, but with a particular bent towards exposing how our conceptual activity distorts or constructs or reveals the true nature of things. Since the claim is that there is some real nature of things to be experienced – or, there are correct and incorrect ways of taking our experiences and the world they represent – and since this is in fact the goal and claim of the Buddhist view, no Buddhist can rest with a mere phenomenology divorced from truth-claims.[3]

Shape-changing Vasubandhu's most fitting intellectual successor was Diṅnāga (fl. early sixth century CE). *The* Buddhist 'logician', hailed for breaking significantly new ground in Indian epistemology and logic as a whole, Diṅnāga cannot be pinned down precisely as Sautrāntika or Yogācāra. Taking on board Vasubandhu's trenchant critique, Diṅnāga largely brackets questions of ontology – in particular, as to the reality or otherwise of mind-independent objects – and attends strictly to the objects we know we have available to us: the contents of our experiences. These, he says, come in two kinds, each with their proper mode of cognition: one is particulars, which bear an uncanny resemblance to Vasubandhu's 'consummate nature', and are available through perception; the other is generalities, generated by conceptualizing. One of the persistent questions, for Diṅnāga and for Dharmakīrti who came after him, was how these two relate. If these are, one way or another, all that we have available to us, then we must attend to how we might best get on with these. But how do we understand and deploy the contents of experience so as to move forwards on the path to enlightenment? The philosophy of mind or cognition that Diṅnāga offers will be set out in §I, together with his account of the corresponding 'objects' (or contents) of experience; his account of reasoning follows in §II. The difficulty of how concepts can be validated by, generated from, or in any way related to an ultimate reality that is itself non-conceptual will occupy us in §IV and §V.

With Vasubandhu's transition from most trenchant Abhidharmika to clearer of the intellectual ground for Yogācāra, we have very little innovative Buddhist philosophy coming from classic Abhidharma, even if Diṅnāga's own position between these two is somewhat indeterminate.[4] The Mādhyamikas, however, were not quiescent in the face of Yogācāra developments, and in the fifth to sixth centuries CE a variety of articulations of Nāgārjuna's Middle Way were offered, competing with each other, but especially competing with the Yogācārins for the claim to offer the best interpretation of the Buddha's teaching, as understood by the Mahāyāna. The Yogācārin's refusal to eliminate all asymmetry from their understanding of ultimate reality with respect to conventional reality led Mādhyamikas to charge them with holding on to a subtle form of self. Bhāviveka, a wide-ranging intellectual whose corpus has largely been lost or neglected, offered a version of the Middle Way that allowed a Mādhyamika to avail herself of the full range of logical tools developed by Diṅnāga in order to articulate and advocate the Madhyamaka view.[5] Candrakīrti, for his part, wishes to rehabilitate the conventional by another means, emphasizing the emptiness of emptiness: the inescapability of our necessarily inadequate concepts. But how and whether Mādhyamikas can themselves avoid the same charge they level against Yogācārins, and yet articulate a coherent position which also escapes the ever-looming charge of 'nihilism', was a matter of controversy among Mādhyamikas, and will be treated in §III. Finally, §VI considers one Mādhyamika's attempt to unite practical and theoretical developments so as to escape the dangers of nihilism and quietism.

I. Perception and conception: the changing face of ultimate reality

Vasubandhu's anti-atomist arguments leave the well-meaning Buddhist in an awkward position. Although he argues for a metaphysical conclusion – about the possible and impossible ways things may actually exist – some of his arguments for the conclusions are epistemological. We can *perceive* neither simples, nor complexes of simples, nor wholes (*VK* 11). This is fully in keeping with the pan-Indic *pramāṇa* tradition, according to which any knowledge claim must be able to be substantiated by some account of how it can come to be known, a *pramāṇa* being, ordinarily, a means of (or instrument for) correct cognition. This is also fully in keeping with the general Buddhist attention to our psychological states and how we get into them, and it gives the *Twenty Verses* and other works a distinctly phenomenological aspect.

But calling the arguments phenomenological offers no escape from the implications lying all too near to the surface of Vasubandhu's atomist critique. If *physical* atoms, simples, can neither be directly perceived nor ground the experience of complex wholes, then the same ought to apply to *all* purported 'atoms' of experience: feelings, desires, perceptions, thoughts. Our mental life can no more be built out of fundamental simples than can the physical world. Just as our apparent experiences of physical, mind-independent reality must be constructed by our way of conceptualizing, so must any experience that we take to be a complex of simpler parts: the analysis is something we *do to* experience, telling us nothing of how it is 'in itself' and, in particular, not grounding any claims that the analysanda are prior, more real building-blocks of that experience.

What counts for purported extra-mental objects counts for *all* objects of experience, even the 'internal' objects that we call the 'contents' of experience: they can be neither simple nor complex. Recall that Vasubandhu's critique of cognizing physical objects claimed that they must be perceived as simple wholes; or perceived as individual smallest elements; or as aggregations of smallest elements. But it turns out that the same applies to all perceptions, no matter whether they are of mind-independent objects or not. Diṅnāga, working in the early sixth century CE, recognizes this, as does his successor, Dharmakīrti, who took up and developed Diṅnāga's epistemology in the first half of the seventh century CE.[6] Their objects of perception are not, therefore, *simples* in the Abhidharmika sense; nothing could be that. Perceptions, rather, are of immediate, undifferentiated, perception-particulars, and "free from conceptual construction" (*PS* I.1.3c).[7] Although perceptibles might be analysed into distinct modes, this is done, Diṅnāga says, "only in response to the view of others" (*PSV* I.1.5); they are not constructed out of these (*PSV* I.1.4c–d). As soon as one asks whether the content of perception is simple or complex, one has already ventured beyond particulars and perceptibles into the realm of generalities and the conceptually constructed. "A thing possessing many properties cannot be cognized in all its aspects by the sense. The object of the sense is the form which is to be cognized [simply] as it is and which is inexpressible" (*PS* I.1.5).

Such perception-particulars have as their distinctive character only that they are themselves: and, indeed, that they are *only* themselves, and not characterized by anything other than their being this perception-particular here now. They are, to use Diṅnāga's term for it, self-characterized, *svalakṣana*.[8] Rendering this as 'perception-particular' is an attempt to capture the assimilation of process and product (or agent and result) that distinguished Diṅnāga's theory of perception from that of other *pramāṇa*-theorists.

A *pramāṇa* is a means, method, tool or instrument of valid cognition. Rather than trading more and less robust conceptions of knowledge, epistemology in classical India disputed the eminently practical question of how one actually got oneself into a reliably true mental state. While the Nyāyaikas offered perception, inference, analogy and testimony, rightly used, as distinct means of valid cognition, the Mīmāṃsā philosophers added to these presumption and absence. The Jaina here joined the Buddhist epistemologists who, tending as usual to maximal minimalism, allowed only two such *pramāṇas*: perception and inference.

> The means of cognition are perception [*pratyakṣa*] and inference [*anumāna*]. (*PS* I.1.2a–b)

> Apart from the particular [*sva-lakṣaṇa*] and the universal [*sāmānya-lakṣaṇa*] there is no other object to be cognized, and we shall prove that perception has only the particular for its object and inference only the universal. (*PSV* I.1.2.b–c)

According to Diṅnāga and his followers, each *pramāṇa* is of a distinct domain, and has a distinctive sort of object: perception is of particulars, *svalakṣana*, or that which is idiosyncratic; inference is of generalities, *sāmāṇya-lakṣana*. This distinction should not be mistaken for a distinction between concrete, sensible particulars (on the one hand) and thoughts (on the other). The 'object' at issue here is always the content of the cognition: the representation of either an object on a realist metaphysics, or simply the mental object on an idealist metaphysics. *Whatever* there may or may not be mind-independently, the distinction is about the kind of mental contents we have: perceptions, which are fully non-conceptual and absolutely particular; and conceptions, which have a generality and repeatability that no particular could have.[9] While they are each distinctive, non-conceptual contents cannot be articulated without falsely implying a generality they do not have. As an illustration, Diṅnāga cites an earlier treatise saying "One who has the ability to perceive perceives something blue, but does not conceive that 'this is blue'" (*PSV* I.1.4a) – for identifying 'this' *as blue* employs a generality.

These generalities are not a domain of independently existing objects; universals are among the first things any Buddhist epistemology would have to give up on, since they are vulnerable to the most basic Abhidharma arguments against the self. That which is characterized as a generality arises only from a mental activity of treating absolutely distinct and unrepeatable particulars as if they are the same; they are thus dependent upon our conceptualizing activity, and constitute conceptual reality. While perception is an immediate experiencing of reality as it is, inference is something the mind does; and on Diṅnāga's account of it, all generalities – that is, all concepts, or anything that refers to or includes indifferently (without distinguishing) several particulars – are the results of inference (see §II).

Thus Diṅnāga is still working within a recognizable descendent of the early Buddhist distinction between ultimate and conventional reality, where the latter has particularly to do with our conceptualizing activity. For Diṅnāga, this is not so much conceptual *construction* (out of real simples), as it is conceptual *structuring* of the immediately perceived. For against the background of general Buddhist minimalism, Diṅnāga's view is minimal in yet another way. The act of perceiving, he says, is not distinct from that which is perceived. And in general:

> [we call the cognition itself] *pramāṇa* ..., because it is [usually] conceived to include the act [of cognizing], although primarily it is a result. We do not admit ... that the resulting cognition [*pramāṇa-phala*] differs from the means of cognition [*pramāṇa*] (*PS* I.1.8c–d, *PSV ad* I.18c–d)[10]

Of course, each perception-particular does have its own 'shape' or form (*ākāra*), distinguishing it from every other activity of perceiving.[11] Diṅnāga distinguishes content (*arthābhāsa*) and activity (*svābhāsa*) aspects of any cognition, also distinguished as the 'apprehensible-form' (*grāyākārya*) and 'apprehension-form' (*grāhakākāra*). These remain, nevertheless, a single moment. "The roles of the means of cognition [*pramāṇa*] and of the object to be cognized [*prameya*], corresponding to differences of [aspect of] the cognition, are [only] metaphorically attributed to the respective factor in each case", Diṅnāga writes (*PSV* I.1.9d).

This unity of cognizing and cognized, of activity and content, may remind us of Vasubandhu's 'other-dependent' nature, for it too was supposed to be characterized by the original but misleading dualism between subjectivity and objectivity: between the cognizing activity and the contents cognized. There is more than a hint of additional echoes of Vasubandhu in the further identification of this only apparent duality with the *pramāṇa-phala*, the fruit or result of cognition (or, the knowledge).

This latter unity, intimated already at *Pramāṇasamuccaya* I.1.8c–d, is picked up again at the end of I.1, when Diṅnāga characterizes all cognition as 'self-cognizing':

> [W]hatever the form in which it [a cognition] appears, that [form] is the object of cognition [*prameya*]. The means of cognition [*pramāṇa*] and its result [*phala*] are respectively the form of subject [in the cognition] and the cognition cognizing itself. Therefore, these three are not separate from one another. (*PS* I.1.10)

B. K. Matilal offers what is perhaps the most minimal reading of the 'cognition cognizing itself' claim. He suggests that with reflexive awareness (*sva-saṁvedana*),

> Diṅnāga only referred to the twofold appearance of the self-cognitive part of the event: the object-appearance (that aspect of a mental occurrence which makes an intentional reference) and the appearance of the cognition itself (the cognizing aspect) ... intend[ing] to emphasize the double feature that self-awareness of such events captures.[12]

That is, 'self-awareness' is another way of capturing the unity of cognizing and content cognized. If this is right, then it is obvious why the fruit of cognizing is not different from the means and object of cognition.

Moreover, this might naturally be expressed as a kind of self-reflexivity. For there to be a cognition–cognized pair is for a single event to have itself as its object. That activity and content are internally related within a single event may be aptly captured by the notion of self-reflection, where the subject and object of cognition are evidently the same, and arise together. And this, the claim is, just is what it is to know; there is no further result to be sought. It does not *cause* knowledge, but *is* the knowing. On this understanding, being self-aware is not a further thing added to a perception: not an extra perception, nor an additional cognizing–cognized pair on top of the original one. It is, rather, the relation the content and activity aspects stand in with respect to each other. This is the sense of asserting the non-difference of the three (object, activity, result).[13] The reflexive relation reminds us that the bifurcation into active and objective aspects is artificial, and the first step down the road to mistakenly 'internalizing' the one and 'externalizing' the other.[14]

Such an understanding of the import of 'reflexive awareness' may rob the Mādhyamikas of one of their favourite arguments against Diṅnāga's epistemology. For they were inclined to argue that the self-perception claim was that for every cognition there was a distinct perception, whose business it was to perceive that cognition. Such a view leads to obvious regress problems: if cognition$_1$ requires being perceived by cognition$_2$ in order to count as a cognition at all, then cognition$_2$ must itself be perceived by some further cognition – cognition$_3$ – in order to be a cognition at all, so that it may do the work of cognizing cognition$_1$ so as to make it a cognition in turn. And yet the same evidently counts for cognition$_3$, and so on. At the same time, they maintain, nothing can illuminate itself, just as a knife cannot cut itself (e.g. *BCA* IX.18–24).

But Diṅnāga anticipated the regress objection, and attempts to forestall it with an argument from memory (*PS* I.1.12), taking as his starting-point the universal agreement that memory is only of that of which there has been prior experience. This agreed fact implies, Diṅnāga argues, that in any recollection, I must actually be cognizant of two things: first, the contents (the Golden Temple); and second, the familiarity of those contents (this is not the first occurrence of a Golden Temple cognition, nor is it just another new cognition). But there was only one previous event I am recalling now: seeing the Golden Temple. Otherwise there would be two distinct recollections going on, each in need of explanation both of its contents and its familiarity. But since memory is only of what has previously been perceived, that one previous event must ground both of the aspects of my current recollecting: both the contents and the familiarity. Otherwise, if there were no basis in previous experience for both of these, I could not claim that it was *recollection* happening here, rather than merely another cognition with contents I judge to be similar. Therefore, the original event must have had contents *and the awareness of them* in the same moment, and in recollection, I am recollecting *both* of these aspects.

Thus Diṅnāga tries to prove the unity of *pramāṇa*, *prameya* and *pramāṇa-phala*: of means, object and result of cognition (or activity, contents and knowledge). Mādhyamikas were unpersuaded by this argument, and did not let the followers of Diṅnāga forget it.[15] For if it successfully avoids regress, it seems to do so by attributing some uniquely mysterious luminosity to cognition. And it is indeed not clear from Diṅnāga's text that he does not mean something of the sort with his self-cognizing aspect of cognition. Later defenders of Diṅnāga, however, were more explicit in insisting that the self-cognition of cognition was not some further thing, on top of the contents and activity of cognizing, and somehow to be added to it as an afterglow.[16] They clearly adopted a more minimal interpretation of Diṅnāga's claim that sidestepped such accusations, and had the additional advantage of looking remarkably like the Yogācāra view of ultimate reality that we developed from Vasubandhu's discussion of the *Three Natures* – with the difference that Vasubandhu seemed to suppose that each experience of ultimate reality is complete (leaves nothing of ultimate reality out) and the same as every other such experience, while both of these presumptions seem not to be the case with Diṅnāga's perception.[17] Indeed, it may seem that it must not be so, for in order for perception to play a role in differentiating everyday experiences, it ought to be different in each case – even if articulating such a difference in any particular case, of course, immediately throws us into the realm of discourse, of conceptual differentiation concealing the true nature of reality, which lacks precisely the boundary lines it is the business of concepts to draw.

All the same, the territory of ultimate reality is precisely where we should want the discussion of perception to lead us. For the epistemological distinction between inference and perception reflects the metaphysical distinction between conventional and ultimate reality. Indeed, given the unity of perceiving and the objects of perception just laid out, it could not be otherwise.

Diṅnāga also wants to retain the original asymmetry of this distinction: if anything can be considered real or true about the contents of our conceptualizing activities – if they are not *purely* illusory – this will be in virtue of their relation to what is ultimately true. And it seems that only if they are not *purely* illusory will we be able to sustain any distinction between a correct, appropriate deployment of concepts and an inappropriate, mistaken one.

Concepts, and the words naming them, are necessarily illusory in a specific sense. Words, by their nature, are such as to be able to apply, without change of meaning, to more than one thing. A word such as 'blue' or 'zebra' that could be used only once would be useless *as a word*. Similarly, if the concept 'zebra' does not equally apply to all zebras, whatever their differences in height, spatial location or comeliness, it would not be effective in its intended purpose. But all that really exists, according to Diṅnāga, are particulars, each one quite distinct from the others, for every genuinely existing thing must be the same as itself and different from every other genuine existent. Perception is the immediate, undifferentiated experience of what really exists. As soon as we ask 'What are these perceptions *like*?', however, the particular escapes us; for as soon as we attempt to analyse and to articulate it, we are obliged to appeal to generalities, which, by their nature, assimilate what in reality are separate entities.

This may not conform to our current everyday notion of 'perception', where we ordinarily suppose that 'I *see* the zebra' and 'Alice *hears* the Queen of Hearts shouting' are unexceptionable cases of perceiving, and one need not, in addition, *believe* that one sees the zebra, or *judge* that one hears the Queen of Hearts.[18] But all these ordinary cases of perceiving involve, Diṅnāga correctly sees, grasping something *as* this or that: taking that which I see to be a *zebra*, taking that which Alice hears to be shouting. Taking some absolutely non-repeatable particular *to be* anything other than itself elides its differences, and this requires some judgement about *which* differences are *dissimilarities* and which are actually *similarities*. Among the infinite possibilities for how to grasp the particular, one must make some decisions about which samenesses and differences are relevant. In this way, what we call perceptions – such as 'I see blue', 'I hear bells' – are already conceptually inflected and infected. "The association of a name, genus, etc." with a perception is conceptual construction (*PS* I.1.3d), so that even the simplest perceptual judgements are *judgements*, not perceptions. The similarities, however, cannot actually be real, for if particulars have real similarities, then these similarities would be repeatable *general* properties, and these are just what Diṅnāga tells us are not ultimately real. In this sense, language, requiring a non-existent sameness across different items, necessarily falsifies.

And yet, even if thoughts expressible by words capture only conceptually contrived unities, it is not irrelevant how we contrive our thoughts. There are legitimate and illegitimate ways of grouping perceptions and the general terms they inspire. If we do not allow this, then we disable the very possibility of philosophy and rational inquiry in the first place: no use of words is better or worse than any other and, if it is truth you want, you are better off doing something else entirely – meditating, perhaps. There might have been Buddhists who thought like this; but they were not the Sautrāntika-Yogācāra Buddhists around and following Diṅnāga. To their minds, the distinction between correct and incorrect deployment of our concepts is interesting and important in its own right and is, moreover, essential to moving from where we are (dwelling thoroughly in the concept-riddled milieus) to where we want to be (appreciating the nature of ultimate reality, so as to eliminate suffering caused by failing to do so).

In general, similarity and dissimilarity are the most basic grounds for drawing things together, or drawing a distinction between them. In drawing on perception-particulars to contrive a conceptually structured reality, we distinguish and relate according to sameness and difference; we did just this above in our description of perception itself. We distinguished the activity of perceiving from its content; we could go on to relate each act of perceiving as similar to every other with respect to its activity. We might distinguish the red, located top-left, from the blue adjacent to it, and relate it as the same colour as the red, located bottom-left.

Every distinction requires some supposed respect in which the things distinguished differ, and these respects are seamlessly treated like properties that might be the same in some other object. To conceptualize is to generalize. And to generalize according to sameness and difference is, as we shall see in the next section, to make a minute inference: to suppose that some contrived and artificial 'samenesses' and 'differences' warrant assimilating current cases to one or the other class. This classifying may distort the essential particularity of any real existent; but it can also be done correctly or incorrectly. And it is in this sense that inference will be *pramāṇa*, if a lesser one. There are standards for correctness and success in discriminating and assimilating.

The difficulty, however, remains in how these standards of correctness are validated by ultimate reality and, in fact, whether they have to be, in the end. Can one be as metaphysically minimalist as the Buddhist epistemologists want to be, and still distinguish correct from incorrect use of concepts? How much could one achieve by considering the nature of inference alone, and disregarding any supposed basis in ultimate reality?

In sum

All we ever actually experience directly are particulars. And every particular is only exactly itself, and has no real relation – and certainly no distinct property 'sameness in kind', nor properties that are in fact shared – with any other particular. The mind, in conceiving the general terms used in inference, must first make very basic inferences: learning the use of a general term is learning to disregard real differences and select among approximations of similarity in ways that follow repeatable, and publicly shared patterns. This brings us to the internal pressure towards the epistemological turn. The problem is this: inference takes place in the medium of language; in fact, all linguistic terms are essentially mini-inferences: "Verbal communication is no different from inference as a means of acquiring knowledge. For it names its object in a way similar to the property of having been produced, by precluding what is incompatible" (*PS* V.1[19])

But language is fundamentally distorting: it involves (i) differentiating what is undifferentiated, and (ii) asserting sameness of what is different. It is thus essentially contrary to perception. How, then, can inference be a *pramāṇa* at all? How could concepts and perceptions be well related, and related in such a way that the latter (partially) grounds the validity of the former?

There are two different but complementary ways of distinguishing the valid uses of reasoning and conceptions from the invalid: first, in terms of the form, relation, and internal structure of the conceptualizing itself; second, by the relation between these and what is ultimately real. The first demands coherence, the second, reality. Articulating the first is an articulation of a theory of reasoning (§II); the second requires asserting, and if possible spelling out, what it is for such reasonings to be well connected to the non-conceptualizable particulars of ultimate reality. We shall look at Diṅnāga's and Dharmakīrti's respective attempts to tackle this problem in §IV and §V, below.

II. Evaluating reasons: Naiyāyikas and Diṅnāga

Although Diṅnāga recognizes the non-conceptual nature of ultimate reality, and consequently the necessarily distorting effect of any conceptual articulation, he is nevertheless not willing to give up on concepts and reasoning altogether. On the contrary, not only does he retain the generally accepted claim that inference (*anumāṇa,* sound reasoning) is a *pramāṇa* (a 'means of knowledge'), but he even contributes significantly to the pan-Indic discussion of sound inference.

In the process of discriminating the sound from the sophistical arguments, Indian philosophers, led by the Naiyāyikas in particular, came to define sound reasoning as consisting in five parts:

1. *Thesis*	It's going to rain.
2. *Reason*	The clouds are black.
3. *Example*	Last Thursday when the clouds looked like that, it rained.
4. *Application*	These clouds here are just like those clouds – black.
5. *Conclusion*	So, (like that other case) it will rain.[20]

Attempts to relate this form to the Aristotelian syllogism have proved largely fruitless, and for good reason.[21] In the *Prior Analytics*, Aristotle is trying to define rules of contextless assembly of information. This is not necessarily how people *make* arguments – for that, one should consult Aristotle's *Rhetoric* and *Sophistici Elenchi*; nor is it a recipe for inquiry – the order of discovery and that of nature (and reason) are different, says Aristotle. The syllogism, for Aristotle, captures absolute relations holding between things; the deductive syllogisms should remain neutral between any contexts in which we might be moved to articulate them.

The Nyāya 'syllogism', by contrast, arose from the context of debate, and interest was explicitly in what it takes to make an argument legitimately convincing to another: to some third party or even a hostile but reasonable interlocutor. How does one formulate an argument that the opponent *cannot* dismiss, but must answer?

First one must (1) state unequivocally what claim is under discussion. This prevents disagreement in what follows from turning on ambiguities, so that interlocutors are simply talking past each other.[22] This also prevents the person defending the thesis from switching horses in midstream, so that the argument ends up leading to a conclusion different from the original claim under dispute. Next, one must (2) adduce a reason or explanation, relevant to the claim made. This rule or principle should be of wider application than the particular claim. Otherwise we have no argument at all, but simply the exceptionalist claim that the thesis is true because it is true. Its way of fitting into a wider, and generally acknowledged, structure of reality should be what gives one reason to believe a claim, and that acknowledgement should be shared by the person not already persuaded of the truth of the thesis. (3) Rules being abstract, however, they are not always immediately clear; and moreover, it is possible to claim something as a general principle that does not in fact aptly relate to how things are. One must, therefore, adduce an example of the application of the principle asserted in the previous step. This clarifies what principle is meant, and establishes at the same time that both parties to the debate agree that there is an actual exemplification of this principle; it is not obscurely incoherent or uninstantiatable. (4) Then, the crucial bit of the argument, one shows that the matter under dispute – the subject of the claim in the first step – is relevantly similar to the example given, so that it should (according to the principle or rule adduced) likewise exemplify the property asserted. (5) Finally, one is entitled to draw the conclusion: a conclusion that the interlocutor must accept unless she can show that there was an error in the previous steps. If there is none, then she would be rightly persuaded to accept the conclusion.

One of Diṅnāga's significant contributions to Indian logic was to simplify and integrate this form. In place of a five-part process, Diṅnāga offers the *trairūpya*: the three marks of a sound basis for inference. This articulation of the inference recognizes that, while it may have successive stages in its presentation, it is a single complex fact that is being asserted, and so evaluated for its validity. Diṅnāga is still interested in the debate context; indeed, chapters III, IV and VI of his *Compendium on Means of Knowing*, the *Pramāṇa-samuccaya*, concern the dialectical context in particular. But these are variants on the basics of what makes a reason a good one, quite generally. According to Diṅnāga, then, a reason, R (*hetu*, *liṇga*) is a sound basis for concluding a further property or fact [P] regarding *x* (the locus, *pakṣa*) when it satisfies three characteristics (*rūpa*):

1. R is in *x* (*pakṣadharmatā* – the quality is in the *pakṣa*); the site of properties, the case at hand
2. R occurs elsewhere, where P is also found (*anvyavyāpti* – the reason occurs [pervades – *vyāpti*] [only] similar cases); the *sapakṣa*, the likeness class
3. R is absent from all cases not like *x* with respect to P (*vyatirekavyāpti* – the *hetu*'s absence from dissimilar cases); the *vipakṣa*, the unlikeness class[23]

The standard example one finds involves whether it is safe to infer from R: 'the sighting of smoke' [the *hetu*], that P: 'there is fire', on yonder hill [the *pakṣa*]. Determining that it is indeed so involves, first, taking all the things similarly situated with respect to fire as that hill yonder and putting them in one class; and taking all things differently situated with respect to fire as that hill yonder. This is a notional division, as yet indeterminate with respect to *which class* is the one of fire-containing cases.

Then we consider the case at hand: that hill yonder has smoke on it. We inspect our two classes – that of those similar, and that of those different with respect to P – and consider whether at least some members of one class have smoke, while all members of the other class lack it. If so, then we know which of those two classes our current case falls into: the class including smoky things. But our original division into two classes was not according to whether they were smoke-having, but according to whether they were fire-having; remember, the similarity class is similarly situated with respect to the property *to be inferred* (in this case, fire). So, *on the basis of the smoke on the hill* (the hill belonging in the class of smoky things), we can safely infer that there is fire on that hill yonder; the hill will be similarly situated with respect to fire as the class of smoky things into which it falls.

In short, the reason (in this case, smoke) is a sound basis for positing the target property (fire) when smoke occurs in at least some members of the similarity class, and none of the members of the dissimilarity class: where similarity and dissimilarity classes are determined according to their possession of the target property (fire). Unlike the Nyāya 'syllogism', this does not so much set out the correct form of legitimate persuasion, as articulate what it is to *have a reason.*

Now, one might worry about redundancies in this account of reasoning. Uddyotakara, the seventh-century CE Nyāya philosopher, and contemporary of Dharmakīrti, brought up such objections in his *Nyāyavārtika.*[24] Diṅnāga himself was perhaps sensitive to these concerns. For instance, the last condition alone seems to say, in effect, that where there is no fire, there is no smoke. And if that is so, this should suffice to legitimize smoke as a ground for inferring fire. The second condition, that is to say, seems to do no work. This is only apparently so, however. Diṅnāga insists on the second condition in order to exclude inferences based on exceptional cases. For example, we cannot reason on the basis that sound is *audible* that it is therefore transitory because there is nothing else to be audible except sound, so the only thing being appealed to as evidence is the thing itself.[25] One has merely restated the assertion, rather than offering a reason. It is only on the basis of there being recognized cases of the co-occurrence of smoke and fire that the *absence* of fire from *every* case of absence of smoke warrants the conclusion 'here, where there is smoke, there is also fire'.[26]

Moreover, many objections can be averted by insisting that in the construction of our similarity and dissimilarity classes, we do not include our current case, for into which of these it falls is precisely what we are trying to discover, or give reason for. We might think of the process in the following way: I see smoke on that hill yonder, and I want to know whether there is also fire there. The question is about fire [P, above]. *Fire*? To decide the question, I notionally divide the world into fire-containing and fire-absent cases; and then I *ask myself* whether either of these is similar – and the other dissimilar – to my current case. Similar in which respect? In respect of the grounds I think I have for inferring fire – in this case, smoke. But I know of several cases of the co-occurrence of smoke and fire (kitchens, matches, campfires); so if one of my two classes is a similarity class, then it will be the one in which fire occurs. Finally, then, I consider whether the other class, the dissimilarity class (excluding fire), has an absence of smoke in all of its members. If so, then I may safely infer from the smoke that there is fire.[27]

What is significant to notice here is the way that drawing an inference involves drawing a line between the *sapakṣa*, the class of objects having the target property, and the class of objects without it (the *vipakṣa*). To infer – that is, to have a correct cognition of what is not directly perceived – is to notionally distinguish and assert similarities. I conceive of one group of things as being alike by sharing the target property, while the other is alike by failing to have the target property. One need not make all aspects of this process of reasoning explicitly present to oneself. But to conclude 'there is fire on yonder hill' from seeing smoke involves having grasped together as relevantly similar several disparate occurrences (and absences) of smoke. This, recall, was precisely what went on in any perceptual judgement.

Thus even the locus of the inference itself (in this case, yonder hill) is conceptually constructed according to this same process of deciding what to regard as relevant similarities and relevant differences. The subject of the inference, conceived of provisionally as the bearer of both the inferential and the inferred properties, is not metaphysically 'more substantial' than, or even of a different kind from, the properties being ascribed to it in our inference. All are equally generalities, artificially superimposing samenesses and differences among perception-particulars. This lack of metaphysical ground to the relata and relations involved in inferences means that we have some measure of flexibility in how we get on with our perceptions in a conceptual way. The smoke can be a property of yonder hill; but it can also bear properties – of opacity, say, and of warmth – for thinking which we would construct our similarity and dissimilarity classes differently.[28] In a move familiar from earliest Abhidharma, it will be our purposes and interests in making the inference that determine which way of treating smoke (in this case) is appropriate: if we want to know about fire on yonder hill, we treat smoke as an inferential property; if we want to know about smoke, whether its opacity implies materiality, then smoke is our locus, or subject, of inference. Perhaps, if we just heard what sounds very much like a match being lit, smoke would be our target property to be inferred.

But we do not want to allow infinite plasticity. It is legitimate to infer fire on the basis of the smoke on the hill, but not on the basis of the house there. Once I have identified the house – which I must do if it is to be the ground of my inference – then I have already selected the cluster of similarities and differences that are to be relevant. When I consider my similarity and dissimilarity classes from before, I recognize that although some in the former class involve houses (some houses burn), so also do some in the dissimilarity class (some houses do not burn); so the house cannot be safe grounds for inferring fire. This much about inference as a *pramāṇa* – as a valid means of cognition – can be established by consideration of the form and nature of inference itself, without any supposition of grounding in non-conceptual ultimate reality.

As an account of what goes on in basic reasoning, this account has the advantage of relating our *use* of concepts to our thinking them at all. There is a single activity, drawing of distinctions and thereby drawing similarities, which is what conceiving (having a concept) is, and which, in further interrelated iterations, is what we *do* with concepts when we want to orient ourselves in the world and try to act with respect to it. There is good ground to call all this conceptual reality, and no need to posit some additional *pramāṇa* to account for the difference between *having* concepts and *using* them, confirming again that "there is no other separate means of cognition for [cognizing] the combination of the two above-mentioned" particulars and generalities (*PS* I.1.2c–d). Nor is there any need, as the Nyāya philosophers would have us do, to complicate our account of perception so that it includes the structured material that we use in our inferences. Perception remains constitutively non-conceptual.

As an *epistemology*, however, we might be dissatisfied. The creation and inspection of our similarity and dissimilarity classes seems highly contingent. That it is contingent on our purposes need not worry us, for then there is still a standard of correctness to which it is answerable: namely, coherence with the conceptual frame in which the purpose has shape and with whatever other concepts and relations are necessary for the purpose to be answered. If I want to know about smoke, this sets the conceptual frame and conditions with which my inferences must cohere. The contingency in this account of inference, and of having a reason, that may worry us, then, is rather the psychological contingency involved in the constructing and inspecting.[29] That is, I may include everything with which I am familiar in either the similarity or the dissimilarity class; but if there is a counter-example (something in the dissimilarity class that shares the *hetu*) of which I know nothing, then all the inspection in the world of my constructed classes could not illuminate me, or prevent me from drawing the inference. For, according to Diṅnāga's three criteria, I am drawing the inference correctly. In fact, the greater my ignorance, the greater my correct inferences.

In the dialectical context of debate, of course, it is the responsibility of the opponent to come up with some such case. But in the purely epistemological context, asking whether R is or is not a good reason – or, what is in effect the same, examining the matter on my own simply because I actually want to know – this will be unavailable and the victory of my ignorance a pyrrhic one indeed. Because in practice, no matter how careful I were to be in the accumulation of further cases and evidence, I could never have all cases available to me for my inspection; all that it would ever be safe for me to infer is that *as far as I know* there are no defeasors. My supposed knowledge must always be provisional and hypothetical. That every case I know of, or even every known case of absence of fire, is also a case of absence of smoke cannot ensure that '*wherever* there is smoke, there's fire', any more than every known case of absence of blackness in a bird being a case of absence of raven-ness guarantees that all ravens are black.

Perhaps Diṅnāga should not be faulted for not solving the problem of induction. Or perhaps he is not even aiming at *certainty*. These matters being thoroughly conventional anyway, perhaps Diṅnāga would not have thought the provisionality of our conclusions a great problem.

It may just be the inevitable consequence of conceptual reality *not* being ultimate, and so not immediately perceived, that it cannot have that kind of certainty, and we are better off doing the best that we can and knowing what would need to be done in order to do better (for instance, to learn more carefully a wider range of cases where defeasors might arise). One might want to think of this as a sceptical position,[30] and for intelligible reasons. After all, on this reading of Diṅnāga, he offers three criteria for knowledge by inference, or reasoning, one of which (the third) cannot ever be satisfied: mere classification of already familiar or existing cases cannot of itself show that no future, or as yet unconsidered, case will not prove to contain the inferential ground but not the inferred property. Until we can claim completeness in our dissimilarity class we cannot claim certainty that our inference is safe; yet it is practically impossible to have surveyed all actual and possible cases. The point of specifying the conditions of knowledge so precisely, then, is (at least in part) to show that such knowledge is in fact impossible, inasmuch as certainty is impossible, since condition 3 can never be known to be satisfied.

Even if this is so, however, and Diṅnāga is aware of it and contented with the implications, there is yet good reason to refrain from calling this position 'sceptical'. First, it would be misleading to call Diṅnāga a sceptic *tout court*, since there *is* on his view perfect knowledge to be had: when cognition is of what is ultimately real, that is, when we perceive without conceptual construction, then we have perfect knowledge. At best, this understanding of Diṅnāga's account of inference could make him a sceptic about *reasoning* (as so understood), but not about the possibility of knowledge. But even with respect to inference, the title of 'sceptic' would lead us astray. For Diṅnāga's conditions give us a clear sense in which inferences can be *improved*, even if not made absolutely certain. The third criterion is,[31] in fact, a specific invitation to do just this, and an indication of how to do it: we increase the safety of our inferences to the extent that we include a wider field of cases.

This has practical implications which differentiate Diṅnāga from any serious sort of scepticism. For the sceptic uses the fact of the impossibility of knowledge as a reason for us to leave off drawing inferences altogether. Our recognition that knowledge is impossible should, according to the sceptic, make us give up the search and accept our ignorance. But the lesson drawn from Diṅnāga's specifications of what makes for a good reason is the opposite of this. Rather than leaving off judging, we ought to use the standards set by the *trairūpya* to assess and improve our judgements. This will, of course, never *be* knowledge of ultimate reality, for that is something approached by a different epistemic mode entirely. But it establishes the framework for discussion of inference in the path to enlightenment. In so far as we are now unenlightened and dwelling thoroughly in a conceptual milieu, we can use this to improve our cognitions, and this not just for the sake of greater practical success in mundane matters, but especially in order to understand better how and why there is no self, what forms suffering takes and what its causes are, so that we might be in a mental condition to be able to directly perceive ultimate reality.

Such a non-sceptical reading of the impossibility of inferential knowledge may yet remain unsatisfactory. Inference is, one might think, already far enough away from truth and reality, just by virtue of dealing in concepts, which necessarily falsify. It cannot afford, in addition, to lose any claim to certainty in its own domain, and still be counted a *pramāṇa*. If Diṅnāga himself did not share this concern, it seems that Dharmakīrti did.[32] Diṅnāga, we said, remains metaphysically fairly agnostic: as metaphysically agnostic as someone claiming the identity of perceiving and perceived can be. Dharmakīrti, by contrast, had fewer reservations. He is sometimes explicitly Yogācāra in his interpretation of Diṅnāga's epistemology; and in contrast to Diṅnāga, he avails himself of causal relations. We shall see this later in their respective treatments of *apoha* (§IV and §V). Here, Dharmakīrti introduces the notion of a real causal relation between the *hetu* (inferential ground or property) and the target property (that which is to be inferred).[33] Whenever our inference is sound, and a ground of inference meets the three criteria Diṅnāga sets out, there is an essential relationship, or natural connection, between the known and the inferred: the sort of relation that holds between causes and their effects.[34] If this is so, then in drawing the inference and establishing that the three conditions are met, I might be confident of a connection between inferential and inferred properties that precludes unknown counter-examples.

Given Nāgārjuna's full-frontal assault on the coherence of causation, one might wonder whether it is wise to invoke it as prodigiously as Dharmkīrti does, even if he is careful to insist that it is not a distinct existing thing in addition to perceptibles. Perhaps Diṅnāga took the better course in restricting himself to the sparse logic of co-occurrence, co-absence, similarity and difference. On the other hand, in this case at least, one may maintain that – as we are discussing conceptual reality anyway – 'cause–effect' is merely the name for these very features of co-occurrence, and so on;[35] and after all, all we need is a serviceable, everyday notion of causation, such as Nāgārjuna's critique leaves in tact. Against this, however, stands the fact that Dharmakīrti's term for this relation is *svabhāva-pratibandha*, 'natural relation', with 'natural' here rendering that metaphysically committing word, *svabhāva*.

Dharmakīrti is not unaware of the problem, and so is careful to specify that the *svabhāvas* – natures or essences – are not particulars, nor of particulars. They describe and belong to conceptual realities: familiar objects such as jugs and trees. Any given conventional entity, or object of conceptual awareness, reliably produces a certain range of collected effects, and no others. Mango seeds, all going well, produce mango trees and mangos; they do not produce tigers, ever.[36] This is the *svabhāva* of the mango seed, virtually defined by its non-accidental causal relations.[37] Dharmakīrti may well say that his *svabhāva*, and so his *svabhāva*-connections, are invulnerable to Madhyamaka critique, for he fully concedes that they are conceptually constructed entities, dependent upon that construction and so in the Madhyamaka sense 'empty'. Their apparent causality is not in the complex, repeatable mango itself; rather, if any of the natural connections among the properties of a conceptually structured entity – like a mango – are really causally efficacious, this is owing only to their relation to real, non-conceptual, causally efficacious particulars.

Such a reply, however, puts additional pressure in turn on the need to substantiate such a connection between ultimate reality (non-conceptually structured particulars) and conventional reality (of conceptually structured items that we can conceive and reason about) – the discussion of which we have postponed to §IV and §V. And in any case, Dharmakīrti's account of how to render Diṅnāgean inferences *certain* will still require real causation of some sort, and so will be vulnerable to the Madhyamaka critique of causation – *if* that critique can be made good.

III. Madhyamaka response to Yogācāra

While Diṅnāga, and after him Dharmakīrti, developed the intellectual inheritance of Vasubandhu and Asaṅga, Nāgārjuna's Madhyamaka did not disappear. His interpretation of 'dependent origination' as 'emptiness', and the resultant claim that all *dharmas* are empty – including that very claim itself – did not encourage the building of systematic accounts of cognition and knowledge to set directly against the Yogācāra. This, in fact, they could claim as a point in their favour, as being more in keeping with the spirit of the Buddha's instruction not to cling to views.[38]

The 'emptiness of emptiness' – that is, the fact that even the dependency of all phenomena is itself dependently arising – has the effect of undermining the asymmetry the Abhidharma philosophers established between ultimate and conventional reality. For while everything was dependently arisen, conventional reality was, according to the Abhidharmika, dependent in yet another way: being dependent upon our conceptualizing for their particular identities (being *a chariot*, rather than a *bookshelf*), they were dependent for their existence and realization on constituents whose identity and realization did not depend upon our conceptualizing activity. If, however, to arise within a causal network at all implies, as Nāgārjuna seemed to claim, this very same *conceptual* dependency, then there is nothing to distinguish *dharmas* (or anything else) as more ultimate than the complex wholes that the Abhidharma denigrates as merely conceptually real.

This means that the whole business of resolving complex wholes into their constituents is a fruitless activity, at least if one hopes thereby to arrive at a better understanding of how the world *really is* (apart from our self-serving conceptualizing). At best, such an exercise can reveal to us only how contingent, and yet how inescapable, our analytical schemas are. Grasping the world in terms of heaps of various types of interacting elements is just another way of grasping the world: a pretty useless one for communicating and satisfying everyday purposes, or a somewhat useful one for showing up the futility of any attempt to lay claim to having grasped something 'more fundamental', more true or real, than our conceptually laden world of everyday experience, and explanatory of it.

To make the argument go through, Nāgārjuna needs two things always to arise together, or to imply each other necessarily (to be logically equivalent): dependency for existence (being or not being), and dependency for essence, or identity (being *this* rather than *that*). It is not an outlandish claim, that to exist at all is to be the very thing that one is. This coincidence is represented in the Aristotelian thought that 'to be is to be a *this*-something'. But this is usually part of a strongly realist metaphysics – it is part of Aristotle's argument for the priority of form (real, structured, intelligible and immaterial – although enmattered – wholes) in the account of being-as-such. Nāgārjuna, by contrast, is attempting to undo all metaphysical asymmetry, not to build it up again in the opposite direction. So he needs these two – 'mere-being' and 'being-this', or existence and essence – to co-occur in a rather different way, for rather different reasons. Thus he argues that all causal dependence is a masked form of conceptual dependence, and what is conceptually dependent has a borrowed, vicarious nature, not an independently specifiable one (no *svabhāva*).

Vasubandhu's Yogācāra aims to separate these claims. Everything is indeed without essence, Vasubandhu agrees. But this does not entail that everything is dependent; for it is possible to lack essence altogether, to lack even the characteristics that might be dependent. Some things, Vasubandhu argues, are empty because their nature is to be merely the misleading way something else appears; sometimes, as Nāgārjuna claimed, a thing is empty because every particular *characteristic* characterizing it is dependent upon preceding qualified moments, none of them the essence or independent of each other; sometimes – rather, in one case only – something is without essence by not having any characteristics at all. It *cannot* be dependent for its characteristics, because it has none and its nature just is this lack of any differentiating characteristics. It cannot, therefore, be dependent in the way Nāgārjuna supposed all things must be. This may be because it is not *a thing* at all. Language fails here. So too with Diṅnāga's ultimate particulars. They are unrepeatable distinct individuals; and yet grasping them as such means refraining from articulating or discriminating any features in them whatsoever. For both, there is a perfectly intelligible sense in which ultimate reality lacks *svabhāva*, without being thereby dependent – and so, in virtue of this, it is entitled to be considered 'ultimate' and not 'conceptual' reality. Thus they retain an asymmetrical metaphysics: there are different ways of being real, one sort dependent upon the other. This dependency is ontological, but only partially explanatory. Ultimate reality grounds *that there is any conventional reality at all*. But the conceptualizing activity of confused mental events explains the specific identity that each dependent nature has.

The task for later Madhyamaka lay in distinguishing itself from some version of this, without becoming nihilism: metaphysical nihilism, since there is no essence (*svabhāva*) to anything, anywhere; and moral nihilism, since this pervasive emptiness should mean that there is no distinction between virtue and vice, correct and incorrect, good and bad.[39] All are equally empty, and empty is what everything ultimately is. "The wise," Candrakīrti tells us, "for whom there is no good or ill, are free" (*MA* VI.42c). One might avoid the threatening nihilism in two ways: (i) by making *something* out of ultimate reality – emptiness *exists*; or (ii) by rehabilitating the reality of conventional distinctions – while conventional reality is in some sense *like* an illusion or dream, it is not in fact merely illusory nor arbitrary and interchangeable as dreams are.

Given the nature of the two truths, one might think that the second option is available only once the first option has been taken. For how does one validate (some) conventions and conceptions (but not all) – how do some distinctions get to be credited as conventionally *real* – without some basis in what, ultimately, really exists (even if this is only part of the explanation)? When Candrakīrti says, for instance, that "from the outset, all phenomena are peace, are unproduced, transcending by their nature every pain" (*MA* VI.112b–c), it may seem that he is in fact following just this strategy of avoiding nihilism by insisting that ultimate reality is, after all, *something*. In fact, he is picking up on *MMK* 18.9, as had Bhāviveka before him:

> "Not known through anyone else, peaceful, not expressed by discursive ideas, non-conceptual, not diverse – this is the definition of reality." [*MMK* 18.9]
>
> Here [reality] is not expressed by discursive ideas, because it is non-conceptual. Because it is not expressed by discursive ideas, it is peaceful. Because it is peaceful, it is accessible only to non-conceptual knowledge. Because it is accessible only to non-conceptual knowledge, it is not known through anyone else. In this way, the nature of reality completely transcends the application of words.[40]

But taking these remarks as straightforwardly referring to some ineffable reality, distinct from ordinary appearances, leads back to a crytpo-Yogācārin or Sautrāntika position. Granting any substantial character to ultimate reality is tantamount to claiming there is a *real* reality behind the experienced one, and our job is to see it. But just that promise of a more real truth, surviving behind the misleading conventional reality and waiting to be discovered, is the sort of presentation of ultimate reality that the Mādhyamika objects to as promising some 'self' that one might cling to.

Bhāviveka and the Yogācāra

Bhāviveka, a mid-sixth-century Mādhyamika, rose to the challenge. After Āryedeva in the second to third centuries CE, there had been few substantial Madhyamaka scholars until Buddhapālita wrote his commentary on the *Mūlamadhyamakakārikā*, probably in the early sixth century CE. This commentary, in Bhāviveka's view, did not avail itself of all available resources in articulating the Madhyamaka position, and so did not take its Buddhist objectors sufficiently seriously.

If the charges of nihilism levelled by Asaṅga and Vasubandhu against the Madhyamaka were to be answered, it required engaging fully with the opposing position as well as articulating the Madhyamaka alternative. For this, Bhāviveka proposed to make use of the pan-Indic terms of debate, and in particular of Dinnāga's analysis of inference, reason and faulty reasoning. These resources allow one to structure one's arguments and identify points of disagreement in a way perspicuous to and acknowledged by all. It being generally agreed that the reason on which one rests one's case must be (i) applicable to the case under examination, (ii) no exception in that respect, and (iii) not equally applicable to opposite cases, Bhāviveka can specify the failings of particular arguments as irrelevant (failing to meet (i)), or promiscuous (admitting counterexamples, failing criterion (iii)). For instance, at *Madhyamakahṛdaya* V.15, Bhāviveka says that if the Yogācārin "thinks that a cognition of material form is incorrect because it has the image of an object, the reason is mistaken and the thesis fails",[41] before going on in the commentary to specify that the reason is mistaken inasmuch as it is contradicted.

Bhāviveka thus engaged not just his Mahāyāna rivals, the Yogācārins, but also the many varieties of non-Mahāyāna Buddhist, whom he called Śrāvakas ('hearers', 'disciples'), and indeed non-Buddhists, devoting separate chapters of his *Madhyamaka-hṛdaya-kārikā* (*Verses on the Heart of Madhyamaka*) to the Sāṃkhyas, the Vaiśeṣikas, the Vedāntins and the Mīmāṃsikas, respectively, and including even a brief treatment of the Jains. Because he follows the typical pattern of setting out the opponent's view before subjecting it to critique, Bhāviveka's *Madhyamakahṛdaya* has proved an invaluable resource for scholars attempting to get a grip on sixth-century intellectual life in all its diversity. It is, for instance, to chapter 4 of the *Madhyamakahṛdaya* that we owe much of the little we do know about the divisions of the Śrāvakas into the canonical eighteen schools.

The Śrāvaka critique of Madhyamaka is, however, generic – and so likewise is Bhāviveka's reply. For the Śrāvakas as a whole object to the Mahāyāna *tout court*, largely on grounds of scriptural authenticity: the Mahāyāna *sūtras* do not date from the time of the Buddha and they are not the Buddha's word (*buddhavācana*). Meeting these charges involves Bhāviveka in interesting matters of hermeneutics. How is authenticity established: by historical transmission or by content? How consistent are the accepted *sūtras*, and how do we explain apparent divergences already present in undisputed texts? The Buddha had openly acknowledged that he tailored his choice of words and topics to his hearer's needs and capacities. The Mahāyāna can draw on this, but must expand vastly the kinds of differences possible between aspirants, and therefore the kinds of expositions of the view of reality and of the final goal that the Buddha endorsed. Just as one may not be ready to hear the no-self view without misconstruing it (*SN* IV.400),[42] so no one contemporaneous with the historical Śakyamuni was ready to hear the still more unfathomable ubiquitous no-self of the *prajñāpāramitā*. Skilfully, the Buddha withheld these obscure but more accurate claims until the ground had been prepared. Then through reliance on and development of the distinction between 'interpretable' (*neyārtha*) and 'definitive' (*nītārtha*) expositions; through insisting that the criterion of authenticity (and for distinguishing the *neyārtha* from the *nītārtha*) was consistency of content rather than historical composition; and through heavy emphasis on the Buddha's own skill in teaching, adopted as a hallmark of Mahāyāna self-understanding of their own ideal practice, the Mahāyāna met Śrāvaka charges of being outside the Buddhist path entirely. Bhāviveka presents the Madhyamaka response in largely these terms, and thus participated in the development of the Buddhist discourse on hermeneutics,[43] the nature of teaching, and the moral psychology of progressing along the path.

It is, however, the Yogācārin that is Bhāviveka's more formidable opponent. For Yogācāra offers a systematic articulation of what taking universal emptiness seriously means, and what it implies. Distinguishing the Madhyamaka position from this, and defending its superiority, requires Bhāviveka to offer moral, metaphysical and epistemological reasons, not just textural and hermeneutical ones.

Bhāviveka's rejoinder to the Yogācāra position in chapter V of the *Madhyamakahṛdaya* may be broken roughly into five parts: verses 10–16 deal with the ultimate as object of cognition; verses 17–54 examine the ultimate as consciousness; verses 55–68 then deal with imagined nature, verses 69–84 with dependent nature, and verses 85–98 with consummate nature, before finally Bhāviveka offers something of how he understands the Madhyamaka approach, in verses 94, 98–114. In this outline, we can see that, in keeping with the *prasaṅga* spirit, Bhāviveka structures his discussion around the principle claims of the Yogācārin.

It is a firm principle of Indian epistemology and metaphysics that something that cannot in any way be cognized cannot plausibly be posited as existing. Vasubandhu appealed to this in his *Twenty Verses*, where his argument against material *dharmas* took the form of arguing that there could be no way at all of cognizing such things. Bhāviveka takes a similar tack in argument against the Yogācāra conception of ultimate reality (*MH* V.10–16). The Yogācārin, he claims, is committed to positing the existence of absences. More specifically, if awareness of consummate reality is the direct perception of non-duality, either that absence of duality exists and is the object of cognition, or it does not exist and so there is no cognition at all. But if this absence of duality exists as the object of (non-conceptual) cognition then there is no reason why every absence should not be an object of (non-conceptual) cognition (*MH* V.14c–d).

Whether this point goes through, or how Bhāviveka thinks it does, requires careful work. But since the Mādhyamika also believes in ubiquitous selflessness, and liberating wisdom as some sort of realization of this, Bhāviveka is also forced to articulate how a Mādhyamika would handle the matter instead. He offers the observation that "the selflessness of *dharmas* is free from all cognitive marks" (*MH ad* V.13c–d), but we might wonder how this should help. Does being free from all cognitive marks mean that Madhyamaka selflessness is not an 'absence' in the way that the Yogācāra ultimate reality as 'non-dual cognition' is an absence? It is not clear why it should do so. Moreover, it seems that being free of cognitive marks should make such selflessness uncognizable *tout court*, in which case we have no reason to believe there is such a thing. The answer comes only at the end of chapter V, where Bhāviveka suggests that the cognizing of selflessness that the Madhyamaka advocates is not so much a matter of seeing *the selflessness*, but rather seeing everything else that is there to be cognized, the correct appreciation of which would include seeing their ultimate insubstantiality.

> According to the Madhyamaka approach, [Reality] is not a real thing and is not apprehended, so for us [reality] can be what [you] have said.

> It is precisely because [reality] is not a real thing (*dravya*) that it cannot be apprehended in its own right.
>
> (*MH* V.99c–d, and comment)

According to Bhāviveka, the Madhyamaka alternative to Yogācāra is not an alternative cognition but, rather, a lack of cognition – refraining from making a cognitive move. This is what it means for Madhyamaka to reject Vasubandhu's third 'nature' (*svabhāva*). We grasp particularities arising within space, but not the space itself within which it arises. "[A supermundane cognition] is non-conceptual, has no object, and has no mark, because it understands the equality of self and other in a single moment with no understanding" (*MH* V.102).

This may look as if it is simply acknowledging that there is no grasping of ultimate reality at all – 'no understanding' of 'no object' is the life of a stone, not a Buddha. If, however, we take seriously the reason offered here – 'because it understands the equality of self and other' – then again the point may be that Madhyamaka distinguishes itself from Yogācāra by refusing to offer an additional thing (indeed, an *absence*, Bhāviveka claims), to be the object of understanding of ultimate reality. Instead, it is the grasping of what is graspable in a particular way – that is, seeing the conventional *as* conventional, as without ultimate reality – and not trying to grasp anything beyond this, that correct insight consists in.

Regarding reality as mind-only, Bhāviveka goes on to observe, is refuted by common sense (*MH* V.17). Such an observation is no argument of course, for Yogācārins never thought they were presenting common sense anyway, but rather analysing and so transforming it. Still, that Bhāviveka is willing to bring the observation as an objection reveals a Madhyamaka deference to common understanding, and implies that his own understanding of the Madhyamaka position is committed to *not* similarly violating common sense. Whatever we are to make of, for instance, Nāgārjuna's critique of causation in *Mūlamadhyamakakārikā* I, Bhāviveka must suppose that our ordinary causal language practices are not undermined.

More serious than contravening common sense, Yogācāra requires the bifurcation of consciousness. They must assert that consciousness is the sort of thing to have two aspects: the form and the content of cognition as we called it in discussing Vasubandhu, and saw again in Diṅnāga's *Pramāṇasamuccaya* (e.g. *PS* I.1.5 and *PS* I.1.9, above). As the Yogācārins themselves might have put it, there is the cognizing and there is the form that cognizing takes as its contents.[44] Only by maintaining this dual nature of cognition can the Yogācārin claim that there is some special realization of ultimate reality that consists in non-duality here. Bhāviveka argues (*MH* V.20–25) that consciousness was never bifurcated into subject–object in the first place: a moment of consciousness has the form of its object, and no other; and independently of objects, there is no consciousness to have or lack a form. Thus, "at the time when a cognition is in the process of arising, bearing the form [*ākāra*] that is called consciousness as object-image, it causes the cognition of the object-form. Therefore, [we] think that the means of knowledge is this cognition while it is arising" (*MH* V.25).

This resistance to reification of aspects of cognition, and so of cognition itself, fits together with Bhāviveka's previous refusal to posit selflessness as an absence or an object of cognition in its own right. There is only the dependently arising way things are. One can describe this as selflessness, and aptly so, because it entails no independent natures or identities. But this is merely a description, not a thing. Seeing it just *is* seeing dependency, and there is no more to it answering to the global noun 'selflessness'. So similarly, the form of consciousness just is the form of its object or contents. There is not some separate existing thing, the consciousness itself, distinct from the forms of its contents.

Bhāviveka needs to offer reasons why subjectivity is not distinct from the form it takes. (It *seems* my awareness of blueness is not identical to the blueness of which I am aware.) But however he will get there, we see another piece of the Madhyamaka view Bhāviveka wants to defend. Consciousness, like everything else, is thoroughly constituted by its conditions. We should not think of ultimate reality either as an object of direct perception, nor as the conclusion of an inference: it "is not a real thing and is not apprehended" (*MH* V.99c–d). Indeed, it seems that one does not properly *think of* ultimate reality at all, on the Madhyamaka view: "it cannot be grasped by the mind in any way" (*MH* V.100d).

Nevertheless, one uses concepts in order to reveal them as mere concepts, and thus follows the Buddha's own practice: "Buddhas use faultless inference in a way that is consistent with tradition to completely reject many different concepts of imagined things" (*MH* V.105). This *via negativa* is likened to removing an eye disease that causes one to see things that were not there (*MH* V.101). Revealing each conditioned thing in all its conditioned, non-essential nature brings the overactive construction of falsifying concepts to an end, so that the mind becomes like space (*MH* V.106) – that is, like ultimate reality itself. In this way, proper attention to and respect for conventional reality is the method of achieving peace from that very reality.

> The understanding of reality depends on conventional usage. The inference that negates concepts depends on what is called correct relative truth [*tathyasamvrtisatya*]. By relying on conventional truth [*vyavahārasatya*], one gradually [*krameṇa*] understands the non-conceptual and inexpressible [*avācya*] ultimate [*paramārtha*]. (*MH* V.110, and comment)

Making reasons your own: Bhāviveka versus Candrakīrti

The Mādhyamikas and the Yogācārins share a view going back to the Abhidharma that assertions require substantial mental engagement, particularly in the isolating of the subject in order to predicate something of it. All the way back in the *Milindapañhā*, we saw a view of ultimate reality as composed of innumerable simples, associating and arising in various ways, which we then gathered together, separated from others, into recognizable objects according to those ways of distinguishing *dharmas* and grouping them together that proved most useful. Isolating and uniting a group of *dharmas* so as to regard them *as* a chariot is a contribution we make to reality, so we called such subjects 'conceptually real' or 'conventionally real'.

For different reasons, both the Yogācārin and the Mādhyamika have critiqued the atomism of Abhidharma thought, resulting for the Yogācārin in an ultimate reality even more significantly undifferentiated than the *dharma* ontology suggested, and for the Mādhyamika in an ultimate reality that is extensionally equivalent to conventional reality. All the more, then, must any identification of a subject of predication involve our mental activity and choices, artificially separating out what is thoroughly interwoven within the texture of reality, in order to assert something *of* it.[45] So the Yogācārins and the Mādhyamikas agree about the structure of assertion: it involves predicating something of a thing. They agree that the object of which something is predicated is not given in nature (or in ultimate reality); they agree that conceptualizing is distorting – it disfigures our experience of ultimate reality, disguises what is ultimately real, or how things ultimately are. And yet Candrakīrti disagrees profoundly with Bhāviveka's willingness to endorse Diṅnāga's position regarding which sorts of statements it is acceptable and useful to make in the course of philosophical inquiry, and so about the place of reason and argument in the project of attaining liberation.

Diṅnāga thinks that as long as we are aware of the provisional use of language, then it can be highly productive of insight and knowledge to reason things through for oneself – that is, to propose theses and hypotheses and to test and explore them for their coherence and accuracy. In this Bhāviveka agreed, and indeed used Diṅnāga's own logical forms in his critique of Yogācāra.[46]

Candrakīrti thinks this is highly dangerous, pernicious even. Proposing theses in one's own voice – even just for investigation, even if you bear in mind that any conceptualizations will be artificial, approximations and distortions – implies commitment to the reality of the entities named. Instead one should confine oneself strictly to the assertions made by others, and to revealing the contradictions inherent in these.

This argumentative strategy is called *prasaṅga*. It is similar to the *reductio ad absurdum* but, while the latter should demonstrate that the proposition under examination is false, the method of *prasaṅga*, in Mādhyamika hands, should show us that the practice of asserting propositions is misguided. According to Candrakīrti, even just to assert a claim provisionally is to be committed implicitly to an existence claim – to be tacitly asserting that the object of predication *exists* – that is, exists as an individual with its own distinct nature. And such a commitment, of course, will positively prevent enlightenment and the appreciation of reality as it is. As Peter Fenner puts it, "discrimination creates entities through a categorical abstraction. Once there is a conceptual discernment of entities, conceptuality [*kalpanā*] is established and from this the full gamut of elaboration [*prapañca*] takes off".[47]

We might think that Candrakīrti's fears here are ludicrously hyperbolic. Surely I can say "the apple is red", and even mean it, without being tacitly committed to apple-essences, existing independently and in their own right. After all, I can speak meaningfully of unicorns and fairies, without supposing they *exist*. Indeed, we might even have thought it was part of Nāgārjuna's own project to show us how everyday language can be left in its place, so long as we resist any temptation to take it literally as a metaphysical claim about how things are. If people took it that way even in everyday thought, Nāgārjuna argues, they would not be able to function as they do. Everyday thought recognizes that sprouts are both the same and not the same as their plants, and it does not bother too much about the contradiction that appears only when these notions – same and different – are made absolute by tying them to a metaphysics of discrete individuals. So if Candrakīrti does not allow a good Madhyamaka to articulate, argue for and defend her position by employing the ordinary methods of reason-giving, he is not only needlessly tying her hands behind her back, but also, one might think, going against Nāgārjuna's insight that ordinary speech – talk of cause, say – does not assert or imply commitment to some strange metaphysical entity (*the cause*) in the first place.

Naturally, the Madhyamaka view is not supposed to be a 'view' like all the others; it should not enjoin on us the assertion of the absolute existence of anything at all. Nevertheless, exploring and explaining even that claim is certainly possible, and all the resources of reasoning should be put in the service of doing so. Bhāviveka was well versed in all varieties of Buddhist thought and, moreover, a keen defender of the Madhyamaka; he is neither naive in commending the full use of reason nor likely to be willing to distort Madhyamaka or sell it short. If thoughtful Mādhyamikas themselves took the view that using arguments involving theses not provided by the opponent was not pernicious – did not commit one to endorsing an invalid existence claim – then this seems indirectly to confirm the supposition that Candrakīrti is just being silly when he insists Mādhyamikas confine themselves to *prāsaṅgika* reasoning. One can perfectly well propose a thesis such as "Giving to worthy renunciants is admirable", while bearing in mind the provisional and distorting nature of any linguistic act.

But it may be that Candrakīrti is motivated in his critique of 'reasoning for oneself' by something more than pure animus against Bhāviveka, his Mādhyamika rival. Diṅnāga and Bhāviveka both think that one can entertain a thought sufficiently to examine it, while still bearing in mind the specific way in which language misrepresents reality. And surely they are right that we can indeed do this. Language works by asserting lines or distinctions between things and unity among diversity – the word 'apple' works only if it picks out a whole cluster of different properties. The question to ask is not whether such a state is possible but, rather, what state are we then in?

This indeed is the nub of the issue, for all Buddhists agree that the point is to get ourselves into the state where we are seeing reality rightly. For the Mādhyamika, this is realizing the emptiness of all things – their dependence and lack of independent existence or essence – and, as for all Buddhists, such realization is not just a matter of learning the truth of a certain proposition. One might follow the logic of the *Mūlamadhyamakakārikā* sufficiently to feel satisfied that she can meaningfully and correctly assert the true proposition "All *dharmas* are empty", but this would not bring one to enlightenment, at least not directly. That requires fully recognizing emptiness in one's whole way of looking at and experiencing the world, appreciating what it means that all *dharmas* are empty. This is not a matter of adopting one proposition among possibly many others but, rather, a reorientation of how one thinks anything at all.

It is this reorientation that, on Candrakīrti's view, is incompatible with even provisionally entertaining a thesis of one's own. Even held at arm's length, assertions artificially individuate – even if only provisionally – so they cannot co-exist with the state of mind we are aiming at. To assert them, and construct arguments out of them, involves *practising* and *reinforcing* the bad habit of taking things to be actually so divided and existing for themselves. When we argue for a position, or entertain any thoughts at all, we are shaping our minds in specific ways, making some ways of looking at engaging with the world more readily available. All such ways of engaging with the world grant it more reality, more substantial individuation, than it has, and they all participate in the habit of 'conceptual proliferation', of making more meaning than is there through elaborating cognitive activity. Realizing reality brings a halt to all such conceptual proliferation:[48] "the very halting of discursiveness is [the] fruit of true analysis" (*MA* VI.117c–d). And silence may be the only proper and full recognition of this.

> This statement is ascertained by reasoning that is just familiar for ordinary people, not for the venerable (*arya*). Does this mean the venerable have no reasoning? Who can say whether or not they do? For ultimate truth is a matter of venerable silence. (*Prasannapadā* 57.5–7[49])

If analysis is required, then, second best to silence, one may only say 'not this', 'not this', without an attempt to formulate alternatives, or even going through the mental motions of constructing the alternatives to be rejected.

We see this summarized by Śāntideva, an eighth-century CE Mādhyamika. At *Bodhicāryāvatāra* IX, he imagines a Yogācārin giving the *tu quoque* reply we had imagined above to Bhāviveka's objection that absences cannot be perceived. Śāntideva's imagined Yogācārin says: "If it is conceived that a phenomenon that does not really exist cannot be perceived then how can a non-entity, which is without basis, stand before the mind?" And Śāntideva's Mādhyamika replies:

> When neither an entity nor a non-entity remains before the mind, then since there is no other possibility, having no objects, it becomes calm. (*Bodhicāryāvatāra* IX.33–34)[50]

Candrakīrti's alternative

If we are not to engage even provisionally in the use of conventional reasoning, how should "conventional reality become the means [by which] the ultimate is reached" (*MA* 80a)? And how, if at all, will Candrakīrti avoid becoming a sort of irrationalist mystic, without thereby becoming a nihilist, dispensing with cognition entirely because there is nothing to cognize?

We cited above two possible strategies for escaping nihilism. But it looks as if Nāgārjuna's claim that emptiness is itself empty forecloses from the outset the first strategy, of avoiding nihilism by giving priority (epistemological or metaphysical) to ultimate reality, for it seems to insist (among other things), that ultimate reality has the *same status* as conventional reality – pervasive emptiness is empty, too – and in particular has that same status in virtue of which it is merely conventional. And yet there is difficulty in adopting the second strategy on its own. For, just to the extent that one succeeds in offering a sense of the *reality* of the conventional as the only reality available, to that same extent one undermines all resources for challenging the conventional, and Buddhism loses any possibility of practical, transformative power.[51]

This is a worry Mādhyamikas were sensitive to, and were made sensitive to by their Yogācāra critics.[52] Asaṅga, in the *Yogācārabhūmi*, argues that without positing a 'dependent nature' distinct from the 'ultimate', "no effort would then be needed to eradicate defilement, simply because the latter would then not exist, and if defilement does not exist, purification would not exist either".[53] And Vasubandhu observes that although "consciousness' character as the construction of that which was not is demonstrated by its being", nevertheless we cannot say that this confused consciousness itself does not exist: "it couldn't be simply non-being because 'Liberation through its extinction is accepted'. Otherwise, bondage and freedom would be contradicted, and this would incur the fault of denying affliction and alleviation."[54]

One attempt to avoid the nihilist implication is to take Candrakīrti's Madhyamaka as a kind of scepticism. We can refuse to reify the 'emptiness' that is ultimate reality, and yet take that very phenomenon seriously, as somehow the 'real point' (the right view, proper appreciation of which is liberating), by taking 'emptiness' as the assertion that all our experience is so irretrievably shot through with our mental fabrications that the project of understanding should be thoroughly abandoned anyway.[55] Remarks such as "in every aspect, ordinary experience has no validity" (*MA* VI.31) lend credence to this sort of reading, which concludes that there is, simply, nothing to know. Such an approach does, of course, lead to familiar circularity and practicability objections to scepticism.[56] If this, or a similar, interpretation of ultimate reality could be made intelligible, it might deal with the threat of metaphysical nihilism, but would still leave the threat of moral nihilism untouched, for that requires some legitimization of some norms of behaviour, thought and attitudes. At best it seems capable of a kind of implacable quietism that requires us to accept whatever happens to pass for 'good' and 'bad' without challenge.

Candrakīrti insists that the conventional *can* be used to approach liberating insight, but it is quite obviously not always so used. If this is to be made good, we must have some way of discriminating correct from incorrect conventional practices. The question "that every Madhyamaka interpretation has to face", as Georges Dreyfus puts it, using the language of Indian Buddhist philosophers, is: "Can Mādhyamikas use the notion of conventional truth without reintroducing the very essentialism that they seek to overcome?"[57] Somehow the Mādhyamika must offer an answer that is neither nihilist nor quietist, and yet distinct from the Yogācāra and Abhidharma positions, which, according to the Mādhyamika, persist in holding on to some sort of 'self'.[58]

Background

In the *Mūlamadhyamakakārikā*, Nāgārjuna directly took on the central resources of current Abhidharma, presenting this critique as a necessary corrective to set Buddhists back on the correct path and supplying intellectual articulation to the growing Mahāyāna movement. He seems to have had one especially energetic disciple, Āryadeva, who was active in establishing Mahāyāna Buddhism according to the lines set out by Nāgārjuna. There was even one commentary of uncertain authorship on the *Mūlamadhyamakakārikā*, such commentaries being the usual medium for extending intellectual discourse.[59] In spite of this, however, the discussion never really seems to have taken off. The Mahāyāna grew and flourished but Nāgārjuna's Madhyamaka articulation of its intellectual grounds seemed to have all but sunk without a trace. Vasubandhu's extended examination of the self in the *Abhdiharmakośabhāṣya* IX engages seriously with non-Buddhist self-theorists and at even greater length with the Buddhist *pudgalavādins*, that substantial portion of Buddhists at the time who thought the person was ultimately real. Nāgārjuna's Madhyamaka, by contrast, warrants only the barest nod of acknowledgement, sandwiched between Pudagalavādins and non-Buddhists:

> Whereas there are those who admit an ineffable *pudgala*, others deny the existence of all the *dharmas*; non-Buddhists imagine a soul apart from all other substances. All these doctrines are wrong and present the same flaw in that they do not lead to liberation. (*AKBh.* IX[60])

It seems Madhyamaka was not a position Vasubandhu felt he had to take seriously.[61] Given Madhyamaka's own refusal to present itself as an alternative system, this is perhaps no surprise.

The clear articulation of a Mahāyāna alternative, in Asaṅga's Yogācāra, ably argued for by Vasubandhu, may have roused proponents of Madhyamaka to action. Around the turn of the fifth to sixth centuries CE, Buddhapālita wrote his fresh commentary on the *Mūlamadhyamakakārikā*. Bhāviveka, a generation later, responded with one of his own, and in this and other works he is critical of Buddhapālita's interpretation of Nāgārjuna. Although an impressive scholar of Buddhism and its competitors, Bhāviveka's work was eventually overshadowed by the enormous success enjoyed outside India by Candrakīrti, who rushed to Buddhapālita's defence, offering a distinctive interpretation of Madhyamaka that came to be considered the correct view by Tibetan inheritors and continuers of the Indian Buddhist tradition.

Candrakīrti's Madhyamakāvatāra

The *Prasannapadā*, the *Clear Words*,[62] is Candrakīrti's definitive commentary on Nāgārjuna's *Mūlamadhyamakakārikā*. More accessible for seeing Candrakīrti's distinctive take on Madhyamaka, however, is his concise *Introduction to the Middle Way*, the *Madhyamaka-Avatāra*, arranged as a discussion of the six Mahāyāna *pāramitās*, or 'perfections': giving, restraint, forbearance, energy, meditation and wisdom (*prajñā*). Presenting the Buddhist path as the perfecting of these six canonical virtues, and dividing the path of the Bodhisattva into stages – from initial aspiration to complete enlightenment – is characteristic of the Mahāyāna.[63] After the first six chapters, Candrakīrti follows with four more on the further perfection of the virtues already described. A concluding eleventh chapter follows, summarizing the whole.

Because it is a *path* that is being described, the order of presentation is not accidental. The first three perfections treated – generosity, self-restraint (*śīla*) and patience – are suitable for everyone, regardless of whether one is aiming at happiness or liberation, and wherever one is on the path, attention to improving these virtues will be beneficial. The last three perfections – energy, concentration and wisdom – discussed in chapters four to six, are relevant specifically to aiming at enlightenment. In fact, the first two of these are aiming at and supporting the third: our energy, zeal or confidence is specifically for the value and possibility of attaining perfect wisdom, and (eventually, if this is different) enlightenment. Our concentration is on whatever insight is constitutive of perfect wisdom, or is conducive to this. This is the same wisdom that Nāgārjuna had warned could be dangerous for someone ill-prepared to try to understand.

Candrakīrti's treatment of the six *pāramitās* is, correspondingly, not even-handed. His remarks on the first three virtues are comparatively brief; there are only seventeen verses on generosity, ten on restraint and thirteen on patience. Energy and concentration then have only eight verses between them. By far the greatest portion of Candrakīrti's attention, two hundred and twenty-six verses, is on the perfection of wisdom. The subsequent chapters detailing further perfection in the Bodhisattva's journey comprise six verses between them. The text is thus properly an introduction to Madhyamaka, for in the perfection of wisdom we learn the specifically Madhyamaka account of what liberating correct view consists in, according to Candrakīrti. Here he articulates his interpretation of the Madhyamaka view of ultimate reality as emptiness, and emptiness itself as empty. In the end, it will only be by understanding this correctly that the other virtues are truly perfected and, with that, perhaps even transcended. Structuring the whole around the distinctively Mahāyāna conception of the Buddhist ethical project, however, has the effect of placing the rarefied questions of metaphysics and mind into their proper ethical context. Metaphysics and epistemology matter – and specifically the Pudgalavādins, Vasubandhu, Diṅnāga and non-Buddhists matter – because liberation matters.

The Madhyamakāvatāra's *perfect wisdom*

Much of Candrakīrti's description of the perfection of wisdom is aimed specifically at his fellow Buddhists. There may be much to say about why one should be a Buddhist at all, but here Candrakīrti is keen to express why Buddhists should be Mādhyamikas. There are two ways of characterizing his dispute with his fellow Buddhists: it could be a philosophical dispute, or it could be a dispute over whether to do philosophy at all. That is, *Madhyamakāvatāra* VI might be offering a proper account of ultimate and conventional reality, for knowing this is what wisdom consists in; or it might rather be presenting the Madhyamaka position as the rejection of all such inquiry and assertions. Candrakīrti has been represented in both ways, and with textual evidence, so it might be that we are best off regarding him as seeking a 'middle way' between these two options. Such a middle way might be, for instance, Kantian in spirit: forcing us to reconceive the very enterprise of thinking philosophically.[64] Or it might be, perhaps, Wittgensteinian: using philosophy in order to get us out of the practice of doing philosophy. As we saw above, "the very halting of discursiveness is the fruit of true analysis" (*MA* VI.117c–d). (Again, both comparisons have been drawn.)

If Candrakīrti is going to sustain Nāgārjuna's rejection of an asymmetrical (foundationalist) view of the two truths, he will, as he himself sees, have to be able to answer the objection: "If things, you say, did not exist in ultimate reality, then conventionally too they would be like a barren woman's son. But this is not the case, you say, and claim phenomena by nature do exist" (*MA* VI.107).

How, Candrakīrti's imagined interlocutor wants to know, can there be dependent reality without some reality on which it depends? But no answer to this question, one might observe, can take it on its own terms without being self-contradictory. To insist, as Candrakīrti does, that everything, including ultimate reality, is *equally* dependently arisen is precisely to reject the idea that between conceptual and ultimate reality there could be any explanatory priority. The question presumes that there must be a ground just where Candrakīrti's claim is that there is none. To offer some explanation of this would be to supply a pseudo-ground precisely where the point is to say there is no such thing. Thus Candrakīrti more or less just asserts, "things are produced dependently ... the argument that all 'arises in dependence' cuts in pieces all mistaken views" (*MA* VI.115).

But in the intervening verses, there has been no *argument* at all.[65] Candrakīrti has only reminded us that, after all, people with peculiar eye diseases have visual experiences not caused by objects resembling the visual experiences (*MA* VI.108), and that dream objects are not caused by the objects dreamt of (*MA* VI.109). Such observations hardly warrant the supposition that we have a grip on how it is that there could be dependent phenomena quite generally without there being, anywhere, some causal-explanatory ground.[66]

Should we conclude that the whole business of giving explanations is defunct? Should we conclude that it is a merely conventional practice – fine on its own terms, for doing a bit of natural science perhaps, but unrelated to the path that leads to enlightenment? Or could pursuing explanations of reality be fruitful for the path, in spite of its necessarily dwelling within the conventional? After all, Diṅnāga and Dharmakīrti would surely concede that explanation is of the sort to belong necessarily to conventional reality. This did not make seeking understanding of ultimate reality, through reasons and arguments for why it must be thus and so, a futile or superfluous exercise. How is the conventional to be relied on at all on the path to enlightenment if not in some such way?

Perhaps the fact that Candrakīrti begins with Nāgārjuna's criticism of causation (from *MA* VI.8–VI.21, VI.32–VI.36), and returns to it repeatedly (e.g. *MA* VI.104, VI.114) suggests that Candrakīrti understands his project as a philosophical one, rather than anti-philosophical, for causation, whether one accepts or rejects it, is a metaphysical and epistemological issue. Moreover, while Candrakīrti's criticism of Diṅnāga's theory of perception in the *Prasannapadā* takes the line that this is just not what the word 'perception' *means*, here in the *Madhyamakāvatāra* Candrakīrti is willing to engage directly: the unconditioned mind that the Yogācārin claims is the ultimate reality cannot, in fact, be so (*MA* VI.45–83).[67] And his expansion on Nāgārjuna's famous opening verse offers considerations of *why* we should not suppose that the effect preexists in the cause: "if you think existent entities can once again arise, the growth of plants and other things could never happen in this world. And seeds would reproduce *themselves*" (*MA* VI.9).

Candrakīrti also offers reasons why we should not adopt the alternative view, that causation is simply from "other", in the sense of 'something or another'. In order to avoid an objectionable arbitrariness in 'other'-causation ("anything could issue forth from anything", *MA* VI.14c), one speculates that certain things have specific *powers*: specific potentialities to generate quite specific effects (*MA* VI.15–16, 18). And Candrakīrti accordingly next repeats arguments against postulating such powers. In these ways, Candrakīrti seems actively engaged in the philosophical project of pursuing clear explanation and greater understanding.

All the same, if this is meant to be a philosophical argument about causation, it is difficult to see what Candrakīrti suggests instead. If it is not anti-philosophical quietism, perhaps his point is that, rather than looking at things in the ordinary way of causes and effects – in which case we should just say about them whatever is ordinarily said, no matter how confused, "and so a man who merely left his seed will say: 'This is the child I fathered'" (*MA* VI.32a–b) – we might instead look at things as they are, in which case "apart from suchness as their nature, nothing else is found" (*MA* VI.35b). There is a real difference in these two different ways of regarding the world, and it is this Candrakīrti likens to the difference between perceiving the same things with and without defective sense-organs (*MA* VI.25): "Whatever is perceived with dimmed, defective sight has no validity compared with what is seen by healthy eyes. Just so, a mind deprived of spotless wisdom has no power to contradict a pure, untainted mind" (*MA* VI.27).

The important point seems to be, then, that instead of thinking that there are two different realities – perhaps even with two different modes of cognitive engagement proper to them, as Diṅnāga suggested – there is only one reality, seen either aright or confused. Seen aright, we see all *as empty* (*MA* VI.36–9); seen confusedly, we make the ordinary useful conceptual distinctions and explanatory moves, relating causes to effects. We can either recognize that nothing is intelligible without reference to things other than itself, so everything is empty of independent nature or identity; or we can pretend that we engage with discrete, independently defined entities coming into various relations with one another.

The lesson to be drawn might be the very pessimistic one that our ways of speaking and thinking are irremediably confused. Without discrete individuals, there are no structured grounding relations; and without structured grounding relations, all pretence at explanation is just that – a pretence. Instead of offering more bad explanations, then, we should acknowledge that there is no explaining to be done. This is philosophical investigation for the sake of ending that sort of inquiry altogether.

But the lesson to be drawn might be slightly less pessimistic if we understand it as the following: what it is to see things as they are instead of as causally related is to acknowledge the necessarily incomplete, because infinitely embedded, nature of whatever we think about, and whatever concepts we think with. 'The tree arises dependently upon the seed' acknowledges the conceptual dependency between tree and seed: that they get their sense and meaning from the very fact that trees arise from seeds and seeds give rise to trees. In this, there is no order of priority between seed and tree.

> If a thing produces an effect, it is indeed a cause. And if no fruit appears, there is no cause and no production. And as for the result, it's only if the cause exists that it comes into being. Tell me, therefore, which derives from which, and what precedes the other? (*MA* VI.168)

I do not grasp something *as a seed* or *as a tree* without already implying this relationship; and yet if I do not grasp it *as a seed*, or *a tree*, then I have not thought anything at all. We might liken this to a critique of the notion of 'the given', particularly when we consider Candrakīrti's criticism of Diṅnāga's conception of 'perception' in the *Prasannapadā*:

> But in the present case — "a jar is perceptible" — there is nothing at all called a jar which is imperceptible, [nothing at all] separately apprehended [*pṛthag upalabdha*] to which perceptibility could figuratively belong ... As it is said [in Āryadeva's *Catuḥśataka*]: "Just as a pot does not exist as separate from things like its form, so, too, form does not exist as separate from [basic elements] like air, etc." (*PP* 70–71)

Everything is experienced *as* ..., or under some description; or, as Kant might put it, there are no 'blind' experiences. Whatever we experience or can experience is *of* something, *as* something. As Bhāviveka already pointed out, with respect to cognitions in particular, there is no characteristic without the characterized. Indeed, what the example should show is that this mutual dependence holds not just between objects of cognition (a tree and a seed), but also between the cognized and the means of cognizing it; it is not a tree unless it is the sort of thing I can engage with in certain sorts of ways (by sight, by touch); and sight and touch are what reveal trees and seeds.[68] Thus everything Diṅnāga noticed about such experiences being necessarily conceptually inflected, hence defined in part by our cognizing activities, was correct. His mistake, Candrakīrti thinks, was to suppose there could be anything else.

Perhaps this is why Candrakīrti enjoins us, "Do not undermine conventions that the world accepts" (*MA* VI.159d). And he famously likens the two truths to the two wings with which one flies into perfect wisdom:

> Like the king of swans, ahead of lesser birds they soar, on broad white wings of relative and ultimate full spread. And on the strength of virtue's mighty wind they fly to gain the far and supreme shore, the oceanic qualities of Victory.
>
> (*MA* VI.226)

"Conventional reality therefore becomes", Candrakīrti claims, "the means ... [by which] the ultimate is reached" (*MA* VI.80a–b).

But "the truth of everyday convention should not be subjected to analysis" (*MA* VI.35c–d), and it could not sustain such analysis if one tried. Indeed, as Dan Arnold puts it "The fact that our ordinary practices cannot be thought to require explanation, then, is proposed by the Mādhyamika as expressing something that is importantly *true*".[69] So how should one *use* conventional reality as a means to ultimate reality, or in fact do anything other than just accept about it that this is what passes for conventionally accepted (*MA* VI.25)? "For our part," Candrakīrti reinterates, "we agree with ordinary convention – memory is the thought that 'I have seen'" (*MA* VI.75c–d), and so generally. But there is nothing transformative in such quietism that puts ordinary opinions beyond critique. It seems that the only difference between Candrakīrti's Mādhyamika and the ordinary person is that the former *sees as conventional* – as provisional, embedded and dependent on our thinking – *and accepts* those things that are simply accepted by the latter.

But this in turn seems undermined by Candrakīrti's claim about everyday talk of planting seeds causing plants to grow (*MA* VI.32c–d), that "in every respect, ordinary experience has no validity" (*MA* VI.31a; c.f. *MA* VI.27, quoted above).

This same tension between revealing the inadequacies of ordinary ways of thinking, and yet accepting them just as they are, *and* finding this somehow useful in realizing ultimate reality, arises in Candrakīrti's discussion of the *pudgalavāda*. His engagement with the Abhidharma Buddhists, including the personalists, at *MA* VI.132–67, likewise involves trying to expose the various inconsistencies that his rivals are supposedly committed to. For those who suppose the aggregates together are the self, for instance, "it follows from your theory that when yogis see there is no self, they fail to understand the final truth of form and other aggregates" (*MA* VI.131a–b). His treatment of the personalists involves appropriating the greater part of their claims, but setting them in a more fitting metaphysical framework so that the suspect claim that the person is ultimately real may be eliminated.

The Pudgalavādin's difficulty was that he wanted to retain Abhidharma metaphysics, but also had an account of the person that did not fit into that – for it was ultimate, by having a real spatiotemporal continuity between its parts, but it was not a substance, as ultimate existents were supposed to be.[70] Candrakīrti argues, however, that the sort of real continuity the Pudgalavādin saw in the person is not special to persons, but just is the non-sameness/non-difference of dependent origination. And the sort of substantiality the person lacked is not to be found anywhere, not in *dharmas* nor any other version of 'ultimate reality'. Thus it is true, as the Pudgalavādin argued, that the person is not the same as its constituents, nor different from them, nor identical to any one of them, and so on. In fact, just as the Pudgalavādins said, the person is conceived on the basis of its constituents dependently arising as they do (*MA* VI.139, VI.150). It is not, for that reason, unsayable (*MA* VI.146–8), or indeed in any way exceptional: "A pot ... you say is indescribable apart from form and other features. The self is also indescribable apart from aggregates" (*MA* VI.148a–c).

And it is important that it is not exceptional. For the Pudgalavādin wished to carve out the special Brahmanical notion of a separate, eternal Self, and suppose that rejecting this sufficed to satisfy the Buddha's instruction not to cling to self. But as Candrakīrti observes, plenty of people engage in the egoism that causes suffering, without having such a philosophical notion of Self.

> Some think that when 'no-self' is understood, this means the refutation of a permanent, existent self. But this could never be the ground of our ego-clinging. How strange to say that understanding this suffices to uproot belief in 'I'. (*MA* VI.140)

> We may see that beings born as beasts for many ages never apprehend a self unborn and permanent. And yet they clearly have a sense of 'I'. (*MA* VI.125a–c; and see *MA* VI.124)

The several observations the Pudgalavādin brings against the Abhidharmika are not themselves wrong. It is rather the exceptionalism of the *pudgalavāda*, which takes itself to have found in the person some unique thing of this peculiar sort, that makes the view even more susceptible to ego-clinging than the *ātmavādins*.

If, however, the self is conventionally real *just like everything else*, and if we should not argue with the world (*MA* VI.159d), or subject it to analysis (*MA* VI.35c–d), then why should we not accept the conventional self as well? Candrakīrti says we must free ourselves from I-thinking, that this is what eliminating ignorance will give us:

> This self will manifest empirically, the fruit of ignorance, as long as it is not subject to analysis. Without a worker, there is no work performed, and likewise without 'I' there is no 'mine'. Perceiving that both 'I' and 'mine' are empty, the yogi will be utterly set free. (*MA* VI.164c–165c)

But at the same time, he wants to insist that we not challenge convention: "Vases, canvas, bucklers, armies, forests, garlands, trees, houses, chariots, hostelries, and all such things that common people designate, dependent on their parts, accept as such. For the Buddha did not quarrel with the world" (*MA* VI.166).

Not just vases and garlands, but also the self is one such thing that common people designate, dependent on their parts. Must we not, then, just accept the self and the clinging that goes with it? If conventional reality is all there is – if nothing survives the sort of conceptual analysis that Vasubandhu made criterial of ultimate reality (*AKBh.* VI.4), so that there is no ultimate reality either to explain or to operate as a constraint on our conventions, nor to serve as a goal towards which we might revise our understandings – then what sense can Candrakīrti give to his claim that insight undoes conventional I-thinking, that conventional reality can become a means to the ultimate, one wing of the swan flying to the further shore, as in his final verse?

When Kant makes his observation about the ineradicability of epistemic categories from our attempts to do metaphysics (or to think anything true at all), he thinks it terribly important nonetheless to validate the objectivity of our experiences. This, indeed, might be thought of as the main burden of his critical task. The distinction between subjective and objective must remain an intelligible one, and we must be able to have confidence that there are recognizable standards of correctness in judgement, if thinking is to be at all possible. In the current case, we want a slightly different distinction, one that would allow us to make out a difference between the conventional validity of forests and the like, and the invalidity, conventional and ultimate, of the 'self' – or at least provide a framework in which such an argument would be possible. For this we need some means of discriminating acceptable from unacceptable conventionally valid truths. Otherwise, it is difficult to see with what right we should eliminate I-thinking and its ego-clinging, and not also tree-thinking and pots-clinging.

Grounds for such a distinction are not forthcoming. For Candrakīrti persists in offering 'what is accepted by the world' as normative:

> We, too, say, What's the use of this hair-splitting, which delves into ordinary discourse? Let it be! Until there is understanding of reality, the conventional – its existence [*sattākā*] come into being [*ātmabhāva*] as projected by nothing but error – is, for those who desire liberation, the cause of the accumulation of the roots of merit that convey [one] to liberation. (*PP* 68)

Similarly, at *Prasannapadā* 75, Candrakīrti seems even to prefer Naiyāyika epistemology to Diṅnāga's, as being truer to 'how we actually talk'. This, however, cannot be a programme for restoring an intelligible sense of objective validity. 'What the world agrees' is just what it is by its inability to withstand critical investigation, and by the consequent unsuitability of subjecting it to examination, supposing thereby to have got at something *more* correct, suitable or valid. 'What is agreed' cannot play the role of explaining that 'the world' is in fact *warranted* in so judging. It cannot, therefore, provide any basis for a distinction among the broad and diverse 'accepted ways of speaking': between those that are rightly accepted and those that might be challenged. They are all equally unchallengeable. 'That sight sees colour', and 'that homosexual relationships are inappropriate' acquire the same unchallengeable status of 'what the world accepts'.

Perhaps we can find sufficient difference between these two types of 'accepted claims' in that *all* the world accepts the former – rejecting it would be unintelligible – whereas only *some* of the world accepts the latter.[71] But I-thinking seems an excellent example of what all the world accepts and, on reflection, finds it unintelligible to reject.[72] So this criterion requires that we leave in place the one conventional style of thinking we ought to let go of.

Beyond this special case (and perhaps a few other, related cases), if I am using 'what the world accepts' as my standard of correctness, I must either be absurdly optimistic about the homogeneity of discourse among people or else I must simply tolerate contradictions, accepting that my ambitions can be no more than descriptive and reproductive of what already is so. 'The world' accepts homosexuality is inappropriate; 'the world' also accepts that homosexuality is appropriate.[73] That is descriptively accurate of 'the world's' views; but if the only permissible project is such description, then even in cases of internal incoherence or dissent between people, the Mādhyamika cannot allow the rational investigation into what *ought* to be said, thought or valued. Given what is at stake in the ordinary world in which such ordinary discourse arises, the Madhyamaka position, as Candrakīrti articulates it, requires an intolerable quietism.

IV. Percepts and concepts: *Apoha* 1 (Diṅnāga)

In the *Theaetetus*, Socrates imagines a discussion with the extreme Heracliteans.[74] Taking their cue from Heraclitus' observation that 'everything flows', these people apparently think not only that "all things move and flow" (*Theaetetus* 182c4), but even that "all things are always in every kind of motion" (182a1–2). Seriously believing this, Socrates contends, must necessarily render the fluxist speechless. First it is noted that individual words presume sameness over time in order to mean anything at all:

> [S]ince not even this abides, that what flows flows white, but rather is in the process of change, so that there is flux in this very thing too, the whiteness ... is it possible to give any name to a colour which will properly apply to it? (182d1–5)

Then this point is generalized to any attempt at expressing such reality in words:

> What has really emerged is that, if all things are in motion, every answer, on whatever subject, is equally correct, both 'it is thus' and 'it is not thus' – or, if you like, 'becomes', as we don't want to use any expressions which bring our friends to a standstill ... One must not even use the word 'thus'; for this 'thus' would no longer be in motion; nor yet 'not thus' for here again there is no motion. The exponents of this theory need to

> establish another language; as it is, they have no words that are consistent with their hypothesis. (183a6–b5)

We might think this problem does not arise for the Buddhist. For the Abhidharmikas, for instance, were happy to concede that, while everything is impermanent and indeed momentary, each white moment gave rise, among other things, to a successor white moment. This is adequate to account both for impermanence, and for the appearance of persistence – for there were indeed 'flowings' of whiteness, one moment of whiteness after another. There was no universal property 'whiteness' that each moment shared, of course; but inasmuch as each moment had a distinctive nature of its own, an identifiable *svabhāva*, the Abhidharmika could – like the modern-day trope-theorist – resort to real similarity between the *svabhāvas* of these distinct moments.

But this picture did not survive the critique of Vasubandhu, and Diṅnāga and later Buddhist epistemologists insist that every moment is *sui generis*. There can be no point on which to compare this or that particular and discover that they have some property in common, for then the common property really existing equally at both moments would itself be permanent, rather than impermanent. But nothing really existing is permanent. Nor can there even be real similarity between diverse moments, because this requires identifying them – and this, Diṅnāga has shown, belongs to our conceptualizing activity, not to the perception-particular as it is. "[I]t is not the case that there exists resemblance. Qualitative resemblance, whether it arise from the transfer of a notion or from the influence of the quality, is absent" (*PS* V.4). Thus, Diṅnāga allows that language is stable, and so relatively 'permanent'. This, indeed, is how we know that it can be at best conventionally true, for whatever ultimately exists does not persist. But "a general term does not express particulars" (*PS* V.2).

Yet it is not clear that allowing only stability of language over shifting, indeterminate particulars – without there being anything that a word picks out in each of the different cases – can suffice to preserve the meaningfulness of language. If each and every particular is wholly distinct from all others, and wholly *sui generis*, then what it is that a word should mean seems opaque and radically unrestricted. First, there are no criteria of correct use (e.g. use 'red' whenever *this colour*, or similar, is at issue), for this would require there to be some identifiable *this colour*, the same in each case, or at least to which others might be similar. And second, if words are ways of carving out bits of reality, distinguishing some into 'same' and some into 'different' – as we saw with inference, and even with basic perceptual judgements like 'This is blue' – and if no particular can in fact be similar to any other (that is, there is no identifiable quality or property they actually have, and so no real similarity), then it seems we should be equally entitled to group together phenomena in any old way. Everything is equally like and unlike everything else.[75]

Yet, according to Diṅnāga, just because thoughts expressible by words capture only conceptually constructed unities, this does not mean that it is irrelevant how we construct things. As we saw in §II, above, there are legitimate and illegitimate ways of grouping perceptions and the general terms they inspire; and, Diṅnāga wants to maintain, it is even interesting and important in its own right to investigate these. Judgement, or inference, is after all a *pramāṇa*, if a lesser one. In our study of inference we saw that similarity and dissimilarity are the most basic grounds for drawing things together, or drawing a distinction between them. When we are making inferences we are concerned with getting it right with respect to the similar and the dissimilar. Even classification or perceptual judgements as minimal as "This is a lamp" or "this is blue" require the recognition of, and classification according to, similarity and non-similarity that we have in inference. It is this recognition and classification that allow me to regulate my behaviour with respect to my perceived environment. I must recognize that this now is relevantly similar to what I previously regarded as a lamp in order to reason that there is therefore a switch or some other mechanism for turning it on and off – and that when on, it ought to give light, and so on.

But it is not clear that Diṅnāga can grant language this regulatory function, when concepts are nothing like perceived reality, and concept application is unconstrained by the nature of perceptual cognitions. Recognition of *this* as a lamp, and so on, seems to require the assertion of real similarities between fundamentally distinct objects. At least, that is required if we want to maintain that there can be right and wrong in our conceptual construction, that conventional falsity is possible, and conventional truth has standards of correctness. Otherwise, it seems, I ought to be able to conceptually carve up perceptual reality in any old way and be no more or less true to how things are.

Diṅnāga hopes to maintain the usefulness of linguistic conventions – without appeal to a metaphysics of properties shared by different objects and without appeal to real similarities that require individuation and determinate identity – by considering concept-boundaries as exclusionary, rather than inclusive. His famous, if obscure, declaration of *anyāpoha*, exclusion-of-other, is that words name their objects "by precluding what is incompatible" (*PS* V.1) – or, as it is most often glossed, "cow means 'not non-cow'". Instead of supposing that the concept cow, and the ability to use it meaningfully, requires gathering together all instances of some common property 'cowness', or recognizing such a thing in each case, we should instead regard 'cow' as excluding all that is not-cow; whatever is left is *cow*, and there is no need to posit some distinct entity within that remainder, 'the cow itself', to serve as the referent of the term.

While the intention not to posit extra entities is attractive, this solution can rapidly appear to be as futile as it is elegant. For how, we must ask, is the excluding to be done? What could operate as the principle of exclusion except some conception of 'cow' to which everything excluded fails to conform? 'Exclusion of the different' instead of 'inclusion of the same' seems only to have shifted the problem around, without actually addressing it.[76] Diṅnāga may even recognize this, for he allows their parity: "Association and dissociation are the two ways that a word expresses its object. They consist respectively in applying to what is alike and in not applying to what is unlike" (*PS* V.34).

There still must be some basis of similarity, real or presumed, between distinct objects in order for a concept to be doing any work at all, and if it is only presumed, then this work looks to be arbitrary and liable to no correctness conditions. The Abhidharmikas and their tropes might not have had any *explanation* of the real similarity that should hold between some tropes and not others; but at least there was real similarity there, and so there was some basis in ultimate reality for carving the multitudinous phenomena in one way rather than another. This could operate as a constraint – one among others, of course – on what could possibly count as 'getting it right'. But Diṅnāga's insistence on the irreducible particularity and distinctness of every ultimately existing thing does not allow him even this much. Nevertheless, Diṅnāga wants to preserve not only perception but also inference – and so concepts – as a *pramāṇa*, a source of valid cognitions. And he wants to do this by observing that 'cow' means 'not non-cow', 'blue' means 'not non-blue', and so on.

This exclusionary theory of meaning brings out the fact that, like inference, deploying concepts carves everything into two classes: the similar and the dissimilar. It emphasizes, moreover, that inclusion and exclusion are complementary faces of a single mental act. To insist that 'blue' means 'not non-blue' is to insist that there is no place to go outside the mental act itself, or related acts, to seek the meaningfulness of 'blue'. Drawing such a line, as for instance '(this is) blue', must, on Diṅnāga's account, be regarded as something like a decision, not a recognition of any shared (or unshared) quality.

It is not perception but decision that I shall consider this class of things to be alike. Being infinitely particular, members of the respective classes have, in fact, nothing in common; and strictly they are as much like each other as unlike, and as like others as like each other. Nevertheless, I decide to consider these as likenesses, and the others not. On the basis of what do I 'decide'? What is the criterion for whether I have got it right? Perhaps it need not be appeal to some non-linguistic fact but, rather, only to other such decisions, to other concepts. For as much as the mental act may be decision-like, rather than perception-like, such 'decisions' are, of course, not for each of us to make completely independently of any meanings of other words, and of any other use of words by others. Such an account has the attraction of rendering it unmysterious how it is that many of our words may, in the course of ordinary use, shift their boundaries in more and less subtle ways, without language-use falling utterly apart.

One might think here of Wittgenstein's observations about 'going on in the same way'. We cannot have a further application rule, prescribing what 'in the *same* way' means, in each case (or in any); this would only introduce the Problem of the Criterion, a problem nearly as old as philosophy itself. And yet (and this I take it is the point), we are quite evidently nevertheless not at a complete loss in actually making such determinations. So the thing to examine is how we *actually do* in fact determine whether someone is going on 'in the same way'. And we discover that we rely on further conventions, tacit expectations, categories and ways of looking at things whose only basis is in practice and in use. Wittgenstein calls this meaning-through-use a 'form of life'; the Buddhists might call it 'conventional reality'. When looking for criteria of correctness of concept application, we look to further conceptual reality, for which we have conventions; these have and need no foundation in some other reality. That suffices.

Of course, it might easily seem not to suffice. For all that conventional reality should be *merely* conventional, in some sense, it should also be *real*, in some sense. This way of understanding the *apoha* claim seems to have saved the particularity of all ultimately real things and the meaningfulness of language, but at the price of the latter becoming utterly untethered from the former. And if the conceptual is utterly untethered from the ultimate, what meaning can we possibly give to its claim to be any kind of reality at all?

Dharmakīrti, Diṅnāga's successor, feels this pressure, and tries to address it.

V. Efficacy: *Apoha* 2 (Dharmakīrti)

Dharmakīrti, working sometime between the mid-sixth and mid-seventh centuries, continued the epistemological tradition inaugurated by Diṅnāga.[77] Among his seven extant works on logic, language, epistemology and metaphysics, the most substantial by far is his *Pramāṇa-Vārttika*, to which he wrote his own commentary, the *Pramāṇavārttika-svavṛtti*. Although ostensibly only elucidating Diṅnāga, Dharmakīrti's *Pramāṇavārttika* is innovative, particularly finding occasions to introduce appeal to causation to cover what he perceives as explanatory gaps. In metaphysics, Dharmakīrti is sometimes thought to be more explicitly Yogācāra and idealist than his intellectual predecessor, although as long as talk remains restricted to non-commital 'particulars' and 'generalities', this will not be evident.[78]

In epistemology, Dharmakīrti takes over Diṅnāga's *apoha* claim, but he is evidently dissatisfied with the minimal interpretation of this, which allows our words to have meaning but at the expense of their bearing any discernible relation to ultimate reality. He introduces therefore an additional criterion of correctness, namely 'efficacy'. If conceptualizing in a particular way turns out to be efficacious – and, in particular, effective in satisfying the expectations consistent with such a way of conceptualizing – then this validates this particular way of conceptualizing reality.

The introduction of the principle of efficacy begins already in Dharmakīrti's exposition of the two truths, which revises Diṅnāga's distinction in the *Pramāṇasamuccaya* between perception-particulars (ultimate reality) and generalities (conventional reality):

> Instrumental cognitions [*pramāṇas*] are of two kinds of objects ... There are two objects because some are similar across

> instances and others are not similar; because some are the objects of words and others are not the objects of words; and because the cognition of some occurs when there are causes other than the object, and the cognition of others does not occur when there are causes other than the object.
>
> (*PV* 3.1–2[79])

This elaboration on Diṅnāga's distinction between that which is perceived and that which is inferred offers two parallel sets of properties: on the one hand, that which is similar across instances, the object of words, the cognition of which is caused by something other than the object; on the other hand, that which is not similar across different instances, is not the object of words, the cognition of which is caused only by itself. The former are what Diṅnāga called 'generalities', and so includes all concepts; the latter are Diṅnāga's perception-particulars. "A single cognition that has various objects should be established to occur. Hence [perception] ... is established to be non-conceptual, since when conceptualizing one object, what one sees is another" (*PV* 3.207).

The very business of seeing something *as* something means taking a particular to be a generality: "what one sees is another". But that one perceives something at all, as an expressible particular or as something other, is due to the causal efficacy of the particular. It has it in itself to give rise to cognition. Thus, according to Dharmakīrti, "that which is capable of telic function [*arthakriyā*[80]] is said to be ultimately real. The other one is said to be conventionally real. They are, respectively, the particular and the universal" (*PV* 3.3).

Suppose we now ask Dharmakīrti how the aptness of concept-application can be grounded in an ultimate reality that admits of no similarity of the sort implied by our concepts.[81] The reply comes in terms of brute facts about causality. Perception-particulars give rise to cognitions of themselves, and nothing else can do that. But they also give rise to *concepts* of various kinds – generalities were the sort of thing to be caused by something *other* than themselves. What Dharmakīrti crucially observes is that we can have similarity of effects, without having to postulate similarity of causes. That is, the particulars need not have real similarities among themselves in order for them to warrant some, but not just any, conceptualizing.

> The nature [*prakṛti*] of [certain] things is such that, although they are different, by their nature [*svabhāva*] some of them

> are restricted to the accomplishment of the same *telos* [*artha*], such as inducing the same judgement or producing an awareness of an object; the sense faculties and so on are examples.
> (*PV* 1.73)

This might seem at first to be about as helpful as Diṅnāga's 'not non-cow', for one might reasonably suppose that there is still some *one thing*, a common property actually shared by all things, namely 'the power to produce *this* effect'. Making the property a power does not seem to help.[82] It is still, as the translation here has it, 'from the nature' of a thing that it has this specific power. Moreover, there is additional real similarity in the effects produced. For if the results of the powers are not in fact the same, then again it looks as if we lack a standard of correctness for conceiving them as such.

Dharmakīrti may be able to evade this, by explaining 'sameness of effects' by reference to desire or expectations. The idea would be that I conceive a desire, and an idea of how I might satisfy it. I so act, and the desire is satisfied – that is, I come to experience the perceptions I expected to. The desire and the expectation are all expressed in generalities, and belong to conventional reality, and this is where the similarities remain. But it is ultimate, non-conceptual reality that links the two, for it will be *because* of the particular nature of ultimate reality that expectation and effect are duly matched. This is the successful action criterion: "having determined the object, when one then acts upon it, that thing's causal capacity is established" (*PV* 2.1a; c.f. *PV* 3.3–5).

Desires, aims through which perceptions become acted on so as to generate expected further perceptions, are themselves conceptual. And any perceived similarity in effect has its root in the similarity of desires and expectation – in things constructed by mental activity. Sameness of effect is a retrospective judgement: an assessment of the relation of my current perceptions to my previous expectations. It is not a separate property rooted in the objects of experience themselves, but in the sameness of judgement.[83] So we should not be worried about discerning or relying on 'real similarity' here – indeed, conceptual reality just is the locus of any similarity, and whatever reality it has. As Tillemans, who likens Dharmakīrti's position to a kind of naturalism, remarks, "It is, in other words, just a brute fact that two distinct particulars can cause the same judgment (e.g., 'this is blue')."[84]

If this correctly characterizes Dharmakīrti's intent, then his preferred example of various medicinal herbs is an apt one, with immediate plausibility. "Further examples are certain medicines which, although they are different from each other, are seen to eliminate fever, either in combination or individually. Other things do not do so" (*PV* 1.74). Whether by paracetamol or by ibuprofen – which are chemically quite distinct, and whose causal paths are distinct – I may reduce pain. So, in general, there can be two quite distinct causal routes to the same result. Or take a more homely example: sometimes there are two eggs in the kitchen because someone ate the other two; sometimes there are two eggs there because someone just brought them in from the henhouse where they were laid. Whatever the causal path, the judgement 'Here are two eggs' is the same. So, similarly, two utterly distinct particulars with nothing in common may be causes of the same conceptual cognition, without supposing that those conceptions could just arise any which way, and so are completely untethered to ultimate reality.

We may well wonder, however, whether the status of the claim here is indeed one of 'brute fact', and indeed whether it is a fact at all. Take, for instance, Plato's critique of the explanatory value of natural sciences in the *Phaedo*. At *Phaedo* 96b–102a, Plato has Socrates set out several constraints on adequate explanation, including two that are relevant here: first, that the same thing cannot be the 'cause' (or real explanation, *aitia*) of opposite effects, for then we would be lacking any explanation of the difference between the two;[85] second, that opposites cannot be considered the proper causes of the same effects – in spite of our eggy example, above, the appearance of such shows only that our explanations are in some way unsatisfactory, imprecise or incomplete.

Now, Plato may not be correct in his claims here. But that he makes them reveals that, whether the essential resemblance is in the effects themselves or in the judgement of the effects,[86] we are not at all in the realm of 'brute facts'. We are, rather, in the philosophical realm of determining, or deciding, what counts as 'explanatory', and 'intelligible'; what reason is, and what it can be satisfied with; where there is explaining to do, and where explanations run out. It is worth noting, then, that if we reflect further on Dharmakīrti's medicinal example, we see that it is precisely by taking up Plato's challenge – so taking it as a regulative principle that like effects ultimately indicate some real likeness in their causes – that the study of medicine has advanced as impressively as it has. Scientific inquiry, taking up Plato's criteria, demands that we consider the case of Dharmakīrti's two fever-reducers as, on some more specific level perhaps, working for the same reasons.

If we find two plants equally good at reducing fever in just the same sorts of cases, then we examine the plants further, in search of the shared characteristic in virtue of which they have their effect, and we look in the expectation that we will find it there.[87] If, as in the case of the analgesics paracetamol and ibuprofen, we discover no such thing, then we are thereby apt to discover that the result was not, in fact, the same after all, but only superficially so. Apparently both paracetamol and ibuprofen reduce pain; actually, however, paracetamol blocks pain receptors, while ibuprofen reduces certain sorts of inflammations.

Dharmakīrti's appeal to essential causation, then, may indeed bring reasoning to an end, but rather too quickly. It may show how a sparse ontology can dispense with real similarities existing ultimately, if we take the sameness of judgement itself to be the 'essentially same effect'. But it does so at the expense of doing away with an explanation that would, on another ontology, be perfectly possible and very useful. And if regarded as the introduction of appeal to 'brute facts', Dharmakīrti's recourse to efficacy seems in fact to do very little work, adding little to Diṅnāga's more modest account beyond the assertion, 'and it really is so'.

On Dharmakīrti's view only particulars are ultimately real, and these are all necessarily different from each other. It is our interest in reducing pain that causes us to treat the results of paracetamol and of ibuprofen as similar, even though they are simply different from each other. There is only apparent similarity in results, just as there is only apparent similarity in any grouping of particulars under a common concept. But this will not help the explanatory project, since by the same reasoning any two instances of using (what is taken to be) paracetamol will likewise be utterly distinct from each other in cause and result.

In our example of the medicinal plants, we had been looking for some explanation of concept-formation, and some standard of correctness in concept-formation. We wanted to know why it is that, given that particulars are all radically distinct, we might nevertheless rightly come to take some of them as being similar. We were offered an answer in terms of sameness of desired results. But if these results, too, are utterly different particulars, then we have only repeated the question: in virtue of what do we group these desired results together as 'the same'? And the claim here may be simply that there is no explanation at all of the sort we are looking for.[88] If we want explanation, then we are in the business of forming concepts and deploying them in systematic ways, just as in our example of medical research. But if we are looking for an explanation of how all this relates to what is itself resistant to all conceptualization, then we must necessarily come up empty-handed. That we are caused by perceptions to form conceptions of certain kinds is just so (it is a 'brute fact'); but this reveals something also about the nature of explanation, and the activity of explaining: it is a thoroughly conceptualizing activity, fully responsive to those norms of explanation, but necessarily incapable of engaging in any way with what is, by its nature, not conceptually structured.[89]

If this is right, then although Dharmakīrti's explanation of the relation between ultimate and conventional reality takes a detour through brute causal efficacy, such claims having no explanatory power, so that his position is ultimately not so different from Diṅnāga's simpler version of *apoha*, which directly insisted that all meaning and truth in language could only be grounded in language itself.[90] And this position, in turn, may not be so different from the Madhyamaka anti-foundationalism. In a way, Diṅnāga does for language – so concepts, so conceptual reality – what Nāgārjuna did for conventional reality – so concepts and language. Taking out any recourse to essences leaves us with essentially a structuralist account of meaning – the meaning of any given term is given by its place in a set of concepts-in-use, that place being defined exclusively by the sheer fact that it excludes all other possible locations in conceptual-linguistic space. It is no wonder that Bhāviveka thought he could make use of his rivals' accounts of conventional reality. But what the Madhyamaka mistook for an ontological point (about the nature of reality), the epistemologists allow instead as a fair point about our understanding, so that the significant difference between the two main philosophical interpretations of Mahāyāna still remains: the inheritors of Vasubandhu's Sautrāntika–Yogācāra synthesis persist in holding out the prospect that there is, after all, a non-conventional reality available to us, even if we can never speak of it.

VI. The path of the Bodhisattva

Like most Buddhist philosophers, Śāntideva (685–763 CE) was also a Buddhist practitioner and teacher. And like many prominent Buddhist practitioner-thinkers, his life attracted a great deal of legend and myth, so that it is difficult retrospectively to distinguish the history from the story. But Śāntideva's story is worth retelling, for it gives us a sense of the spirit in which later readers would pick up his most beloved composition, the *Bodhicāryāvatāra* (*Introduction to the Conduct of the Bodhisattva*).

According to the tale, Śāntideva was – like Śakyamuni himself – born into a royal family, but renounced his crown and his way of life when he came of age. He spent years as a forest meditator, which means his development during this period was independent of the large monasteries that had been becoming established since about the fifth century CE, and through which most Buddhist intellectual life took shape. Acquiring some reputation for wisdom, Śāntideva was invited to court to advise the king. This sojourn as court advisor did not go well – Śāntideva's Buddhist outlook, presumably representing a kind of unworldliness and consequent incorruptibility, did not endear him to his fellow courtiers, who spread poisonous slander about him until he was driven out of court. Śāntideva made his way to Nālandā, the celebrated Buddhist monastic university in the north, in the area of today's Bihar. Only then did he take monastic ordination and begin to study Buddhism formally.

But Śāntideva was scarcely better liked at Nālandā than he had been at court. Evidently his composition of the *Śiskṣa-samuccaya* and the *Sūtra-samucccaya* was on the sly, for he had a reputation for extreme laziness – it was said of him by his fellow monastics that he did nothing but eat, sleep and defecate. The *saṅgha,* the monastic community, expressed its opinion in classic Buddhist intelligentsia fashion – by challenging Śāntideva to feats of intellectual prowess, with the purpose of exposing and humiliating him when he failed. Can Śāntideva recite even a single Buddhist *sūtra*? Śāntideva obliges, offering to recite either a known *sūtra* or an original composition. Thinking to expose the shameless Śāntideva even more, the monks request an original composition.

Śāntideva then begins to recite the *Bodhicāryāvatāra*. As he recites, he begins to levitate, rising further into the air as he unfolds further chapters. It is said that even after his body disappeared from sight above Nālandā, his voice completed the recitation of his text, until – at the last verses of the masterful composition – he vanished altogether into the air above and was not seen in Nālandā again. Śāntideva dwelt in forests and forest monasteries thereafter. The *Bodhicāryāvatāra* became a classic.

The *Bodhicāryāvatāra* exemplifies the dialectic between phenomenology and metaphysics in the service of ethical praxis and development. Like Candrakīrti's *Madhyamakāvatāra*, the Mādhyamika Śāntideva's exposition is arranged around the six *pāramitās*, or 'perfections' – generosity, restraint, patience, energy, meditation and wisdom – with two significant differences. First, Śāntideva devotes the first four chapters to the praise, encouragement and development of *bodhicitta* – serving here for the first *pāramitā* of generosity, or giving (*dāna*). Like Candrakīrti, Śāntideva ends up with eleven chapters, including a dedicatory chapter at the end; but he builds more into his exposition of beginning the journey along the path, rather than describing its refinements at the far end, as Candrakīrti does. And this is, in one respect, only indicative of a second significant difference: Candrakīrti was quite happy to allow only a handful of cryptic verses, or sometimes even just one verse, to do the work of expressing the *pāramitā* under discussion. Not so Śāntideva, who devotes substantial attention to each of the *pāramitās* in turn, so that the whole is much more balanced than the *Madhyamakāvatāra*, which put the greater energy and weight into articulating the perfection of wisdom. On the one hand, we may think it perfectly in order that a Madhyamaka text should take such care to articulate the Mādhyamika's preferred version of wisdom, for it is after all this that distinguishes Madhyamaka from other forms of Buddhism. On the other hand, we saw that just this approach in the *Madhyamakāvatāra* left particularly acute questions of the coherence of moral improvement and the status of the standard virtues, ethical principles and aims, on the Madhyamaka view.

Śāntideva's interest in ethical development pervades his text, not just in its structure, but in his particular way of handling the virtues. This development is above all an 'inner', or psychological development – a reorientation of perspective and patterns of mind, and thus of the affects. The philosophical interest and the moral work happen in our ways of thinking, feeling and looking at the world – appropriate action of other sorts follows as a matter of course. Thus where a Seneca will offer you rules of thumb, so that you can roughly conform your behaviour in most cases to what is approximately correct, and then learn to judge more subtly with experience,[91] Śāntideva will work directly and consistently on our ways of looking at and responding to the world and ourselves, so that we become in each case increasingly able to perceive situations in ways that proper motivations and appropriate responses are immediate and obvious.

Replacing *dāna*, giving, with *bodhicitta* is indicative of this 'phenomenological' approach.[92] While *dāna*, the typical word for the virtue of generosity, indicates as much the giving of some thing to another as the state of mind with which one gives, *bodhicitta* is specifically a mental quality. It is, indeed, the mental quality *sine qua non*. Literally translated as something like 'awakened mind' or 'enlightenment-mind', *bodhicitta* is a mental state of aliveness to suffering (the first Noble Truth) as an active concern to eliminate it. Before one has understood suffering so as to eradicate it, *bodhicitta* is the firm aspiration to attain this state. *Bodhicitta* also names this state once fully realized, or perfected. True generosity is the enlightenment-mind dedicated to giving happiness and relief from suffering to all beings. Śāntideva begins by recommending this quality of attention to us as an aspiration, and then describes its benefits – and the harms of its absence – so as to cultivate within the reader a firm commitment to *bodhicitta*. This will be the basis for all that follows, and should be understood as the perspective from which reflection on further *pāramitās* takes shape.

When he turns to consider the remaining perfections, Śāntideva continues the focus on what it is like to be in the mental states from which good and bad actions of body, speech and mind arise. So, for instance, the chapter on restraint – a virtue most naturally associated with behaviour – is called "Guarding Introspection", and focuses on taming the mind. "Those who wish to protect their practice", it begins, "should zealously guard the mind" (*BCA* V.1). And illuminating the logic in this is one of the most famous images in Buddhist ethics:

> Where would there be leather enough to cover the entire world? The earth is covered over merely with the leather of my sandals. Likewise, I am unable to restrain external phenomena, but I shall restrain my own mind. What need is there to restrain anything else? (*BCA* V.13–14)

Patience or forbearance in the face of situations that might naturally give rise to frustration, anger or resentment is quite naturally handled by attention to the quality of mental states, the painful unpleasantness of anger contrasted with the calm that is possible instead. Here the discussion attends to changing our way of apprehending situations so that it becomes *unnatural* and perplexing that anger would arise. It is not angry *behaviour* that should no longer arise, but the anger itself. Thus attention throughout remains concertedly focused on what our experiences are like: our current experiences, full of confusion and tempted by self-absorption and laziness, and alternative experiences possible for us from this state. It is no surprise that the cultivation of energy (vigour, zeal), meditation and wisdom attend to our phenomenological states, and how to improve these. Increasingly through the chapters, this improvement will depend upon coming to have a better and better understanding of no-self, and emptiness.

The work is *protreptic*, actively trying to turn us from where we misguidedly are at the moment towards where we ought to be. This makes the *Bodhicāryāvatāra* dialectically dense, for at different moments it will be engaging different levels and varieties of misguided attention, offering remedial mental exercises and observations suited specifically to reorienting *that* inadequate way of thinking. What Śāntideva relies on to shift our attention in one verse, therefore, may be inconsistent with what he says elsewhere, when he is addressing rather more refined mistakes; we should in each case take his assertions not as definitive assertions of the truth, but rather as true only so far as they are useful.[93] This must not, however, become a licence to arbitrary inconsistency. The measure of consistency will be in whether we can understand each version of Śāntideva's recommendations as successive refinements, suitable for bringing a specific familiar mindset into an improved condition.

The chapter on patience or forbearance is a good example of this notion of consistency as successive refinement. Śāntideva begins with a homily on the evils and dangers of lacking forbearance and giving way to anger: people distrust you, it creates suffering, and is in any case unnecessary. "There is nothing whatsoever that remains difficult as one gets used to it. Thus, through habituation with slight pain, even great pain becomes bearable" (*BCA* VI.14). He then cites examples of everyday trivial things that can give rise to frustration and annoyance: mosquitoes, thirst, a serious rash are agreed to be insignificant. We should likewise consider the discomforts of bad weather, illness and even captivity insignificant (*BCA* VI.15–16). We should not be some version of the timid person who faints at the sight of blood (*BCA* VI.17); and in order to build up the necessary toughness of mind, we should recall that our real battle is not with external circumstances but with the mental afflictions – it is over these that we must be victorious (*BCA* VI.18–20).

Śāntideva then turns attention to less trivial vexations, which are harder to dispel. Often it is persons with whom we lose patience, and for good reason: they behave badly towards us (*BCA* VI.21–72). To this sort of 'justified anger', Śāntideva recommends several alternative considerations in perspective: (i) we should regard the offending behaviour as arising owing to natural causes, like bile (*BCA* VI.22; 39–41); therefore, (ii) recall there is nobody there *deciding* to get angry (*BCA* VI.23–33). This provides Śāntideva an opportunity to introduce no-self into the discussion, where it does some psychological-ethical work. (iii) Whatever could warrant an angry response should be of the sort also to warrant a compassionate response (*BCA* VI.35–8); and so (iv) we might try exchanging ourselves for others – we, too, have inflicted harm out of anger or spite, overcome by greed or pride or resentment, and have reaped only misery for our pains, as will our current tormenters likewise (*BCA* VI.42–9).

Notice how naturally we have moved from minimizing the significance of what pertains to ourselves to adopting a no-self interpretation of our experience; and then from this no-self perspective to regarding whatever suffers with equal compassion, in order to build a foundation of mental fortitude where we are undisturbed by irritations, resentments or indignation. To develop this further, and address more refined disturbances connected with reputation and honour, Śāntideva extends this compassion based on no-self, and interchangeability of each with all, by observing that all are equally deserving of my delighting in their joys, and having compassion for their sorrows (*BCA* VI.96). This should relieve us of any need to feel righteously indignant over temple desecration because, after all, "the Buddhas and the like are free from distress" (*BCA* VI.64). Our focus is now properly on the *suffering*, not on indignities against things I am attached to. If perfected, this new perspective, which we have gradually built up, should enable us to deal appropriately even with "some king's man [who] tyrannizes the populace" (*BCA* VI.128); even indignation on behalf of others should give way to concerned recognition of root causes of suffering and what might be done to alleviate them.

With this practical-phenomenological bent, it is no wonder perhaps that in the *Bodhicāryāvatāra* it is the perfection of meditation, rather than the perfection of wisdom, that receives the longest exposition (although the difference is not great). Śāntideva's intent is to work us into a perspective, not convince us of an argument. The phenomenological practice is not a myopic scrutiny of 'inner states', without regard for the world they purport to be presenting. Rather, the process includes increasing attention to, and refinements on *how we perceive the world.* After all, "the Sage taught this entire system for the sake of wisdom" (*BCA* IX.1).

Yet in the end Śāntideva is still a Mādhyamika – he devotes substantial attention to critique of Yogācāra in chapter IX, on the perfection of wisdom, and also addresses objections from Abhidharma and other unspecified critics. So none of the foregoing reflections should be taken as assertions about how the world ultimately is; they are conventional designations. Still, they are recommendations on how to regard the world, invitations to a certain outlook. These ways of looking are commended to our attention not because they specify definitively how things are, but because they get us out of thinking of things as they are not: "Analysis is created as an antidote to that false notion [of 'feeling', created by conceptual fabrication]" (*BCA* IX.92).

If we had wondered earlier, looking at Candrakīrti, just how a Mādhyamika could insist on the conventionality of all intellectual exercise, including perception (*BCA* IX.6), on the futility of Diṅnāga–Dharmakīrti style inference as a *pramāṇa*, and on the usefulness of the conventional for attaining liberating insight, we have in Śāntideva a concrete demonstration of this. Increasing insight into emptiness does not require us to abandon conceptualizing where this is useful:

> [*Qualm*:] If no sentient being exists, for whom is there compassion?
> [*Mādhyamika:*] For one who is imagined through delusion, which is accepted for the sake of the task.
> [*Qualm*:] If there is no sentient being, whose is the task?
> [*Mādhyamika:*] True. Effort, too, is due to delusion. Nevertheless, in order to alleviate suffering, delusion with regard to one's task is not averted. (*BCA* IX.75–6)

But we should never mistake such conceptualizing for a *pramāṇa*, however second-tier, for it does not give us knowledge. And recognizing this is crucial. The difference between common delusion and wisdom is not in whether appearances are conceptually rich, but in whether we believe the claim the appearances make to represent things truly. "Ordinary people see and imagine things as real and not illusory. It is in this respect that there is disagreement between the contemplatives and the ordinary people" (*BCA* IX.5).

It is in this way that our exercises have brought us closer to the perfection of wisdom. Rather than getting a firmer and firmer handle on the correct way of understanding reality, we have had increasing practice in letting go of one way of looking at things in order to adopt another. We have seen by doing it how the criterion of 'better' in ways of looking is usefulness in alleviating suffering. We have seen as well how trying to latch on to 'selves' – personal or impersonal – consistently creates frustration, intellectually and emotionally, rather than alleviating it. "Grasping onto the 'I', which is a cause of suffering, increases because of the delusion with regard to the Self. If this is the unavoidable result of that, meditation on identitylessness is the best" (*BCA* IX.77).

Any use of the intellect, Śāntideva reminds us, belongs to the conventional (*BCA* IX.2), including any attempt to explain, examine or understand emptiness – presumably even this meditation on identitylessness. Such efforts are not, however, in vain, because suffering too belongs to the conventional, and we can alleviate it only if we can recognize how it arises in the first place. The Mādhyamika has a way of articulating the path, and progress along it, according to a sound Buddhist principle: uses of intellect are beneficial and comparatively refined to the degree that they alleviate suffering, and we should grant none of them any more credence than this. Closely related to not clinging to our favoured conceptualizations is learning how not to grasp the world in terms of distinct individuals, autonomous and separately defined. Carried to its completion, this project would indeed involve abandoning intellect altogether. But this could only go along with the complete extinguishment of all suffering, for we conceived of this journey from the first through the motivation of *bodhicitta*, the committed care for all suffering. Meanwhile, there is still plenty of work for the intellect to do, for there is as yet no end of suffering.

> There are incomparable, violent, and boundless oceans of suffering ... (*BCA* IX.158)

> [W]hen might I bring relief to those tormented by the fire of suffering ...? When shall I respectfully teach emptiness and the accumulation of merit – in terms of conventional truth and without reification – to those whose views are reified?
> (*BCA* IX.166–7)

Epilogue

Also at Nālandā, perhaps just slightly after Śāntideva's ill-fated sojourn there, was the Mādhyamika Śāntarakṣita. Śāntarakṣita's stay was a happier one – he became a teacher there and, by some accounts, even the head of the great monastic university. His learning was prodigious; working more in the manner of Bhāviveka than Candrakīrti, Śāntarakṣita mastered not only the various forms of Buddhist philosophy, but also the increasingly important and energetic non-Buddhist rivals.

We encountered the Naiyāyika Uddyotakara's trenchant critique of classical Abhidharma *anātmavāda* in Chapter 6. A contemporary of Dharmkīrti and perhaps Candrakīrti, Uddyotakara was part of a general intensification of intellectual activity in the seventh century, involving not just Buddhists, but also non-Buddhists, particularly those working within the various Brahmanical traditions. Śaṅkara-ācārya, who would later come to have enormous influence on Indian philosophy with his contribution to Advaita Vedānta, dates from around this period, as do the two most incisive commentators on the Mīmāṃsā giant Śabara (fourth century CE): Kumārila and Prabākara. Taking the interpretation of Vedic injunctions as their special domain of inquiry, the Mīmāṃsakas developed an elaborate hermeneutics that began to stray increasingly into epistemological territory. These epistemological endeavours were in obvious ways orthogonal to the Buddhist project, aimed as they were at proving the necessary validity of the Vedas. But their consequent concern to identify where in the cognizing process error crept in, and their related interest in rejecting any supposed epistemological priority in perception, formed part of the philosophical context within which Diṅnāga's followers debated Mādhyamikas.[1] The Nyāya cause would be taken up in the ninth century by Vācaspati Miśra, and then by Jayana Bhaṭṭa.[2] Roughly contemporaneous with Udayana (fl. 984), whose defence of the *ātmavāda* was so trenchant it became known as the 'Disgrace of the Buddhists', the Vaiśeṣikas came to voice with Śridhara's *Nyāyakandalī.*

Arising in the midst of this philosophical excitement, it is no wonder that Śāntarakṣita took an active interest in mastering the various positions of non-Buddhists, and their arguments against Buddhists. He did not just engage in defensive manoeuvres, but went out to meet his opponents on their own ground: his compendious *Tattvasaṃgraha* is organized according to the classical categories not of Abhidharmikas (as was Nāgārjuna's *Mūlamadhyamakakārikā*, six centuries earlier), but rather of Nyāya-Vaiśeṣikas and other Brahmanical schools. Śāntarakṣita begins, for instance, with a refutation of primordial nature (*prakṛti*) as the first principle (a Saṁkhya view), then of God as the first principle (a Nyāya view), and then of the Yoga claim that both together are the first principle of all things. After considering and rejecting the various going conceptions of *ātman* in turn, Śāntarakṣita devotes chapters to the examination of substance (*dravya*), quality, action, generality, particularity, and inherence: that is, to the Vaiśeṣika categories. After significant discussion of the *pramāṇas*, Śāntarakṣita closes with a consideration of the Jaina view, and of the Cārvākā materialism before examining specific views about intrinsic validity and omniscience. Only the latter two were of specific concern to Buddhist epistemologists, the last arising when considering what sort of 'all-knowing' (*sarvajñā*) should characterize the Buddha: if it concerns several objects taken together, then it is conceptual and constructed; or else there is some one thing that all existents share, a sort of realism that is ordinarily anathema to Buddhist metaphysics.[3]

In the *Madhyamaka-alaṃkāra* (and its auto-commentary, or *vṛtti*), Śāntarakṣita offers to each of the non-Buddhist categories essentially the same destructive argument: anything existing must be either one or many; but each of these supposed existents – substance, particular, universal, *prakṛti*, and so on – cannot be either. They are therefore non-existent, incoherent and useless as categories of thought. Or it may be better to say that the very enterprise of thinking, taken as one of uncovering a more fundamental structure of reality than the one we experience, is what is ultimately under critique here. At any rate, the organizing role and space Śāntarakṣita devotes to non-Buddhists is a testament to the rising prominence of the latter, and that they could not be ignored by someone seriously wanting to defend the Buddhist view. In canvassing rival views, Śāntarakṣita is not entirely original – Vasubandhu engages directly with Nyāya-Vaiśeṣika views in his 'appendix' or book IX to the *Abhidharmakośabhāṣya*, the "Refutation of the Person"; and for nearer precedent, Diṅnāga defends his own theory of perception in part by treating each of his rivals in turn in book I of the *Pramāṇasamuccaya*, and Bhāviveka likewise engages seriously with non-Buddhist thought. Both Diṅnāga and Bhāviveka seem to have influenced Śāntarakṣita deeply, in more respects than this. But taking non-Buddhists as the interlocutors around which to structure his presentation of his particular interpretation of the Buddhist view indicates the prominence and tenacity of those interlocutors by Śāntarakṣita's time. All the same, this attention to meeting non-Buddhist positions with reason and argument does not mean that Śāntarakṣita spared his fellow Buddhists: the *Tattvasaṃgraha* also devotes a section to refuting the *pudgalavāda,* evidently still a going view in spite of its later scarcity; and the *Madhyamakālaṃkāra* criticizes Buddhists who would claim that consciousness is truly singular, and so escapes the destructive neither-one-nor-many dilemma.[4]

Candrakīrti's insistence on the validity of 'what the world says', and his refusal to allow any assessment of these in terms of better or worse reasons and arguments, left his version of Madhyamaka with a particularly acute problem of what it could actually *mean* to use conventional reality for the sake of realizing ultimate reality and, indeed, what it could mean to progress along a path towards any goal at all. Śāntideva's *Bodhicāryāvatāra* may offer a pragmatic suggestion of how this could actually be done, yet it must be admitted that Śāntideva engages in plenty of reason-giving as a method of recommending one conceptual construction of reality over another; as with Bhāviveka, we should understand the provisional status of such arguments, and not take them to be closer approximations to descriptions of ultimate reality, but rather equally (and necessarily) inadequate conceptual constructions that are better and worse as they are more and less able to diminish suffering through a proper appreciation of emptiness. Śāntarakṣita openly embraces the usefulness of conventional language, and even inference and argument in the service of coming to realize the Madhyamaka version of ultimate reality. But he goes one better than Bhāviveka, who delighted in using Diṅnāga's own method of argument against him. Śāntarakṣita not only employs inferences, but actually incorporates Yogācāra views into Madhyamaka, offering a Mahāyāna synthesis of what had been, up to that point, explicitly rival interpretations of the *bodhisattva* ideal: the perfection of wisdom and emptiness.

How such a synthesis of fundamentally antagonistic views is possible deserves close consideration. But some of Śāntarakṣita's syncretic ambitions are realized through what might be considered his distinctive version of what it is for a Mādhyamika to rely on conventional truth to realize ultimate reality. For Śāntarakṣita seems to have been the first Buddhist explicitly to offer a progressive analysis of previously rival Buddhist views, coordinating positions that arose in dispute with each other. He does this by imposing on them an order from the most preliminary to the most refined interpretations of those core Buddhist commitments of impermanence, no-self and dependent arising.

Thus, the best antidote to the mistakes of everyday thinking and the naive Abhidharma alternative is a bit of bracing Sautrāntika critique, which insists we refrain from having recourse to metaphysical categories that are doing no work, are incoherent or could not do the work intended of them. This was the sort of internal critique that Vasubandhu brought against the Vaibhāṣikas in his commentary (*bhāṣya*) on his own Vaibhāṣika text (the *Abhidharmakośa*). But as Vasubandhu himself saw, such a minimalist Abhidharma position is itself in need of critique, and Śāntarakṣita agrees that such a critique leads to a Yogācāra, mind-only view. He even grants, as Bhāviveka and Candrakīrti were unwilling to, that "All causes and effects are consciousness alone. And all that this establishes abides in consciousness" (*MAl* 91).

But this consciousness-only view is after all just an improved conception of conventional reality. It is not, contrary to Vasubandhu's claims, consummate nature, but just another antidote to even more refined versions of self-thinking and self-clinging. The full elimination of such mistaken conceptual grasping requires abandoning even the recognition of the non-duality of subject and object, for Yogācāra non-duality grants undue priority to mind, retaining something to be clung to. Therefore "On the basis of 'mind alone', we should know that outer things do not exist. On the basis of the method set forth here, we should know mind is utterly devoid of self" (*MAl* 92).

Admittedly, Vasubandhu was already speaking of progressive refinements in our comprehension of non-duality in his exposition of the path to consummate reality. So Śāntarakṣita's staged progression, although granting priority ultimately to Madhyamaka, is not as such a distinctively Madhyamaka idea. Yogācārins, too, use conventional reality in the service of understanding ultimate reality; and Vasubandhu had already suggested that this might take the form of progressively refined understandings of no-self, from those that he himself had superseded in his Vaibhāṣika past to that of Asaṅga's Yogācāra.

Śāntarakṣita's distinction here, then, is not just that he puts Madhyamaka, rather than Yogācāra, at the terminus of the path. Nor is it even just his non-adversarial manner of setting out these transitions, as a set of related thoughts that anyone might move through in an orderly progression along the path – although this is part of Śāntarakṣita's distinctive contribution, and one that would come to be enormously influential in Tibet, where Śāntarakṣita later established the country's first Buddhist monastery at the end of the eighth century. Related to the ecumenical and dynamic spirit of allowing the usefulness of competing Buddhist views was Śāntarakṣita's incorporation of Yogācāra positions into his understanding of the best final – if still conventional – conception of reality. Not only does he accept the Yogācārin's point – in spite of Bhāviveka's critique – that the nature of the object of awareness is not-different from the nature of consciousness, but he also accepts Diṅnāga's view of cognition as self-cognizing, and offers an insightful interpretation and defence of the claim.[5] Śāntarakṣita also continues the Buddhist epistemologist's defence of inference as a legitimate *pramāṇa*, and likewise of conceptions as having a criterion of correctness, via his contribution to the ongoing discussion of *apoha*, or 'exclusion'. He does this, however, while still insisting that none of this is an account of ultimate reality, which can have no account. In contrast to Dharmakīrti's view that causal efficacy is the mark of the ultimately real, Śāntarakṣita maintains the Madhyamaka insistence on the causally efficacious being a mark of the dependent, the transient, the conventional.

Śāntarakṣita's dynamically protreptic arrangement of Buddhist views into a hierarchy describing an intellectual journey became especially influential in Tibet, where he was invited by King Trisong Detson (Tib. Khri srong lde brtsan, 755–97 CE) to establish Buddhism on a firm intellectual foundation. Establishing Tibet's first monastery at Samye (Tib. bSam yas), Śāntarakṣita returned to India. It was his learned student Kamalaśīla who was later sent to Tibet to defend Śāntarakṣita's version of Madhyamaka – and of Buddhist thought generally – against the rival form of Buddhism propounded by the Chinese monk known as Mahāyāna. Mahāyāna's Buddhism was an early version of Ch'an (later to become Zen), and was distinctive for its assertion that enlightenment was instantaneous, or sudden. The implications of this for Śāntarakṣita-style Buddhism were enormous, for if enlightenment is sudden then there is no need for mental cultivation, nor for the arduous progression along the path from Abhidharmika to Sautrāntika to Yogācāra (Cittamātra) to Madhyamaka. There is no need to progressively refine one's understanding, for enlightenment comes – if at all – quite out of the blue, and not through reasoned consideration of the nature of reality.

Such a view is even more challenging for the value of ethical discipline, or anything like Śāntideva's *bodhisattva* path. For where enlightenment comes suddenly out of the blue, so too does liberation. And if liberation is attained thus, then again there is no need for the painful discipline of generosity, restraint, patience and the rest of the perfections or precepts. Along some such lines Kamalaśīla argued; his interpretation won over the king, who banished the adherents of the Ch'an view, and gave institutional support to Kamalaśīla, who remained in Tibet to continue teaching and writing. In addition to his *Tattvasaṃgrahapañjikā* (a commentary on Śāntarakṣita's *Tattvasaṃgraha*), and the *Madhyamakālaṃkārapañjīka* (a commentary on the *Madhyamakālaṃkāra*), Kamalaśīla wrote three treatises on gradual enlightenment, *Bhāvanakrama.* Although Kamalaśīla came to a sticky end – murdered, apparently – his assiduous exposition and elaboration of Śāntarakṣita's Mahāyāna established the progressive and hierarchical integration of Indian Buddhist debates within Tibet.

The epistemological tradition started by Diṅnāga continued to flourish in its own right, as its central commitments were challenged by Buddhists and non-Buddhists alike. While Mādhyamikas and Mīmāṃsakas doubted the priority granted to perception over inference, Naiyāyikas came to challenge the adequacy of an account of perception that allowed nothing determinate to be perceived. Contemporary with Kamalaśīla, Dharmottara continued the defence and development of Diṅnāga and Dharmakīrti, with his commentaries on Dharmakīrti's *Pramāṇaviniścaya* and *Nyāyabindu* (the *Pramāṇaviniścayatīkā* and *Nyāyabindutīkā*, respectively), and in several independent texts. In these extensions and elaborations of the Buddhist epistemological project, Dharmottara wrestles, for instance, as in his *Apohaprakaraṇa*, with the persistent difficulty of connecting concepts and percepts without positing real universals, unwilling to abandon either the priority of perception or the validity of inference.[6] His *Kṣaṇabhaṅgasiddi* reinvigorates the debate over the strictly momentary existence of reality, defending it against problems this raises about, for instance, the coherence of causation.

This defence was taken up by the later Buddhist epistemologist, Ratnakīrti (*c.* 1000–1050 CE), who offered his own *Kṣaṇabhaṅgasiddi*, which made full use of the ever more sophisticated resources of Buddhist logic, including various forms of negation and correlation.[7] Like his teacher Jñānaśrīmitra, Ratnakīrti criticizes Dharmottara's interpretation of Dharmakīrti, arguing, for instance, that there is a kind of universal that can be directly perceived, thus attempting to counter Nyāya objections that Buddhist perception is blind and dumb, because it cannot after all ground any reliable association between words deployed in inference, and what the objects they should refer to are actually like. Ratnakīrti was himself a towering systematic thinker, and this defence of momentariness was part of a defence of the Buddhist view that included as well a critique of Nyāya theories of inference, and of Brahmanical conceptions of god generally.[8]

Much was innovative, and very sophisticated, in these final three centuries of Buddhist philosophy in India. And yet the terms of debate, and the positions to defend, had already been laid out in the first millennium of Buddhism. Given his disinterest in, and denigration of, philosophical debate, it is no wonder that Candrakīrti's peculiar brand of Madhyamaka seems to have had less influence on this period of Buddhist thought, when Nyāya and Mīmāṃsā critics were pressing Buddhists to think harder, more carefully and more cleverly about just what exactly 'no-self', dependent origination and transience meant, and just how the inevitable implications of these views could accommodate everyday experiences and thoughts we know ourselves to have. The metaphysical concerns of Yogācārins in dispute with Abhidharmikas were preserved and continued, as were the Madhyamaka concerns with an emptiness that encompassed even Yogācāra 'consummate nature'. But it was Bhāviveka's intellectually engaged Madhyamaka that attracted philosophical proponents; and it was relatively easy for some of these to allow the ultimate metaphysical picture of Madhyamaka to prevail, while taking a serious intellectual interest in the nature of reasoning, the possibility of knowledge and of other minds, the source of error and the standards of validity in thinking – an interest, that is, in the epistemological project of Diṅnāga, who himself retained a certain element of metaphysical agnosticism or even indifference.

It is more surprising that when Buddhist thought migrates to Tibet a second time, with the arrival of Dīpaṁkaraśrījñāna (known as Atiśa) in the mid-eleventh century, it is Candrakīrti's Madhyamaka that becomes definitive of the highest and final interpretation of the Buddha-*dharma*. The banishment of the Chinese monk Mahāyāna, and the consequent support of Kamalaśīla's insistence on gradual enlightenment had been a decisive turn in favour of everyday ethics as promoting the ultimate goal of enlightenment. At the same time, it was a crucial affirmation of philosophical reflection, and the process of giving and grasping reasons, as essential to the path towards what may itself ultimately be the direct, inexpressible realization of reality as it is. Within this highly intellectual culture, Candrakīrti somehow became established as the pinnacle of Śāntarakṣita's graded development of Buddhist views: the view one has when all the errors of other views have been purified. Because the structures of Buddhist intellectual life in India were eventually destroyed quite comprehensively through war and social upheaval (in the twelfth to thirteenth centuries), this Tibetan appropriation of Indian Buddhist philosophical debate played an enormous role in determining which texts and authors were preserved, what place they were given, and what shape the future development of these views would take.

Śāntarakṣita's syncretism had already dampened or cloaked some of the disputatious character of Buddhist intellectual life in India; the lack of realist and theist thinkers in Tibet, such as Nyāya and Mīmāṃsā in India, left Buddhist thought there to develop without robust critique from outside. Tibetan philosophers did, however, persist in pursuing the careful epistemological and metaphysical distinctions, and the sophisticated debates over the relations between meaning, knowing and reality, that characterized the final period of Buddhist thought in India, making significant contributions through sophisticated reinterpretations and debates of their own over these matters.

Meanwhile, the intellectual life of Buddhism in India seems to have been mostly dispersed: eastwards to China, south to Sri Lanka and points east, as well as north into Tibet. The last significant Buddhist contributor within India was Mokṣākaragupta, working some time in the late eleventh to thirteenth centuries CE. His (*Bauddha*)*Tarkabhāṣa*, which survives in Sanskrit and also in a more complete Tibetan translation, follows Diṅnāga's programme fairly closely, but is enriched and informed by the intervening centuries of innovation and debate. Thus its books are divided into treatments of perception, reasoning 'for oneself' and reasoning 'for others', and include discussion of the self-cognition of cognition, the non-difference of cause and effect of knowing, the *trairūpya* analysis of inference, and the exclusion theory of meaning (*apoha*). But these discussions involve distinctions and rejoinders to objections that Diṅnāga and even Dharmakīrti could not have anticipated. Mokṣākaragupta distinguishes, for instance, between two kinds of universal; he takes up the debate over whether the contents of perception are with or without 'form' (*sākāravāda* or *nirākāravāda*); and he feels obliged to give an explicit defence of why both the second and third of the marks of sound inference are necessary. In addition to explicit argument in favour of the *trairūpya* over the Nyāya five-limbed form of inference, Mokṣākaragupta directly engages the Naiyāyikas Trilocana and Vācaspatimiśra. Mokṣākaragupta rounds out his discussion, which might be thought of as a survey of Buddhist epistemology,[9] with the requisite Buddhist rejection of God, nature and self-causation as metaphysical and explanatory principles, before examining a Buddhist account of omniscience, and the views of Vaibhāṣika, Sautrāntika, Yogācārin and Mādhyamika in turn, just as Śāntarakṣita had set out. The nuances in articulation and defence of positions after this would be left to philosophers outside India, working primarily in languages other than Sanskrit and its related vernaculars.

Background information

APPENDIX ONE

The languages of Buddhism

Siddhartha Gautama was probably teaching in the fifth to fourth centuries BCE, although this date is disputed. He lived and taught in northern India, in the area that is now the state of Bihar, and in Nepal. The scholarly language of the sub-Continent at that time, and in the millennia following, was Classical Sanskrit – a later form of the language of the Vedas. Gautama spoke and taught in his local dialect/s, one [set] of the many vernaculars of Sanskrit [called *prākrits*], and not in Sanskrit.

This tradition of communicating in the local language, rather than the scholarly language, continued – and may have been a deliberate statement against reverence accorded any specific language, of the kind the Brahmans accorded Sanskrit. Thus, the oldest record of the Buddha's teaching which has come down to us was written in Pāli, another *prākrit*, possibly closely related to the Buddha's own vernacular.

As Buddhism spread, texts were translated into and composed in any number of local languages, including Chinese and Tibetan. As Buddhists in India became more philosophically engaged – with each other across different language-areas, and with non-Buddhists within the Brahamanical tradition – they began composing their works in Classical Sanskrit. The earliest texts this book treats were originally written in Pāli; the rest in Classical Sanskrit.

Because Pāli and Sanskrit are closely related, many words are similar, and variations between them easily recognized. In the main, Pāli simplifies consonant conjuncts, vowels and sibilants; 's'- and 'r'-sounds can tend to go astray. For instance:

PĀLI:	*kamma*	*sutta*	*dhamma*	*atta*	*satta*	*khandha*	*dukkha*
SANSKRIT:	*karma*	*sūtra*	*dharma*	*ātman*	*satva*	*skandha*	*duḥkha*

Sanskrit is an Indo-European language, sharing much of its basic structure and function with Greek, Latin and modern related languages. Verbs are conjugated, nouns declined, substantives easily formed from adjectives and participles, shades of meaning expressed by tenses. The phonetics of Sanskrit (and Pāli) are also largely familiar to speakers of European languages. Variations, and explanations of diacritical marks, are as follows:

- Vowels with a line over them are twice as long as the same vowel without a line.
- 'ś' is pronounced as 'sh' is in English
- 'c' is pronounced as 'ch' is in English
- 'ñ' is pronounced 'ny', as in Spanish ñ
- 'ṅ' is pronounced 'ng', and is sometimes written out as 'ng'
- 'h' after a consonant (e.g. 'dh') indicates aspiration only; it does not change the quality of the consonant. Thus, 'th' and 'ph' are not as in English. 'th'/ 'dh'/ 'ph' are pronounced as 't'/ 'd' / 'p', but with breath.
- Consonants with a dot underneath are pronounced as those without a dot, but with the tongue pointing to the roof of the mouth. Generally one does not make the difference in English.

Basic analysis of Sanskrit phonetics, established by the grammarian Pāṇini (sometime between the seventh and fourth centuries BCE):

	unvoiced		voiced		nasal	liquids	sibilants		vowels
	un-asp.	asp.	un-asp.	asp.		semi-vowels			
gutteral	k	kh	g	gh	ṅ	y		h	a/ā
palatal	c	ch	j	jh	ñ	r			ṛ/ṝ
retroflex	ṭ	ṭh	ḍ	ḍh	ṇ		ṣ		ḷ
dental	t	th	d	dh	n	l	ś		i/ī
labial	p	ph	b	bh	m	v/w	s		u/ū

APPENDIX TWO

Intellectual context

Writing and speaking

India of the Buddha's time, and the centuries following, was predominantly an oral culture. Script was known, but writing was not common. Instead a highly sophisticated and literary culture was transmitted orally. This included an analysis of the phonetics and grammar of Sanskrit, by the grammarian Pāṇini (probably around the sixth century BCE) unparalleled in any Indo-European language until the twentieth century. Even in the centuries following the Buddha, as writing became more widespread, practices of memorization and recitation, of debate and personal dialogue – in teaching, learning and intellectual life – remained preferred.

Texts and teaching

The Vedas are the oldest texts in India. They contain mostly hymns, myths and ritual formulae. Written in an older form of Sanskrit (now aptly called 'Vedic Sanskrit'), by the time of Pāṇini the language of these texts was distant enough from spoken Sanskrit to require interpretation at times.

Attached to the Vedas are several related texts of three sorts, *Brahmāṇas*, *Aranyakas* and *Upaniṣads*. The first of these are essentially commentaries on the Vedas; the second sort, "The Wilderness Books", also have largely to do with religious practice. In both of these, views about the nature of the universe are implicit. In the *Upaniṣads*, especially, we see speculative thought in earnest – reflection on the nature of human beings, the structure and origin of the universe and life, its purposes and meaning.

Several themes are characteristic of the Vedic world-view:

- A moralized version of reincarnation, sometimes called the doctrine of *karma* and rebirth.
- Microcosm–macrocosm coordination: the structure of the universe, of society and the self are in some sense similar, and *interrelated*.
- Ritual efficacy: ritual practice is an obligatory means of keeping the universe well ordered.
- Societal order is a part of cosmic order, and sustains it. It is therefore hierarchical and *fixed*.
- Brahman is the fundamental principle of reality.
- The cycle of rebirth and re-death is ultimately unattractive; the wise seek liberation from this.
- Liberation (*mokṣa*) is found through understanding, especially understanding the Self (*ātman*).

Dissenters

Śakyamuni challenged some but not all of these prevalent beliefs. He seems to have accepted the view that people are reborn into circumstances fitting the quality of their actions (but see Stephen Batchelor for a dissenting voice). But he rejected both the social order, and the supposition that our orderly behaviour – adherence to scriptural injunction and ritual – made a difference to the order of the universe or to our own well-being. He rejected the claim of the Vedas to any kind of authority.

Śakyamuni was not the only dissenter. Jainism, with its emphasis on non-violence, pre-dated the Buddha, and also rejected the world-view of the Vedas and their prescriptions. The materialist Cārvākas were so notorious that very little of their own work has survived, and we know them primarily through criticism of them by others.

In a case of 'victors write the history', those thinking within the Brahmanical tradition are commonly referred to as orthodox; those working outside it are 'heterodox'. Had the convention been established in the third century BCE, when the Buddhist Emperor Aśoka united most of the sub-Continent, Buddhism would have been 'orthodox'.

APPENDIX THREE

The Abhidharma

The early Buddhist texts are typically grouped into three kinds, known as the three *Pitakas* ('baskets' or collections) – together the *Tripitaka*:

The *Sutta Pitaka* comprises the *nikayas*, collections of the discourses of the Buddha:

1. The *Samyutta Nikāya* (the *Connected Discourses*)
2. The *Majjhima Nikāya* (the *Middle-Length Discouses*)
3. The *Dīgha Nikāya* (the *Longer Discourses*)
4. The *Anguttara Nikāya* (the *Gradual* or *Enumerated Discourses*)
5. The *Khuddaka Nikāya* (the *Minor Discourses*)

The *Vinaya Pitaka* comprises all texts concerned with monastic discipline, which could vary in details according to sect. It is a rich source for examples of moral reasoning.

The *Abhidharma* (or *Abhidhamma*) *Pitaka* is the 'Higher Teaching', where the Buddha's teachings are distilled, organized and sometimes explored. The texts of the Pāli Abhidharma canon are:

1. The *Dhammasaṅgaṇi* (the *Enumeration of Phenomena*, translated under the title *Buddhist Psychological Ethics*)
2. The *Vibhaṅga* (the *Book of Analysis*)
3. The *Dhātukathā* (*Discussion of Elements*)
4. The *Puggalapaññatti* (*Concept of Persons* or *Designation of Human Types*)
5. The *Kathāvatthu* (*Points of Controversy*)
6. The *Yamaka* (the *Book of Pairs*)
7. The *Paṭṭhāna* (*Conditional Relations*)

There were variations on the *Sutta-Pitaka*, just as in the *Vinaya* texts, with different early Buddhist groups recognizing only partially overlapping subsets of each others' *sūtras* as authentic. The Pāli canon is that of the Theravādins. The only other extant Abhidharma canon is that of the Sarvāstivādins, preserved only in Chinese translation. Some included the *Milindapañhā* – purporting to recount a dialogue between a Buddhist monk and a Greek King of Bactria – in the *Sutta Pitaka*.

As those following the Buddha's teachings after his *parinirvāṇa* attempted to find the best systematic interpretation of those teachings, they inevitably disagreed, with different groups advocating different positions, as well as different monastic rules and different authentic discourses of the Buddha. While monastic groups most often split up or stayed together according to their agreement, or disagreement, on the *Vinaya* rather than on points of doctrine or conviction, the intellectual disagreements were clearly articulated, carefully differentiated and labelled. While the number '18' is oft-repeated, there are in fact many more named groups and positions. Below are some of those one is most likely to encounter in discussions of Buddhist philosophy:

1. Theravāda	5. Sammitīya	9. Vaibhāṣika
2. Mahāsāṅghika	6. Mahisāśaka	10. Sautrāntika
3. Vajjiputtaka	7. Vibhajjavāda	11. Dārṣṭāntika
4. Vātsīputrīya	8. Sarvāstivāda	12. Pudgalavāda

Distinctions between the schools are fine, names change over time, and relations between them are both complex and disputed, with some names "likely to have been informal schools of thought in the manner of 'Cartesians,' 'British Empiricists,' or 'Kantians'" (Gethin, *Foundations of Buddhism*, 52); or they might name a position, as does 'consequentialist'. Thus, for instance, the *pudgalavāda* was a doctrine (*vāda*) attracting adherents from within various schools (including 3, 4, and 5, above).

For our purposes, the most relevant schools are the closely related *Sarvāstivādins* (Pan-realists, who defended the reality of past and future events) and Vaibhāṣikas (adherents to the interpretation of the *Mahā-Vibhaṣa*, the Great Commentary); and the Sautrāntikas (*sūtra*-followers), responsible for the doctrine of momentariness.

Today's Theravādins (from Sthaviravādin) are the only Abhidharma school continuously extant. The fifth-century commentaries of Buddhaghosa, working in Sri Lanka, are invaluable expositions of the Theravāda. André Bareau, *Les Sectes bouddhique du petit Véhicule* (Paris: Efeo, 1955) is the definitive study.

APPENDIX FOUR

Snapshot of Indian philosophy

Buddhist philosophy neither grew up nor developed in an intellectual vacuum. As Buddhist philosophers' claims became more systematic and precise, so too did the objections of their non-Buddhist opponents, who were meanwhile developing systematic views of their own. Public debates, sometimes sponsored by local aristocrats and kings, were an important part of the intellectual context. Buddhist and non-Buddhist philosophers alike knew that they had to make their views persuasive to those who did not already agree with them, and made efforts to demonstrate that their respective positions were the most credible to the impartial mind.

The history and development of these philosophical debates and discussions is hard to track precisely. But a common snapshot overview of the main participants in philosophical discussion over a period of more than two millennia lists six recognized Brahmanical schools. Each school has its own foundational *sūtra*, setting out the domain of concern and the main principles of that discipline. Such divisions can tend to mark a difference in interest and emphasis, rather than outright competing philosophical systems – although they often disagree with each other on particular points, they also often work co-operatively on the philosophical enterprise. To a certain extent, the divisions are sometimes not unlike the distinctions in contemporary analytic philosophy between, say, epistemology, metaphysics, phenomenology, applied ethics, and so on.

Hindu, Brahamanical, or 'Vedic' Schools of Thought

Name	Author	Date	Root text	Primary focus
Grammarian	Pāṇini	7th to 4th c. BCE	*Aṣṭādhyāyī*	linguistics, semantics, language
Sāṁkhya	Iśvarakṛṣṇa	2nd c. CE	*Sāṁkhya-Kārikā*	dualist metaphysics; Nature analysed into three *guṇas* (qualities)
Vaiśeṣika	Kaṇāda	1st c. BCE	*Vaiśeṣika-Sūtra*	categorial metaphysics
Nyāya	Gautama Akṣapada	1st c. CE	*Nyāya-Sūtra*	logic, epistemology, philosophy of language
Yoga	Patañjali	2nd c. BCE	*Yoga-Sūtra*	practices for realizing Self
(Pūrva) Mīmāṁsā	Jaimini	1st c. CE	*Mīmāṃsā-Sūtra*	Vedic hermeneutics, epistemology
Vedānta:				
Uttara-Mīṃāmsā	Bādarāyaṇa	2nd c. BCE	*Vedānta-Sūtra*	metaphysics of *Ātman* and *Brahman*
Advaita-Vedānta	Śaṅkara	11th c. CE	commentaries	– monism
Viśiṣta-Advaita-Vedānta	Rāmānuja	11th c. CE	on Vedas, Upaniṣads,	– qualified non-dualism
Dvaita-Vedānta	Madhva	12th c. CE	etc.	– dualist

Notes

1. The Buddha's suffering

1. For details of the intellectual background and context of the Buddha's teaching, see Appendix 1 and Appendix 2.
2. For an overview of the *abhidharma* that developed in the period just after the Buddha, see Appendix 3.
3. For a guide to Sanskrit phonetics, see Appendix 1.
4. See *AN* 3.69, PTS i.201–5, "Mula Sutta" (Roots). Greed is often more broadly called 'desire', but this generic term raises questions, particularly in the European philosophical context, where 'desire' is taken to be simply whatever motivational element there is in a mental state, and that without which there would be no action. For extensive philological discussion of words and roles for desire in the Pāli canon, see David Webster, *The Philosophy of Desire in the Buddhist Pāli Canon* (Abingdon: RoutledgeCurzon, 2005).
5. The "Right View Sutra" (*MN* 9) has ignorance caused by 'taints' or cankers (*āsavas*), including sense-desires, and ignorance is the cause of these cankers: "with the arising of the taints there is the arising of ignorance" (MN 9.66); and "with the arising of ignorance there is the arising of the taints. With the cessation of ignorance there is the cessation of the taints" (MN 9.70). (Just to complicate matters, ignorance is itself an *āsava*.) Here, at least, the urge to name any one of the three roots of suffering as *the* foundation is resisted. Phenomenologically, they can each cause each other. In the pragmatics of interrupting this mutual causation, however, eliminating ignorance is both a good way in and necessary for the definitive elimination of the three.
6. For a brief sketch of the non-Buddhist intellectual and cultural background in which Buddhism arose, see Appendix 2.
7. *MN* 72, "Aggi-Vacchagotta Sutta" (To Vacchagotta on Fire).
8. For the canonical exploration of the practices of Hellenistic philosophy, see Pierre Hadot, *Philosophy as A Way of Life*, Michael Chase (trans.) (Oxford: Blackwell, 1995).
9. It is worth comparing this conception of emotions and their relations to

judgements with the ancient Stoics of Greece and Rome. While the Buddhists may not, like the Stoics, think that emotions are just how certain judgements feel in creatures like us, they do share the optimism that destructive emotions can be eliminated through cognitive therapy, through altering the way we look at the world. So not being ignorant of the first two Noble Truths means in particular being able to recognize the suffering in things and its causes.

10. *MN* 9.15 contains a version of the canonical formulation of suffering (cf. *AN* 6.63, PTS iii.410).
11. Indeed, in the case of pleasure, there may be no equivalent to the 'brute pain' described above. There may be an asymmetry between pleasure and pain regarding their necessary cognitive richness, and our consequent control over determining the quality of our pleasures.
12. This is nearly tautologically true. One might want to point out that sometimes I do not want the desires I have: I crave a cigarette, but do not want to crave a cigarette. In such cases, it makes sense to say, "I do not want to get what I want". But in order to make sense of this, we must shift between different orders of desire. (Harry Frankfurt, "Freedom of the Will and the Concept of a Person", *Journal of Philosophy* 68 [1971], 5–20 [reprinted in *Free Will*, Gary Watson (ed.), 322–36 (Oxford: Oxford University Press, 2003)] is the *locus classicus* for discussion of second-order desires.) Within any single order of desires, the claim is trivially true.
13. Much of this material is closely related to my paper "Metaphysical Suffering, Metaphysics as Therapy", in *Making Sense of Suffering: An Inter-Disciplinary Dialogue on Narrative and the Meaning of Suffering*, N. Hinerman & M. Sutton (eds), 37–52 (Oxford: Inter-Disciplinary Press, 2012). While that paper and this chapter have gone in different directions, they share a common origin, and the discussion here has benefited from the opportunity to present and revise "Metaphysical Suffering, Metaphysics as Therapy" for the interdisciplinary conference "Making Sense of Suffering" (Prague, November 2010). My thanks and gratitude to the participants and organizers of the conference for their thoughtful comments.
14. "When one is touched by a painful feeling, if one sorrows, grieves and laments, weeps beating one's breast and becomes distraught, then the underlying tendency to aversion lies within one" (*MN* 148, "Chachakka Sutta", §28).
15. Peter Harvey brings out this connection between Self and control in *The Selfless Mind: Personality, Consciousness and Nirvana in Early Buddhism* (Richmond: Curzon Press, 1995), ch. 2, 49–50.
16. Thus Buddhaghoṣa, a fifth-century CE Theravādin, describes "not-self in the sense of having no core" as "the absence of any core of self conceived as a self, an abider, a doer, an experiencer, *one who is his own master*" (*Vsm.* XX.16).
17. David Webster draws out this same point from a consideration of dependent arising: "That things come about due to causes seems, on first glance, obvious – almost a truism. What makes it a notion which is the basis of meditation, and seen as complex and hard to grasp, is that it calls on no external aspect. There is no first cause, and no guiding agency. Furthermore, it is not a teleological principle – it has no aim" (Webster, *The Philosophy of Desire*, 147).
18. Rupert Gethin, in a different context, says of suffering: "As the first truth, its reality must be fully understood [*pariññeyya*]" ("Can Killing a Living Being Ever

Be an Act of Compassion? The Analysis of the Act of Killing in the Abhidhamma and Pali Commentaries", *Journal of Buddhist Ethics* 11 [2004]: 167–202, esp. 189–90).

19. The quote is from the *Milindapañhā*, a text written several centuries after the Buddha's passing away, but it refers to incidents recorded in the Discourses (all helpfully noted by I. B. Horner in her translation, *Milinda's Questions* [Oxford: Pali Text Society, 1996], from which this translation is drawn). Webster wonders "whether the distinction between an unenlightened and an enlightened being can be understood in terms of the types of *dukkha* they can be subject to (the enlightened normally being considered as capable of suffering only physical *dukkha*)" (*The Philosophy of Desire,* 159). Although this was the 'normal view', it was disputed: later Mahāsaṅghikas held rather different views about the Buddha's body; it was itself merely a useful appearance and so too its 'pains'. See André Bareau, *Les Sects bouddhiques du petit véhicule* (Paris: École Française d'Extrême-Orient, 1955), 57–61; see also Bibhuti Barhuah, *Buddhist Sects and Sectarianism* (New Delhi: Sarup & Sons, 2000), 7–8.

2. Practice and theory of no-self

1. For incisive discussion of the importance for Socrates of knowing oneself, rather than knowing others, see Raphael Woolf, "Socratic Authority", *Archiv für Geschichte der Philosophie* 90 (2008), 1–38.
2. The *Alcibiades* is a 'Platonic' dialogue in that it is written in the Platonic tradition, even if it is not written by Plato himself. Julia Annas ("Self-knowledge in Early Plato", in *Platonic Investigations,* D. J. O'Meara [ed.], 111–38 [Washington, DC: Catholic University of America Press, 1985]) and Nicholas Denyer (*Plato: Alcibiades* [Cambridge: Cambridge University Press, 2001]) take the *Alcibiades* to be quite probably written by Plato; other scholars mostly not.
3. See Aristotle, *Metaphysics* XII.7, *de Anima* III.2, and *Nicomachean Ethics* X.7. Klaus Oehler explores the connection between self-knowing and the highest end in his "Aristotle on Self-Knowledge", *Proceedings of the American Philosophical Society* 118(6) (1974): 493–506.
4. For an excellent discussion of the original indeterminacies in the early *sūtras* see Leonard Priestley, *Pudgalavāda Buddhism: The Reality of the Indeterminate Self* (Toronto: Centre for South Asian Studies, University of Toronto, 1999), ch. 1. For two modern scholars who deny that outright rejection of self was an original part of the Buddha's teachings, rather than a later accretion or interpretation of those teachings, see Lambert Schmidthausen, "Spirituelle Praxis und philosophische Theorie im Buddhismus", *Zeitschrift für Missionswissenschaft und Religionswissenschaft* 57 (1973), 161–86, and Erich Frauwallner, *Geschichte der indischen Philosophie,* vol. 1 (Salzburg: Otto Müller, 1953), 217–25.
5. Peter Harvey notes "that Self is practically equivalent to 'what pertains to Self', I, mine, 'I am'", discussing a text from the *Khuddaka Nikaya, Niddesa* II.278-82, in particular (*The Selfless Mind,* 50). Vasubandhu confirms this. In his comment on V.9a–b of the *Abhidharmakośa,* he responds to the objection that "the view of self has two parts: to say 'I' and to say 'mine'", by observing "If the idea of 'mine' were different from the idea of 'I', then the ideas expressed in the other

grammatical cases, such as *mayā* (by me) or *mahyam* (to me) would thus constitute so many new views. Thus all belief in a self and in things pertaining to a self is totally included in the error of self" (*AKBh.* V.9).

6. Compare Plato's discussion of the psychological effects of thinking of things as 'mine' in the *Republic* (V.462a–464d).
7. Iris Murdoch writes in a similar vein, that we require "methods of dealing with the fact that so much of human conduct is moved by mechanical energy of an egocentric kind. In moral life the enemy is the fat, relentless ego" ("On 'God' and 'Good'", in *The Sovereignty of Good* [London: Routledge, 2001], 51; first published in *Anatomy of Knowledge*, M. Greene [ed.], 233–58 [London: Routledge & Kegan Paul, 1969]).
8. Put more colloquially, people with self-directed desires mostly seem not to be very happy, just to the extent they have such desires. The happiness argument offers an explanation for this phenomenon.
9. Translation from *Buddhist Advice for Living and Liberation: Nagarjuna's Precious Garland*, Jeffery Hopkins (trans.) (Ithaca, NY: Snow Lion Publications, 1988), 97.
10. Christopher Gowans, *Philosophy of the Buddha: An Introduction* (London: Routledge 2003). Gowans also holds unquestioningly that the Buddhist view is one of *denial* of the existence of a metaphysical entity, 'the substantial self'.
11. Thanissaro Bhikkhu emphasizes this in his "No-self or Not-self?", www.accesstoinsight.org/lib/authors/thanissaro/notself2.html), also available in his book, *Noble Strategy: Essays on the Buddhist Path* (Valley Center, CA: Metta Forest Monastery, 1999).
12. 'Soul' here translates the Pāli *jīvaṃ*, 'living principle' ('life-principle' in the previous quote from the *Milindapañhā*), often understood as one of the functional equivalents of 'I', or self. See Buddhaghoṣa's gloss on *puggala* as '*attā satto jīvo*' in his commentary on the *Kathāvatthu*, I.1 (*Kathāvatthuppakaraṇa-Aṭṭhakathā*, translated as *The Debates Commentary*, B. C. Law [trans.] [Oxford: Pali Text Society, (1940) 1999]).
13. See discussion of the *pudgalavāda*, and of Aristotle below.
14. See in particular *SN* 22.59. PTS iii.66–8, the Discourse on the Characteristic of Nonself.
15. This is a standard argument in the Christian tradition for denying change to God, and is present already in Aristotle's discussion of the prime unmoved mover, in *Metaphysics* XII.
16. Such strongly held intuitions about our phenomenology are what really give traction to Kant's ethics; see, for instance, his use of the gallows example (*Critique of Practical Reason*, 30).
17. *Chāndogya Upaniṣad* 13.2. Translation from *A Sourcebook in Indian Philosophy*, S. Radhakrishnan and C. A. Moore (eds) (Princeton, NJ: Princeton University Press, 1957), 72. This is one of the older *Upaniṣads*. Similar attention to seeking the self can be found in the (pre-Buddhist) *Bṛhadāraṇyaka Upaniṣad*, for instance, and the (possibly post-Buddhist) *Katha Upaniṣad* (both can be found in *The Early Upanishads: Annotated Text and Translation*, P. Olivelle [ed.] [Oxford: Oxford University Press, 1998]).
18. For philosophical discussion of the Vedic seeking of self in the *Upaniṣads*, see J. Ganeri, *The Concealed Art of the Soul: Theories of Self and Practices of Truth in Indian Ethics and Epistemology* (Oxford: Clarendon Press, 2007), ch. 1.

19. Buddhaghoṣa has detailed discussion in his *Visuddhimagga*, chapter XIV, including lists of the *saṁskāras* (XIV.133), as well as the other aggregates. For mature Abhidharma articulation of the five *skandhas*, see also Vasubandhu's more concise *Discussion of the Five Aggregates* (translated in *Seven Works of Vasubandhu, the Buddhist Psychological Doctor*, Stefan Anacker [trans.] [New Delhi: Motilal Banarsidass, 1984]).
20. "In one way of presentation I have spoken of two kinds of feelings, and in other ways of presentation I have spoken of three, of six, of eighteen, of thirty-six, and of one hundred and eight kinds of feelings. So the Dhamma has been shown by me in different ways of presentation" (*MN* 59, "Bahuvedaniya Sutta" [The Many Kinds of Feeling], §5, Nyanaponika's much more concise translation, at accesstoinsight.org). See also *SN* 36.22, PTS iv.231–2; *MN* 137.
21. Alternatives include the twelve *āyatanas* (sense-bases) and the eighteen *dhātus* (elements), largely discriminated according to their mode of apprehension. For detailed discussion, including the purposes specific to each analysis, see Y. Karunadasa, *The Dhamma Theory: Philosophical Cornerstone of the Abhidhamma* (Kandy, Sri Lanka: Buddhist Publication Society, 1996), www.abhidhamma.org/dhamma_theory_philosophical_corn.htm (accessed November 2013).
22. For a fine discussion of this, see Peter Harvey, *The Selfless Mind*, ch. 2; and again see Thanissaro Bhikkhu, "No-self or Not-self?" and, in greater detail, his "The Not-self Strategy", www.accesstoinsight.org/lib/authors/thanissaro/notself-strategy.html (accessed May 2013).
23. Translated in *Epictetus: The Discourses as Reported by Arrian*, W. A. Oldfather (trans.), books I–II (Cambridge, MA: Harvard University Press, [1925] 2000).
24. The most infamous of these passages is the Buddha's outright refusal to answer the explicitly posed question "Is there a self?" (*SN* 44.10, PTS iv.400); the forty-fourth chapter of the *Connected Discourses*, the *Abyākatasaṁyutta* (*Connected Discourses on the Undeclared*), is a wealth of similar instances. For discussion of the unanswered questions, see Stephen Collins, *Selfless Persons: Imagery and Thought in* Theravada *Buddhism* (Cambridge: Cambridge University Press, 1990), §4.2.
25. See my "Persons Keeping Their Karma Together", in *The Moon Points Back: Analytic Philosophy and Asian Thought*, J. Garfield, G. Priest and K. Tanaka (eds) (New York: Oxford University Press, forthcoming) for discussion of the *pudgalavāda*.
26. Miri Albahari argues to the contrary that the Buddhist *sūtras* do endorse a sort of witness-consciousness, much like the Brahamanical Self (see "Witness Consciousness: Its Definition, Appearance and Reality", *Journal of Consciousness Studies* 16 [2009]: 62–84; and in detail *Analytical Buddhism: the Two-Tiered Illusion of Self* [Basingstoke: Palgrave Macmillan, 2006]).
27. Priestley offers an excellent overview of the ambiguities in the no-self claims in the Buddha's discourses and in early Buddhism, in the first chapter of his *Pudgalavāda Buddhism*. The second chapter of this monograph is an outstanding overview of the *pudgalavāda* itself.
28. More on Abhidharma texts and their relation to the *Discourses of the Buddha*, and on varieties of Abhidharma, can be found in Appendix 3.
29. That is, a metaphysics distinguishing 'substance', 'property', 'relation', 'action', for instance, as various interrelated *ways* of being, as one finds, say, in Aristotle. "It is a cardinal doctrine of Abhidharma Buddhism that there is a single kind of thing", writes Ganeri (*Philosophy in Classical India* [London: Routledge, 2001],

101): that is to say, only one category of existent, although there is, of course, variety within this single kind of being; see also Paul Williams, "On the Abhidharma Ontology" (*Journal of Indian Philosophy* 9 [1981]: 227–57). This will be explored in more detail in Chapter 6.

30. According to Buddhaghoṣa's fifth-century commentary on the *Kathāvatthu* (*The Debates Commentary* [*Kathāvatthuppakaraṇa-Aṭṭhakathā*], I.1.[8]), to exist really and ultimately means, "that which is not to be apprehended as not fact, like magic, a mirage and the like; actual" (real), and "that which is not to be accepted as hearsay; highest sense" (ultimate). Vasubandhu's account at *Abhidharmakośa* 6.4 contrasts that which remains after analysis, even mental analysis (*paramārthasat*), with that which does not resist analysis (*saṁvṛtisat*); Dharmakīrti (*Pramāṇavārttika* 2.3, 3.3) makes the distinction according to whether or not something is capable of causal influence. For Candrakīrti's definition, see *Prasannapadā* 24.8 (selections translated as *Lucid Exposition of the Middle Way,* Mervyn Sprung [trans.] [London: Routledge & Kegan Paul, 1979]); for Śāntideva's, see *Bodhicaryāvatāra* IX.2 (translated as *A Guide to the Bodhisattva Way of Life,* B. A. Wallace & V. A. Wallace [trans.] [Ithaca, NY: Snow Lion Publications, 1997]). For general discussion, see Mervyn Sprung (ed.), *The Problem of Two Truths in Buddhism and Vedānta* (Dordrecht: Reidel, 1973).
31. This is a question that exercised Plato greatly, especially in the *Parmenides,* the *Sophist* and the *Philebus.*
32. Mark Siderits, who calls conventional realities 'convenient designators' and (more tendentiously) 'conceptual fictions', writes, "we can expect that our convenient designator for that substance will pick out a different set of *dharmas* on different occasions. There is no collection of *dharmas* that our name for the conceptual fiction will always pick out. So we cannot say precisely which ultimately real things the concept corresponds to" (*Buddhism as Philosophy: An Introduction* [Aldershot: Ashgate, 2007], 130).
33. The *Dhammasangani,* the *Vibhanga* and the *Dhatukatha* are exemplary in this respect, though philosophically unsatisfying, as might be expected.
34. Mental cultivation as described by Buddhaghoṣa in his *Visuddhimagga* takes both material and immaterial objects, and even at times attends to the mental aspect of attending to such objects. The five aggregates (*Vsm.* XIV) arise in the context of understanding and purification of view.
35. Ganeri, *Philosophy in Classical India,* 99–111, attributes the view specifically to later Buddhists; but also "the basic Abhidharma ontology is an ontology of tropes or property-particulars. So dividing something into its constituents just is a matter of dissolving it into its (particular) properties" (Ganeri, *The Concealed Art of the Soul,* 172).
36. This was not universally agreed among Buddhists, some of whom (like the Theravādins) suppose each *dharma* to have exactly seventeen moments (although what this means is disputed). Vasubandhu's argument for momentariness at *AKBh.* IV.2b–3b includes arguments against several alternative Buddhist explanations. The main arguments for the view are discussed by Siderits, *Buddhism as Philosophy,* §6.4.
37. Caution with the notion of 'substance' is advisable. Inasmuch as they are really existing individuals, and constitute whatever else is real, *dharmas* play the role of traditional 'substances'. They do so, however, outside the structures of the

metaphysical picture that gave rise to the traditional notion of substance, so they do not perform other standard roles thought to belong to substances: for instance, being 'that in which other things inhere but which does not itself inhere in anything else'. Thus it is not surprising to find Siderits, for instance, write with equal validity, "An atom, then, is not a substance. Nothing is a substance, for the category is just a conceptual construction" (*Buddhism as Philosophy*, 115). The trouble with sticking to 'atom' as a translation of *dharma*, however, is that it inevitably brings to mind the ordinary meaning of 'atom' today, as a figure within modern scientific theory, and *those* atoms, as we now know, have parts and are very much divisible.

38. *Avaktavya* is constructed in the same way as 'ineffable', from the root *vac-*, 'to speak'.
39. See Webster, *The Philosophy of Desire,* for extensive discussion of the question; the latter half of chapter 4 in particular studies the link between ignorance and desire in creating suffering experience.
40. See Chapter 1, n. 5.

3. *Kleśas* and compassion

1. *Nyāyadarsana of Gautama, with Bhasya, Vartika, Tika and Parisuddhis,* A. Thakur (ed.) (Mittula Institute, 1967), vol. 1, 150, quoted in Arindam Chakrabarti, "Is Liberation (mokṣa) Pleasant?", *Philosophy East and West* 33 (1983): 167–82, 167.
2. F. Nietzsche, *Twilight of the Idols,* "What I Owe the Ancients", 5, in *The Portable Nietzsche,* W. Kaufmann (trans.) (New York: Viking 1954).
3. The word used throughout the list is *sukha,* an untranslatable word meaning pleasure, joy, happiness, bliss depending on what qualifies it. It is best understood etymologically and by contrast with *duḥkha.* The *su-* prefix in *sukha* is related to the Greek *eu-* prefix – it asserts goodness of that to which it is prefixed, in contrast to the prefix *duḥ,* cognate with the Greek *dus/dys,* which asserts badness. *Sukha* and *duḥkha* are thus direct opposites, indicating good and bad states respectively, whatever those turn out to be.
4. "Discusion of points of doctrine also led to the development of different interpretative schools of thought (*vāda's*)", writes Peter Harvey. "Originally, these could not be a cause of schism, as the only *opinion* a monk could be condemned for was the persistent claim that there is nothing wrong with sensual pleasure (*Vin.*IV.134–5). Early on, it seems that adherents of a particular school of thought could be found among members of various monastic fraternities, but perhaps by the second century BC monastic fraternities started to become known for the specific doctrinal interpretations common among their members. By 100 AD at least, schisms could occur over points of doctrine, and the distinction between a 'fraternity' and a 'school' faded" (*An Introduction to Buddhism: Teachings, History and Practices* [Cambridge: Cambridge University Press, 1990], 74, citing *Vinaya Piṭaka*]).
5. See *Abhidharmakośabhāṣya* (*Commentary on the Treasury of Abhidharma*) II.26–27 for Vasubandhu's list of *kleśas.*
6. *Muditā* translates as sympathetic joy, appreciative joy: delight at the well-being of others.

7. *Vsm.* II.ix.1 addresses one "who wants to develop firstly loving-kindness among these".
8. Thus consequentialism – and so Jeremy Bentham's utilitarianism as well as Epicurus' hedonism – is teleological. It should be no surprise, then, that the main rival to the 'virtue ethics' interpretation of Buddhist ethics is the consequentialist one. One of the most robust defences of the consequentialist line is Charles Goodman's recent *Consequences of Compassion: An Interpretation and Defense of Buddhist Ethics* (Oxford: Oxford University Press, 2009). He focuses specifically on the much later Madhyamaka Buddhist Śāntideva, who may well have taken the basic teleology of his predecessors in a specifically consequentialist direction. The case is much less persuasive regarding, for instance, the fourth-century CE Yogācārin Asaṅga.
9. Because Damien Keown's understanding of 'virtue ethics' focus narrowly on neo-Aristotelianism, I think he misses out some of the possibilities and subtleties of Buddhist ethics (see his *The Nature of Buddhist Ethics* [New York: St Martin's Press, 1992]); this accounts in particular for his inability to accommodate what often looks like a genuine 'otherworldly' character of Buddhist ethics, incompatible with taking as the ultimate aim flourishing or fulfilling our human nature, on any description. For we do not look to human nature to inform us of what *nirvāṇa* is, or that it is good for us; and the fully attained state leaves real doubt about whether it is *me* that it is good for, or whether there is even anything recognizable as me (see below for further remarks). Martha Nussbaum, "Aristotle on Human Nature and the Foundations of Ethics", in *World, Mind and Ethics: Essays on the Ethical Philosophy of Bernard Williams*, J. E. J. Altham & Ross Harrison (eds), 86–131 (Cambridge: Cambridge University Press, 1995) offers a reading of Aristotle's ethics in which the difference here is particularly sharp.
10. So, in particular, the Buddhists do not – like some modern-day Aristotelians – aim at, or value especially, narrative unity; nor even express success as the attainment of a certain *structure* of soul, as Plato does.
11. James P. McDermott picks out those few exceptional places where *nirvāṇa* is claimed to be a reward for meritorious action in his "*Nibbāna* as a Reward for *Kamma*", *Journal of the American Oriental Society* 93 (1973), 344–7.
12. There is a great deal of discussion about how best to translate *kuśala*. Outside the indeterminate contexts at issue, *kuśala* seems centrally to carry connotations of wholesome, proficient, wise, skilful. It is very often translated as the latter in Buddhist ethical contexts, and as L. S. Cousins persuasively argues, rightly so; see "Good Or Skilful? Kuśala in Canon and Commentary", *Journal of Buddhist Ethics* 3 (1996), 136–64. Keown's reasons for preferring a generic 'good' over 'skilful' are motivated by philosophy rather than philology; but it is unnecessary for his case, since 'skilful' does not imply consequentialist ethics, but only teleological ethics, which all virtue ethics are anyway (*Nature of Buddhist Ethics*, esp. 119–20). For extra-Buddhist use of *kuśala*, see P. Tedesco, "Sanskrit *Kuśala* – 'Skilful, Welfare'", *Journal of the American Oriental Society* 74 (1954), 131–42; for discussion of its use in Buddhist ethics, see Peter Harvey, "Criteria for Judging the Unwholesomeness of Actions in the Texts of Theravāda Buddhism", *Journal of Buddhist Ethics* 2 (1995): 140–51.
13. Martin T. Adam's excellent "Groundwork for a Metaphysic of Buddhist Morals:

A New Analysis of *Puñña* and *Kuśala*, in Light of *Sukka*", *Journal of Buddhist Ethics* 12 (2005), 62–85, from which I borrow some of the schematic way of setting out the relation between *puñña* and *kuśala*, goes further by arguing that whatever is *kuśala* is also *puñña*. The argument is ingenious, but creates difficulties (not entirely allayed by the author's good efforts) for the accomplished person who has *kuśala* characteristics, but no longer generates further results of action, meritorious or otherwise. The more conservative view I outline above is fairly standard – see for example Bhikkhu Thich Nhat-Tu, "in this higher status of attainment (*nibbāna*), the sphere of *puñña* is left behind while that of *kuśala* remained the same as the sphere of *nibbāna*. This is the reason why the Pali canon describes an *Arahat* as one who is being freed from or is having passed beyond *puñña* and *pāpa* (*puññapāpapahīṇa*) but not good (*kuśala*) and evil (*akuśala*) [*Dhp.* 39; *S.* II. 82; *Sn.* [*Suttanipāta*] 520; 790]" ("*Kuśala* and *Akuśala* as Criteria of Buddhist Ethics", *Buddhism Today*, www.buddhismtoday.com/english/ethic_psy/004-tnt-kusala.htm [accessed July 2013]).

14. The translation is somewhat modified from Giuseppe Tucci's edition and translation, "The *Ratnāvalī* of Nāgārjuna", *Journal of the Royal Asiatic Society of Great Britain and Ireland* (1934), 307–25.
15. *MN* 11, for instance, but also, for example, *MN* 112, *SN* 12.61 (PTS ii.95) and elsewhere.
16. Vasubandhu offers a taxonomy of those afflictive states that are to be abandoned through seeing the truth alone, those that are abandoned through this together with meditation or mental cultivation generally, and those that are abandoned through mediation alone (*AKBh.* V.1–5). Of the six, or seven, fundamental afflictive states – attachment (to pleasures, and to existence), anger, pride, ignorance, wrong views, and doubt – it is perhaps unsurprising that those directly consisting in misunderstanding are largely to be abandoned through correct grasping of the four Noble Truths (*AKBh.* V.4) alone, while the directly affective afflictions require meditative training (*AKBh.* V.5a).
17. See Georges Dreyfus's excellent discussion of "Meditation as Ethical Activity", *Journal of Buddhist Ethics* 2 (1995), 28–54, for further discussion of the relation between mediation and the moral life.
18. The translation is of the *Dhamma-Saṅghaṇi* (Oxford: Pali Text Society, [1900] 1974).
19. See for instance Jay Garfield, "Mindfulness and Ethics: Attention, Virtue and Perfection", *Thai International Journal of Buddhist Studies* 3 (2012), 1–24, and "What is it Like to be a Bodhisattva?: Moral Phenomenology in Śāntideva's *Bodhicaryāvatāra*", *Journal of the International Association of Buddhist Studies* 33 (2012), 333–57; Daniel Lusthaus, *Buddhist Phenomenology* (London: Routledge-Curzon, 2002) and Christian Coseru, "Naturalism and Intentionality", *Asian Philosophy* 19 (2009): 239–64, favour a phenomenological interpretation of later Sautrāntika and Yogācāra Buddhist views and, while this is a claim about metaphysics, it cannot be disconnected from one's understanding of Buddhist meditational-ethical practice.
20. Vasubandhu summarizes the consequences of a *kleśa* as follows: (1) it makes firm its root, preventing the possession one already had of the *kleśa* from being broken; (2) that is, it continues to reproduce itself [establishes itself in a series]; (3) it makes one fit for the arising [or abiding] of the *kleśa* [makes one unapt

to change]; (4) it engenders its offspring, e.g. hatred engenders anger, etc.; (5) it leads to action; (6) it aggregates its causes, namely, incorrect judgement; (7) it causes mistaken understanding; (8) it bends the mental series towards the object or towards rebirth; (9) it brings about a falling away of good; (10) it becomes a bond and prevents surmounting of the sphere of existence to which it belongs (paraphrase of *AKBh.* V.1; see also Vasubandhu's discussion of *kleśas* at *AKBh.* II.26-30).

21. These connections are formalized as the so-called Twelvefold Chain of Dependent Origination, although the earliest occurrences include fewer links: seven or eight in the *Dīgha Nikāya*'s "Brahmajāla Sutta", verse 3.71; ten in *DN* 14; nine in *DN* 15. "The Analysis of Dependent Arising Sutta" has the canonical twelve: "And what, bhikkhus, is dependent origination? With ignorance as condition, volitional formations [come to be]; with volitional formations as condition, consciousness; with consciousness as condition, name-and-form; with name-and-form as condition, the six sense bases; with the six sense bases as condition, contact; with contact as condition, feeling; with feeling as condition, craving; with craving as condition, clinging; with clinging as condition, existence; with existence as condition, birth; with birth as condition, aging-and-death, sorrow, lamentation, pain, displeasure, and despair come to be. Such is the origin of this whole mass of suffering. This, bhikkhus, is called dependent origination" (*SN* 12.1, PTS iii.1). There are both psychological and metaphysical readings of these links and, because of the phenomenological character of Buddhist ethical practice, tending even in some forms towards idealism, these are not always entirely distinct. In Anuruddha's late (eighth- to twelfth-century CE) *Abhidhammattha Sangaha* (VIII.3-10), we see the facility with which Buddhist teachers might break the chain down in different ways, revealing different aspects, to illuminate various points.
22. Melford Spiro's *Buddhism and Society* (New York: Harper & Row, 1971) is responsible for the terminology, and much of the subsequent discussion of Buddhism as practised that has arisen in these terms. McDermott claims that "the paths to the goals of *Nibbana* and better rebirth were originally incompatible with each other in Theravada Buddhist thought" ("Nibbāna as a Reward for Kamma", 344), but concedes some early attempts to "harmonize the ultimate and proximate goals".
23. Their criticisms, then, were rather like the charge of egoism that modernity so regularly brings against the *eudaimonism* of antiquity, although, given the shared commitment to no-self, are rather difficult to make out fairly in those terms. For incisive discussion of the particular inappropriateness of the charge in the Buddhist case, see Roy Perrett, "Egoism, Altruism and Intentionalism in Buddhist Ethics", *Journal of Indian Philosophy* 15 (1987), 71–85.
24. "I considered: 'This Dhamma that I have attained is profound, hard to see and hard to understand, peaceful and sublime, unattainable by mere reasoning, subtle, to be experienced by the wise. But this generation delights in attachment, takes delight in attachment, rejoices in attachment. It is hard for such a generation to see this truth, namely, specific conditionality, dependent origination. And it is hard to see this truth, namely, the stilling of all formations, the relinquishing of all acquisitions, the destruction of craving, dispassion, cessation, Nibbāna. If I were to teach the Dhamma, others would not understand me, and

that would be wearying and troublesome for me.' ... Considering thus, my mind inclined to inaction rather than to teaching the Dhamma" (*MN* 26, "Ariyapariyesana Sutta" [The Noble Search], §19).

25. The birth of the Mahāsaṅghikas is murky, and developed over many centuries, beginning, as far as we can tell, with a rejection of some conservative verdicts of Buddhist Elders at the Second Council, at Vesālī (about a century after the Buddha's *parinirvāṇa*), developing subsequently a critique of the Arhat implicit in Mahadeva's 'five points', and a corresponding elevation of the Buddha by contrast. There were several Mahāsaṅghika sects, so that the evolution of this liberal-minded older form of Buddhism into the Mahāyāna is in fact much more difficult to trace than I describe here. Bart Dessein offers scholarly consideration of the question ("The Mahāsaṇghikas and the Origin of Mahayana Buddhism: Evidence Provided in the *Abhidharmamahāvibhāṣaśāstra*", *The Eastern Buddist*, new series, 40 [2009], 25–61). Harvey's *An Introduction to Buddhism* (Cambridge: Cambridge University Press, 1990) devotes a few pages to the arising of the Mahāsaṅghikas (pp. 87–9); more detail can be found in Bareau, *Les Sects bouddhiques du petit vêhicule*, II.1. A. K. Warder remarks briefly on the relation between Mahāyāna and Mahāsaṅghika, a claimed pedigree that dates back to the sixth-century Buddhist translator Paramārtha (*Indian Buddhism* [Delhi: Motilal Banarsidass, 1970], esp. 335–7).
26. The 'perfection of wisdom' (*prajñāpāramitā*) literature is of uncertain heritage. Several different *sūtras* of different lengths bearing that name seem to have been in circulation at various points. While the *prajñāpāramitā* literature is not itself philosophy, it influenced philosophers, particularly Nāgārjuna, discussed in Chapter 4.
27. Plato, *Apology*, in *Five Dialogues*, G. M. A. Grube (trans.), J. Cooper (rev.) (Indianapolis, IN: Hackett, 2002), with small revisions.
28. See also the claim in *Gorgias* 511a–512e, in *Complete Works*, J. Cooper & D. S. Hutchison (eds) (Indianapolis, IN: Hackett, 1997), that it is better for the wicked man himself if he is seriously disabled and impoverished, so that he might be restricted in his wicked activities.
29. The line is from Alexander Pope's *Essay on Man* (London: Routledge, 1993), which runs together love of God and love of all mankind.
30. R. F. Holland, "Is Goodness a Mystery?", in his *Against Empiricism: On Education, Epistemology and Value*, 93–109 (Oxford: Blackwell, 1980), 107.
31. "Moral Luck" and "Persons, Character, and Morality", both reprinted in Bernard Williams, *Moral Luck* (Cambridge: Cambridge University Press, 1981), are good examples, but it is a persistent theme in Williams's work.
32. See Susan Neiman, *Moral Clarity: A Guide for Grown-up Idealists* (Boston, MA: Houghton Mifflin Harcourt, 2008), esp. chs 6 and 10.
33. Might there be a third sort, moral badness, where emotions are wrong because they arise from, embody or lead to 'moral badness'? Not really. Apart from divine command theories, most ethical views aim to explain moral badness in terms of pleasure, reason, truth, knowledge or variants on the same, and since the Buddhists emphatically reject both divine command and intuitionism (a sort of nominal rationalism, or divine command without the 'divine'), we should expect some explanation of the badness of the emotions in terms of (a) or (b), or a combination of them.

4. The second Buddha's greater vehicle

1. The translation follows Thich Nhat Hanh, *The Heart of Understanding* (New Delhi: Full Circle Publishing, 1997).
2. On Nāgārjuna's relation to the *prajñaparamitā* literature, and a sound study of Madhyamaka in its historical intellectual context, see David Seyfort Ruegg, *Literature of the Madhyamaka School of Philosophy in India* (Wiesbaden: Harrassowitz, 1981).
3. The translation, slightly adapted, is by Ron Epstein, *The Heart of Prajna Paramita Sutra*, 2nd edn (Burlingame, CA: Buddhist Text Translation Society, 2002).
4. The *Eight-Thousand Verse Prajñāpāramitā Sūtra* describes the emptiness teachings as the 'second turning of the wheel of *dharma*' (v. 203, IX.3 of *The Perfection of Wisdom in Eight Thousand Lines & its Verse Summary*, E. Conze [trans.] [San Francisco, CA: Four Seasons Foundation, 1990]). As a description of Madhyamaka in particular, this may have become popular only later; it was entrenched by the time of the fourteenth-century Tibetan Mādhyamika, Tsongkhapa.
5. And perhaps rightly, at least according to Thomas Wood's *Nāgārjunian Disputations* (Honolulu, HI: University of Hawai'i Press, 1994), which argues that the position of the *Mūlamadhyamakakārikā* is indeed that, in the final analysis, nothing exists. How exactly this relentless eliminativism relates to *ucchedavāda*, the 'doctrine of cutting off', which is often translated as nihilism, is complex. But eliminativism is intelligibly 'nihilist' in the metaphysical sense; and Buddhist critics of Nāgārjuna ascribed the *ucchedavāda* to him for the extreme view, opposite of eternalism, that ultimately there is nothing.
6. David Burton (*Emptiness Appraised: A Critical Study of Nāgārjuna's Philosophy* [Richmond: Curzon Press, 1999]), is less optimistic: although he did not intend it, Nāgārjuna ends up a nihilist in spite of himself.
7. In this chapter, translations of the *Ratnāvalī* are, where possible, based on "The Ratnāvalī of Nāgārjuna", G. Tucci (trans.), *Journal of the Royal Asiatic Society of Great Britain and Ireland* 66 (1934): 307–25 and 68 (1936): 237–52, 423–35, which includes the Sanskrit as well as a translation. Where the Sanskrit is unavailable, the translations are based on Hopkins's translation of the Tibetan in *Buddhist Advice for Living and Liberation.*
8. I elaborate the contrast, and what exactly it means for faith to be a virtue in Buddhism in "Faith Without God", in *Thomism and Asian Cultures,* Alfredo P. Co & Paolo A. Bolaños (eds) (Manila: University of Santo Tomas Publishing House, 2012).
9. See my "Happiness and the Highest Good in the *Ratnāvalī*", in *Moonpaths: Ethics and Emptiness,* The Cowherds (New York: Oxford University Press, forthcoming) for detailed discussion of this point.
10. Āryadeva echoes this thought at *Catuḥśataka* XII.12, "For an unwise person, the apprehension of ego (*ahaṃkāra*) is better than the theory of selflessness".
11. The Abhidharma Buddhists who did not take to the Mahāyāna.
12. See Bhikkhu Bodhi's introduction to the *Aṅguttara Nikāya*, 54–6, where he offers texts from the *nikāyas* to show that even earliest Buddhism believed not only in a symbiotic relationship between monastic and lay communities, but also that this relationship could benefit lay members by leading them towards liberation, and not just happiness or a better rebirth.

13. This critique seems to be one that returns later in Vasubandhu's critique of atomism in the *Twenty Verses*.
14. Compare *Vigrahavyāvartanī* 29: "If I had any thesis, the fault would apply to me; but I do not have any thesis, so there is indeed no fault for me" (translated as *The Dispeller of Disputes*, Jan Westerhoff [trans.] [Oxford: Oxford University Press, 2010]; lightly modified from his commentary-embedded rendering). See also *MMK* XIII.8: "The victorious ones have said that emptiness is the relinquishing of all views. For whomever emptiness is a view, that one will accomplish nothing."
15. For one classic such characterization of Nāgārjuna's Madhyamaka as "extreme scepticism" and "the merciless condemnation of all logic, and the predominance given to mysticism and revelation", see Theodor Stcherbatsky, *Buddhist Logic*, vol. 1, Bibliotheca Buddhica 26 (Leningrad: Izdeatel'stov Akademii Nauk S.S.S.R., 1932), 12.
16. It may, however, have its background in textual considerations. Compare, for instance, this from *SN* 12.17, PTS ii.19–20: "'How is it, Master Gotama: is suffering created by oneself?' ('Not so, Kassapa,' the Blessed One said.) 'Then, Master Gotama, is suffering created by another?' ('Not so, Kassapa' …) How is it then, Master Gotama: is suffering created both by oneself and by another?' ('Not so, Kassapa' …) 'Then, Master Gotama, has suffering arisen fortuitously, being created neither by oneself nor by another?' ('Not so, Kassapa,' the Blessed One said.)" This style of refusing to endorse positions is particularly characteristic of the Buddha's discussion of self, which is why there can be dispute about whether the Buddha actually asserted the non-existence of self.
17. Compare *Vigrahavyāvartanī* 22.
18. "It has been a regular occurrence in the history of physics, metaphysics, and psychology," Karunadasa quotes Nyanaponika Thera observing, "that when a whole has been successfully dissolved by analysis, the resultant parts come again to be regarded as little Wholes" (*The Dhamma Theory*, 5–6). One might compare Plato's *Philebus* 16d, where he actively recommends that we do just that. Karunadasa thinks some Abhidharma thought escapes this charge: "In the Pali tradition it is only for the sake of definition and description that each *dhamma* is postulated as if it were a separate entity; but in reality it is by no means a solitary phenomenon having an existence of its own. This is precisely why the mental and material *dhammas* are often presented in inter-connected groups" (*ibid.*). This point is good so far as it goes, but it may not answer Nāgārjuna's charge. Nāgārjuna implies there is something suspect even in supposing *dharmas* can be distinguished 'for the sake of definition'; and if they could be, then it would be mysterious why, as Karunadasa claims "the factors into which the apparently composite things are analysed (*ghana-vinibbhoga*) are not discrete entities" (which is, after all, different from being a 'solitary phenomenon') (*ibid.*). For this, more careful thinking about the relation between essence and existence is required.
19. See Richard Hayes, "Nāgārjuna's Appeal", *Journal of Indian Philosophy* 22 (1994), 299–378, for a full exposition of the equivocation charge. Hayes offers considerable philological detail, among which it is perhaps helpful to observe that the '*bhāva*' in *svabhāva* is liable to the same multivalence as 'being' in English, or *ousia* in Greek. 'X's being' can be 'X's existence' or 'X's nature'; and we require an argument to show that these two meanings cannot be distinguished,

if that is in fact the case. Jan Westerhoff's "philosophical introduction", in *Nāgārjuna's Madhyamaka* (Oxford: Oxford University Press, 2009), offers extended consideration of the multivalence of *svabhāva*, and of Nāgārjuna's use of it to argue to an anti-foundationalist conclusion.

20. You can also see why the alternative is mysticism. If nothing has an essence, nor is an essence, then this is tantamount to saying that there is no definite thing that it is at all. Either way, it looks as if language – which is a stable system for ascribing definite and distinct natures to distinct entities – will not be a suitable medium for describing reality. But language is the only tool we have for coming to understand anything. It is the inescapable condition of our understanding. How, then, will Nāgārjuna bring us to seeing and understanding this conclusion? How do we use rational speech, concepts, and so on in order to show that conceptualization as such is arbitrary, not grounded in, or justified by, reality? The rejection of individuals may well explain Nāgārjuna's preference for the *via negativa* in argument.
21. See for instance Anuruddha's *Abhidhammattha Sangaha* III.16–22 and VIII.16–17.
22. That the crucial step is to demonstrate that the notion of causation, on any formulation at all, is conceptually dependent is argued well by Mark Siderits, "Causation and Emptiness in Early Madhyamaka", *Journal of Indian Philosophy* 32 (2004), 393–419. Such a position is incompatible with the gloss Garfield offers of *MMK* I, in his commentary, to the effect that it is only causes that are found inadequate, while 'conditions' escape critique. If this were the force of *MMK* I, it would fall wide of its mark, for many Abhidharmikas were not particularly invested in a strong notion of *cause* as opposed to an amalgam of conditions in the first place (on which see *Vsm* 542; and also recent comments in Harvey, *An Introduction to Buddhism*, 54–5, and Webster, *The Philosophy of Desire in the Buddhist Pāli Canon*, 147–9). Siderits claims that the conceptual dependency of causation infects that which is causally related; but exactly how this should work bears further consideration.
23. Think of Aristotle's requirement that to exist is to be a 'this-something': a determinate, distinct individual (*Metaphysics* VII.3).
24. And think here of the claim in Plato's *Sophist* that to be is to be able to act or be acted upon (*Sophist* 247d–e).
25. Georges Dreyfus identifies such a tension in later Buddhist epistemologists who were the intellectual heirs of the view Nāgārjuna is criticizing. In *Recognizing Reality: Dharmakīrti's Philosophy and Its Tibetan Interpretations* (Albany, NY: SUNY Press, 1997), 73–4, Dreyfus describes an ambiguity in the concept of existence between (i) to exist is to be causally efficacious; and (ii) to exist is to be an object of valid cognition (*prameya*), which includes the non-functional.
26. This is perhaps what Siderits, "Causation and Emptiness", §4, gets at in saying that the purported intrinsic nature of any existing thing *qua* existing involves essential reference to its causal relatedness. Causal relatedness itself is a conceptual construction, and since even thinking of something as existing requires reference to this construct, the constructedness – or emptiness – of 'cause' infects the purported 'existent'. To claim that something exists now amounts to claiming that its very essence contains mere conceptual construction – empty of real existence – at its core.

27. Note the regularity with which Nāgārjuna claims his arguments "refuted both 'it is' and 'it is not'" (*MMK* XV.7).
28. The example is taken from Plato, although the point is one readily granted independently of Plato's particular concerns. The fact that we have a single word 'barbarian' does not imply there is a single feature all items picked out by that term share. That we have a single term, 'barbarian', to pick out all non-Greeks does not indicate some *metaphysical* difference between Greeks and barbarians.
29. The moral undertones acquire more body when we see Nāgārjuna's successor, Āryadeva, claiming that "Regression even from moral conduct is preferable", presumably because that pertains to merely conventional reality, "but regression from the [right] view is never preferable" (*CŚ* XII.11).

5. Karmic questions

1. We might contrast this with the Stoics, for instance, who instead write the coincidence into the very nature of *happiness*, reconceiving ordinary notions so radically as to insist that happiness consists *entirely* in virtue, so that the two may never diverge.
2. Whether this was the *origin* of belief in rebirth is not so clear; see Gavin Flood, *An Introduction to Hinduism* (Cambridge: Cambridge University Press, 1996), ch. 4, esp. 75–6. But a moralized notion of rebirth does seem distinctive of the subcontinent (shared possibly in a minor strand of the Greek philosophical tradition, see Thomas McEvilley, *The Shape of Ancient Thought* [NewYork: Allworth Press, 2002], ch. 4), and such a view entwines *karma* and rebirth in a relationship of mutual support.
3. Thus a significant strand in European scholarship takes Indian theories of *karma* as the perfect solution to the so-called 'problem of evil', for which, see Max Weber, *Essays in Sociology*, H. H. Gerth & C. Wright Mills (trans. and ed.) (New York: Oxford University Press, 1946), 359. The view is still discussed, its perfection as a solution recently challenged by Whitley R. P. Kaufman, "Karma, Rebirth, and the Problem of Evil", *Philosophy East and West* 55(1) (2005), 15–32, and treated insightfully regarding the Buddhist tradition by Roy Perrett, "Karma and the Problem of Suffering", *Sophia* 24(1) (1985), 4–10.
4. It is additionally difficult because this highly schematic exposition of the *karma* claim glosses over significant variations on the view. Karl Potter sets out the variables and permutations in views of *karma* in "How Many Karma Theories Are There?", *Journal of Indian Philosophy* 29 (2001), 231–9.
5. This point is dwelt on at length in the *Milindapañhā*, in the context of whether the Buddha could experience pain after he was enlightened. The text takes the view that these were pains, but *mere* pains; and were not the fruition of previous action, but were due to entirely physical causes (*Milindapañhā* 134–8, §IV.i.8, PTS 134–8). Even one's death can be 'untimely' when due to such physical causes (*MP* IV.viii.6, PTS 303).
6. The *Kathāvatthu* makes it clear that knowledge of particular karmic connections would require the complete omniscience of a Buddha (*KV* V.10).
7. Such searching implies a mean and calculating mindset: "I am willing to pay with so much suffering for the evil I wish to do, but not more. If only I could know!"

8. "It is generally accepted that an emphasis on the role of *cetanā* [intention] in the action of *kamma* was the Buddha's contribution to the concept of *kamma*," writes James Paul McDermott in *Development in the Early Buddhist Concept of Kamma/Karma* (New Delhi: Munshiram Manoharlal, 1984), 28. While "it is not so clear that the *Upaniṣads* made no connection between intention and *karman*," he goes on, "... Only in Buddhism could the intentional impulse (*cetanā*) be defined as *kamma*" (*ibid*.: 29).
9. "*Cetanā* [intention]," writes Karin L. Meyers ("Freedom and Self-Control: Free Will in South Asian Buddhism", PhD dissertation, University of Chicago [2010]), "is essentially the movement of mind towards a particular object or end'. The Abhidharma literature has an elaborately specified view here, distinguishing and relating different components in the mental processes conditioning the 'action' that attracts *karmic* results. For a full discussion, see Webster, *The Philosophy of Desire in the Buddhist Pāli Canon*, esp. 120–25, 152–7. "Greed and craving", Webster writes, "do not arise spontaneously, but are ... the result of a process of our perception of 'reality'" (*ibid*.: 156).
10. Vasubandhu lists as the *samskāras* associated with *cittas* (mental events), "contact, mental attention, feelings, cognitions, volitions, zest, confidence, memory or mindfulness, meditational concentration, insight, faith, inner shame, dread of blame, the root-of-the-beneficial of lack of greed, the root-of-the-beneficial of lack of hostility, the root-of-the-beneficial of lack of confusion, vigor, tranquillity, carefulness, equanimity, attitude of non-harming, attachment, aversion, pride, ignorance, views, doubt, anger, malice" and he says that "among these, the first five occur in every *citta*". Volition (intention) itself is "mental action which impels a *citta* towards good qualities, flaws, and that which is neither" (*Discussion of the Five Aggregates*, in Anacker, *Seven Works of Vasubandhu*, 66–7).
11. P. A. Payutto writes, "In the English language, we tend to use the word when we want to provide a link between internal thought and its resultant external actions. For example, we might say, 'I didn't intend to do it,' 'I didn't mean to say it' or 'she did it intentionally.' But according to the teachings of Buddhism, all actions and speech, all thoughts, no matter how fleeting, and the responses of the mind to sensations received through eye, ear, nose, tongue, body, and mind, without exception, contain elements of intention. *Intention is thus the mind's volitional choosing of objects of awareness*; it is the factor which leads the mind to turn towards, or be repelled from, various objects of awareness, or to proceed in any particular direction; it is the guide or the governor of how the mind responds to stimuli; it is the force which plans and organizes the movements of the mind, and ultimately it is that which determines the states experienced by the mind. One instance of intention is one instance of kamma" (*Good, Evil and Beyond: Kamma in the Buddha's Teaching*, Bruce Evans [trans.] [Bangkok: Buddha Dharma Education Association, 1992], 7, emphasis added).
12. For discussion, see McDermott, *Development of the Early Buddhist Conception of Kamma/Karma*, 26–31. Earlier, at *AN* 98–113 (PTS i.17), a number of similar mental factors, or what we might call intentional states or attitudes, are considered likewise the greatest cause of harm, for example, heedlessness, laziness, strong desire, non-contentment, careless attention, lack of clear comprehension.
13. From the *Jaina Sutras*, Herman Jacobi (trans.) (Varanasi: Motilal Banarsidass, 1964), 414–15.

14. Gethin excludes the object intended entirely from the evaluation of the intention: "For the Theravāda Buddhist tradition there is in the end only one question one has to ask to determine whether an act is wholesome (*kusala*) or unwholesome (*akusala*): is it motivated by greed, hatred, and delusion, or is it motivated by nonattachment, friendliness, and wisdom" ("Can Killing a Living Being Ever be an Act of Compassion?", 190). See also Keown's *The Nature of Buddhist Ethics*, which emphasizes intention to the detriment of consequences in Buddhist moral thought generally; Goodman, *Consequences of Compassion*, inverts the emphasis.
15. This is one way of making sense of why, in the *Milindapañhā*, Nāgasena says that the person who grasps the glowing iron pot not knowing it is hot will get burned worse that someone who sees that it is hot, and touches it nonetheless (*MP* III.vii.8, PTS 84). This exposition does, however, radically simplify what was a very complex discussion in the Abhidharma and Vinaya texts, about when, how and to what degree which sorts of awareness were factors for mitigation (*MP* IV.ii.6 alludes to this discussion).
16. The same set of related issues is also discussed in the intra-Buddhist debate set out in the first part of the *Kathāvatthu*, or *Points of Controversy*.
17. See *Nyāya-Sūtra* 4.1.10, where "rebirth is impossible without a self", and Vatsyāyana's commentary on it.
18. Buddhaghoṣa goes into great detail about the exact causal connections, at *Vsm.* XVII.163–4.
19. A host of related objections are raised by Vasubandhu's imagined opponents in the final pages of the "Appendix", or Book IX, of his *Abhidharmakośabhāṣya*.
20. Cf.: "all beings are the owners of their actions, heirs to their actions, born of their actions, related through their actions, and have their actions as their arbitrator. Whatever they do, for good or for evil, to that will they fall heir" (*AN* 5.57, PTS iii.71, trans. by Thanissaro Bhikkhu at www.accesstoinsight.org).
21. For further discussion of the *pudgalavāda* as concerned with *karma*, see McDermott, *Development in the Early Buddhist Concept of Kamma*, 84–6. See also my "Persons Keeping Their Karma Together", §4–5.
22. But note: *not* holding the phenomena together; it is not an agent, or an efficient cause. See also Thich Thiên Châu, *The Literature of the Personalists of Early Buddhism*, Sara Boin-Webb (trans.) (Delhi: Motilal Banarsidass, 1999), esp. 161, for discussion of the *pudgalavāda* as concerned with preserving continuity.
23. Not all Buddhists were careful to stick to this. Śāntideva is a prominent example of one who does not; some of his Tibetan commentators seem even to *emphasize* the claim that even causally connected phenomena are distinct persons at distinct times. To the extent they emphasize this, and legitimize talk of persons as wholes at a time and not as causal continuities, the old objection returns with new force. In his essay "On Altruism and Rebirth", in *Altruism and Reality: Studies in the Philosophy of the Bodhicāryāvatāra* (Delhi: Motilal Banarsidass, 2000), 50, Paul Williams brings out sharply how this gives rise to the dreaded implication "that one person does the deed and another gets the result": dreaded because this is tantamount to conceding that actions have no reasonable consequences at all. Williams observes, "Rationally Śāntideva, rGyal tshab rje and others are in a dilemma. The more they stress otherness between this life and future lives, the more they open themselves up to the reply that there is no need to concern ourselves with future lives. After all,

one who argues that we have no need to concern ourselves with contemporary others will not stop at denying the need to concern ourselves with future lives. The more it is argued that there is a need to concern ourselves with future lives because it will be us, the less grounds there can be for arguing a concern with contemporary others" (*ibid.*).

24. Spiro, *Buddhism and Society*, is the source of the distinction, although he is careful to complicate it: "To say that there are three systems of Buddhism in Burma (or in Thailand or Ceylon) does not mean that there are three kinds of Buddhists in these societies; rather all three systems are found in varying degrees in all Buddhists" (*ibid.*: 13). Collins relates this distinction between *kammic* and *nibbanic* Buddhism to the Buddhist distinction between conventional and ultimate reality. This suggestion preserves the connection and continuity between "the two poles to which Buddhist thought and practice can be oriented" (Collins, *Selfless Persons*, 153).
25. See also *MN* 57, "The Dog-Duty Ascetic", where the same point is more directly tied to the volition for abandoning action of all kinds.
26. This was the complex *eudaimonist* dynamic discussed in Chapter 3.
27. For further elaboration of this point, through examples of actual appeals and omissions of appeal to *karma*, see my "'... And None of Us Deserving the Cruelty or the Grace': In Search of the Buddhist Job", public talk at the Einstein Forum conference on the Book of Job, 2012.
28. See their excellent "Narrative, Sub-Ethics, and the Moral Life: Some Evidence From Theravāda Buddhism", *Journal of Religious Ethics* 24(2) (1996), 305–27, esp. 318–22.
29. David Loy emphasizes the forward-looking character of "karma-as-how-to-transform-my-life-situation-by-transforming-my-motivations-right-now", taking the doctrine of *karma* to be an invitation to consider how to do just that ("How to Drive Your *Karma*", in *Money, Sex, War, Karma: Notes for a Buddhist Revolution*, 53–63 [Somerville, MA: Wisdom Publications, 2008]). He looks at similar issues in the concrete situation of juridical practices in Tibet in "How to Reform a Serial Killer: The Buddhist Approach to Restorative Justice", *Journal of Buddhist Ethics* 7 (2000), 145–68, where he also writes that "in traditional Tibet, as Buddhist a society as any has been, *karma* was never used to justify punishment" (*ibid.*: 147).
30. Again, this is discussed in more detail in my '"...and None of Us Deserving the Cruelty or the Grace"'.
31. See Hallisey and Hanson, "Narrative, Sub-Ethics, and the Moral Life", whose discussion of Bandhula (treacherously murdered along with his sons) concludes that "If we take seriously a story like this, we need to wonder whether there is an important gap between the well-known explanatory functions of karma, analyzed so well in modern scholarly literature, and the actual experience of karma in ordinary life. We feel that this story is quite realistic in its portrayal of an ordinary experience of karma, with all its unresolved contradictions between responsibility and innocence: innocent Bandhula got what he deserved" (*ibid.*: 318). The particular story they refer to is found in *Dhammapadaṭṭakathā* IV.3 (*Commentary on the Dhammapadā*, E. W. Burlingame [trans.] [Cambridge, MA: Harvard University Press, 1921], 42).
32. This is notwithstanding the energetic work of Ian Stevenson and Jim Tucker.

Literal rebirth also raises difficult philosophical questions of individuation and identity, which can challenge the coherence of the very idea.

33. "Rebirth, the law of karma, gods, other realms of existence, freedom from the cycle of birth and death, unconditioned consciousness: these were all ideas that *predated* the Buddha. For many of his contemporaries, such notions would have been uncritically accepted as a description of how the world worked. They were not, therefore, intrinsic to what he taught, but simply a reflection of ancient Indian cosmology and soteriology" (*Confessions of a Buddhist Atheist* [New York: Spiegel & Grau, 2010], 100).
34. Beware the argument from 'surely'. According to Lusthaus, the '*karmic* problem' is the central characteristic feature of Buddhism, and "It is no accident that where, for various reasons, a Buddhist school rejects this style of karmic analysis, it must also relinquish claim to a large segment of Buddhist soterical rhetoric. For instance, Mādhyamika and Ch'an, once they have jettisoned karmic classification, are compelled to utter such non-soteric pronouncements as 'no one obtains nirvana' or 'there is nothing to attain', etc. Simply put, without karmic analysis any Buddhist soteric claim would be without foundation and incoherent" (*Buddhist Phenomenology*, 181).
35. See for instance, Loy, "How to Drive your *Karma*"; Damien Keown, "Karma, Character and Consequentialism", *Journal of Religious Ethics* 24 (1996), 329–50; and Dale Wright, "Critical Questions Towards a Naturalized Conception of *Karma*", *Journal of Buddhist Ethics* 12 (2005), 78–93. Naturalizing *karma* is also the ambition of Owen Flanagan's recent monograph *The Boddhisattva's Brain: Buddhism Naturalized* (Cambridge, MA: MIT Press, 2011), though Flanagan's emphasis is more on the natural sciences.
36. "Just as my body is composed of the food eaten," writes Loy, "so my character is composed of conscious choices" ("How to Drive your Karma", 61–2). "People are 'punished' or 'rewarded' not for what they have done but for what they have become, and what we intentionally do is what makes us what we are" (*ibid.*). Potter observes in this context that "if the maturation of karma is dispositional – one's character conditioning one's experience and/or one's future acts without determining them absolutely – the theory may not seem terribly "unrealistic", since it is plausible to suppose that one's past actions create habits which determine our subsequent character and through that condition our experiences and/or actions" ("How Many Karma Theories Are There?", 234).
37. See Kathāvatthu VII.7–8; and, for discussion, McDermott, *Development in the Early Buddhist Concept of Kamma/Karma*, 87–90.
38. See Wright, "Critical Questions Towards a Naturalized Conception of *Karma*".
39. E.g.: "So too, bhikkhus, there are certain recluses and Brahmins whose doctrine and view is this: 'There is no harm in sensual pleasures ... this is the way of undertaking things that is pleasant now and ripens in the future as pain" (*M.* 45.4–6), and McDermott, *Development in the Early Buddhist Conception of Kamma*, 89, for discussion.
40. McDermott summarizes the position of the *Kathāvatthu*: "One of the most striking of these refinements was seen in the Theravādin's repeated insistence that the result [*vipāka*] of kamma is a matter of subjective experience, that material effects *per se* do not arise directly because of human action" (*Development in the Early Buddhist Conception of Kamma*, 102).

6. Irresponsible selves, responsible non-selves

1. More will be said about the Sautrāntikas in Chapter 7.
2. For a snapshot of non-Buddhist Indian philosophy, see Appendix 4.
3. Indeed, the two are often referred to together as the Nyāya-Vaiśeṣika, taken as representing a single view. Brahmanical traditions with different interests making common cause is not unusual. In fact, the traditional taxonomy of 'six orthodox systems' can also be presented as three pairs: Saṁkhya–Yoga, Nyāya–Vaiśeṣika, and Mīmāmsā–Vedānta (sometimes called Old and New Mīmāmsā). Such a taxonomy is too tidy but it forcefully illustrates the fact that intellectual practices were often distinguished by area of interest and methodology, and so did not necessarily regard each other as offering competing answers to the same questions. A brief overview of non-Buddhist Indian philosophy can be found in Appendix 4. For detailed philosophical treatment of the metaphysical sides of these investigations see Stephen Phillips, *Classical Indian Metaphysics: Refutations of Realism and the Emergence of "New Logic"* (La Salle, IL: Open Court, 1995).
4. For Nāgārjuna, this account of what does in fact exist will not do. But in so far as anything at all exists, for Nāgārjuna, too, it is the same sort of thing: its ultimate reality is to be empty of 'inherent nature' (*svabhāva*). Any categorial schema of the sort the Vaiśeṣika philosophers advocate is an attempt to resolve by different means just the sorts of paradoxes Nāgārjuna raises in the *Mūlamadhyamakakārikā.*
5. We might compare this to medieval discussion of *haecceity*, or 'thisness' (a non-qualitative property responsible for individuation), introduced into philosophical discourse by Duns Scotus (for an overview see Richard Cross, "Medieval Theories of Haecceity", in *Stanford Encyclopedia of Philosophy*, http://plato.stanford.edu/entries/medieval-haecceity [accessed July 2013]).
6. B. K. Matilal has a concise philosophical exposition in his *Logic, Language and Reality* (New Delhi: Motilal Banarsidass, 1985), §4.1. For full discussion, see the introduction in Karl Potter (ed.) *Indian Metaphysics and Epistemology: The Tradition of Nyāya-Vaiśeṣika up to Gangeśa* (New Delhi: Motilal Banarsidass, 1977).
7. See Ganeri, *Philosophy in Classical India*, ch. 3, for one intriguing exposition of the developed Vaiśeṣika view.
8. We saw Nāgārjuna's recognition of the same, in the *Ratnāvali* (cited in Chapter 2), where, for him, it is a reason to count the aggregates themselves as selfless: "The Buddha, who utters exclusively what is good to creatures, has stated them to be the offspring of the error that there is an 'I' and a 'mine' ... The *skandhas* [aggregates] forming a person are originated from the assumption of personality, but this personality is, from the standpoint of the absolute truth, unreal ... If one considers *skandhas* as unreal, the assumption of personality is abandoned; when the assumption of personality is abandoned, there is no more room for the *skandhas*" (*Ratnāvalī* I.27-30, trans. Tucci, modified).
9. *Discussion of the Five Aggregates*, in Anacker, *Seven Works of Vasubandhu*, 74. Compare Buddhaghoṣa's "the absence of any core of self conceived as a self, an abider, a doer, an experiencer, one who is his own master" (*Vsm.* 610), quoted in Ch. 1, n. 16.
10. Another reason, of course, would work in the opposite direction: speech and

argument have to be well grounded in reality if they are to be able to lead us to truth. Vaiśeṣika metaphysics provided the real grounds for Nyāya logic, epistemology, and philosophy of language.

11. The *vāda* tradition distinguished between friendly, instructive debate, contentious but constructive debate, and hostile, destructive debate, outlining aims and methods of each. This simplified version of the schema is discussed with great nuance in Matilal, *Logic, Language and Reality*, §1.2.
12. See B. K. Matilal, *Perception: An Essay on Classical Indian Theories of Knowledge* (Oxford: Clarendon Press, 1986) for a thorough introduction to, and investigation of, *pramāṇa* theory and its development through critique. For treatment of the later logic, epistemology and philosophy of language of the Navya-Nyāya, see Jonardon Ganeri, *Semantic Powers* (Oxford: Clarendon Press, 1999).
13. Sometimes called the 'Appendix' because, although it appears at the end of the commentary (the *bhāṣya*), it is (rather unusually) not commenting on any part of the root text itself.
14 The translation is Matthew Kapstein's, from the appendix to his *Reason's Traces* (Boston, MA: Wisdom Publications, 2001), 350; the following translations of Vatsyāyana and Uddyotakara are from the same source.
15. See Ganeri, *Philosophy in Classical India*, ch. 1, for early formulations of sound inference; see also again Matilal, *Logic, Language and Reality*. Buddhists make a distinctive contribution to this discussion later, most notably with Diṇnāga (fl. early sixth century CE), and those whose work followed on from his. This will be discussed in Chapter 8.
16. Vatsyāyana does not need all desires to be like this. Perhaps it is possible (although unusual, and difficult to articulate) to desire something never before experienced. All the argument needs is that there are undeniably desires of this sort.
17. See also *NS* III.i.26, where longing and aversion are due to anticipation, which requires memory.
18. This is why, as we shall see, the seventh-century Naiyāyika Uddyotakara will insist in this context that the Buddhists have only explained *difference*, not unity; and that thus the Buddhists are committed to supposing that Yajñadatta can recall what Devadatta perceived.
19. But not all. For an Indian philosopher willing to maintain that seeking knowledge is impossible, see discussion of the paradox of inquiry (familiar in the Greek tradition as Meno's paradox), in A. D. Carpenter & J. Ganeri, "Can You Seek the Answer to this Question?", *Australasian Journal of Philosophy* 88 (2010), 571–94.
20. Whether the Naiyāyikas Vasubandhu presents there are directly taken from Vatsyāyana or not, the arguments he attributes to them are essentially the same.
21. So writes Bhikkhu Ñāṇamoli in his note on *Visuddhimagga* XIV.59, which discusses the life-faculty *dharma*.
22. Paul Williams explores this objection in his *Altruism and Reality: Studies in the Philosophy of the Bodhicāryāvatāra* (London: Routledge, 1997; reprinted New Delhi: Motilal Banarsidass, 2000). According to Ganeri, *The Concealed Art of the Soul*, 187, essentially the same objection is made to Parfit's attempt to do without any mechanism for stream-individuation. I discuss this dialectic in the context of philosophical motivation for the *pudgalavāda* in "Persons Keeping Their Karma Together".

23. Two acute studies of the most sophisticated Nyāya objection of this kind, and possible Buddhist replies, are Arindam Chakrabarti, "I Touch What I Saw", *Philosophy and Phenomenological Research* 52 (1992), 103–16, and Jonardon Ganeri, "Cross-Modality and the Self", *Philosophy and Phenomenological Research* 61 (2000), 639–58.
24. See, for instance, J. David Velleman, "So It Goes", The Amherst Lecture in Philosophy, Lecture 1 (2006), www.amherstlecture.org/velleman2006/index.html (accessed July 2013).
25. Arindam Chakrabarti construes the Nyāya argument in this way, in "I Touch What I Saw".
26. Of course, I might simply remember someone having told me this; but this will not change the problem very much. I shall have to coordinate a greater range of experiences in order to find the testimony both intelligible and motivating.

7. The third turning: Yogācāra

1. Mostly, as it turns out, from Vasubandhu's own use of the term in identifying his dissent from Vaibhāṣika positions in the *Abhidharmakośabhāṣya* (see Robert Kritzer, "Sautrāntika in the *Abhidharmakośabhāṣya*", *Journal of the International Association of Buddhist Studies* 26[2] [2003] 331–84, esp. 367).
2. *Abhidharmakośavyākhyā* 11.29–30, quoted by Kritzer, "Sautrāntika in the *Abhidharmakośabhāṣya*", 380.
3. *Abhidharmakośabhāṣya* III.1, on which, see Pruden's note 16; see also critical distancing from Abhidharma texts and views at, e.g., *AKBh.* I.20, I.42d; III.28a–b.
4. See L. Cousins, "On the Vibhajjavādins: the Mahiṃsāsaka, Dhammaguttaka, Kassapiya and Tambapaṇṇiya Branches of the Ancient Theriyas", *Buddhist Studies Review* 18 (2001), 131–82; Colette Cox, *Disputed Dharmas: Early Buddhist Theories on Existence – An Annotated Translation of the Section on Factors Dissociated from Thought from Saṅghabhadra's Nyāyānusāra* (Tokyo: International Institute for Buddhist Studies, 1995) and "Mainstream Buddhist Schools", in *Encyclopedia of Buddhism*, R. Buswell (ed.), 501–7 (New York: Macmillan, 2004). Étienne Lamotte's indispensable study, *History of Indian Buddhism: From the Origins to the Śaka Era*, has been translated by Sara Boin-Webb (Paris: Louvain-la-Neuve, 1988).
5. See Erich Frauwallner *On the Date of the Buddhist Master of the Law Vasubandhu* (Rome: Instituto Italiano per il Medio ed Estremo Oriente, 1951). Padmanabh S. Jaini offers a very helpful *précis* of Frauwallner's argument, along with some textual evidence against the thesis that the author of the *Abhidharmakośabhāṣya* is different from the author of the Yogācāra pieces attributed to Vasubandhu, in "On the Theory of Two Vasubandhus", *Bulletin of the School of Oriental and African Studies* 21 (1958), 48–53.
6. Central *sūtras* are the *Tathāgagarbha Sūtra* and the *Ratnagotravibhāga*. The *tathāgatagarbha* does not seem at first to have influenced Buddhist intellectuals very much, but it did go on to have considerable influence in the development of Buddhist views and practice, particularly in Chinese Buddhism, and to an uneven extent in Tibet. The view essentially is that all sentient beings have (or are,

depending on the text) Buddha Nature, already perfected within them; enlightenment is a matter of eliminating whatever covers over this pristine nature. This Buddha Nature is sometimes called self (*ātman*) in some texts, although usually only dialectically, in order to orient potential Hindu converts in where to find what they might have been seeking in the Self. The *tathāgatagarbha* was also associated by some Yogācārins with the *ālayavijñāna*, or 'store-consciousness' (on which see the following note). Some Mādhyamikas associated themselves with the notion: David Ruegg cites Kamalaśīla, an eighth-century Madhyamaka-Yogācāra syncretist, as discussing the "*gotra* and *tathāgatagarbha* theories, thus assuring them a much more prominent place in later Madhyamaka thought than they had occupied in the words of the earlier Mādhyamikas" (*The Literature of the Madhyamaka School of Philosophy in India*, 95; see also 31–5, 54–7). Paul Williams offers a concise overview of the *tathāgatagarbha* in the Mahāyāna in *Mahāyāna Buddhism: The Doctrinal Foundations* (London: Routledge, 1989), ch. 5.

7. Yogācāra is wider and more complex than Vasubandhu, and other Yogācārins did not necessarily see themselves as interpreters of Vasubandhu, or as required to conform to his texts (see Lusthaus, *Buddhist Phenomenology*, for broad – if idiosyncratic – treatment of Yogācāra, including as it developed in China). My scope here is narrower, so in what follows I shall mean by 'Yogācāra' that view as it is laid out in these texts of Vasubandhu, hence the absence of discussion here of *the ālaya-vijñāna*, a *leitmotif* for Yogācāra in general. For a good general overview of Yogācāra Buddhism, see Williams, *Mahāyāna Buddhism*, ch. 4. For an excellent philosophical overview of Vasubandhu, see Jonathan C. Gold, "Vasubandhu", *Stanford Encyclopedia of Philosophy* (Winter 2012 Edition), Edward N. Zalta (ed.) http://plato.stanford.edu/entries/vasubandhu/ (accessed July 2013).
8. For 'existence' the text actually says 'the three realms' (*traidhātukaṁ*), which is a way of referring to this world, the world of higher beings and that of lower beings, or, in short, since all these realms are like ours in being transient and, in some sense, suffering, it is a conventional moniker for *saṃsāra*. It may have more specific meditational overtones, familiar to monastic readers, as Anacker suggests (*Seven Works of Vasubandhu*, 76 n. 12), but we do not need this here. Because he chooses this expression, it is unlikely that Vasubandhu intends – as my own unhappy translation of the phrase might suggest – that we are dealing here with a definition of 'exist'. One might translate here 'reality', or 'experienced reality'; no other translation seems any better at avoiding false implications and unwarranted presumptions.
9. George Cronk's rendering here is rather free, but to the point (G. Cronk (ed.), "Rendition of Vasubandhu's *Twenty Verses on Consciousness-Only*", www.bergen.edu/phr/121/vasubandhugc.pdf [accessed July 2013]). Anacker translates more inflatedly, but sticks more closely to the text: "It's just like in the case of the scope of Buddhas, which comes about through the ineffable Self. Thus both of these knowledges, because of their inherent non-knowledge, are not like an object, because it is through the state of an appearance of something which appears differently than it does later that there is a state of non-abandonment of the discrimination between object apprehended and subject apprehendor" (*Seven Works of Vasubandhu*, 174). Carmen Dragonetti and Fernando Tola

manage to translate the 'self' away entirely, rendering *ātman* as 'nature' (*Being as Consiousness: Yogācāra Philosophy of Buddhism* [New Delhi: Motilal Banarsidass, 2004]).

10. This should put paid to the suggestion that, for Vasubandhu at least, the *anātmavāda* was just a 'linguistic taboo', as Collins (*Selfless Persons*, 77), has argued, for "preserv[ing] the identity and integrity of Buddhism as a system separate from Brahmanism" (*ibid.*: 183) – as if the issue were not discerning reality but merely quibbling over the words we chose, regardless of meaning.
11. Indeed, they are so much in keeping with it that Robert Kritzer has argued that even in the *Abhidharmakośabhāṣya* Vasubandhu was, perhaps, crypto-Yogācāra. See "Sautrāntika in the *Abhidharmakośabhāṣya*" and his *Rebirth and Causation in the Yogācāra Abhidharma* (Vienna: Arbeitskreis für Tibetische und Buddhistische Studien, Universität Wien, 1999).
12. A serious look at a less clearly classifiable text, like the *Karmasiddhiprakaraṇa* (*Demonstration of Action*) – which Lamotte (*History of Indian Buddhism*, 40ff.) takes to be Sautrāntika, while Anacker takes it to be Yogācāra – would force one to adopt a view on the matter and, for the reasons given, I think the traditional account of a single philosopher who changed his views over time is more sustainable.
13. Diṅnāga, for instance, uses the same format for his discussion of perception (*pratyakṣa*) in his *Pramāṇasamuccaya*, or *Compendium on Pramāṇas* (means of knowing), translated by Masaaki Hattori as *On Perception: The Pratyakṣa-paricceda [Chapter] of Diṅnāga's Pramāṇasamuccaya* (Cambridge, MA: Harvard University Press, 1968).
14. The translation is a modification of Anacker's, using his edition of the Sanskrit, also included in *Seven Works of Vasubandhu*. Subsequent passages from the *Twenty Verses* are taken from the same, unless otherwise noted.
15. Indeed, one might argue – as in fact the later Mādhyamika Bhāviveka did argue – that such experiences as of objects without objectual support are only possible in dreams because at some point we did indeed have experiences of objects (with objectual support); see Bhāviveka, *Madhyamakahṛdaya IV and V*, in *Bhāviveka and His Buddhist Opponents*, Malcolm David Eckel (trans.) (Cambridge, MA: Harvard University Press, 2008).
16. For this same claim, compare Leibniz's *Monadology*: "(1) The *monad*, of which we will be speaking here, is nothing but a simple substance, which enters into composites; *simple*, meaning without parts. (2) And there must be simple substances, because there are composites; for the composite is nothing but a collection, or *aggregatum*, of simples" (*Monadology*, R. Franks & R. S. Woolhouse [trans.], in Leibniz, *Philosophical Texts* [Oxford: Oxford University Press, 1998]).
17. Interestingly, the *Nyāya-Sūtra* IV.2.4–25 brings similar problems of composition with atomism; and Vatsyāyana has already elaborated these in his commentary when Vasubandhu composes his *Twenty Verses*.
18. The alternative would be to make sense of Aristotle's continuum as not just a theoretical construct or set of possibilities, but as the nature of extended things. This, in turn, requires individuation, even of basic physical existents, to come from some other source.
19. This is just one reason why, I think, it is inaccurate to represent the *Twenty Verses* as advocating a 'mere epistemic idealism', like, for instance, Trivedi, who

uses the distinction, and the association with Kant, to place Vasubandhu's view in the *Twenty Verses* within the company of mere agnostics; see Saam Trivedi, "Idealism and Yogacara Buddhism", *Asian Philosophy* 15 (2005), 231–46.

20. Can this minimal, *a posteriori* account of the distinctness of persons suffice to get everything Buddhists – Abhidharma or Mahāyāna – want to get from appeal to distinct causal streams? I argue in "Persons Keeping Their Karma Together" that some Buddhists, at least, thought not, and that this motivated the *pudgalavāda*.
21. So this is more radical than the view Paul Williams famously condemns, in his reading of Śāntideva's *Bodhicāryāvatāra* VIII.101–103, for requiring 'free-floating' pains; Paul Williams, "The Absence of Self and the Removal of Pain: How Śāntideva Destroyed the Bodhisattva Path", in *Altruism and Reality: Studies in the Philosophy of the Bodhicāryāvatāra* (London: Routledge, 1997; reprinted New Delhi: Motilal Banarsidass, 2000), esp. §9.
22. Mark Siderits discusses the objection in *Buddhism as Philosophy*, 172–3, but offers a rather different solution, having argued that all current impressions can only be caused by previous actions, so that for any experience, there must be an intentional action standing behind it somewhere in the causal streams of *dharmas*.
23. That is, solipsism may be avoided here by allowing mental events that do not belong to any person in any sense at all. Peter Strawson has challenged the coherence of the idea, arguing that "states, or experiences, one might say, *owe* their identities as particulars to the identity of the person whose states or experiences they are" (*Individuals* [London: Routledge, 1959], 97).
24. Berkeley, for instance, presuming substantially distinct individuals, appeals to those ideas that are also thought by God, as opposed to those that are not (*Treatise Concerning the Principles of Human Knowledge*, §§29–33).
25. See for instance Alex Wayman, "The Yogācāra Idealism", *Philosophy East and West* 15 (1965), 65–73, and Trivedi, "Idealism and Yogacara Buddhism". More carefully, but also problematically, Dan Lusthaus argues for a phenomenological reading that manages to evade metaphysical considerations altogether (at length, in *Buddhist Phenomenology*, and in "What is and isn't Yogācāra" www.acmuller.net/yogacara/articles/intro-uni.htm [accessed July 2013]). Lusthaus argues emphatically against treating Yogācāra as a kind of idealism. At best, in his view, "questions about the ultimate reality of non-cognitive things are simply irrelevant and useless for solving the problem of karma" (*Buddhist Phenomenology*, 172; see also 188), which he takes to be the defining question of Buddhism. Lusthaus's argument concerns the Yogācāra tradition broadly, particularly the Chinese versions of it. For trenchant and convincing critique of this as an adequate interpretation of either texts or tradition, see Lambert Schmidthausen, *On the Problem of the External World in the Ch'eng Wei Shih Lun* (Tokyo: International Institute for Buddhist Studies, 2005), who nevertheless agrees with Lusthaus's "view that the teaching of *vijñaptimātra* is not basically a theoretical aim in itself but a 'therapeutic device', a soteric strategy, directed against attachment and appropriation" (*ibid.*: 11). But this, of course, does not answer the question of how important metaphysics is to that aim.
26. *Thirty Verses*, v. 29; the phrase is Anacker's translation, and a notion that plays a significant role in his interpretation of Vasubandhu.
27. The central transformative insight is explained in this way by Asaṅga

(*Mahāyānasaṃgraha*, translated into French as *La Somme Du Grand Véhicule*, Étienne Lamotte [trans.] [Louvain: Bureaux du Muséon, 1938–39], 2:28, 9:2). For discussion see Gadjin Nagao, "Connotations of the Word *Āsraya* (Basis) in the *Mahāyāna-Sūtralaṃkāra*", in *Mādhyamika and Yogācāra: A Study of Mahāyāna Philosophies*, Leslie S. Kawamura (trans.) (Albany, NY: SUNY Press, 1991).

28. Gold, "Vasubandhu", makes this concession to the Vasubandhu-as-not-idealist camp. I actually think it is an unnecessary concession, as even the positive views, including 'consummate nature' do not seem to introduce anything ontologically different from mentality. But if one cannot, strictly, count consummate nature as either mental or as non-mental, it might perhaps after all be wise to refrain from calling the view, including ultimate reality or consummate nature, 'idealist'.
29. Translations of the *Thirty Verses* and of the *Treatise on the Three Natures* are modified from Anacker's translations in *Seven Works of Vasubandhu*, consulting the Sanskrit in the same.
30. A recent translation of the former can be found in Jay Garfield and William Edeglass (eds), *Buddhist Philosophy: Essential Readings* (Oxford: Oxford University Press, 2009). A concordance of English translations of the latter text, with the Sanskrit original and Tibetan translation, prepared and made available by Richard Nance, can be found at www.nagaraprathama.com/uploads/3/6/5/7/3657511/trimsika_nance_rev.pdf (accessed July 2013).
31. This was not the only grounds on which Yogācārins faced charges of being crypto-*ātmavādins*. Their much-discussed view that there was a distinct kind of consciousness, called variously the *ādānavijñāna* (appropriating-consciousness) and the *ālayavijñāna* (store-consciousness) – a sort of unconscious form of consciousness explaining memory, and results that follow an action after some interval of time – tended to attract similar criticism, in spite of the fact that this form of consciousness was every bit a stream of momentary events as any other form of mental event. The Yogācāra *Saṃdhinirmocanasūtra* explains that the tendency of foolish people to mistake the *ādāna/ālaya-vijñāna* for a self was the reason the Buddha did not teach of it openly (see Kritzer, "Sautrāntika in the *Abhidharmakośabhāṣya*", 379).
32. And this is why it would be misleading to suppose that consummate nature is, just as any Mādhyamika would be happy to agree, simply the absence of the imagined nature in the dependent nature. It is rather the precondition for dependent nature, whether full of imagined entities or recognizing their illusoriness.
33. This also explains epistemological commitments that arise in later Yogācārins: Diṅnāga and Dharmakīrti, for instance, hold that every moment of consciousness is reflexive. While content of a particular kind is presented, the fact of awareness here and now is thereby also made apparent.
34. Indeed, in Vasubandhu's analogy of the wood somehow forming the basis of the mass hallucination of an elephant (*TSN* 30), the piece of wood stands for consummate nature, just as wood, *hule*, does duty for Aristotle in trying to construct a notion of 'matter'.
35. "[T]he residues of a 'dual' apprehension will not come to an end … even with the consciousness, 'All this is cognition-only', because this also involves an apprehension" (*TK* 26d–27c).

36. These are the reasons Aristotle cites in *Metaphysics* Z.3 for rejecting matter's claim to be substance.
37. This should not imply that the very concept of cognition commits us to the contested claim that there always *is* some determinate content or another to every moment of any mode of awareness. Perhaps it is possible – although certainly unusual – for a moment of awareness to have no content; but then we are forced to say that it has nothing at all for its content: *not* that there is no content-aspect, but that this content-aspect is 'filled', if you like, by nothing at all.
38. Indeed, one might be tempted to ask Nāgārjuna just what justified his own claim that the ultimate emptiness of reality was itself *dependent* upon other. On the reading offered here, this is just the claim that Vasubandhu is challenging.
39. Notwithstanding this, it is worth noting that in other strands of Yogācāra, influenced more by the *tathāgatagarbha* view, such styles of thinking do indeed seem to have gained traction; if it is against these that the Mādhyamika raises his objection, it may yet have some point. However, reflection on Vasubandhu shows that a Yogācārin need not, and ought not, go down that route.

8. The long sixth to seventh century: epistemology as ethics

1. Cox gives translation and detailed discussion of Saṅghabhadra in *Disputed Dharmas*.
2. See Matilal, *Language, Logic and Reality*, §§1.2–1.5 for discussion.
3. As Lusthaus says, with perhaps a little hyperbole, "since the soteric efficacy of Buddhism itself rested on the question of correct cognition, there could be no more momentous endeavour than epistemology" (*Buddhist Phenomenology*, 6); and "epistemology is a necessary cause of Awakening" (*ibid.*: 173).
4. Sthiramati and Dharmapāla, among others, seem to have carried on the Abhidharmic psychology strain within Vasubandhu's Yogācāra thought into the next century, but as Lusthaus puts it, "the Abhidharma direction atrophied, and by the eight century had been eclipsed by" the epistemologists working in Diṅnāga's mould, and syncretists that blended this with Tathāgatagarbha thought (*Buddhist Phenomenology*, 7; see also Williams, *Mahāyāna Buddhism*, 311 n. 46).
5. The scholar's precise name has been obscured through time and transmission. Very often, at least in anglophone literature of the twentieth century, he went by the name Bhāvaviveka, a name often shortened (especially in Tibetan-influenced discourse) to Bhāvya. Malcolm David Eckel's recent edition and commentary indicates scholarly consensus now building towards 'Bhāviveka' as the correct rendering (*Bhāviveka and his Buddhist Opponents* [Cambridge, MA: Harvard University Press, 2008], 88 n. 1).
6. For Dharmakīrti's direct engagement with this, see his *Pramāṇa-Vārttika* 3.194–210, translated by John Dunne (*Foundations of Dharmakīrti's Philosophy* [Boston, MA: Wisdom Publications, 2004], §7: *PV* 3.194–224).
7. And again at the commentary (*vṛtti*) on I.1.3d and on I.1.4a–b, where Diṅnāga concludes, "It is established that perception is free from conceptual construction". Translations of the first chapter of Diṅnāga's *Pramāṇa-samuccaya*

(*Compendium of Means of Knowing*) are from Masaaki Hattori, *Dignāga, On Perception* (Cambridge, MA: Harvard University Press, 1968), with some minor modifications especially of extra words supplied in parenthesis. Hereafter cited as *PS*. Hattori translates Diṅnāga's own commentary, or *vṛtti*, on the *Pramāṇasamuccaya* alongside the main text; citations of the commentary are abbreviated *PSV*, and locations specified by the verse number of the main text.

8. Such a view of perception has been compared to sense-data theories by, for instance, B. K. Matilal, in *Perception.*
9. We may find it interesting to consider here Kant's strikingly similar distinction: "An objective perception is cognition [*erkenntnis*] (*cognitio*). This is either *intuition* or *concept* (*intuitus vel conceptus*). The former relates immediately to the object and is single, the latter refers to it mediately by means of a feature which several things may have in common" (*Critique of Pure Reason*, N. Kemp Smith [trans.] [New York: St Martin's Press (1929), 1965], A320/377; I put 'cognition' where he has 'knowledge'). Whether Diṅnāga could or would want to distinguish, as Kant does, among immediate experiences those that are objective (intuitions) and those that are subjective (sensations), is worth considering in the context of two further demands Diṅnāga places on perception: first, that they be of non-conceptual ultimate reality; second, that they somehow ground linguistic, conventional reality.
10. See also *PS* I.3.3c–d, where the Naiyāyikas are criticized for maintaining the distinctness of the means (activity) and results of cognition.
11. According to Matilal, it is in fact Dharmakīrti whom tradition credits with originating the 'Buddhist idealist' view that "each awareness ... [has] a *form* [*ākāra*] by which it is distinguishable and identifiable. This form is in each case the form of the apprehensible ... and what thereby distinguishes itself from the apprehension, *viz.* the awareness itself. It is self-awareness which combines them" (*Perception*, 339). Because Dharmakīrti presents his work as an exposition of Diṅnāga's thought, it is often difficult to distinguish between interpretation, extrapolation and innovation.
12. *Ibid.*, 150.
13. Dan Arnold describes Dharmakīrti's interpreter, Dharottara, in this context as "having in mind the relationship between the object intended [*vyavasthāpya*] and an intending [*vyavasthāpaka*] subject", as opposed to a causal, producer–produced, relation (*Buddhists, Brahmins, and Belief* [New York: Columbia University Press, 2005], 47). He cites later Buddhists making the content–cognizing distinction. According to the eleventh-to-twelfth-century Mokṣākaragupta, "the property of knower in relation to what is known is ... [the relation of] intended and intentional"; and the self-awareness joining these two is, as Śāntarakṣita and Kamalaśīla had already observed, just "this fact of its being not-unconscious". "There can be no self-cognition of the cognition in the sense that it is the action and also the active agent, because one and the same entity, which is impartite in form, cannot have three characters [*viz.*, of the cognized, the cognizer and the cognition]. Hence the only right view is that the 'self-cognition' of the cognition is due to its being of the very nature of consciousness" (Śāntarakṣita, *Tattvasaṃgraha, with the Commentary of Kamalaśīla,* Ganganatha Jha [trans.] [New Delhi: Motilal Banarsidass, (1939) 1986], 2000–2002).

14. If our observation, above, of the resemblance between Diṅnāga's epistemology and Vasubandhu's Yogācāra metaphysics were apt, then this understanding of self-cognizing would be picking up on Vausbandhu's consummate nature, which is logically prior to, but expressed in, the mode–content bifurcation.
15. According to Dan Arnold, rightly so. His engaging treatment of the post-Diṅnāga debate on this point, likening it illuminatingly to the post-Kantian discussion of the transcendental unity of apperception, holds that Diṅnāga himself cannot avoid the regress charge ("Is *svasaṃvitti* Transcendental? A Tentative Reconstruction Following Śāntarakṣita", *Asian Philosophy* 15 [2005], 77–111).
16. See *ibid.* for discussion of these later interpreters.
17. Bruce Hall's translation and edition of the first chapter of the *Abhidharmakośabhāṣya* notes in relation to v. 16a, that "this 'cognition' [*vijñānaskandha*] of the Abhidhārmikas corresponds to the 'direct perception' [*pratyakṣa*] of the Diṅnāga-Dharmakīrti school of Buddhist Logic, while 'idea' [*saṃjñā*] corresponds to 'inference' [*anumāna*]" ("Vasubandhu on 'Aggregates, Spheres, and Components: Being Chapter One of the *Abhidharmakośa*'", PhD dissertation, Harvard University [1983], 84 n.). See also Peter Fenner, "A Study of the Relationship Between Analysis (*vicara*) and Insight (*prajna*) Based on the Madhyamakavatara", *Journal of Indian Philosophy* 12 (1984), 139–97, in which he discerns a line stretching into Madhyamaka as well: "According to the *Abhidharmakośa* (1.14b) *saṁjñā* is apprehending the features [*nimitta, mtshan-ma*] and this is echoed exactly by Candrakīrti in the MA (6.202) … According to the *Abhidharmakośa* (1.44) consciousness [*vijñāna*] apprehends just the bare object [*vastumātra-grāhaṇam*] while recognition [*saṁjñā*] takes the process further by apprehending the features" (*ibid.*: 145–6).
18. Candrakīrti levels this objection against Diṅnāga's theory of perception, in the *Prasannapadā*, his commentary on the *Mūlamadhyamakakārikā*, at 23.28–25.28. "This word '*pratyakṣa*' [perception] is established in the world. It is, however, used by us just as it is in the world. That derivation [of yours] being made only by setting aside the correct worldly categories, however, what would be established is the setting aside of an established word. And it thus follows that there would be no perception" (*PP* 25.10–12). How, and how much, what is 'established in the world' should weigh with us is a central part of Candrakīrti's understanding of Madhyamaka, as we shall see below. The translation is from Mark Siderits's treatment of Candrakīrti's objections to Diṅnāga's epistemological project, in "The Madhyamaka Critique of Epistemology II", *Journal of Indian Philosophy* 9 (1981), 121–60, which are largely sympathetic to the Mādhyamika. Dan Arnold offers a readable translation of the whole section, as "Materials for a Madhyamaka Critique of Foundationalism: An Annotated Translation of *Prasannapadā* 55.11 to 75.13", *Journal of the International Association of Buddhist Studies* 28(2) (2005), 411–67.
19. Translations of *Pramāṇasamuccaya* II and V are taken from Richard Hayes, *Dignaga on the Interpretation of Signs* (Dordrecht: Kluwer, 1988). Although the verse here seems specifically aimed at rejecting the claim that testimony might be a third *pramāṇa*, Diṅnāga later refers back to this initial claim in drawing a conclusion with much wider scope: "Therefore, we have established the truth of what was said at the outset of this discussion, namely, that a word expresses its own object by precluding what is incompatible in a way similar to

[an inferential sign such as] the property of having been produced [indicates a property such as the fact of being transitory]" (*PS* V.11, at Hayes's 11.3.0).

20. One can still see Uddyotakara formatting his argument against the Buddhist no-self view in this way in his seventh-century CE sub-commentary (*vārtika*) on Vatsyāyana's commentary (*bhāṣya*) on the *Nyāya-Sūtra* (for translation of which, see Kapstein, *Reasons Traces*, 378–90, esp. 382); a schematic gloss of *NV* I.1.10 would be – THESIS: Not [memory is without foundation]; REASON: All effects have foundation; EXAMPLE: Visible form, for instance, is an effect grounded in a visible object; APPLICATION: Memory is one such effect; CONCLUSION: Memory occurs only with such a foundation.
21. For a good collection of classic essays treating the so-called 'Indian syllogism', from H. T. Colebrook's 1924 essay to B. K. Matilal's "Introducing Indian Logic", see Jonardon Ganeri (ed.), *Indian Logic: A Reader* (New York: Routledge, 2001).
22. "The greatest part of the questions and controversies that perplex mankind, depending on the doubtful and uncertain use of words, or (which is the same) indetermined ideas", John Locke writes, in his "Epistle to the Reader" prefacing the *Essay Concerning Human Understanding*, P. H. Nidditch (ed.) (Oxford: Clarendon Press, [1975] 1979), xvi. "If men had such determined ideas in their inquiries and discourses, they would both discern how far their own inquiries and discourses went, and avoid the greatest part of the disputes and wranglings they have with others" (*ibid.*).
23. Diṅnāga did not discover these criteria *ex nihilo*. Hayes, *Dignaga on the Interpretations of Signs*, 145–9, discusses the state of play as Diṅnāga inherited it (perhaps, according to Katsura 1986c7, from Asaṅga), and credits Diṅnāga specifically with recognizing that condition 2 must be existentially quantified ('there is some other occurrence'), while condition 3 must be universally quantified ('in all cases', or 'not in any cases').
24. See *NV* I.1.5 (Ganganatha Jhā [trans.] [Allahabad: E. J. Lazarus, 1910–1920], 188–94). Discussion of this can be found in Hayes, *Dignaga on the Interpretation of Signs*, 149–54.
25. The example is raised at *Pramāṇasamuccaya* II.7, translated in Hayes, *Interpretation of Signs*, ch. 6; a translation of the first twenty-five verses of *PS(V)* II can be found in Richard Hayes's excellent survey and overview of Diṅnāga's epistemology, "Dinnaga's Views on Reasoning (*svarthanumana*)", *Journal of Indian Philosophy* 8 (1980), 219–77.
26. One can also generate a converse worry about the redundancy of the third condition by reading the second condition as already saying that the target property (fire) is found *only* in cases where the *hetu* (smoke) is present. This obviously would already entail the third condition, rendering it otiose. One would think it a good reason not to read the second condition in this way, except that Diṅnāga does say things at his comment on *PS* II.5 that lend themselves to this reading.
27. This is what Tom Tillemans calls the 'traditional' reading, contrasting it with a reading put forward primarily by Gelugpa philosophers in Tibet ("On *Sapakṣa*", in his *Scripture, Logic, Language: Essays on Dharmakirti and his Tibetan Successors*, 89–116 [Boston, MA: Wisdom Publications, 1999]; originally published in *Journal of Indian Philosophy* 18 [1990]: 53–79). Although there is less textual support for the Gelugpa reading, it avoids, according to Tillemans, awkward logical implications of the traditional reading.

28. Hayes, *Interpretation of Signs*, 15, discusses this flexibility.
29. Diṅnāga acknowledges just this contingency at *PS* V.30, where he argues that "it is not necessary to say that a verbal symbol applies to every instance of what is similar, because in some cases it is not possible to express an extension that is unlimited. But it is possible to say that it does not occur in the dissimilar – although it too is unlimited – simply on the basis of its not being observed to apply to any dissimilar instance" (quoted in Hayes, *Dignaga on the Interpretation of Signs*, 182–3).
30. Richard Hayes does so, for instance (*ibid.*: 163–7).
31. Or the second, if it is the demand that the two properties co-arise *only* in the similarity class.
32. "Veiled within Dharmakīrti's notion of *svabhāva* as nature", John Dunne writes, "is a strong rejection of random (*ākasmika*) causality and thus a strong commitment to the regularity of causality" (*Foundations of Dharmakīrti's Philosophy*, 161).
33. See, for instance, his *Pramāṇa-vārttika*, and its auto-commentary, 1.34–37 (helpfully translated in John Dunne's Appendix of Translations in *Foundations of Dharmakīrti's Philosophy*).
34. There are in fact two forms of such 'natural connections', one of which is the producer–produced type and the other an invariable concomitance due to a thing's nature; but this latter is also a way of being implicated in a causal structure (as discussed below). See Dunne, *Foundations of Dharmakīrti's Philosophy*, part 3, for detailed and illuminating discussion of Dharmakīrti's 'natural connection' (*svabhāva-pratibandha*).
35. This is what Dharmakīrti seems to argue in *On Relations (The Philosophy of Relations); Containing the Sanskrit text and English translation of Dharmakīrti's Sambandha-Parīkṣa with Prabhācandra's Commentary,* V. N. Jha (trans.) (New Delhi: Sri Satguru Publications, 1990).
36. This may recall the Aristotelian dictum 'man begets man'. Since this is, for Aristotle, a consideration in favour of formal causation, and real natural forms, which any Buddhist would eschew, the association should remind us that Dharmakīrti's philosophical task is precisely to explain what warrants or grounds Diṅnāgean appeals to mere constant conjunction, *without* postulation of any ultimately real, non-perceptible, rationally structured entities such as Aristotelian forms, universals or selves.
37. Dunne describes it as "a relationship between an entity's nature-*savbhāva* and its participation in a present causal complex or its arisal from a past causal complex" (*Foundatins of Dharmakīrti's Philosophy*, 163), and refers us to Dharmakīrti's auto-commentary on his *Pramāṇa-vārttika* (*PVSV* 1.7).
38. See the advice in "To Long Nails": "A wise person among them considers that 'If I were to grasp and insist firmly on this view … I would clash with these two. Where there is a clash, there is dispute. Where there is a dispute, quarreling. Where there is quarreling, annoyance. Where there is annoyance, frustration.' Envisioning for himself clash, dispute, quarreling, annoyance, frustration, he both abandons that view and does not cling to another view. Thus there is the abandoning of these views; thus there is the relinquishing of these views" ("Dighanaka Sutta", *MN* 74). See also: "When ignorance is abandoned and true knowledge has arisen in a bhikkhu, then with the fading away of ignorance and the arising of true knowledge he no longer clings to sensual pleasures, no longer

clings to views, no longer clings to rules and observances, no longer clings to a doctrine of self. When he does not cling, he is not agitated. When he is not agitated, he personally attains Nibbana" ('Shorter Discourse on the Lion's Roar', *Cūlasīhanāda sutta, MN* 11).

39. Although perhaps, as Claus Oetke argues ("'Nihilist' and 'Non-nihilist' Interpretations of Madhyamaka", *Acta Orientalia* 57 [1996], 57–104), and Thomas Wood at greater length (*Nāgārjunian Disputations* [Honolulu, HI: University of Hawai'i Press, 1994]), trying to avoid metaphysical nihilism – modern-day eliminativism about all things – is an interpretive mistake, for this was indeed the view Nāgārjuna was after. The unpalatable moral implications remain, and require making sense of such claims as: "when, through right knowledge, one has suppressed any notion of existence and non-existence, one is beyond merit and demerit" (*Ratnāvalī* I.45).
40. The passage is translated by Eckel, *Bhāviveka and his Buddhist Opponents*, 52, and taken from Bhāviveka's commentary on the *Mūlamadhyamakakārikā*, the *Prajñāpradīpa*.
41. Translations of Bhāviveka's *Madhyamakahṛdaya* are taken from Eckel, *Bhāviveka and his Buddhist Opponents*.
42. "And if, when I was asked by him, 'Is there no self?' I had answered, 'There is no self,' the wanderer Vaccagotta, already confused, would have fallen into even greater confusion, thinking, 'It seems that the self I formerly had does not exist now'" (*SN* 44.10, PTS iv.401).
43. For scholarly discussion of this, see Donald S. Lopez (ed.), *Buddhist Hermeneutics* (Honolulu, HI: University of Hawai'i Press, 1992).
44. This is referred to as the *sākāravāda* – the 'with aspect' view, that is the position that consciousness has aspects; and it is contrasted with the *nirākāravāda* (held by Nyāya-Vaiśeṣika, the Mīmāmsā, and the Jains; and among Buddhists by the Vaibhāṣikas). This is discussed with respect to Dharmakīrti by Dreyfus, *Recognizing Reality*, 338–44.
45. See Fenner, "A Study of the Relationship between Analysis (*vicāra*) and Insight (*prajñā*)", for discussion.
46. "Yogācāra, on the other hand, attempts, as did Candrakīrti's 'opponent'" – presumed to be Bhāviveka – "to maintain clear-cut distinctions between those things which are conventionally real and those things which are truly chimeric. What is *paramārthic* should not be a matter of truth claims; but that doesn't foreclose making *samvṛtic* truth-claims" (Lusthaus, *Buddhist Phenomenology*, 455).
47. Fenner, "A Study of the Relationship between Analysis (*vicāra*) and Insight (*prajñā*)', 146.
48. "*Nirvāṇa* is the reversal of elaboration accomplished by a ceasing of discriminations" (*ibid.*: 147).
49. Translated in Arnold, "Materials for a Mādhyamika Critique of Foundationalism". Subsequent quotes from the *Prasannapadā* are taken from the same.
50. This and subsequent translations of the *Bodhicāryāvatāra* are taken from *A Guide to the Bodhisattva Way of Life*, Wallace & Wallace (trans.).
51. This is what Tom Tillemans aptly characterizes as the 'dismal slough' a Mādhyamika may land in, which concern he discusses trenchantly in "How Far Can a Madhyamaka Buddhist Reform Conventional Truth?", in *Moonshadows*, The Cowherds, 151–65 (New York: Oxford University Press, 2011).

52. Guy Newland discusses the Tibetan Mādhyamika Tsongkapa's treatment of this worry in his "Weighing the Butter, Levels of Explanation, and Falsification", in *Moonshadows*, The Cowherds, 57–71: "For if conventional minds were *completely* nonanalytical, how would one distinguish between virtue and nonvirtue?" (*ibid.*: 60).
53. This is Paul Hoornaert's gloss on *Yogācārabhūmi, Viniścaya-saṃgrahanī* 15, in "An Annotated Translation of *Madhyamakahṛdayakārikā/Tarkajvāla* V", Kanazawa University Repository for Academic Resources, Departmental Bulletin Papers 19 (1999), 127–59. Eckel cites another passage from the *Yogācārabhūmi*, quoted by Bhāviveka at *MH* V.82–83ab, which seems to criticize the Madhyamaka metaphysical position as "the worst kind of nihilis[m]" (*Bhāviveka and his Buddhist Opponents*, 65).
54. Vasubandhu, *Commentary on the Separation of the Middle from the Extremes*, I.4 (in *Seven Works of Vasubandhu*, Anacker (trans.)).
55. Ganeri calls this 'external protreptic', as opposed to the 'internal proteptic' with which he credits Candrakīrti: "Dharmapāla's [external protreptic] method does not, as Candrakīrti's did, have stages and levels; it is not described in terms of an intellectual journey. There is no biographical story of moral progression. The hoped-for effect of *this* exercise is that the audience gives up believing at all" (*The Concealed Art of the Soul*, 117). Some Mādhyamikas did indeed go in this direction, and much attention has been given in recent scholarly literature to comparisons between Madhyamaka and ancient Greek scepticism: see Thomas McEvilley, "Pyrrhonism and Madhyamaka", *Philosophy East and West* 32 (1982), 3–35); Adrian Kuzminsky, "Pyrrhonism and the Madhyamaka", *Philosophy East and West* 57 (2007), 482–511); Jay Garfield, "*Epoché* and *Śūnyatā*: Scepticism East and West", *Philosophy East and West* 40 (1990), 285–307); and, for a Tibetan Mādhyamika who went in this direction, see Georges Dreyfus, "Can a Mādhyamika be a Skeptic? The Case of Patsab Nyimadrak", in *Moonshadows*, The Cowherds, 89–113.
56. Dreyfus, "Can a Mādhyamika be a Skeptic?", articulates the difficulties; see also Dreyfus & Garfield, "Madhyamaka and Classical Greek Skepticism", in *Moonshadows*, The Cowherds, 115–30. Both are optimistic that the difficulties facing 'Pyrrhonnian' scepticism are not insurmountable. For subtle discussion of the various senses of 'scepticism', and which may be appropriate or inappropriate in characterizing Candrakīrti, see Arnold, *Buddhists, Brahmins, and Belief*, 131–42.
57. Dreyfus, "Can a Mādhyamika be a Skeptic?", 113.
58. According to Tillemans, "How Far Can a Mādhyamika Reform Conventional Reality?", this is something *a* Mādhyamika may be able to do, and other Mādhyamikas did; but it is not available to the Mādhyamika who follows Candrakīrti in dismissing the relevance of the critical tools of Diṅnāga and Dharmakīrti.
59. See chapters 7 and 8 of Jonardon Ganeri's *Lost Age of Reason* (Oxford: Oxford University Press, 2011) for illuminating and detailed articulation of the genre of commentary, its species, and the various ways in which they extend philosophical investigations in the Sanskrit discourse.
60. In a note to his translation, Pruden calls this "the only reference to the Madhyamaka system that the work of Vasubandhu contains" (book IX, n. 111).
61. And, according to Hayes (as we discussed in Chapter 4), for good intellectual reason: the arguments Nāgārjuna offers against essence, says Hayes, rest on

an equivocation on the Sanskrit word *svabhāva*; and while the evidentness of the fallacy might be lost in translation, it was too perspicuous among Sanskrit-speaking intellectuals to warrant further scrutiny.

62. Parts of the *Clear Words* have been translated into English by Mervyn Sprung as *The Lucid Exposition of the Middle Way* (London: Routledge & Kegan Paul, 1979).
63. Asaṅga's *Yogācārabhūmi* sets out the stages (*bhūmi*) of development up to the *bodhisattva* stage, the trajectory of which is then set out according to the cultivation of the *pāramitās*. Śāntideva's *Bodhicāryāvatāra* will roughly follow Candrakīrti's *Madhyamakāvatāra* in setting out the *bodhisattva* path according to cultivation of the perfections.
64. Arnold, *Buddhists, Brahmins and Belief*, offers an articulation of a Kantian reading of Candrakīrti, and the Madhyamaka project as a whole, proposing "a reconstruction of Mādhyamika arguments as transcendental arguments" (*ibid.*: 139).
65. Arnold more sympathetically observes that "Candrakīrti's deference to the conventional *is itself the argument* … there is nothing 'more real' than the world as conventionally described" (*ibid.*: 117). How to make sense of such deference as an argument is, however, difficult.
66. For instance, the eye disease case depends upon the eye being in such-and-such a condition, and various causal factors operating such as to generate black lines. There is something 'really there' and really causing the experience: the eye, the visual cortex and laws of physics describing causes and effects of relevant components. Such a strongly realist picture may indeed be problematic; but Candrakīrti's example does not suffice to show in what way it might be, nor to show that we all ordinarily accept cases of dependent arising, causal explanation, that do not grant priority to the cause on which the arising depends, or that we could do so pervasively rather than merely vicariously (the dream example being a likely candidate for what can arise without objects only because we have experiences caused by objects).
67. Candrakīrti seems to address himself to Vasubandhu in *MA* VI.61–6 and *MA* VI.72 and to Diṅnāga in *MA* VI.73–6.
68. Arnold argues in detail for a reading of Madhyamaka as arguing that "the terms involved in causal explanation turn out to be … intelligible only with reference to phenomena they supposedly explain"; and generally, "explananda, therefore, can never be thought finally to drop out of any explanation" ("Nāgārjuna's 'Middle Way': A Non-Eliminative Way of Understanding Selflessness", *Revue Internationale de Philosophie* 64 [2010], 367–95, esp. 371); and also in "The Deceptive Simplicity of Nāgārjuna's Arguments Against Motion", *Journal of Indian Philosophy* 40 (2012), 553–91, which is devoted to showing that *Mūlamadhyamakakārikā* II pursues the same strategy with respect to motion that is pursued throughout the *Mūlamadhyamakakārikā*, namely, to argue "that any attempt to *explain* motion … turns out itself to be intelligible only insofar as we already understand motion" (*ibid.*: 555). In his translation of *Prasannapadā* 55.11–75.13, Arnold approvingly quotes Claus Oetke as saying the "means of knowledge cannot be what they are, namely means of knowledge, without the existence of that for which they are means, whereas the objects of knowledge cannot be what they are, i.e. *prameyas*, if there are no *pramāṇas*" ("Materials for a Madhyamaka Critique of Foundationalism", 437 n. 87).
69. Arnold, *Buddhists, Brahmins, and Belief*, 139.

70. I set out and defend this reading of the *pudgalavāda* in "Persons Keeping Their Karma Together".
71. This may remind us of a similar move made to try to solve the normative question in the *Euthyphro*, where it is the gods' agreement, and not human agreement, that should set the standard of what must be accepted.
72. Strawson's Kantian inspired reflections on the topic in *Individuals* are an excellent example of arguments for the sheer unintelligibility of forgoing I-thinking; some of Williams's arguments in "The Absence of Self and the Removal of Pain" are another. The nice thing about the Strawson example is that he *also* thinks that it is either unintelligible or immoral to eliminate the 'reactive attitudes', such as anger, indignation and resentment, which Buddhists generally – and Śāntideva in particular – will argue that we should eliminate, and will be free of when we are free of erroneous I-thinking.
73. The example is chosen to reflect the changing standards of what the Buddhists themselves included under acceptable and unacceptable sexual relations for a lay-person, between the earliest less restrictive times, and later views. For illuminating discussion of the issue, see José Cabezón, *Buddhism, Sexuality and Gender* (Albany, NY: SUNY Press, 1992). His lecture on the subject is available at hwww.shedrub.org/videoplayback.php?vid = 39 (accessed July 2013).
74. Translations from *The Theaetetus of Plato*, M. J. Levett (trans.), M. F. Burnyeat (rev.) (Indianapolis, IN: Hackett, 1990).
75. To a certain extent, this is a problem that already arises on the Abhidharma picture that, like contemporary trope-theory, rejects appeal to universals and so must instead suppose there to be 'real similarity' between property-particulars, without that consisting in their sharing properties.
76. And so argued Diṅnāga's non-Buddhist critics Uddyotakara and Kumārila. Even the Yogācāra–Madhyamaka syncretist Śāntarakṣita seems to have agreed. Dreyfus describes Śāntarakṣita's position as "the understanding of the positive element is primary and prior; the negative import is understood later, by implication" (*Recognizing Reality*, 247). It is a challenge that contemporary interpreters have attempted to take up. Tillemans's discussion of what he calls the 'top-down' approach to addressing the relation of concepts to content, in "How to Talk About Ineffable Things", in *Apoha, Buddhist Nominalism and Human Cognition*, Arindam Chakrabarti, Mark Siderits & Tom Tillemans (eds) (New York: Columbia University Press, 2011), is a clear and excellent guide to further discussion in this area.
77. Dharmakīrti's thought has been the subject of two relatively recent comprehensive treatments in English: Dreyfus, *Recognizing Reality*; and Dunne, *Foundations of Dharmakīrti's Philosophy*, the latter of which also has translations of selected texts into English. Tillemans offers a reasonably concise overview of Dharmakīrti's thought in his *Stanford Encyclopedia of Philosophy* contribution on Dharmakīrti.
78. Dreyfus, in his magisterial work on Dharmakīrti, takes Diṅnāga and Dharmkīeri together in offering a sophisticated alternative attitude towards ontological commitment: "They are ontologists only insofar as their epistemology requires them to be. They even seem to feel free to alternate between several conflicting metaphysical standpoints. For example, in most parts of their works, Diṅnāga and Dharmakīrti adopt a so-called Sautrāntika standpoint, presupposing the

existence of external objects. In other parts of their works, however, they shift their ontological framework and move to a Yogācāra rejection of external objects. Such an unusual attitude towards ontological commitments is not due to confusion or lack of logical rigor but to the nature of their project. For them, ontology remains subordinated to epistemology. Hence, they feel free to shift their ontological framework following a strategy that I will describe as an ascending scale of analysis" (*Recognizing Reality*, 49).

79. This and further translations of Dharmakīrti's *Pramāṇavārttika* (*PV*) and *Pramāṇavārttika-svavṛtti* (*PVSV*) are taken from John Dunne, *Foundations of Dharmakīrti's Philosophy*, sometimes excluding Sanskrit that he includes in brackets.
80. 'Causal efficacy', 'useful/purposive action'; see Esho Mikogami, "Some Remarks on the Concept of *Arthakriyā*", *Journal of Indian Philosophy* 7 (1979), 79–94, for critical elucidation of *arthakriyā* in Dharmakīrti's philosophy and that of those who followed him.
81. Or, as Tillemans, "How to Talk About Ineffable Things", puts it, how schema and content, once distinguished, are nevertheless able to be properly related.
82. See, for instance: "even if Dharmakīrti stresses the sameness of effect as the warrant for the application of the same term to multiple entities, he is in the end also appealing to a sameness of cause. In other words, if we can call certain entities 'water-jugs' because they have the same type of effects, we are at the same time saying that those entities have come from the same type of causes. In short, we are appealing to those entities' nature-*svabhāvas*: the totality of their causal characteristics" (Dunne, *Foundations of Dharmakīrti's Philosophy*, 163).
83. See *PVSV* I.137–142, where "a person applies expressions to something with some purpose in mind"; and "the capacity to refer to things depends on the speaker's wishes" so that intention fixes meaning (c.f. *PVSV* I.40–42). As Dunne describes it, "Dharmakīrti claims that a universal is constructed on the basis of the exclusion of all the entities in question from those that do not have the expected causal characteristics. Dharmakīrti recognizes, however, that if certain things – such as those called 'water-jugs' – are excluded from others because those others do not have the expected causal characteristics, one is also asserting that all the things we call 'water-jugs' have the *same* causal characteristics: they all have the causal characteristics expected of a 'water-jug'. For Dharmakīrti, this amounts to the claim that, in the case of all water-jugs, we may identify at least some of their causes as the 'same' [*eka*], and most importantly, we may likewise identify at least some of their effects as the 'same'." But when Dharmakīrti appeals to 'sameness of effect', "those cognitive images are all the same because they all produce the same effect, namely, a judgement", and that is all the 'sameness' of cause amounts to (*ibid.*: 119–21).
84. Tillemans, "How to Talk About Ineffable Things", 28.
85. This becomes, in later European tradition, the Principle of Sufficient Reason (as, for instance, in Leibniz). See David Sedley, "Platonic Causes", *Phronesis* 43 (1998), 114–32, for detailed discussion of the *Phaedo* passage here as concerned with constraints on explanation.
86. Dunne prefers the latter in *Foundations of Dharmakīrti's Philosophy*; Dreyfus sticks with the former: "Dharmakīrti argues that, despite being distinct, things can produce similar results on the basis of which abstract properties are

constructed. These similarities are not our own projection but exist essentially or naturally, as is made clear by Dharmakīrti's use of the term *svabhāvena* ... Various medicinal plants ... can cure fever through their natural therapeutic powers. The common element in these plants is their remedial effect. Nothing over and above such resemblances regarding their medicinal effects is required to explain how these plants are all remedies" (*Recognizing Reality*, 149).

87. This is, remember, a regulative principle, acting according to which furthers our understanding and knowledge. It is not a claim that we are guaranteed always to be satisfied in our search.
88. So in "Key Features of Dharmakīrti's *Apoha* Theory" (in *Apoha*, Charkrabarti *et al.* [eds]), John Dunne clarifies that it is not just sameness of judgement that is the result (judging then that 'this is blue', and judging now that 'this is blue'); rather the result is a single judgement of sameness. But if this judgement is *always* literally mistaken, because no two particulars are in fact the same, then we have done nothing but state that some things induce a 'this is the same as that' judgement, without explanation. There is no standard of correctness, and so no correctness. Dunne writes, "We can pose the question 'but *why* do those objects all produce cognitions that can lead to the same judgement?' And Dharmakīrti can answer, 'because it is their nature to do so' (*ibid.*: 98). Parimal Patil offers as Dharmakīrti's the minimalist (non)explanation "because it does" in his "Constructing the Content of Awareness", in *Apoha*, Charkrabarti *et al.* (eds), 156.
89. In a more optimistic reading of Dharmakīrti, Mark Siderits thinks that double-negation can offer some response to the difficult question of "how there can be exploitable patterns in a world of unique particulars" ("Introduction, in *Apoha*, Charkrabarti *et al.* [eds], 47).
90. Dreyfus's assessment of this deadlock is more pessimistic: "We require something stronger than mere causal link; namely, that conceptions apprehend the same object (the snowy mountain) as perceptions. Such a cognitive cooperation between perception and conception, however, is impossible on Dharmakīrti's system, based as it is on a radical dichotomy between conception and perception: Whereas perception apprehends real individual things, thought and language relate only to conceptual quasi-entities. Thus there seems to be no way for Dharmakīrti to account for the cooperation his system requires" (*Recognizing Reality*, 272). The Tibetan inheritors of Dharmakīrti, whom Dreyfus discusses in chs 8–10, were also dissatisfied with this way of treating the issue of the reality or otherwise of resemblances, and of 'generalities' and wholes. And they took it in different directions: "The reason Tibetans found the realist interpretation compelling ... relates to the inherent difficulty anti-realism faces in accounting for human reasoning" (*ibid.*: 201).
91. See Seneca, *Epistles* 94, 95.
92. This description of Śāntideva's approach in the *Bodhicāryāvatāra* is offered by Garfield, "What Is It Like To Be A Bodhisattva?".
93. This, I suggest, is the best way to handle the scholarly storm started off by Paul Williams's dissection of *BCA* VIII.101–3 ("The Absence of Self and the Removal of Pain"). Śāntideva is offering a way of looking at things that is helpful for people who are a certain way along the path of understanding no-self, and trying to incorporate that so that it fully informs their immediate perceptions of, and

responses to, conventional reality. He is not trying to make an argument that takes as a premise an assertion about what is ultimately true.

Epilogue

1. Dan Arnold brings this out in *Buddhists, Brahmins and Belief*.
2. Perhaps it was the other way round; even relative chronology is difficult to determine. For discussion of these dates, particularly those of Vācaspatimiśra, and references to further scholarly consideration of the matter see Yuichi Kajiyama, *An Introduction to Buddhist Philosophy: An Annotated Translation of the Tarkabhāṣā of Mokṣakaragupta*, Memoirs of the Faculty of Letters, Kyoto University, vol. 10 (1966), 8–10; reprinted as *Wiener Studien Zur Tibetologie Und Buddhismuskunde*, vol. 42 (Vienna: Arbeitskreis Für Tibetische Und Buddhistische Studien, Universität Wien, 1998).
3. See Funayama Toru, "Perception, Conceptual Construction and Yogic Perception in Kamalaśīla's Epistemology", *Chun-Hwa Buddhist Journal* 18 (2005), 273–97, for discussion of the issues at stake. For wider consideration of the context and nuances of the argument, see Sara L. McClintock, *Omniscience and the Rhetoric of Reason: Śantarakṣita and Kamalaśīla on Rationality, Argumentation, and Religious Authority* (Boston, MA: Wisdom Publications, 2010).
4. For further discussion of Śāntarakṣita's distinctive mode of argumentation in the *Madhyamakālaṃkāra*, see James Blumenthal, "The 'Neither-One-nor-Many' Argument of Śāntarakṣita: A Classical Buddhist Argument on the Ontological Status of Phenomena", in *Buddhist Philosophy: Essential Writings*, William Edelglass & Jay Garfield (eds), 46–60 (New York: Oxford University Press, 2009). For an English translation of the text, see Blumenthal, *The Ornament of the Middle Way: A Study of the Madhyamaka Thought of Śāntarakṣita* (Ithaca, NY: Snow Lion Publications, 2004) or *The Adornment of the Middle Way*, Padmakara Translation Group (trans.) (Boston, MA: Shambhala, 2005).
5. See Chapter 8, note 13; *TS* 2000–2002.
6. Some of Dharmottara's innovations in this area are brought to an anglophone audience by Helmut Krasser, "Dharmottara's Theory of Language in his *Laghuprāmāṇyaparikṣa*", *Journal of Indian Philosophy* 23 (1995), 247–71, which offers discussion and detailed gloss of his German introduction and translation, *Dharmottaras kurze Untersuchung der Gültigkeit einer Erkenntnis, Laghuprāmāṇyaparikṣā* (Vienna: Obersetzung, 1991).
7. See Stephen Phillips, *Ratnakīrti's Proof of Momentariness by Positive Correlation (Kṣaṇabhaṅgasiddhi Anvayatmika): Transliteration, Translation, and Philosophic Commentary* (New York: Columbia University Press, 2013).
8. For exemplary exposition of Ratnakīrti's view, see Parimal Patil, *Against a Hindu God* (New York: Columbia University Press, 2009).
9. Yuichi Kajiyama, who translated the *Tarkabhāṣa* into English, even sees it as a suitable introduction to Buddhist logic – hence the unlikely title for Mokṣākaragupta's discussion of logic, *An Introduction to Buddhist Philosophy*.

Bibliography

Primary sources

Discourses

The Connected Discourses of the Buddha: A Translation of the Saṃyutta Nikāya, Bhikkhu Bodhi (trans.) (Boston, MA: Wisdom Publications, 2000).

The Middle-Length Discourses of the Buddha: A Translation of the Majjhima Nikāya, Bhikkhu Bodhi and Bhikkhu Ñāṇamoli (trans.) (Boston, MA: Wisdom Publications, 1995).

The Long Discourses of the Buddha: A Translation of the Dīgha Nikāya, M. Walshe (trans.) (Boston, MA: Wisdom Publications, [1940] 1999).

The Numerical Discourses of the Buddha: A Translation of the Aṅguttara Nikāya, Bhikkhu Bodhi (trans.) (Boston, MA: Wisdom Publications, 2012).

Unattributed

The Dhammapada, G. Fronsdal (trans. and annot.) (Boston, MA: Shambhala, 2005).

Dhamma-Saṅghaṇi. Translated as *A Buddhist Manual of Psychological Ethics*, C. A. F. Rhys Davids (trans.) (Oxford: Pali Text Society, [1900] 1974).

Dhammapadaṭṭakathā (Commentary on the Dhammapadā), E. W. Burlingame (trans.) (Cambridge, MA: Harvard University Press, 1921).

The Jaina Sutras, H. Jacobi (trans.), Sacred Books of the East, vol. 45 (Oxford: Clarendon Press, 1895). Reprinted (Varanasi: Motilal Banarsidass, 1964).

Kathāvatthu. Translated as *Points of Controversy, Or Subjects of Discourse*, S. Z. Aung & Mrs R. Davids (trans.) (Oxford: Pali Text Society, [1915] 1974).

Milindapañhā. Translated as *Milinda's Questions*, I. B. Horner (trans.) (Oxford: Pali Text Society, [1963–64] 1996).

The Perfection of Wisdom in Eight Thousand Lines & its Verse Summary, E. Conze (trans.) (San Francisco, CA: Four Seasons Foundation, [1973] 1990).

Other primary sources

Anuruddha. *Abhidhammattha Sangaha (Compendium of Philosophy)*, S. Z. Aung (trans.), C. A. F. Rhys Davids (rev. and ed.) (Oxford: Pali Text Society, [1910] 1995).

Aristotle. *Complete Works*, J. Barnes (ed.), 2 vols (Oxford: Oxford University Press, 1984).

Āryadeva. *Catuḥśataka (on the Bodhisattva's Cultivation of Merit and Knowledge)*, K. Lang (trans.) (Copenhagen: Akademisk Forlag, 1986).

Asaṅga. *Mahāyānasaṃgraha*. Translated as *La Somme Du Grand Véhicule*, É. Lamotte (trans.) (Louvain: Bureaux du Muséon, 1938–39) [French].

Bhāviveka. "*Prajnapradipa*: A Translation of Chapter Two: Examination of the Traversed, the Untraversed, and that which is Being Traversed," W. L. Ames (trans.). *Journal of Indian Philosophy* 23 (1995): 295–365.

Bhāviveka. *Madhyamakahṛdaya IV and V*. In *Bhāviveka and His Buddhist Opponents*, M. D. Eckel (trans.) (Cambridge, MA: Harvard University Press, 2008).

Buddhaghoṣa. *Kathāvatthuppakaraṇa-Aṭṭhakathā*. Translated as *The Debates Commentary*, B. C. Law (trans.) (Oxford: Pali Text Society, [1940] 1999).

Buddhaghoṣa. *Visuddhimagga*. Translated as *The Path of Purification*, Ñaṇamoli Bhikkhu (trans.) (Onalaksa, WA: Pariyatti Publishing, [1975] 1991).

Candrakīrti. *Madhyamakāvatāra (in the Emptiness of Emptiness)*. Translated by C. W. Huntington Jr. with G. N. Wangchen (Honolulu, HI: University of Hawai'i Press, 1989).

Candrakīrti. *Madhyamakāvatāra*. Translated as *Introduction to the Middle Way*, Padmakara Translation Group (trans.), J. Mipham (comm.) (Boston, MA: Shambhala, 2002).

Candrakīrti. *Prasannapadā*. Selections translated as *Lucid Exposition of the Middle Way*, M. Sprung (trans.) (London: Routledge & Kegan Paul, 1979).

Dharmakīrti, *Pramāṇavārttika* (*Commentary on the Pramāṇas*). Selections translated by J. Dunne in *Foundations of Dharmakīrti's Philosophy* (Boston, MA: Wisdom Publications, 2004).

Dharmakīrti. *On Relations (The Philosophy of Relations); Containing the Sanskrit text and English translation of Dharmakīrti's Sambandha-Parīkṣa with Prabhācandra's Commentary*, V. N. Jha (trans.) (New Delhi: Sri Satguru Publications, 1990).

Dharmottara. *Laghuprāmāṇyaparikṣā I (Dharmottaras Kurze Untersuchung Der Gültigkeit Einer Erkenntnis)*, H. Krasser (trans.) (Vienna: Verlag der Österreichischen Akademie der Wissenschaften, 1991).

Diṅnāga. *Pramāṇasamuccaya I*. Translated as *On Perception: The Pratyakṣa-paricceda [Chapter] of Diṅnāga's Pramāṇasamuccaya*, M. Hattori (trans.) (Cambridge, MA: Harvard University Press, 1968).

Diṅnāga. *Pramāṇasamuccaya II and V (with Explanatory Chapters and Notes)*, in R. P. Hayes, *Dignaga on the Interpretation of Signs* (Dordrecht: Kluwer, 1988).

Epictetus. *Discourses*. Translated as *Epictetus: The Discourses as Reported by Arrian*, W. A. Oldfather (trans.), books I–II (Cambridge, MA: Harvard University Press, [1925] 2000).

Gautama. *Nyāyadarsana of Gautama, with Bhasya, Vartika, Tika and Parisuddhis*, A. Thakur (ed.) (Darbhanga: Mithila Research Institute, 1967).

Gautama. *Nyāya-Sūtra With Nyāya-Vārṭika*, G. Jhā (trans.) (Allahabad: E. J. Lazarus, 1910).

Nāgārjuna. *Mūlamadhyamakakārikā (Fundamental Wisdom of the Middle Way),* J. Garfield (trans. and comm.) (Oxford: Oxford University Press, 1995).

Nāgārjuna. *Ratnāvalī.* Translated in *Buddhist Advice for Living and Liberation: Nagarjuna's Precious Garland,* J. Hopkins (ed. and trans.) (Ithaca, NY: Snow Lion Publications, 1988).

Nāgārjuna. "The Ratnāvalī of Nāgārjuna", G. Tucci (trans.). *Journal of the Royal Asiatic Society of Great Britain and Ireland* 66 (1934): 307–25 and 68 (1936): 237–52, 423–35.

Nāgārjuna. *Vigrahavyāvartanī.* Translated as *The Dispeller of Disputes,* J. Westerhoff (trans.) (Oxford: Oxford University Press, 2010).

Plato. *Complete Works,* J. Cooper & D. S. Hutchison (eds) (Indianapolis, IN: Hackett, 1997).

Plato. *Five Dialogues,* G. M. A. Grube (trans.), J. Cooper (rev.) (Indianapolis, IN: Hackett, 2002).

Plato. *The Theaetetus of Plato,* M. J. Levett (trans.), M. F. Burnyeat (rev.) (Indianapolis, IN: Hackett, 1990).

Ratnakīrti. *Kṣaṇabhaṅgasiddhi Anvayatmika (Ratnakīrti's Proof of Momentariness by Positive Correlation),* S. Phillips (trans. and comm.) (New York: Columbia University Press, 2012).

Śāntarakṣita. *Madhyamakālaṃkāra.* Translated as *The Adornment of the Middle Way,* Padmakara Translation Group (trans.) (Boston, MA: Shambhala, 2005).

Śāntarakṣita, *Tattvasaṃgraha, with the Commentary of Kamalaśīla,* G. Jha (trans.) (New Delhi: Montilal Banarsidass, 1939).

Śāntideva. *Bohicāryāvatāra.* Translated as *A Guide to the Bodhisattva Way of Life,* B. A. Wallace & V. A. Wallace (trans.) (Ithaca, NY: Snow Lion Publications, 1997).

Seneca. *Epistles,* R. M. Gummere (trans.), Loeb Classical Library 77 (Cambridge, MA: Harvard University Press, [1925] 2000).

Uddyotakara. *Nyāya-Vārṭika.* See Gautama. *Nyāya-Sūtra With Nyāya-Vārṭika.*

Vasubandhu. *Abhidharma-Kośa-Bhāṣya,* L. de la Vallée Poussin (trans. Skt. to French and ed.) & L. M. Pruden (trans. French to English), 4 vols (Berkeley, CA: Asian Humanities Press, 1988–90).

Vasubandhu. *Seven Works of Vasubandhu, the Buddhist Psychological Doctor,* S. Anacker (trans.) (New Delhi: Motilal Banarsidass, 1984). Includes: *Method for Argumentation; Five Aggregates; Discussion for the Demonstration of Action; Twenty Verses* (and commentary); *Thirty Verses; Commentary on the Separation of the Middle From the Extremes; Treatise on the Three Natures.*

Vatsyāyana, *Nyāya-bhāṣya.* See Gautama. *Nyāya-Sūtra With Nyāya-Vārṭika.*

Secondary sources

Adam, M. T. "Groundwork for a Metaphysic of Buddhist Morals: A New Analysis of *Puñña* and *Kusala,* in Light of *Sukka*". *Journal of Buddhist Ethics* 12 (2005): 62–85.

Albahari, M. *Analytical Buddhism: The Two-Tiered Illusion of Self* (Basingstoke: Palgrave Macmillan, 2006).

Albahari, M. "Witness Consciousness: Its Definition, Appearance and Reality". *Journal of Consciousness Studies* 16 (2009): 62–84.

Alt, W. "There Is No Paradox of Desire in Buddhism". *Philosophy East and West* 30(4) (1980): 521–8.
Ames, W. L. "The Notion of *svabhāva* in the Thought of Candrakīrti". *Journal of Indian Philosophy* 10 (1982): 161–77.
Anacker, S. (ed. and trans.) *Seven Works of Vasubandhu, the Buddhist Psychological Doctor.* (New Delhi: Motilal Banarsidass, 1984).
Annas, Julia. "Self-Knowledge in Early Plato." In *Platonic Investigations*, D. J. O'Meara (ed.), 111–38 (Washington, DC: Catholic University of America Press, 1985).
Arnold, D. *Buddhists, Brahmins, and Belief* (New York: Columbia University Press, 2005).
Arnold, D. "The Deceptive Simplicity of Nāgārjuna's Arguments Against Motion". *Journal of Indian Philosophy* 40 (2012): 553–91.
Arnold, D. "Is *svasaṃvitti* Transcendental? A Tentative Reconstruction Following Śāntarakṣita". *Asian Philosophy* 15 (2005): 77–11.
Arnold, D. "Materials for a Madhyamaka Critique of Foundationalism: An Annotated Translation of *Prasannapadā* 55.11 to 75.13". *Journal of the International Association of Buddhist Studies* 28 (2005): 411–67.
Arnold, D. "Nāgārjuna's 'Middle Way': A Non-Eliminative Way of Understanding Selflessness". *Revue Internationale de Philosophie* 64 (2010): 367–95.
Arnold, D. "On Semantics and Saṃketa: Thoughts on a Neglected Problem with Buddhist *Apoha* Doctrine". *Journal of Indian Philosophy* 34 (2006): 415–78.
Bareau, A. *Les Sects bouddhique du petit véhicule* (Paris: École Française d'Extrême-Orient, 1955).
Barhuah, B. *Buddhist Sects and Sectarianism* (New Delhi: Sarup, 2000).
Batchelor, S. *Confessions of a Buddhist Atheist* (New York: Spiegel & Grau, 2010).
Berkeley, G. *Treatise Concerning the Principles of Human Knowledge*, K. Winkler (ed.) (Indianapolis, IN : Hackett, [1710] 1982).
Betty, L. S. "Nāgārjuna's Masterpiece: Logical, Mystical, Both or Neither". *Philosophy East and West* 33(2) (1983): 123–38.
Blumenthal, J. "The 'Neither-One-nor-Many' Argument of Śāntarakṣita: A Classical Buddhist Argument on the Ontological Status of Phenomena". In *Buddhist Philosophy: Essential Writings*, W. Edelglass & J Garfield (eds), 46–60 (New York: Oxford University Press, 2009).
Blumenthal, J. *The Ornament of the Middle Way: A Study of the Madhyamaka Thought of Śāntarakṣita (including translation of the Madhyamakālaṃkāra)* (Ithaca, NY: Snow Lion Publications, 2004).
Bond, G. D. "The Development and Elaboration of the *Arahant* Ideal in the Theravāda Buddhist Tradition". *Journal of the American Academy of Religion* 52 (1984): 227–42.
Bronkhorst, J. "Dharma and Abhidharma". *Bulletin of the School of Oriental and African Studies* 48(2) (1985): 305–20.
Burton, D. *Buddhism, Knowledge and Liberation* (Aldershot: Ashgate, 2004).
Burton, D. *Emptiness Appraised: A Critical Study of Nāgārjuna's Philosophy* (Richmond: Curzon Press, 1999).
Cabezón, J. *Buddhism, Sexuality and Gender* (Albany, NY: SUNY Press, 1992).
Cabezón, J. "Development of the Doctrine of Sexual Misconduct". Paper presented at a symposium on Buddhist Ethics, Kathmandu 2009: www.shedrub.org/video-playback.php?vid = 39 (accessed July 2013).

Carpenter, A. D. "'... And None of Us Deserving the Cruelty or the Grace': In Search of the Buddhist Job". Public talk, Einstein Forum conference on the Book of Job, 2012.

Carpenter, A. D. "Faith Without God". In *Thomism and Asian Cultures*, A. P. Co & P. A. Bolaños (eds) (Manila: University of Santo Tomas Publishing House, 2012).

Carpenter, A. D. "Happiness and the Highest Good in the *Ratnāvalī*". In *Moonpaths: Ethics and Emptiness*, The Cowherds (New York: Oxford University Press, forthcoming).

Carpenter, A. D. "Metaphysical Suffering, Metaphysics as Therapy." In *Making Sense of Suffering: An Inter-Disciplinary Dialogue on Narrative and the Meaning of Suffering*, N. Hinerman & M. Sutton (eds), 37–52 (Oxford: ID Press, 2012).

Carpenter, A. D. "Persons Keeping Their Karma Together". In *The Moon Points Back: Analytic Philosophy and Asian Thought*, J. Garfield, G. Priest & K. Tanaka (eds) (New York: Oxford University Press, forthcoming).

Carpenter, A. D. & J. Ganeri. "Can You Seek the Answer to this Question?" *Australasian Journal of Philosophy* 88 (2010): 571–94.

Chadha, M. & N. Trakakis. "Karma and the Problem of Evil: A Response to Kaufman". *Philosophy East and West* 57(4) (2007): 533–56.

Chakrabarti, A. "Is Liberation (*mokṣa*) Pleasant?" *Philosophy East and West* 33 (1983): 167–82.

Chakrabarti, A. "I Touch What I Saw". *Philosophy and Phenomenological Research* 52 (1992): 103–16.

Chakrabarti, A. "Seeing Without Recognizing? More on Denuding Perceptual Content (Comment and Discussion)". *Philosophy East and West* 54(3) (2004): 365–7.

Chakrabarti, A., M. Siderits & T. Tillemans (eds). *Apoha, Buddhist Nominalism and Human Cognition* (New York: Columbia University Press, 2011).

Châu, T. T. *The Literature of the Personalists of Early Buddhism*, S. Boin-Webb (trans.) (Delhi: Motilal Banarsidass, 1999).

Cho, S. "Selflessness: Toward a Buddhist Vision of Social Justice". *Journal of Buddhist Ethics* 7 (2000): 76–85.

Collins, S. *Selfless Persons: Imagery and Thought in* Theravada *Buddhism* (Cambridge: Cambridge University Press, 1982).

Collins, S. "What are Buddhists Doing when they Deny the Self?" In *Religion and Practical Reason: New Essays in the Comparative Philosophy of Religions*, F. E. Reynolds & D. Tracy (eds), 59–86 (Albany, NY: SUNY Press, 1994).

Conze, E. *Buddhist Thought in India: Three Phases of Buddhist Philosophy* (London: Allen & Unwin, 1962).

Conze, E. (ed. and trans.) *The Large Sutra on Perfect Wisdom with the Divisions of the Abhisamayālaṅkāra* (Berkeley, CA: University of California Press, 1975).

Conze, E. "The Ontology of the *prajñāpāramitā*". *Philosophy East and West* 3 (1953): 117–30.

Coseru, C. "Naturalism and Intentionality". *Asian Philosophy* 19 (2009): 239–64.

Cousins, L. S. "Good or Skilful? Kusala in Canon and Commentary". *Journal of Buddhist Ethics* 3 (1996): 136–64.

Cousins, L. S. "Person and Self." In *Buddhism into the Year 2000*, Khlong Luang Khlong Sam (ed.), 32–47. (Los Angeles, CA: Dhammakaya Foundation, 1994).

Cousins, L. S. "On the Vibhajjavādins: the Mahiṃsāsaka, Dhammaguttaka, Kassapiya and Tambapaṇṇiya Branches of the Ancient Theriyas". *Buddhist Studies Review* 18 (2001): 131–82.

Cox, C. *Disputed Dharmas: Early Buddhist Theories on Existence – An Annotated Translation of the Section on Factors Dissociated from Thought from Saṅghabhadra's Nyāyānusāra* (Tokyo: International Institute for Buddhist Studies, 1995).

Cox, C. "From Category to Ontology: The Changing Role of Dharma in Sarvāstivāda Abhidharma". *Journal of Indian Philosophy* 32 (2004): 543–97.

Cox, C. "Mainstream Buddhist Schools". In *Encyclopedia of Buddhism*, R. Buswell (ed.), 501–7 (New York: Macmillan, 2004).

Cronk, G. (ed.) "Rendition of Vasubandhu's *Twenty Verses on Consciousness-Only*". www.bergen.edu/phr/121/vasubandhugc.pdf (accessed July 2013).

Cross, R. "Medieval Theories of Haecceity". *Stanford Encyclopedia of Philosophy* (Fall 2010 Edition), E. N. Zalta (ed.), http://plato.stanford.edu/entries/medieval-haecceity (accessed July 2013).

Denyer, N. *Plato: Alcibiades* (Cambridge: Cambridge University Press, 2001).

Dessein, B. "The Mahāsaṇghikas and the Origin of Mahayana Buddhism: Evidence Provided in the **Abhidharmamahāvibhāṣaśāstra*". *The Eastern Buddhist*, new series, 40 (2009): 25–61.

Dragonetti, C. & F. Tola. *Being as Consiousness: Yogācāra Philosophy of Buddhism* (New Delhi: Motilal Banarsidass, 2004).

Dragonetti, C. & F. Tola. "The *Trivabhāvakārikā* of Vasubandhu". *Journal of Indian Philosophy* 11 (1983): 225–66.

Dreyfus, G. "Can a Mādhyamika be a Skeptic? The Case of Patsab Nyimadrak." In *Moonshadows*, The Cowherds, 89–113 (New York: Oxford University Press, 2011).

Dreyfus, G. "Meditation as Ethical Activity". *Journal of Buddhist Ethics* 2 (1995): 28–54.

Dreyfus, G. *Recognizing Reality: Dharmakīrti's Philosophy and Its Tibetan Interpretations* (Albany, NY: SUNY Press, 1997).

Dreyfus, G. *The Sound of Two Hands Clapping* (Berkeley, CA: University of California Press, 2003).

Dreyfus, G. & C. Lindtner. "The Yogacara Philosophy of Dignaga and Dharmakirti". *Studies in Central and South East Asian Religions* 2 (1989): 27–35.

Dreyfus, G. & J. Garfield. "Madhyamaka and Classical Greek Skepticism." In *Moonshadows*, The Cowherds, 115–30 (New York: Oxford University Press, 2011).

Dreyfus, G. & S. L. McClintock (eds) *Svatantrika-Prasangika Distinction, What Difference Does a Difference Make?* (Boston, MA: Wisdom Publications, 2003).

Duerlinger, J. *Indian Buddhist Theories of Persons* (London: RoutledgeCurzon, 2003).

Dunne, J. *Foundations of Dharmakīrti's Philosophy* (Boston, MA: Wisdom Publications, 2004).

Dunne, J. "Key Features of Dharmakīrti's *Apoha* Theory." In *Apoha, Buddhist Nominalism and Human Cognition*, A. Chakrabarti, M. Siderits & T. Tillemans (eds), 84–108 (New York: Columbia University Press, 2011).

Dunne, J. "Realizing the Unreal: Dharmakīrti's Theory of Yogic Perception". *Journal of Indian Philosophy* 34 (2006): 497–519.

Eckel, M. D. *Bhāviveka and His Buddhist Opponents* (including translation of *Madhyamakahṛdaya* IV and V) (Cambridge, MA: Harvard University Press, 2008).

Epstein, R. *The Heart of Prajna Paramita Sutra,* 2nd edn (Burlingame, CA: Buddhist Text Translation Society, 2002).

Fenner, P. G. "Candrakīrti's Refutation of Buddhist Idealism". *Philosophy East and West* 33 (1983): 251–61.

Fenner, P. "A Study of the Relationship Between Analysis (*vicara*) and Insight (*prajna*) Based on the Madhyamakavatara". *Journal of Indian Philosophy* 12 (1984): 139–97.

Flanagan, O. *The Boddhisattva's Brain: Buddhism Naturalized* (Cambridge, MA: MIT Press, 2011).

Flood, G. *An Introduction to Hinduism* (Cambridge: Cambridge University Press, 1996).

Franco, E. "A New Era in the Study of Buddhist Philosophy". *Journal of Indian Philosophy* 34 (2006): 221–7.

Franco, E. "On *Pramāṇasamuccayavṛtti* 6a-b, Again". *Journal of Indian Philosophy* 33 (2005): 631–3.

Frankfurt, H. "Freedom of the Will and the Concept of a Person". *Journal of Philosophy* 68 (1971): 5–20. Reprinted in *Free Will,* G. Watson (ed.), 322–36 (Oxford: Oxford University Press, 2003).

Frauwallner, E. *Geschichte Der Indischen Philosophy,* vols 1 and 2 (Salzburg: Otto Müller Verlag, 1953–56).

Frauwallner, E. *On the Date of the Buddhist Master of the Law Vasubandhu* (Rome: Instituto Italiano per il Medio ed Estremo Oriente, 1951).

Ganeri, J. *The Concealed Art of the Soul: Theories of Self and Practices of Truth in Indian Ethics and Epistemology* (Oxford: Clarendon Press, 2007).

Ganeri, J. "Cross-Modality and the Self". *Philosophy and Phenomenological Research* 61 (2000): 639–58.

Ganeri, J. (ed.) *Indian Logic: A Reader* (New York: Routledge, 2001).

Ganeri, J. *The Lost Age of Reason* (Oxford: Oxford University Press, 2011).

Ganeri, J. *Philosophy in Classical India* (London: Routledge 2001).

Ganeri, J. "Self-intimation, Memory and Personal Identity". *Journal of Indian Philosophy* 27 (1999): 469–83.

Ganeri, J. *Semantic Powers* (Oxford: Clarendon Press, 1999).

Garfield, J. "Dependent Arising and the Emptiness of Emptiness: Why Did Nagarjuna Start with Causation?" *Philosophy East and West* 44 (1994): 219–50.

Garfield, J. "*Epoché* and *Śūnaya*: Scepticism East and West". *Philosophy East and West* 40 (1990): 285–307.

Garfield, J. *The Fundamental Wisdom of the Middle Way: Nāgārjuna's Mūlamadhyamakakārikā.* Translation with commentary (Oxford: Oxford University Press, 1995).

Garfield, J. "Mindfulness and Ethics: Attention, Virtue and Perfection". *Thai International Journal of Buddhist Studies* 3 (2012): 1–24.

Garfield, J. "Turning a Madhyamaka Trick". *Journal of Indian Philosophy* 36 (2010): 507–27.

Garfield, J. "What is it Like to be a Bodhisattva: Moral Phenomenology in Śāntideva's *Bodhicaryāvatāra*". *Journal of the International Association of Buddhist Studies* 33 (2012): 333–57.

Garfield, J. & W. Edelglass (eds) *Buddhist Philosophy: Essential Readings* (Oxford: Oxford University Press, 2009).

Gethin, R. "Can Killing a Living Being Ever Be an Act of Compassion? The Analysis of the Act of Killing in the Abhidhamma and Pali Commentaries". *Journal of Buddhist Ethics* 11 (2004): 167–202.

Gethin, R. "The Five *khandhas*: Their Treatment in the Nikāyas and early Abhidhamma". *Journal of Indian Philosophy* 14 (1986): 36–54.

Gethink R. *Foundations of Buddhism* (Oxford: Oxford University Press, 1998).

Gethin, R. "He Who Sees Dhamma Sees Dhammas: Dhamma in Early Buddhism". *Journal of Indian Philosophy* 32 (2004): 513–42.

Gold, J. C. "No Outside, No Inside: Duality, Reality and Vasubandhu's Illusory Elephant". *Asian Philosophy* 16 (2006): 3–16.

Gold, J. C. "Vasubandhu". *Stanford Encyclopedia of Philosophy* (Winter 2012 Edition), E. N. Zalta (ed.) http://plato.stanford.edu/entries/vasubandhu/ (accessed July 2013).

Goodman, C. *Consequences of Compassion: An Interpretation and Defense of Buddhist Ethics* (Oxford: Oxford University Press, 2009).

Goodman, C. "Consequentialism, Agent-neutrality, and Mahayana Ethics". *Philosophy East and West* 58 (2008): 17–35.

Goodman, C. "Resentment and Reality: Buddhism on Moral Responsibility". *American Philosophical Quarterly* 39 (2002): 359–72.

Gopnik, A. "Could David Hume have Known about Buddhism? Charles Francois Dolu, the Royal College of La Flèche, and the Global Jesuit Intellectual Network". *Hume Studies* 35 (2009): 5–28.

Gowans, C. W. "Medical Analogies in Buddhist and Hellenistic Thought: Tranquility and Anger". *The Royal Institute of Philosophy Supplement* 66 (2010): 11–33.

Gowans, C. W. *Philosophy of the Buddha: An Introduction* (London: Routledge, 2003).

Hadot, P. *Philosophy as a Way of Life,* M. Chase (ed. and trans.) (Oxford: Blackwell, 1995).

Hall, B. "Vasubandhu on 'Aggregates, Spheres, and Components: Being Chapter One of the *Abhidharmakośa*'". PhD dissertation, Harvard University (1983).

Hallisey, C. "Ethical Particularism in Theravāda Buddhism". *Journal of Buddhist Ethics* 3 (1996): 32–43.

Hallisey, C. & A. Hansen. "Narrative, Sub-Ethics, and the Moral Life: Some Evidence from Theravāda Buddhism". *Journal of Religious Ethics* 24(2) (1996): 305–27.

Hanh, Thich Nhat. *The Heart of Understanding* (New Delhi: Full Circle Publishing, 1997).

Harvey, P. *An Introduction to Buddhism: Teachings, History and Practices* (Cambridge: Cambridge University Press, 1990).

Harvey, P. *The Selfless Mind: Personality, Consciousness and Nirvāṇa in Early Buddhism* (Richmond: Curzon Press, 1995).

Harvey, P. "Criteria for Judging the Unwholesomeness of Actions in the Texts of Theravada Buddhism". *Journal of Buddhist Ethics* 2 (1995): 140–51.

Harvey, P. "Self-Development and Self-Transcendence in Theravada Buddhist Thought and Practice". *Wisdom Books Reading Room.* www.wisdom-books.com/FocusDetail.asp?FocusRef=21 (accessed July 2013).

Harvey, P. "Vinaya Principles for Assigning Degrees of Culpability". *Journal of Buddhist Ethics* 6 (1999): 271–91.

Hattori, M. "*Apoha* and *Pratibhā*." In *Sanskrit and Indian Studies: Essays in Honour of Daniel H.H. Ingalls*, M. Nagatomi, B. K. Matilal, J. M. Masson & E. Dimock (eds), 61–73 (Boston, MA: D. Reidel, 1979).

Hayes, R. P. *Dignaga on the Interpretation of Signs* (Dordrecht: Kluwer, 1988).
Hayes, R. P. "Dinnaga's Views on Reasoning (*svarthanumana*)". *Journal of Indian Philosophy* 8 (1980): 219–77.
Hayes, R. P. "On the Reinterpretation of Dharmakirtis Svabhavahetu". *Journal of Indian Philosophy* 15 (1987): 319–32.
Hayes, R. P. "The Question of Doctrinalism in the Buddhist Epistemologists". *Journal of the American Academy of Religion* 52(4) (1984): 645–70.
Hayes, R. P. "Nagarjuna's Appeal". *Journal of Indian Philosophy* 22 (1994): 299–378.
Herman, A. L. "Ah, But There Is a Paradox of Desire in Buddhism: A Reply to Wayne Alt". *Philosophy East and West* 30(4) (1980): 529–32.
Holland, R. F. "Is Goodness a Mystery?" In his *Against Empiricism: On Education, Epistemology and Value*, 93–109 (Oxford: Blackwell, 1980).
Hoornaert, P. "An Annotated Translation of *Madhyamakahṛdayakārikā/Tarkajvāla* V". Kanazawa University Repository for Academic Resources, Department Bulletin Papers 19 (1999): 127–59.
Hopkins, J. *Buddhist Advice for Living and Liberation: Nagarjuna's Precious Garland* (Ithaca, NY: Snow Lion Publications, 1988).
Hopkins, J. *Meditation on Emptiness* (London: Wisdom Publications, 1983).
Huntington, C. W. "The Nature of the Mādhyamika Trick". *Journal of Indian Philosophy* 35 (2007): 103–31.
Huntington, C. W. with G. N. Wangchen. *The Emptiness of Emptiness (Including a Translation of the Madhyamakāvatāra)* (Honolulu, HI: University of Hawai'i Press, 1989).
Huxley, A. "The Kurudhamma: From Ethics to Statecraft". *Journal of Buddhist Ethics* 2 (1995): 191–203.
Iida, S. *Reason and Emptiness: A Study in Logic and Mysticism (Including a Sanskrit Edition of Bhāviveka's Madhyamakahṛdaya-Kārikā and Its Commentary*. (Tokyo: Hokuseido Press, 1980).
Ingalls, D. H. H. "Śaṇkara's Arguments against the Buddhists". *Philosophy East and West* 3(4) (1954): 291–306.
Jacobi, H. (trans.). *The Jaina Sutras* (Oxford: Clarendon Press, 1895; reprinted Varanasi: Motilal Banarsidass, 1964).
Jaini, P. S. "On the Theory of Two Vasubandhus". *Bulletin of the School of Oriental and African Studies* 21 (1958): 48–53.
Kajiyama, Y. *An Introduction to Buddhist Philosophy: An Annotated Translation of the Tarkabhāṣā of Mokṣakaragupta.* Memoirs of the Faculty of Letters, Kyoto University, vol. 10 (1966). Reprinted as *Wiener Studien Zur Tibetologie Und Buddhismuskunde*, vol. 42 (Vienna: Arbeitskreis Für Tibetische Und Buddhistische Studien, Universität Wien, 1998).
Kant, I. *Kritique der praktischen Vernunft.* Translated as *Critique of Practical Reason*, M. Gregor (ed. and trans.) (Cambridge: Cambridge University Press, 1997).
Kant, I. *Kritique der reinen Vernunft.* Translated as *Critique of Pure Reason*, N. Kemp Smith (trans.) (New York: St Martin's Press [1929], 1965).
Kapstein, M. "Mereological Considerations in Vasubandhu's 'Proof of Idealism'." In *Reasons Traces*, ch. 7 (Boston, MA: Wisdom Publications, 2001).
Kapstein, M. *Reason's Traces* (Boston, MA: Wisdom Publications, 2001).
Karunadasa, Y. *The Dhamma Theory: Philosophical Cornerstone of the Abhidhamma.* Kandy, Sri Lanka: Buddhist Publication Society, 1996. www.abhidhamma.org/dhamma_theory_philosophical_corn.htm (accessed May 2013).

Katsura, S. "On Trairūpya Formulae." In *Buddhism and its Relation to Other Religions: Essays in Honour of Dr. Shozen Kumoi on his Seventieth Birthday*, 161–72 (Kyoto: Heirakuji Shoten, 1986).

Katz, N. "Does the 'Cessation of the World' Entail the Cessation of Emotions?" *Pali Buddhist Review* 4 (1979): 53–65.

Kaufman, W. R. P. "Karma, Rebirth, and the Problem of Evil". *Philosophy East and West* 55(1) (2005): 15–32.

Keira, R. *Madhyamika and Epistemology: A Study of Kamalasila's Method for Proving the Voidness of All Dharmas; Introduction, Annotated Translations and Tibetan Texts of Selected Sections of the Second Chapter of the Madhyamakaloka* (Vienna: Arbeitskreis für tibetische und buddhistische Studien Universität Wien, 2004).

Keown, D. "Karma, Character and Consequentialism". *Journal of Religious Ethics* 24 (1996): 329–50.

Keown, D. *The Nature of Buddhist Ethics* (New York: St Martin's Press, 1992).

King, R. "*Vijñāptimātratā* and the Abhidharma Context of Early Yogācāra". *Asian Philosophy* 8 (1998): 5–17.

Kochumuttom, T. A. *A Buddhist Doctrine of Experience : A New Translation and Interpretation of the Works of Vasubandhu, the Yogācārin* (New Delhi: Motilal Barnarsidass, 1989).

Koichi, T. "Vasubandhu and the Yogacarabhumi". *The Eastern Buddhist* 36(1–2) (2004): 236–42.

Kragh, U. T. *Early Buddhist Theories of Action and Result: A Study of Karmaphalasambudha - Candrakīrti's Prasannapadā Verses 17.1–20* (Vienna: Arbeitskreis für tibetische und buddhistische Studien Universität Wien, 2006).

Krasser, H. "Are Buddhist Pramāṇavādins non-Buddhistic? Dignāga and Dharmakīrti on the Impact of Logic and Epistemology on Emancipation". *Hōrin: Vergleichende Studien zur japanischen Kulture* 11 (2004): 129–46.

Krasser, H. *Dharmottaras kurze Untersuchung der Güiltigkeit einer Erkenntnis, Laghuprāmāṇyaparikṣā* (Vienna: Obersetzung, 1991).

Krasser, H. "Dharmottara's Theory of Language in his *Laghuprāmāṇyaparikṣa*". *Journal of Indian Philosophy* 23 (1995): 247–71.

Kritzer, R. *Rebirth and Causation in the Yogācāra Abhidharma* (Vienna: Arbeitskreis für Tibetische und Buddhistische Studien, Universität Wien, 1999).

Kritzer, R. "Sautrāntika in the *Abhidharmakośabhāṣya*". *Journal of the International Association of Buddhist Studies* 26(2) (2003): 331–84.

Kuan, Tse-Fu. "Clarification on Feelings in Buddhist *Dhyāna/Jñāna* Meditation". *Journal of Indian Philosophy* 33 (2005): 285–319.

Kuzminsky, A. "Pyrrhonism and the Madhyamaka". *Philosophy East and West* 57 (2007): 482–511.

Lamotte, É. *History of Indian Buddhism: From the Origins to the Śaka Era*, S. Boin-Webb (trans.) (Paris: Louvain-la-Neuve, 1988).

Lang, K. *Āryadeva's Catuḥśataka: On the Bodhisattva's Cultivation of Merit and Knowledge* (Copenhagen: Akademisk Forlag, 1986).

Leibniz, G. W. *Monadology*, R. Franks & R. S. Woolhouse (ed. and trans.). In Leibniz, *Philosophical Texts* (Oxford: Oxford University Press, 1998).

Lipman, K. "The Cittamātra and its Mādhyamika Critique: Some Phenomenological Reflections". *Philosophy East and West* 32 (1982): 295–308.

Locke, J. *Essay Concerning Human Understanding*, P. H. Nidditch (ed.) (Oxford: Clarendon Press, [1975] 1979).
Lopez, D. S. (ed.) *Buddhist Hermeneutics* (Honolulu, HI: University of Hawai'i Press, 1992).
Lovejoy, A. O. "The Buddhistic Technical Terms *upādāna* and *upādisesa*". *Journal of the American Oriental Society* 19 (1988): 126–36.
Loy, D. R. "How to Drive Your *Karma*." In *Money, Sex, War, Karma: Notes for a Buddhist Revolution*, 53–63 (Somerville, MA: Wisdom Publications, 2008).
Loy, D. R. "How to Reform a Serial Killer: The Buddhist Approach to Restorative Justice". *Journal of Buddhist Ethics* 7 (2000): 145–68.
Lusthaus, D. *Buddhist Phenomenology* (London: RoutledgeCurzon, 2002).
Lusthaus, D. "What Is and Isn't Yogācāra". www.acmuller.net/yogacara/articles/intro-uni.htm (accessed July 2013).
Matilal, B. K. *Logic, Language and Reality* (New Delhi: Motilal Banarsidass, 1985).
Matilal, B. K. *Perception: An Essay on Classical Indian Theories of Knowledge* (Oxford: Clarendon Press, 1986).
McClintock, S. L. *Omniscience and the Rhetoric of Reason: Śantarakṣita and Kamalaśīla on Rationality, Argumentation, and Religious Authority* (Boston, MA: Wisdom Publications, 2010).
McCrae, L. & P. Patil. "Traditionalism and Innovation: Philosophy, Exegesis, and Intellectual History in Jñānaśrīmitra's *Apohaprakaraṇa*". *Journal of Indian Philosophy* 34 (2006): 303–66.
McDermott, A. C. "Asaṅga's Defense of *ālayavijñāna*". *Journal of Indian Philosophy* 2 (1973): 167–74.
McDermott, J. P. *Development in the Early Buddhist Concept of Kamma/Karma* (New Delhi: Munshiram Manoharlal, 1984).
McDermott, J. P. "*Nibbāna* as a Reward for *Kamma*". *Journal of the American Oriental Society* 93 (1973): 344–7.
McEvilley, T. "Early Greek Philosophy and Madhyamaka". *Philosophy East and West* 31 (1981): 141–64.
McEvilley, T. *The Shape of Ancient Thought: Comparative Studies in Greek and Indian Philosophies* (New York: Allworth Press, 2002).
McEvilley, T. "Pyrrhonism and Madhyamaka". *Philosophy East and West* 32 (1982): 3–35.
Meyers, K. L. "Freedom and Self-Control: Free Will in South Asian Buddhism".PhD dissertation, University of Chicago (2010).
Mikogami, E. "Some Remarks on the Concept of *Arthakriyā*". *Journal of Indian Philosophy* 7 (1979): 79–94.
Murdoch, I. "On 'God' and 'Good'". In *The Sovereignty of Good*, 45–74. London: Routledge, 2001. First published in *Anatomy of Knowledge*, M. Greene (ed.), 233–58 (London: Routledge & Kegan Paul, 1969).
Nagao, G. "Connotations of the Word *Āsraya* (Basis) in the *Mahāyāna-Sūtralaṃkāra*". In *Mādhyamika and Yogācāra: A Study of Mahāyāna Philosophies*, L. S. Kawamura (trans.), 75–82 (Albany, NY: SUNY Press, 1991).
Nance, R. *Concordance of English Translations of Vasubandhu's Thirty Verses, With Sanskrit Original and Tibetan Translation.* www.nagaraprathama.com/uploads/3/6/5/7/3657511/trimsika_nance_rev.pdf (accessed July 2013).
Nance, R. "On What Do We Rely When We Rely on Reasoning?". *Journal of Indian Philosophy* 35 (2007): 149–67.

Nayak, G. C. "The Madhyamaka Attack on Essentialism: A Critical Appraisal". *Philosophy East and West* 29 (1979): 477–90.

Neiman, S. *Moral Clarity: A Guide for Grown-Up Idealists* (Boston, MA: Houghton Mifflin Harcourt, 2008).

Newland, G. *The Two Truths* (Ithaca, NY: Snow Lion Publications, 1992).

Newland, G. "Weighing the Butter, Levels of Explanation, and Falsification." In *Moonshadows*, The Cowherds, 57–71 (New York: Oxford University Press, 2011).

Nhat-Tu, Thich. "*Kuśala* and *Akuśala* as Criteria of Buddhist Ethics". *Buddhism Today*. www.buddhismtoday.com/english/ethic_psy/004-tnt-kusala.htm (accessed July 2013).

Nietzsche, F. *Beyond Good and Evil*, W. Kaufmann (trans.) (New York: Vintage, [1966] 1989).

Nietzsche, F. *On the Genealogy of Morals; and Ecce Homo*, W. Kaufmann (trans.) (New York: Vintage, [1967] 1989).

Nietzsche, Friedrich. *Twilight of the Idols*, W. Kaufmann (trans.). In *The Portable Nietzsche* (New York: Viking, 1954).

Nussbaum, M. "Aristotle on Human Nature and the Foundations of Ethics". In *World, Mind and Ethics*, J. E. J. Altham & R. Harrison (eds), 86–131 (Cambridge: Cambridge University Press, 1995).

Oehler, K. "Aristotle on Self-Knowledge". *Proceedings of the American Philosophical Society* 118(6) (1974): 493–506.

Oetke, C. "'Nihilist' and 'Non-nihilist' Interpretations of Madhyamaka". *Acta Orientalia* 57 (1996): 57–104.

Oetke, C. "On MMK 24.8". *Journal of Indian Philosophy* 35 (2007): 1–32.

Olivelle, P. (ed. and trans.). *The Early Upaniṣads: Annotated Text and Translation* (New York: Oxford University Press, 1998).

Olsen, R. F. "Candrakīrti's Critique of *Vijñānavāda*". *Philosophy East and West* 24 (1974): 405–11.

Patil, P. *Against a Hindu God* (New York: Columbia University Press, 2009).

Patil, P. "Constructing the Content of Awareness."In *Apoha, Buddhist Nominalism and Human Cognition*, A. Chakrabarti, M. Siderits & T. Tillemans (eds), 149–169 (New York: Columbia University Press, 2011).

Patil, P. "On What it is that Buddhists Think About: *Apoha* in the RATNAKÎRTI-NIBANDHÂVALI". *Journal of Indian Philosophy* 31 (2003): 229–56.

Payutto, P. A. *Good, Evil and Beyond: Kamma in the Buddha's Teachings*, B. Evans (trans.) (Bangkok: Buddha Dharma Education Association, 1993).

Perrett, R. "The Bodhisattva Paradox". *Philosophy East and West* 36 (1986): 55–9.

Perrett, R. "Egoism, Altruism and Intentionalism in Buddhist Ethics". *Journal of Indian Philosophy* 15 (1987): 71–85.

Perrett, R. "Karma and the Problem of Suffering". *Sophia* 24(1) (1985): 4–10.

Phillips, S. *Classical Indian Metaphysics: Refutations of Realism and the Emergence of "New Logic"* (La Salle, IL: Open Court, 1995).

Phillips, S. "Dharmakīrti on Sensation and Causal Efficacy". *Journal of Indian Philosophy* 15 (1987): 231–59.

Phillips, S. "Perceiving Particulars Blindly: Remarks on a Nyāya-Buddhist Controversy". *Philosophy East and West* 54 (2004): 389–403.

Phillips, S. *Ratnakīrti's Proof of Momentariness by Positive Correlation (Kṣaṇabhaṅga-*

siddhi Anvayatmika): Transliteration, Translation, and Philosophic Commentary (New York: Columbia University Press, 2013).

Pind, O. H. *Dignāga's Philosophy of Language: Dignāga on Anyāpoha* (Vienna: Universität Wien, 2009).

Pope, A. *Essay on Man* (London: Routledge, 1993).

Potter, K. (ed.) *Indian Metaphysics and Epistemology: The Tradition of Nyāya-Vaiśeṣika up to Gangeśa* (New Delhi: Motilal Banarsidass, 1977).

Potter, K. "How Many Karma Theories Are There?" *Journal of Indian Philosophy* 29 (2001): 231–9.

Priest, G. & J. Garfield. "Nāgārjuna and the Limits of Thought." In *Beyond the Limits of Thought*, 249–70 (Oxford: Clarendon Press, 2002).

Priestley, L. C. D. C. *Pudgalavāda Buddhism: The Reality of the Indeterminate Self* (Toronto: Centre for South Asian Studies, University of Toronto, 1999).

Radhakrishnan S. & C. A. Moore (eds). *A Sourcebook in Indian Philosophy* (Princeton, NJ: Princeton University Press, 1957).

Robinson, R. "Did Nāgārjuna Really Refute All Philosophical Views?" *Philosophy East and West* 22 (1972): 325–31.

Ruegg, D. S. *The Literature of the Madhyamaka School of Philosophy in India (A History of Indian Literature)* (Wiesbaden: Harrassowitz, 1981).

Ruegg, D. S. "Does the Mādhyamika Have a Thesis and a Philosophical Position." In *Buddhist Logic and Epistemology*, B. K. Matilal & R. D. Evans (eds), 229–37 (Dordrecht: Reidel, 1982).

Ruegg, D. S. "The Uses of the Four Positions of the Catuṣkoṭi and the Problem of the Descrition of Reality in Mahāyāna Buddhism". *Journal of Indian Philosophy* 5 (1977): 1–71.

Rupp, G. "The Relationships between *nirvāṇa* and *saṃsāra*: An Essay on the Evolution of Buddhist Ethics". *Philosophy East and West* 21 (1971): 55–68.

Sanderson, A. "The *Sarvāstivāda* and its Critics: *Anātmavāda* and the Theory of *Karma*." In *Buddhism into the Year 2000*, Khlong Sam & Khlong Luang (eds), 32–47 (Patumthani: Dhammakaya Foundation, 1994).

Schmithausen, L. *On the Problem of the External World in the Ch'eng Wei Shih Lun* (Tokyo: The International Institute for Buddhist Studies, 2005).

Schmithausen, L. "Spirituelle Praxis und Philosophicsche Theorie im Buddhismus". *Zeitschrift für Missionswissenschaft und Reliongswissenschaft* 57 (1973): 161–86.

Sedley, D. "Platonic Causes". *Phronesis* 43 (1998): 114–32.

Segal, P. "Nāgārjuna's Paradox". *American Philosophical Quarterly* 29 (1992): 79–85.

Siderits, M. "The Madhyamaka Critique of Epistemology I". *Journal of Indian Philosophy* 8 (1980): 307–35.

Siderits, M. "The Madhyamaka Critique of Epistemology II". *Journal of Indian Philosophy* 9 (1981): 121–60.

Siderits, Mark. *Buddhism as Philosophy: An Introduction* (Aldershot: Ashgate, 2007).

Siderits, M. "Causation and Emptiness in Early Madhyamaka". *Journal of Indian Philosophy* 32 (2004): 393–419.

Siderits, M. "Perceiving Particulars: A Buddhist Defense (Comment and Discussion)". *Philosophy East and West* 54(3) (2004): 367–82.

Silk, J. A. "Good and Evil in Indian Buddhism: The Five Sins of Immediate Retribution". *Journal of Indian Philosophy* 35 (2007): 253–86.

Spiro, M. *Buddhism and Society: A Great Tradition and Its Burmese Vicissitudes*, 2nd

edn (Berkeley, CA: University of California Press, 1982; first published New York: Harper & Row, 1971).
Sprung, M. *Lucid Exposition of the Middle Way* (London: Routledge & Kegan Paul, 1979).
Sprung, M. (ed.) *The Problem of Two Truths in Buddhism and Vedānta* (Dordrecht: Reidel, 1973).
Stcherbatsky, T. *Buddhist Logic*. Bibliotheca Buddhica, vol. 26. Leningrad: Izdeatel'stov Akademii Nauk S.S.S.R., 1932.
Stcherbatsky, T. *Central Conception of Buddhism and the Meaning of the Word 'Dharma'* (New Delhi: Motilal Banarsidass, 1970).
Stcherbatsky, T. *The Soul Theory of the Buddhists (with Sanskrit Text)* (New Delhi: New Bharatiya Book Corp., 2003).
Strawson, P. F. "Freedom and Resentment". *Proceedings of the British Academy* 48 (1962): 187–211.
Strawson, P. *Individuals* (London: Methuen, 1959).
Tedesco, P. "Sanskrit *Kuśala* – 'Skilful, Welfare'". *Journal of the American Oriental Society* 74 (1954): 131–42.
Thanissaro Bhikkhu. *Noble Strategy: Essays on the Buddhist Path* (Valley Center, CA: Metta Forest Monastery, 1999).
Thanissaro Bhikkhu. "The Not-self Strategy" (2010). www.accesstoinsight.org/lib/authors/thanissaro/notselfstrategy.html (accessed May 2013).
Thanissaro Bhikkhu. "No-self or Not-self?" (2011). www.accesstoinsight.org/lib/authors/thanissaro/notself2.html (accessed November 2013). Originally published in *Noble Strategy: Essays on the Buddhist Path* (Valley Center, CA: Metta Forest Monastery, 1999).
The Cowherds. *Moonshadows* (New York: Oxford University Press, 2011).
Tillemans, T. J. F. "How Far Can a Madhyamaka Buddhist Reform Conventional Truth?" In *Moonshadows,* The Cowherds, 151–65 (New York: Oxford University Press, 2011).
Tillemans, T. J. F. "How to Talk About Ineffable Things." In *Apoha, Buddhist Nominalism and Human Cognition,* A. Chakrabarti, M. Siderits & T. Tillemans (eds), 50–63 (New York: Columbia University Press, 2011).
Tillemans, T. J. F. "On *Sapakṣa*". In his *Scripture, Logic, Language: Essays on Dharmakirti and his Tibetan Successors,* 89–116 (Boston, MA: Wisdom Publications, 1999). Originally published in *Journal of Indian Philosophy* 18 (1990): 53–79.
Tillemans, T. J. F. "Trying to be Fair to Mādyamika Buddhism". The Numata Yehan Lecture in Buddhism, University of Calgary (2001).
Toru, F. "Perception, Conceptual Construction and Yogic Perception in Kamalaśīla's Epistemology". *Chun-Hwa Buddhist Journal* 18 (2005): 273–97.
Trainor, K. "Seeing, Feeling, Doing: Ethics and Emotions in South Asian Buddhism". *Journal of the American Academy of Religion* 71(3) (2003): 523–9.
Trivedi, S. "Idealism and Yogacara Buddhism". *Asian Philosophy* 15 (2005): 231–46.
Tucci, G. *Minor Buddhist Texts,* 3 vols (Rome: Ist. Ital. per il Medio ed Estremo Orient, 1956–1971).
Tucci, G. *Pre-Dinnāga Buddhist Texts on Logic* (Baroda: Oriental Institute, 1929).
Tucci, G. "The *Ratnāvalī* of Nāgārjuna". *Journal of the Royal Asiatic Society of Great Britain and Ireland* (1934): 307–25; (1936): 237–52, 423–35.

Velleman, J. D. "So It Goes". The Amherst Lecture in Philosophy Lecture 1 (2006). www.amherstlecture.org/velleman2006/ (accessed July 2013).
Venkataramanan, K. "*Saṃmitīya-nikāya-śāstra*" (translation). *Visvabharati Annals* 5 (1953): 153–243.
Vernezze, P. "Moderation or the Middle way: Two Approaches To Anger". *Philosophy East and West* 58 (2008): 2–16.
Vetter, T. "On the Authenticity of the *Ratnāvalī*". *Asiatische Studien/Études Asiatique* 46 (1992): 492–506.
Vetter, T. "Zum Problem der Person in Nāgārjunas Mūla-Madhyamamka-Kārikā." In *Offenbarung als Heilserfahrung im Christentum, Hinduismus, und Buddhismus*, W. Strolz & S. Ueda (eds), 167–84 (Freiburg, Basel, Vienna: Stiftung Oratio Dominica, 1982).
Visvader, J. "Reply to Wayne Alt's "There is No Paradox of Desire in Buddhism"". *Philosophy East and West* 30(4) (1980): 533–4.
Warder, A. K. "Dharmas and Data". *Journal of Indian Philosophy* 1 (1971): 272–95.
Warder, A. K. *Indian Buddhism* (Delhi: Motilal Banarsidass, 1970).
Warder, A. K. "Objects". *Journal of Indian Philosophy* 3 (1975): 355–62.
Watanabe, F. *Philosophy and Its Development in the Nikāyas and Abhidhamma* (New Delhi: Motilal Banarsidass, 1983).
Wayman, A. "The Yogācāra Idealism". *Philosophy East and West* 15 (1965): 65–73.
Weber, M. *Essays in Sociology*, H. H. Gerth & C. Wright Mills (trans. and ed.) (New York: Oxford University Press, 1946).
Webster, D. *The Philosophy of Desire in the Buddhist Pāli Canon* (Abingdon: RoutledgeCurzon, 2005).
Wetlesen, J. "Did Śāntideva Destroy the Bodhisattva Path?". *Journal of Buddhist Ethics* 9 (2002): 34–88.
Westerhoff, J. (trans.) *The Dispeller of Disputes* (Oxford: Oxford University Press, 2010).
Westerhoff, J. "Nāgārjuna's Catuṣkoṭi". *Journal of Indian Philosophy* 34 (2006): 367–95.
Westerhoff, J. *Nāgārjuna's Madhyamaka* (Oxford: Oxford University Press, 2009).
Williams, B. A. O. *Moral Luck* (Cambridge: Cambridge University Press, 1981).
Williams, P. "The Absence of Self and the Removal of Pain: How Śāntideva Destroyed the Bodhisattva Path". In *Altruism and Reality: Studies in the Philosophy of the Bodhicāryāvatāra* (London: Routledge, 1997; reprinted New Delhi: Motilal Banarsidass, 2000).
Williams, P. *Altruism and Reality: Studies in the Philosophy of the Bodhicāryāvatāra* (London: Routledge, 1997; reprinted New Delhi: Motilal Banarsidass, 2000).
Williams, P. "On Altruism and Rebirth." In *Altruism and Reality: Studies in the Philosophy of the Bodhicāryāvatāra* (London: Routledge, 1997; reprinted New Delhi: Motilal Banarsidass, 2000).
Williams, P. *Mahāyāna Buddhism: The Doctrinal Foundations* (London: Routledge, 1989).
Williams, P. "On the Abhidharma Ontology". *Journal of Indian Philosophy* 9(3) (1981): 227–57.
Wood, T. *Nāgārjunian Disputations* (Honolulu, HI: University of Hawai'i Press, 1994).
Woolf, R. "Socratic Authority". *Archiv für Geschichte der Philosophie* 90 (2008): 1–38.
Wright, D. "Critical Questions Towards a Naturalized Conception of *Karma*". *Journal of Buddhist Ethics* 12 (2005): 78–93.

Index

abhidharma (higher teachings) 2, 29, 38, 45, 74, 90–91, 139, 246–7
  Abhidharma account of reality 197–8
  Abhidharmika 82, 85, 119, 134–6, 166, 215
Abhidharmakośabhāṣya *see under* Vasubandhu
Adam, Martin T. 258n13
agency 16–19
anatta/anātman *see* no-self
anger 227, 229
anyāpoha (exclusion-of-other) 217
Aranyakas, the 244
Arhat (the accomplished person) 62–5, 69
Aristotle 20, 121, 130, 163–4, 190–91, 281n36
  on identity of whole and parts 41
  Prior Analytics 181
  on substances 84
  virtue ethics 56
Arnold, Dan 210, 278n13
Āryadeva 73, 169
asceticism 28, 67
Athens 11
Atiśa (Dīpaṁkaraśrījñāna) 239
atomism *see dharmas*
aversion *see* suffering, roots of

Batchelor, Stephen 112, 245
Berkeley, George 156
Bhāviveka x, 155, 171, 192, 193–8, 198–202, 277n5
  on dreams 274n
  Madhyamakahṛdaya 193, 194–5
bodhisattva (awakened being) 64–5, 69
Brahmāṇas, the 244
Brahmanical philosophers 28, 67, 82, 130, 141, 211, 232–3, 238, 242
Buddha Nature 272n6
Buddha, the 3, 25, 30, 32, 64, 108, 242, 245
  on asceticism 67
  "did not quarrel with the world" 212
  discourses of the Buddha *see sūtras*
  experience of pain 19, 265n5
  interpretable vs definitive statements of 77, 144, 194
  and *karma* 112
  legend of 1
  and reincarnation 32, 64, 77, 268n33
Buddhaghoṣa 37, 42, 45, 50, 53, 252n16
Buddhapālita 169
Buddhism **xvi–xvii**
  development in India **xviii**, 117, 238–9
  establishment in Tibet 236–7, 239

and Greek philosophy 3, 42, 44, 55–6, 58, 60, 62, 115, 121, 251n9
kammic and *nibbanic* 63, 106, 112–13
reading Buddhist philosophers 5
as religion 4
see also specific entries
bundles 103, 122–3, 127, 133–4
Burden, the 32, 77

Candrakīrti x, 80, 85, 110, 170, 192, 198–202, 238–9, 279n18
on dependent existence 206–7
interpretation of Madhyamaka 204–14
on language 199–201
Madhyamaka-Avatāra 204–5
normativity of common opinion 213
on perfection of wisdom 205, 206–14
Prasannapadā 204
on ultimate vs conventional reality 208, 210–12
Cārvākas 245
catuṣkoti *see* tetralemma
causation 6, 26, 59, 86, 152, 188–9, 207–8, 221–3, 264n22, 264n26, 284n66, 286n83
and identity 128, 267n23
and inference 188
reality a matter of degree of 154–5
and the self 28
see also dependent origination
change
identity through change 27–8, 40–41
and suffering 27
chariot principle, the 43–4, 118, 198
cognition 175–6, 195, 277n37
mode of vs content of 161–2, 165–6, 196–7, 208, 278n13
pramāṇas 171–2, 173–5
as self-cognizing 174–7, 236
compassion 71, 107, 140, 229
complex wholes *see under* mereology
concepts 214–19, 224, 235
as illusory 178–9, 199
conceptual reality *see under* reality
consciousness 141, 163–4, 197, 235, 276n31, 276n33
dual nature of 196–7
non-conceptual 80, 167
reflexive awareness 176
vijñāna 29, 141
convention, linguistic 38–40, 104, 216
conventional vs ultimate reality *see under* reality
craving *see* suffering, roots of
critical philosophy 199
critique of naturalist explanation 222
cross-modal unity 125–7, 129–31, 131–4, 134–6

delusion *see* suffering, roots of
dependent origination 6, 15, 26, 45, 59, 85–7, 89, 151, 167, 189–95, 252n17, 260n21
Descartes, René 162
desire 15, 22, 126–7, 251n4
altered by belief 13
in construction of reality 46–7
elimination of 48, 53
second-order desires 252n12
in Uddyotakara's account of self 132–3
determinable, ultimate 163–5
dhamma *see dharmas*
Dharmakīrti ix–x, 170, 172, 188–9, 219–24, 276n33, 281n36
"Buddhist idealism" 278n11
on "efficacy" 221–3
dharmas (absolute simples) 44–7, 81–5, 85–7, 119, 131, 178, 180, 190–91, 195
Abhidharmika conception of 82, 263n18
Buddha-*dharma* 78, 188, 239
dharma-atomism 147–8, 171–2
as events 45
merely conceptual (*prajñapti*) 138
mind-independent 143–5
as substances 90–91, 256n37
translation of 256n37
unnecessary *dharmas* 138

Dharmottara 237
Diṅnāga ix–x, 172–80, 180–89, 238, 276n33, 281n36
 anyāpoha (exclusion-of-other) 217, 224
 on cognition as self-cognizing 174–7
 on experience 170, 172, 278n9
 on language/concepts 198–9, 215–19
 Pramāṇasamuccaya 175
 trairūpya 182–5
Diogenes of Sinope 3
Dīpaṁkaraśrījñāna (Atiśa) 239
dissatisfaction 8
dreams 146–7, 152–4, 274n15
duḥkha *see* suffering
 translation of 8

Eightfold Path, the 11–12, 54, 60
 "seeing things as they are" 6
 substantive moral claim of 12
eliminativism 37
emotion 54, 69–71, 251n9, 261n33
kleśas (afflictions) 52–3, 259n20
emptiness 74, 78–9, 81, 87–8, 90, 139–40, 192
 "emptiness of emptiness" 190
 Middle Way arguments for 79–81, 200
 three kinds of 159–60
enlightenment 12, 53, 64, 107–8, 141, 188, 201, 205, 272n6
 bodhicitta 226–7
 Kamalaśīla's view on 236–9
 sudden 237
Epictetus 31–2
epistemology ch. 8, 186
 "cognition is the knowing" 175–6
 concerned with life 3
 epistemological turn in Buddhism ix
 inferential knowledge 188
 and moral philosophy 12
ethics 3, 56–7, 62, 70
 consequentialist ethics 100, 258n8, 258n12
 eudaimonist ethics 55, 260n23
 and metaphysics 3–4, 12, 48, 70
 phenomenological ethics 61
 teleology in 54–7, 258n8, 258n12
 virtue ethics 56, 258n8, 258n9, 258n12
exercises, spiritual 28, 48, 60–61, 62–3, 163, 228, 230–31
 and sudden enlightenment 237
existence 86–7
experience 209
 contents of neither simple nor complex 172
explanation 207–8, 222–4
extinguishment (of suffering) 10, 57, 60; *see also* suffering, elimination of

faith 75
Fenner, Peter 199
fire, metaphor of 10
four Noble Truths *see* Noble Truths
freedom 80
Gautama Buddha *see* Buddha, the
God 67
Gokulikas, the 54
Gowans, Christopher 23
greed *see* suffering, roots of
Greek philosophy
 and Buddhist philosophy 3, 42, 44, 55–6, 58, 60, 62, 115
 see also specific entries

Hallisey, Charles 109
Hanson, Anne 109
happiness argument, the 21, 33
happiness 7, 21, 55–6, 57–9, 63, 75–6, 94, 265n1
 sukha 75, 257n3
Harvey, Peter 253n5, 257n4
hatred *see* suffering, roots of
hermeneutics 194, 232
holism and anti-holism 81, 118–19

idealism ix, 145, 152–3, 156, 158, 166
identification, to appropriation 22, 106
identity 42, 86, 127, 156, 166

and causation 128, 267n23
function as criterion of 41–3
personal identity 103
and memory 126–7
and reincarnation 103
through change 24, 27–8
ignorance *see* suffering, roots of
impermanence 15
impotence 16–19
Indian philosophy 248–9
individuals 26, 31–2, 39, 41, 43–5, 56, 83, 87–8, 121; *see also dharmas*
induction, problem of 186
inference 173–4, 177–80, 181–9, 216
pan-Indic rules of 181, 182, 193, 280n26
trairūpya 182–5
inherence 121
intention 11, 93, 95, 98–9, 113–14, 138, 152
intentional object 99, 100–102

Jainism 99–100, 245
Jain objection to *karma* 99–100
Jñānaśrīmitra 238
joy 7
of enlightenment 53

Kamalaśīla 236–9
kamma see karma
Kant, Immanuel 66, 94, 100–101, 130, 150, 155–6, 210, 212, 278n9
transcendental idealism 150
unity of apperception 130
karma viii–ix, ch. 5
and action 93–5
explanation of 93–4
as intention 99, 108, 138, 266n8
Jain objection to 99–100
knowledge of 97–8, 109
and moral quietism 108–11
as natural property 94
"never part of Buddhist view" 112
and no-self 102–5, 105–8, 111–13
and reincarnation 95, 112–13
Vasubandhu's discussion of 138, 146–7, 152–4

Kathāvatthu, the 50–52
Buddhaghoṣa's commentary on 50, 254n12, 256n30
Keown, Damien 258n9, 258n12
King Milinda 24
kleśas (afflictions) 52–3, 259n20
knowledge *see* epistemology
kuśala (wholesome) practices 59, 78, 258n13
translation of 258n12

language 87–8, 191, 199–200, 264n20
as distorting understanding 178–80, 200, 215
Leibniz, G. W. 149, 274n16
liberation 10, 48, 75, 237
life vii–viii, 68–9
embracing life 49–51, 69
"how should I live?" 3
see also saṃsāra
linguistic convention 38–40
love 66–7
Lusthaus, Dan 274n25

Madhyamaka viii, x, 72–4, 81, 82, 85, 91, 139–40, 159–60, 161, 171, 189, 189–92, 193–8, 200, 202, 224, 226, 234–9
Candrakīrti's account of 204–14
critique of *dharma*-atomism 198
Mādhyamika regress objection to Diṅnāga 176–7
Mādhyamikas 169, 171
Mahāsaṅghikas 64, 261n25
Mahāyāna (monk) 236–7
Mahāyāna (the Greater Vehicle) 65, 77–8, 139–40, 142–3, 194, 203–4, 204–5, 224, 237–9
and Abhidharma Buddhism 142
materialism and *dharma*-atomism 44
Matilal, B. K. 175
meditation 61–2, 62–3, 82, 106, 229, 259n16
memory 126–7, 132, 176
mereology 38–41, 118, 263n18
complex wholes viii, 36, 39, 40, 46, 56, 60, 81–2, 172, 190

identity of whole and parts 40–41
"nothing complex can be ultimately real" 43
metaphysics
categorial metaphysics 118–23, 149
and elimination of suffering 18–19
and ethics 3–4, 12, 48, 70
minimalist 119–20
"path to happiness is the practice of" 19
practical exercises in 29
Middle Way *see* Madhyamaka
Milindapañhā, the 24, 35–7, 102, 118, 198, 253n19, 265n5
mindfulness 11
minimalism ix, 38, 119, 122, 138, 142, 179
mokṣa *see* liberation
Mokṣākaragupta 239–40, 278n13
moral improvement argument, the 25–6, 32
moral philosophy *see* ethics
moral psychology 8–9, 116
and liberation 237
morality
and *karma* 95, 102–5, 105–8, 108–11
moral motivation 115
moral transformation 57
and responsibility viii, 102–5
Mūlamadhyamakakārikā, the *see under* Nāgārjuna
Murdoch, Iris 254n7
mysticism 264n20

Nāgārjuna viii, 22–3, 59, ch. 4, 139, 162, 166, 270n4, 270n8, 277n38
and Abhidharma 74, 78–9, 82
on dependent origination 189–95
on *dharmas* 81–4
"as holding no views at all" 79, 263n14
Mūlamadhyamakakārikā, the 72, 79, 83, 86, 262n5
Ratnāvali (*The Precious Garland*) 59, 73, 74–8, 89
Nāgasena 19, 35–7, 38

naturalist explanation, critique of 222
Neiman, Susan 69
neyārtha/nithārtha *see* Buddha, the, interpretable vs definitive statements of
Nietzsche, Friedrich Wilhelm 20, 49, 50, 65
Beyond Good and Evil 50
Ecce Homo 49
objection to Buddhism 48–50, 54, 65–8
nihilism 74, 106, 140, 160, 191–2, 262n5, 282n39
moral nihilism 91–2
Nikāyas, the 52
nirvāṇa 53, 57, 60, 62–3, 69, 87, 258n9
"with remainder" 62
identified with *saṃsāra* 87–9, 208–14
Noble Truths 5–6, 6–10, 12–14, 14–19, 51, 54, 70
nominalism 35–7, 39, 46
no-self viii, ch. 2, 195, 229
habit of mind vs metaphysical claim, vii 32, 35–43
and *karma* 102–5, 105–8, 111–13
practice of 30, 31
and responsibility ix, 102–5
self's vulnerability to external influences 28
Numerical Discourses 99
Nyāya ix, **xvi–xvii**, 102, 118, 119, 122, 123
Nyāya-Vaiśeṣika metaphysics 149
on sound inference 181–9
Nyāya-Sūtra 124

other-dependent nature 158

pain 7–8
asymmetry with pleasure 252n11
Pāli 242–3
paramārthasat 38; *see also* reality, ultimate reality
pāramitās (perfections) 64, 204–5, 226–7

"perfection of wisdom" literature 261n26
parantra 158
particulars *see topics under dharmas*
as *sui generis* 215
parts and wholes *see* mereology
Payutto, P. A. 266n11
perception 143, 173–4, 176–9, 207, 224
framed by belief 13
perfections 78
personalists *see pudgalavāda*
personhood 104–5
phenomenology 163, 170, 172, 227
Plato 20, 55, 115, 265n28
Apology 65–6
definition of being 264n24
Theaetetus 130, 214–15
Timaeus 163, 166
Republic 158
Phaedo 222
Philebus 263n18
revisionary ethics 55
pleasure 252n11
danger of sense pleasures 51–2
possessiveness 21–2
prajñāptisat (conceptual reality) 39
pramāṇas 173–5, 180, 185, 219–20, 230
pramāṇa tradition 171–2
prasaṅga 199
Pratītyasamutpāda *see* dependent origination
properties viii
pudgalavāda 33, 105
Pudgalavādins, the 46, 105, 210–12
puñña and *pāpa* (merit and demerit) 58, 258n13

Ratnakīrti 238
Ratnāvali (*The Precious Garland*) *see under* Nāgārjuna
realism 142–5, 284n66
reality 39, 44, 74, 80, 143–7
Abhidharma account of 197–8
conceptual reality 39, 44, 108, 135, 172, 174, 185, 187, 189
constructed vs other-dependent 158–60, 161–3
conventional vs ultimate 38–40, 43, 81, 85–8, 91, 108, 118–19, 119, 138, 157, 174, 177, 189–92, 196, 198, 206–7, 210–12, 219–21, 236, 256n30, 256n32
experience of 156, 163, 167, 177, 187–8
impossibility of making statements about 81, 163
mind-independent 143–57, 157–61
"nothing complex can be ultimately real" 43
seen aright vs confused 208
ultimate reality 38, 43–6
receptacle, as in the *Timaeus* 163, 166
reflection 11
reincarnation 58, 98, 103, 245, 265n2
Buddha's remarks on 32, 64, 77, 269n33
and *karma* 95, 112–13
and personal identity 103, 267n17, 268n32
religion 4
"revolution at the basis" 155, 157
Rhys Davids, C. A. F. 61
A Buddhist Manual of Psychological Ethics 61
right view 11, 99; *see also* Eightfold Path
rūpa (form) 29, 61

Śakyamuni *see* Buddha, the
saṃbodhisukha (joy of awakening) 53
saṁjñā (cognition) 29
saṃsāra 15, 62, 87, 110
"three realms" 273n8
saṁskāras 29, 266n10
saṁvṛttisat *see* reality, conventional vs ultimate
Saṃyutta Nikāya 25, 34
Saṅghabhadra 169
Sanskrit 242–3
Śāntarakṣita 232–40, 278n13, 285n76
Śāntideva x, 201–2, 224–31, 267n23, 287n93
Bodhicāryāvatāra 201–2

sarvaṁ duḥkhaṃ *see* suffering, "all is suffering"
Sautrāntikas (*sūtra*-followers) 137
scepticism 154, 187
Sceptics, the 80–81
self, the ch. 2, 122, 123–4, 165–6, 212–13
absence of *see* no-self
argument for existence of ix; *see also* Nyāya
bundle-theory 127, 133 *see also* bundles
and change 27–8
clinging to self as causing suffering 21, 231
cross-modal unity 125–7, 129–31, 131–4, 134–6
delusion 13
"I am that" 165
"know thyself" 20–21, 31
as "metaphysical glue" 32, 127
process self vs substance self 23, 134
as substance 123, 134
transformation of ix
"true self" 28, 141
Uddyotakara on 129–30
Vaiśeṣika view on 122
Vatsyāyana's argument for existence of 124, 125–7, 128, 141
vulnerability to external influences 28
see also pudgalavāda
see also under Vasubandhu
self-determination, illusion of 17
"Shorter Exposition of Action" 95, 105, 109
Siddhartha Gautama *see* Buddha, the
Siderits, Mark 256n32, 256n37, 264n26
silence 201
simples, absolute *see dharmas*
skandhas (heaps) 29, 45, 152, 255n19, 270n8
and cross-modal unity 133
Socrates 3, 20, 65
solipsism 147, 151, 156
sophistry 170
space 196
spatially extended objects 139
Śrāvakas ("hearers", "disciples") 193–4
Stoics 21, 31–2, 60, 115, 252n9, 265n1
Strawson, P. F. 285n72
substance 120, 123
Suddhodana (father of the Buddha) 1
suffering 2, 5–6, 6–10, 12–14, 14–19, 27, 54, 55
and agency 16–19
"all is suffering" 7, 14, 15–16, 51, 90
anatomy of 14–19
causes of viii, 8–9, 13, 60; *see also* suffering, roots of
Christian view of 27
and clinging to the self 21
elimination of viii, 10, 11, 18–19, 60, 157, 166–7, 231
ignorance of 13
"is a fact before it is a feeling" 9
and *karma* 110–111
as lack of control 15, 20
metaphysical suffering 15–16
pain 7–8
paschein and *poiein* 16
roots of 8–9, 13, 22, 47, 62
ubiquity of 9
see also Noble Truths
sufficient reason, principle of 13
sukha 257n3
śūnyatā *see* emptiness
Sūtrakṛtāṅga 100
sūtras 1
discourses of the Buddha 2, 77, 137, 246–7
"Greater Discourses of the Full Moon Night" 26–7
"Heart Sūtra" 72, 73–4
"Nibbedhika Sutta" 98
"Right View Sūtra" 13, 47, 101, 251n5
"Snake Sūtra" 13, 21, 26, 34, 52
śāstras vs *sūtras* 137
"Tittha Sūtra" 110

sutta *see sūtras*
svabhāva (distinct nature) 45, 189, 215
absence of 164, 270n4
translation of 263n19
svalakṣana ("self-characterized") 173

teleology 58
in ethics 54–7
tetralemma viii, 79–80
Thanissaro Bhikku 8
Theravāda, the 65
Theravādin, the 50, 52, 114–15
third turning, the ch. 7
Tibet
establishment of Buddhism in 236–7, 239
first monastery in 236
transcendental idealism 150
transformation, moral 57
tropes viii, 44, 166
truth 67–8
two truths, the 38, 76, 91, 192, 206, 210, 219, 256n30; *see also* reality, ultimate vs conventional

Uddyotakara 129–30, 131, 183, 232
universals 174
Upaniṣads, the 10, 28, 244
Chāndogya Upaniṣad 28
"ultimate determinable" 163–5
ultimate reality 38, 43–6

Vaibhāṣikas 117, 137–8
Vaiśeṣikas 118, 119–22, 123
and Aristotelian metaphysics 121
on the self 122
Vajirā 33
Vasubandhu ix, x, 43, 53, 58, 74, 103, 117, 131–2, ch. 7, 169–71, 259n16
Abhidharmakośa 43, 117, 123–4, 139
Abhidharmakośabhāṣya 117, 123, 131, 234, 272n5
on atomism 171–2
on constructed vs other-dependent nature 158–60, 161–3, 175
on conventional vs ultimate reality 119
A Demonstration of Action 138
on dreaming 153–4
as follower of Mahāyāna/Yogācāra 141–2, 191, 273n7
and idealism ix, 152–6, 158–9, 276n28
on *karma* 138, 146–7, 152–4
on *kleśas* 259n20
list of *samskāras* 266n10
on the lower realm 146
and perfected nature 160–63, 170
"revolution at the basis" 155, 157
on the self 122, 128–9, 130–31, 165–6, 166–8, 253n5
on spatial objects 139
on three kinds of emptiness 159–60
Thirty Verses 157–61
Treatise on the Three Natures 157–61, 177
Twenty Verses 141, 142–50, 157, 195
Vatsyāyana, argument for existence of the self 124, 125–7
vedanā (feeling) 29
Vedas, the 244–5
vijñāna *see* consciousness
virtue 58, 66
Visuddhimagga (the *Path of Purification*) 37, 42, 104

Weber, Max 93
Webster, David 252n17, 253n19
wholes, complex *see under* mereology
Williams, Bernard 68
Williams, Paul 267n23, 287n93
Wittgenstein, Ludwig 87–8, 206, 218
worthlessness argument, the 27–9, 33, 36
Wright, Dale 113

Xuanzang (Hsüan-tsang) 33

Yaśomitra 137
Yogācāra 135, ch. 7
critique of *dharma*-atomism 198

and idealism 156–7, 275n25
and nature of consciousness 196–7, 276n31
and phenomenology 163
"third turning of the wheel of Dharma" 74, 139, 160
Yogācārins 140–42, 169–71, 191, 195–6, 238, 273n7, 277n39